LEGAL RESEARCH
IN A NUTSHELL

NINTH EDITION

By

MORRIS L. COHEN
Librarian (Retired) and Emeritus Professor of Law
Yale Law School

KENT C. OLSON
Director of Reference, Research and Instruction
University of Virginia Law Library

THOMSON
™
WEST

Mat #40578515

COPYRIGHT © 1968, 1971, 1978, 1985, 1992, 1996 WEST PUBLISHING CO.
© West, a Thomson business, 2003
© 2007 Thomson/West
    610 Opperman Drive
    St. Paul, MN 55123
    1–800–328–9352
Printed in the United States of America

ISBN 978–0–314–18007–0

TEXT IS PRINTED ON 10% POST CONSUMER RECYCLED PAPER

In memory of

Meredith Olson Murnyak (1951-2006)

and

Douglas J. Olson (1953-2006)

*

PREFACE

Nearly forty years have now passed since the first edition of *Legal Research in a Nutshell* in 1968. Legal research then required access to a law library's extensive sets of reporter volumes, but today most research can be performed just as effectively from anywhere with an Internet connection. For many years Westlaw and LexisNexis have been among the most important legal information resources, but they have been joined in recent years by a wide range of free and subscription-based websites. Finding an answer to a legal question is easier than ever. Finding a correct and complete answer requires as much skill as it did in the era of print dominance.

With each edition the *Nutshell* focuses more and more on electronic research methods, but it continues to devote attention to printed, or "traditional," legal resources. Keyword retrieval and search engines have not fully supplanted the sophisticated editorial tools that form the basis of our legal literature. Many online sources are based on printed works and incorporate their structure and logic. An understanding of their purpose and scope is required for effective research, whether in print or electronic media. Successful research also appreciates the computer's ability to perform searches impossible with print materials, and its power to retrieve information unavailable on a local library's shelves. An integrated approach to print and electronic sources pervades most of this text and shapes the actual practice of modern legal research.

This book presents legal materials in the order in which they are often consulted by beginning researchers.

The first five chapters provide an introductory overview and cover essential secondary and primary sources in American law. General background sources such as legal encyclopedias and law review articles are discussed at the outset, just as they are usually the first sources consulted in research. Case law sources and research methods are discussed next, in keeping with the central place of court decisions in the American legal system and in legal education, followed by a discussion of constitutional and statutory law. The next five chapters cover areas such as legislative history, administrative regulations, court rules, and current awareness resources. While these topics are more specialized than the basic case law and statutory sources, they are just as important in many research situations. The final two chapters provide a brief introduction to research in international and foreign law. These topics may be beyond the scope of many introductory courses in legal research, but no consideration of legal resources is quite complete without recognizing the place of the United States in a larger community. The discussion of international and foreign law resources reflects their increased role in practice and in scholarship.

As noted earlier, the book covers a wide range of government and commercial Internet sites in addition to printed resources and Westlaw and LexisNexis databases. The Internet is notoriously fluid, of course, and yesterday's valuable site may be today's dead link. All addresses listed were still valid as of April 2007, and the *Nutshell*'s companion website <www.virginia.edu/nutshell> provides a regularly updated set of links to all sites mentioned in the text. Its links can reduce both frustration caused by obsolete references and time spent carefully typing lengthy URLs.

This is the first edition of *Legal Research in a Nutshell* prepared without the active involvement of Morris Cohen. He has hardly retired from legal scholarship, but graduating from this basic course has allowed him to focus more on his specific interests in legal history and bibliography. In many ways, however, the book remains his in both content and spirit. It is an honor to be able to carry on the work of a true Giant in a Nutshell.

For her help in preparing this edition, I am deeply indebted to Elizabeth Lambert, reference librarian at Harvard Law School. She carefully edited the manuscript several times, spotted errors and inconsistencies, and generally provided counsel and encouragement. She in turn would like to thank her supportive and helpful colleagues at Harvard Law School, in particular the members of the Anglo American and International Legal Studies reference departments.

Kent C. Olson

Charlottesville, Virginia
April 2007

*

OUTLINE

LEGAL
RESEARCH
IN A NUTSHELL

NINTH EDITION

*

CHAPTER 1

THE RESEARCH PROCESS

---

§ 1–1. Introduction

Legal research is an essential component of the practice of law. It is the process of identifying the rules that govern an activity and finding materials that explain or analyze those rules. These resources give lawyers the knowledge with which to provide accurate and insightful advice, to draft effective documents, or to defend their clients' rights in court. Ineffective research wastes time and money, and inaccurate research leads to malpractice.

Determining what law applies to a particular situation is a skill requiring expertise in legal analysis. Lawyers must be able to analyze factual situations, determine the relevant fields of legal doctrine, and apply rules developed by courts, legislatures, and administrative agencies. Finding these rules is a skill requiring expertise in legal research and the effective use of the law library's extensive array of online and printed resources. Successful research provides the information and knowledge necessary for confidence in one's legal analysis.

Legal research involves the use of a variety of resources, some created by lawmaking bodies such as courts and legislatures, and others by scholars and practicing lawyers. Successful research demands an understanding of which resources to consult in each situation. Experienced researchers know which sources are authoritative or useful for what purposes, and how to use these sources most effectively. Versatility and flexibility are needed, as no single approach can work every time.

§ 1–2. The Sources of the Law

The law consists of those recorded rules that society will enforce and the procedures by which they are implemented. These rules and procedures are created in various ways. Statutes are enacted by elected representatives, for example, while common law doctrines are shaped over the course of many years in court decisions. These are just two of many sources of the law, but the distinction between statutory and common law is one of several dichotomies and classifications that characterize the legal system.

The law has numerous sources, from the United States Constitution to the pronouncements of municipal agencies. Both federal and state governments have lawmaking powers, and in each case three branches—legislative, executive, and judicial—share in this responsibility. As the elected voice of the citizens, the legislature raises and spends money, defines crimes, regulates commerce, and generally determines public policy by enacting statutes. Some of these statutes are broadly worded statements of public policy, while others regulate activity in minute detail.

The executive branch is charged with enforcing the law, but in doing so it too creates legally binding rules. The president and most governors can issue executive orders, and administrative agencies provide detailed regulations governing activity within their areas of expertise. Agencies also act in a "quasi-judicial" capacity by conducting hearings and issuing decisions to resolve particular disputes. These *administrative law* sources are less familiar to law students and the public than statutes and court decisions, but they may be just as important in determining legal rights and responsibilities. Attorneys in heavily regulated areas such as securities law or telecommunications may work more frequently with agency pronouncements than with congressional enactments.

The judicial branch plays a complex role in this system. Judges apply the language of constitutions and statutes to court cases, which often involve circumstances that could not have been foreseen when the laws were enacted. In most instances, these judicial interpretations become as important as the text of the provisions they interpret. The courts have determined, for example, that sexual harassment is a form of employment discrimination under the Civil Rights Act of 1964 even though those words never appear in the statute. Through the power of *judicial review*, asserted by Chief Justice Marshall in *Marbury v. Madison*, the courts also determine the constitutionality of acts of the legislative and executive branches.

Judges also create and shape the *common law*. In a common law system such as ours, the law is expressed in an evolving body of doctrine determined by judges in specific cases, rather than in a group of prescribed abstract principles. As established rules are tested and adapted to meet new situations, the common law grows and changes over time.

An essential element of the common law is the doctrine of precedent, or *stare decisis* ("let the decision stand"). Under this doctrine, courts are bound to follow earlier decisions. These provide guidance to later courts faced with similar cases, and aid in preventing further disputes. People can study earlier cases, evaluate the legal impact of planned conduct, and modify their behavior to conform to existing rules. Although the law changes with time, precedent is designed to provide both fairness and stability. It is the importance of judicial decisions as precedent that gives them such a vital place in American legal research.

The first year law school curriculum sorts legal issues another way, into distinct areas of doctrine such as contract, tort, and property. In doing so, it provides law students with a framework for analyzing legal situations and applying a particular body of rules. While real life does not always divide so neatly into issues of contract or tort, legal materials generally follow this paradigm. A lawyer with a case involving injury from a defective product, for example, may need to research breach of warranty issues in texts and articles on contracts as well as strict liability and negligence issues in the tort literature.

Other distinctions that pervade legal thinking include *civil* and *criminal law, substance* and *procedure*, and *state* and *federal jurisdiction.* Law students must learn how legal issues fit into these dichotomies, not only to solve problems but to know where to look for answers. It is necessary, however, to learn how to classify a question without pigeonholing the situation too narrowly. Analysis within a particular doctrinal area can clarify a specific issue, but most situations contain issues from a number of areas. A lawyer who does thorough research on causation issues but forgets about the statute of limitations or service of process is one who loses cases.

§ 1–3. The Forms of Legal Information

Effective legal research requires more than knowledge of the nature of the legal system. An understanding of the ways in which legal information is disseminated is also needed. Several characteristics have affected the research process. Laws are published chronologically, requiring both resources compiling current laws and access to historical sources. Legal literature comprises both official, primary statements of the law and an extensive body of unofficial secondary writings. Information is accessible both in print and electronically, creating a wide range of research choices.

a. Current and Historical Information

The legal system is created over the course of time, and the law in force today is a combination of old and new enactments and decisions. The United States Constitution has been in force for more than 200 years, and many judicial doctrines can be traced back even farther. Other laws are just days or weeks old, as legislatures, courts, and executive agencies address issues of current concern.

These laws have been published as they were issued, whether in volumes of legislative acts or court reports, or through electronic dissemination. They retain their force and effect until they are expressly repealed or overruled. To determine the law that governs a particular situation, the researcher may need access to all of these sources, no matter how old or new they may be.

This has led to the creation of a complex collection of resources designed to provide topical access to this vast body of material. Today the most widely used approach is keyword searching in databases containing the full text of thousands of court decisions or other documents. More traditional means of access to court opinions include digests classifying summaries of points from cases; texts and reference works summarizing and comparing similar cases; and citators allowing researchers to trace doctrines forward in time. For access to statutes and regulations, laws in force are arranged by subject in codes which are accessible online by keyword or in print through extensive indexes. Even laws no longer in force, however, may also be important in interpreting documents or resolving disputes, so historical resources are needed as well. Some older materials have been digitized and are available online, but many others can be found only in print.

It is just as important for lawyers and others interested in the legal system to keep up with new developments, and an extensive body of resources exists to provide current information. New statutes, regulations, and court decisions are issued by the government and by commercial publishers, both in print and through electronic means. Newsletters, looseleaf services, websites, and blogs provide notice of and analyze these new developments. In addition, the codes and texts lawyers use are updated regularly to reflect changes. New documents can be incorporated into a database within minutes of their release. Many print publications are updated through the use of *pocket parts* supplements which fit inside the back covers of bound volumes, while others are issued in looseleaf binders so that they can be updated with supplementary inserts or replacement pages.

b. Primary and Secondary Sources

Legal sources differ in the relative weight they are accorded. Some are binding authority, while others are only persuasive in varying degrees or are useful only as tools for finding other sources. Each source must be used with a sense of its place in the hierarchy of authority. A decision from one's state supreme court has more authority than a scholarly article, but an influential article may have more persuasive force than rulings of courts in other jurisdictions.

The most important distinction is between *primary* and *secondary sources*. Primary sources are the official pronouncements of the governmental lawmakers: the court decisions, legislation, and regulations that form the basis of the legal doctrine. Not all primary sources have the same force for all purposes. A decision from a state supreme court is mandatory authority in its jurisdiction and must be followed by the lower state courts. A state statute also must be followed within the state. Other primary sources are only persuasive authority; a court in one state may be influenced by decisions in other states faced with similar issues, but it is free to make up its own mind. A statute or regulation from one state is not even persuasive authority in another state.

Works which are not themselves the law, but which discuss or analyze legal doctrine, are considered secondary sources. These include treatises, hornbooks, *Restatements*, and practice manuals. Much of the most influential legal writing is found in the academic journals known as *law reviews*. Secondary sources serve a number of important functions in legal research. Scholarly commentaries can have a persuasive influence on the lawmaking process by pointing out flaws in current legal doctrine or suggesting solutions. More often, they serve to clarify the sometimes bewildering array of statutes and court decisions, or provide current awareness about developing legal doctrines. Finally, their footnotes provide extensive references to primary sources and to other secondary material.

c. Print and Electronic Resources

Most of the resources to be discussed in this book first appeared in printed form, and developed as print publications over several decades or even centuries. Detailed editorial systems such as digests, citators, and annotated codes were created to make sense of the jumble of primary sources. In recent years, of course, more and more material has become available electronically. Lawyers now do more research online than in print, but books still have some advantages. The astute researcher knows how to take advantage of both media.

Electronic research has significantly affected the legal research process. The computer can integrate a variety of tasks that are conducted with separate print sources, such as finding cases, checking the current validity of their holdings, and tracking down secondary commentary. The ability to search the full text of documents for specific combinations of words means that researchers are not limited to the choices of editors who create indexes and digests. Each research situation presents a unique set of factual and legal topics, and the computer makes it possible to find documents which address this specific confluence of issues.

Yet editors have hardly been put out of work. Researchers forced to work only with an uncontrolled mass of electronic data can quickly find themselves drowning in unsorted information. Tools such as digests and indexes, whether used online or in print, continue to provide the invaluable service of sorting material by subject and presenting it in a comprehensible fashion.

Computerized research has also blurred the distinctions among different types of information and broadened the scope of legal inquiry. Case law research, for example, was traditionally a process quite distinct from research in secondary commentary or social sciences. Using electronic databases, it is much more convenient and natural to switch from one source to another and back again, bringing to legal research more empirical experience and a wider range of scholarly commentary. Hypertext links between documents make it possible to follow various leads and ideas as they arise, rather than following one linear research path.

Two major commercial database systems, Westlaw <www.westlaw.com> and LexisNexis <www.lexis.com>, are widely used in law schools and in legal practice as comprehensive legal research tools. Westlaw and Lexis-Nexis, however, are available only to subscribers and other paying customers. Law students generally have access through their school's subscriptions, but for other researchers these can be expensive tools. (Much of the information in these databases may be available to university faculty and students through LexisNexis Academic <web.lexis-nexis.com/universe/> or Westlaw Campus Research <campus.westlaw.com>.)

Other commercial online research systems may provide lower-cost alternatives to Westlaw and LexisNexis for access to primary sources. These systems generally provide reliable access to case law and statutes, but offer a smaller range of secondary sources and other features. Some of these, such as Loislaw <www.loislaw.com> and VersusLaw <www.versuslaw.com>, are available free to law students.

Free Internet sites, particularly those provided by the federal and state governments, can also be valuable sources of legal information. While some sites provide access to statutes and recent case law, the most useful sites provide access to previously hard-to-find resources such as legislative documents, administrative agency materials, and court documents. The Internet also provides an invaluable means of linking scholars and researchers through websites, blogs, and electronic mail.

One advantage of major commercial services such as Westlaw or LexisNexis is that the information they provide is generally (but not always) accurate and up to date. Even government sites can present obsolete information without indicating that it is no longer current, and other websites can be biased, selective in coverage, or dangerously out of date. A diligent researcher always assesses the currency and reliability of information found online before relying on it as an accurate statement of the law.

§ 1–4. Legal Language

One of the tasks facing law students is mastering a new way of speaking and writing. The law has developed its own means of expression over the centuries. Latin words and phrases are still prevalent, from the familiar writs of *certiorari* or *habeas corpus* to doctrines such as *res ipsa loquitur*, and even everyday words such as *infant* or *issue* may have specialized meanings in legal documents.

A good law dictionary is needed to understand the language of the law. The leading work, *Black's Law Dictionary* (8th ed. 2004), edited by Bryan A. Garner, provides definitions for more than 40,000 terms, and includes pronunciations and nearly 3,000 quotations from scholarly works. It can be used to find new legal terminology and to define older terms found in historical documents. *Black's* is also available in a somewhat shorter abridged edition (2005), a considerably smaller pocket edition (3d ed. 2006), and a digital edition (2006). It can also be searched as the BLACKS database on Westlaw.

Some lawyers continue to use *Ballentine's Law Dictionary* (3d ed. 1969), which is also available online through LexisNexis. *Ballentine's* was once the major competitor to *Black's*, but it is now considerably out of date and lacks many modern legal terms and usages. Several other, shorter dictionaries can also be found in law libraries and bookstores. Among the best are Steven H. Gifis *Law Dictionary* (5th ed. 2003), and Daniel Oran *Oran's Dictionary of the Law* (3d ed. 2000). Two dictionaries that are available both in print and as free Internet resources are *Merriam-Webster's Dictionary of Law* (1996) <dictionary.lp.findlaw.com> and *Real Life Dictionary of the Law* (1995) <dictionary.law.com>.

Bryan A. Garner, editor of *Black's Law Dictionary*, is also author of *A Dictionary of Modern Legal Usage* (2d ed. 1995, earlier ed. available on LexisNexis), which focuses on the way words are used in legal contexts. It is an entertaining guide to legal language's complexities and nuances, with definitions and essays providing articulate advocacy for clear and simple writing. *Mellinkoff's Dictionary of Legal Usage* (1992) is a complementary work providing examples of usage and distinctions among related terms.

A variety of other language reference works exist. William C. Burton, *Burton's Legal Thesaurus* (4th ed. 2006) helps writers choose correct terms, and can aid researchers in identifying and choosing words when searching in indexes or preparing online searches. Fred R. Shapiro, *Oxford Dictionary of American Legal Quotations* (1993) is the most scholarly of several sources providing access to the most memorable uses of legal language. It is arranged topically, with precise citations to original sources and indexes by keyword and author.

§ 1–5. Legal Citations

A second hurdle in understanding legal literature is understanding the telegraphic citation form used in most sources. Before reading *Tarasoff v. Regents of the University of California*, a researcher must be able to decipher "551 P.2d 334 (Cal. 1976)" and understand that "551" is the volume number, "334" the page number, and "P.2d." the abbreviation for the *Pacific Reporter, Second*

Series, a source for California Supreme Court opinions. This form may seem obscure at first, but in a very succinct manner it provides the information necessary to find the source and to evaluate the scope of its precedential value. All case citations, for example, identify not only where a case can be found but also the issuing court and the date of decision.

This citation form is centuries old, but the standard guide to its present use is *The Bluebook: A Uniform System of Citation* (18th ed. 2005), published by the Harvard Law Review Association. *The Bluebook* establishes rules both for proper abbreviations and usage of signals such as "cf." and "But see." The Association of Legal Writing Directors' *ALWD Citation Manual* (3d ed. 2006) is used in numerous law schools and by a few journals as a more straightforward and easier-to-learn alternative to the *Bluebook*. Cornell Law School's Legal Information Institute publishes an online *Introduction to Basic Legal Citation* <www.law.cornell.edu/citation/>, a handy, concise guide that incorporates both *Bluebook* and *ALWD* rules.

Even though most research is done electronically, *The Bluebook* and other citation systems generally require citation to page numbers in printed sources if the material is published in that form. Some electronic resources provide page images mirroring the printed version, while others (including Westlaw and LexisNexis) indicate the printed page numbers in the text of the electronic documents. In some instances, however, for a complete citation it may still be necessary to track down the original printed version in the library.

Recent years have seen a trend towards citations to legal authorities that do not depend on reference to a

Abbreviations

particular volume and page number, and that thus can be used whether documents are retrieved in print or online. A *public domain citation* system assigns official numbers to documents such as court decisions sequentially as they are issued, and also numbers each paragraph so that references to specific portions of the text can be identified. This approach has been endorsed by the American Bar Association, and if a public domain citation is available its use is required by the *Bluebook*. Only a few jurisdictions, however, have adopted rules requiring paragraph numbers or other public domain citation features. The American Association of Law Libraries (AALL) has issued a *Universal Citation Guide* (2d ed. 2004) providing rules for a uniform public domain format.

No matter what citation rules are followed, part of the puzzle is simply deciphering the abbreviations in order to identify sources. Reference works such as *Black's Law Dictionary* and the *Bluebook* contain tables listing the major abbreviations found in legal literature, but these are hardly comprehensive. Cases and law review articles contain numerous abbreviations and citations that are cryptic even to experienced researchers. Specialized abbreviation dictionaries, such as Mary Miles Prince, *Bieber's Dictionary of Legal Abbreviations* (5th ed. 2001, available on LexisNexis) and Donald Raistrick, *Index to Legal Citations and Abbreviations* (2d ed. 1993), provide extensive coverage of both common and obscure abbreviations. The most convenient source for deciphering abbreviations may be the free online Cardiff Index to Legal Abbreviations <www.legalabbrevs.cardiff.ac.uk>, which can be searched by abbreviation or title keyword.

§ 1–6. Beginning a Research Project

Often the hardest part of the research process is finding the first piece of relevant information. Once one document is found, it usually can lead to a number of other sources. Cases cite earlier cases as authority; a statute's notes provide useful leads to decisions, legislative history documents, and secondary sources; and law review articles cite a wide variety of sources. Finding the first piece of the puzzle, though, can be a challenge.

Where does a researcher begin when working on a new problem? To some extent, this is a matter of personal preference and familiarity with particular tools. It makes sense to start with material which you can use most effectively. There are, however, some guidelines that can make for better choices.

Before looking anywhere, step back and study the problem carefully. If possible, determine whether the jurisdictional focus is federal or state. Be sure you understand the terms in which the problem is stated; if not, consult a good dictionary or other reference source. Formulate tentative issues, but be prepared to revise your statement of the issues as research progresses and you learn more about the legal background.

It is generally best to begin research by going to a trustworthy secondary source—a legal treatise or a law review article. The mass of primary sources retrieved by keyword searching can be overwhelming, and using a subject index or digest to find statutes or cases on point is often frustrating. Primary sources can be confusing, ambiguously worded documents. Access to secondary materials, on the other hand, is usually easier and more straightforward. These materials try to explain and analyze the law. They summarize the basic rules and the leading authorities and place them in context, allowing the researcher to select the most promising primary sources to pursue.

The choice of the appropriate starting point should be influenced by the nature of the problem. When researching an issue that fits within a traditional area of legal doctrine, begin by consulting a subject treatise or hornbook in the area. A good treatise explains the major issues and terminology, and provides a context in which related matters are raised or considered. The names of some of the most famous treatises, such as *Corbin on Contracts* or Wright & Miller's *Federal Practice and Procedure*, are familiar to most law students. Treatises in other areas can be found by using a law library's online catalog or asking a reference librarian.

If no treatise is available, a legal encyclopedia such as *American Jurisprudence 2d* or *Corpus Juris Secundum* can be a useful first step. These works attempt to cover the entire field of legal doctrine, so their focus is rather diffuse. They do, however, outline the basic rules in each area and provide extensive references to court decisions.

When researching a new or developing area of law, start by looking for a recent periodical article. A law review article can provide an overview of the field, references to important cases and statutes, and a relatively current perspective. Articles from hundreds of law journals are available in online full-text databases. Even more up to date than law reviews are sources such as legal newspapers, newsletters, and blogs.

When it is apparent that the issue to be researched is statutory in nature, it may be most efficient to begin with the annotated code. This is particularly the case in areas with substantial governmental regulation, such as antitrust, banking, labor, or taxation. The statutory language may not provide a clear overview of the field, but an annotated code leads directly to most of the other relevant primary sources and may provide references to secondary sources as well. Specialized services in areas such as securities or taxation often combine the statutory text with editorial explanatory notes.

Despite most researchers' inclination to begin their research online, resources such as treatises and annotated codes may actually be easier to understand in print, where it is simpler to scan headings, get an overview of an area, and learn about related issues without incurring online search charges. The computer databases of Westlaw or LexisNexis can certainly be effective starting points if you are generally familiar with an area of law and are researching a narrow question or a particular combination of issues, but it is still necessary to choose an appropriate database from the array of cases, statutes, law review articles, and other resources.

Free Internet sites are not comprehensive, but they can provide places to start if more thorough resources are not readily available. Several websites provide directories organizing legal material by jurisdiction and topic. Among the most popular are FindLaw <www.findlaw. com> and Cornell Law School's Legal Information Institute <www.law.cornell.edu>. These sites provide links to primary sources, blogs, journals, and numerous other sources. Google <www.google.com> and other Internet search engines can also find relevant sites, although it may be difficult to evaluate results and weed out superficial or misleading information. Search engines limited to legal sites, such as LawCrawler <lawcrawler.findlaw. com>, may yield more focused results.

Finally, sometimes the first research step does not involve using either books or databases. Instead it may be more efficient to send an e-mail or make a telephone call. Government agencies and professional associations are staffed with experts who can answer questions, provide invaluable references, or send essential documents. It's usually best to do one's homework first, and to make sure that the information isn't posted on the agency's or organization's website. Directories and websites can be used to identify contact persons at legislative offices, administrative agencies, and nongovernmental organizations.

These various options are the sorts of choices one must make in any research process. It is important to remember that professional help may be available to guide you in the choice of the first resource. Law librarians are trained to provide just this sort of assistance. While they are not permitted to interpret the law or provide legal advice to library users, librarians can assist patrons in determining how best to identify and track down the relevant sources.

§ 1–7. Online Research Basics

The methods of legal research using books vary widely, depending on factors such as the size of the work and the extent of its index, and approaches to specialized resources such as digests and annotated codes will be discussed in later chapters. Online legal research, on the other hand, has several basic characteristics no matter what type of sources are being explored.

Most researchers these days are familiar with Internet search engines such as Google, which can search for documents containing a combination of keywords or a specific phrase. This approach may be adequate for searching the Internet for information, but legal research requires identifying relevant documents from the thousands or millions of documents in a database. The online databases of Westlaw and LexisNexis permit much more powerful and focused searches, allowing the use of features such as synonyms, truncation, and proximity connectors.

Whether to use Westlaw or LexisNexis for particular research (if a choice is available) is a decision based in part on personal preference and in part on the features and materials they offer. Each has advantages, and familiarity with both will make for more successful research. Law schools generally have subscriptions allowing their students unlimited use of both databases, and most larger law firms subscribe to at least one of these services.

For other researchers, however, these commercial online systems may be unavailable or prohibitively expensive. Other options are available. Many college and university libraries subscribe to LexisNexis Academic, with many of LexisNexis's features, and other commercial services are available at lower cost. Generally these services and products provide access in similar ways to Westlaw and LexisNexis, although their interfaces and search engines may be less flexible and sophisticated.

a. Westlaw

One of the first choices confronting an online researcher is the selection of an appropriate database. Westlaw
has a wide selection of databases, some limited to particular jurisdictions or specific subject areas and others
providing comprehensive access. Whether to limit research to a particular jurisdiction or topical area depends
upon a variety of factors, including cost (searches in
large databases are generally more expensive), the purpose of the research, and the value of information from
other jurisdictions or in other subjects.

Several means are available for choosing an appropriate database. The introductory Westlaw screen includes a
"Search these databases" box. Typing keywords such as
"products liability" in the box will retrieve a list of
suggested databases from which to choose. Westlaw also
provides an online directory, listing databases by jurisdiction and subject. Exhibit 1–1 on page 32 shows part of
Westlaw's online directory, indicating some of its federal
case law databases. The *i* icon after the name of each
database leads to an explanation of its scope of coverage.
The directory is also available as the IDEN database,
which can be searched to find databases containing specific publications or with particular terms in their descriptions.

Westlaw offers two basic methods of searching: natural
language, and terms and connectors (or Boolean). Each
of these search methods has its strengths. A natural
language search allows the researcher to enter a phrase,
or a combination of words (e.g., *Are handgun manufacturers liable for injuries to shooting victims?* or simply
handgun manufacturer liability). The computer assigns
relative weights to the terms in a query, depending on

how often they appear in the database. It then retrieves a specified number of documents which appear most closely to match the query, giving greater weight to the less common terms. Not all terms will necessarily appear in every document retrieved, but one can specify "required terms" that *must* appear in all documents.

A terms and connectors search can provide greater precision in retrieval, but it does require learning a structured search syntax. Specific terms or phrases are joined by logical connectors such as *and*, or by proximity connectors specifying the maximum number of words that can separate the search terms (e.g., */10*) or specifying that the words appear in the same sentence (*/s*) or the same paragraph (*/p*). In Westlaw, an *or* connector is understood between two adjacent terms. The search *handgun firearm*, for example, searches for documents containing either the word *handgun* or the word *firearm*. To search for a phrase such as "products liability," it is necessary to place the phrase in quotation marks. A terms and connectors search screen is shown in Exhibit 1–2 on page 33.

Another aspect of terms and connectors searching is the use of the truncation symbols *!* and ***. An exclamation point is used to find any word beginning with the specified letters. *Manufactur!*, for example, will find *manufacturer*, *manufactured*, and *manufacturing*. Without the truncation symbol, only the word itself and its plural form are retrieved. *Manufacturer* will retrieve *manufacturers*, but not *manufactured* or *manufacturing*. The asterisk is less frequently used, but represents a particular character or a limited number of characters. *Legali*e* will retrieve either the American *legalize* or the

British *legalise*, and *hand*** will retrieve *hand*, *handy* or *handle* but not *handgun*.

Whether natural language or terms and connector searching is used, the terms entered will determine what documents are retrieved. Since more than one term can usually be used to denote a particular concept, it is important to enter synonyms or related terms. One court decision may use the word *ambiguous*, another *vague*, and a third *unclear*. Whether searching with terms and connectors or natural language, it is important to use synonyms and related concepts. Westlaw provides help in identifying additional terms with an online thesaurus. For *handgun*, for example, it provides such terms as *firearm*, *pistol*, and *weapon*. In a terms and connector search, these alternates are simply typed one after the other, as in *handgun firearm weapon /p manufacturer*; in a natural language search, alternate terms are included in parentheses after the term to which they relate, as in *handgun (firearm weapon) manufacturer liability*.

One major difference between the two types of searching is that a natural language search always retrieves the same number of documents, unless it includes mandatory terms. (The number is something you determine on the Preferences–Search Method screen, and can be anywhere from 1 to 100.) The display shows the documents that best match the query, in order of relevance. A terms and connectors search, on the other hand, can retrieve anywhere from nothing to thousands of cases, depending on how well the search is prepared and how often the terms appear in the database. The number of retrieved documents can be a useful indication of whether an appropriate search was performed. In a natural language search, the first few documents may be right on point but the degree of relevance can drop off precipitously. It is important to recognize when relevance declines, and to be aware that reading every document retrieved will usually be a waste of time. The effectiveness of a search depends on the quality of the resulting documents, not their quantity.

Researchers generally develop a preference for natural language or terms and connectors search methods, but they are best suited for different purposes. Because natural language searching retrieves documents based on how frequently search terms appear, it is ideal for finding documents on issues revolving around frequently used terms such as "summary judgment." Many cases mention the standards for summary judgment, but the few decisions focusing on it in depth would be retrieved first as most relevant. Terms and connectors searches require documents to match a request exactly, so this approach is generally preferable when searching for a particular phrase or a precise combination of terms. It is often fruitful to perform similar searches using both methods.

An important feature of Westlaw searching is the use of document fields. These are specific parts of a documents, such as the title of an article or the name of the judge writing an opinion. Limiting a search to a particular field can produce a much more specific result. A search in a case database for *bell* retrieves any decisions mentioning a person named Bell or simply using the word *bell* anywhere in the opinion. A title search, *ti(bell)*, retrieves only those cases where one of the parties is named Bell.

Some fields allow research that is virtually impossible by other means. It would be a lengthy and tedious process manually to find all opinions written by a particular judge, but online databases can easily retrieve a complete list of a judge's opinions with searches such as *ju(molloy)*. The researcher can examine a judge's decisions on a particular topic by combining this request with other search terms. The entire list of available fields is shown in a drop-down box on the terms and connectors search screen, as shown in Exhibit 1–2 on page 33.

Once a search is entered, Westlaw displays a list of retrieved documents showing the context in which the search terms appear and the beginning of the first document. Buttons at the bottom of the screen allow the researcher to go to that part of the document with terms matching the search query or to the next document. Natural language search results also include a *Best* button to focus on that part of the document that most closely matches the query. Exhibit 1–3 on page 34 shows the display for a query about handgun manufacturer liability, including the text of the U.S. District Court case *City of New York v. Beretta U.S.A. Corp.*

In addition to the documents retrieved by the search, Westlaw also displays a "Results Plus" list suggesting secondary sources and finding tools based on the concepts in the search or the terms in a specific document retrieved. These references to legal encyclopedias and other sources may provide helpful background or lead to additional research resources.

If a completed search retrieves too many cases, you can narrow the focus of inquiry by using the *Locate* feature. This allows you to examine the retrieved set of documents for specific terms, whether or not they were included in the initial request. Instead of identifying a new set of cases replacing the original search result, *Locate* searches for and highlights particular terms among the retrieved documents. This feature is particularly valuable if each new search costs money, because it does not incur an additional search charge. (Another time-and money-saving feature is Research Trail, which allows you to return to searches from earlier in the same day without additional charges and saves searches for two weeks.)

It is also possible, of course, to edit a query by adding new terms or to pursue new topics, perhaps in another database. Clicking on "edit query" provides a new search screen, including a "change database(s)" link to specify other resources to check.

One valuable Westlaw feature which many students overlook is the ability to save a search and have the system automatically run it to check for new material on a daily or weekly basis. This feature, WestClip, is available only with terms and connectors searches, not natural language. It can be accessed by clicking on the "Add Search to WestClip" link at the top of the full screen list of search results, and provides for notification by e-mail or when you sign onto Westlaw. WestClip provides a very convenient way to stay abreast of developments in a specific case or in an area of interest.

Most legal documents cite extensively to other documents, such as cases, statutes, and law review articles, and it is often important or helpful to examine these other sources. Westlaw's display includes hypertext links to these other sources if they are available online. A researcher using book sources would have to make notes for possible future reference, but a Westlaw researcher can follow these leads as they arise. Clicking on a hyperlink opens up a new "link viewer" window, making it easy to return to the original citing document.

Westlaw provides links not only from a document to the resources it cites, but also from a document to later sources that cite it. This is done through the KeyCite feature, which is an integral part of Westlaw's document display. If later citing documents are available, the display includes a small "C" (or other symbol) at the top of the document and a "Citing References" link to the left. Clicking on either of these links will lead to a list of cases, law review articles, court documents, and other sources that make some reference to the document being viewed. This is an invaluable way to find related materials and to bring research forward in time.

If a document has been frequently cited, KeyCite provides several ways to focus retrieval. *Limit KeyCite Display* can be used to see only particular types of documents, references from specific jurisdictions, or (using the *Locate* feature) those documents using specific keywords. In the same way that WestClip provides automatic notification of new documents matching a particular search, KeyCite Alert is a service that provides notice of any new citations to an important document. You can limit a KeyCite Alert to specific *Locate* terms, providing an easy way to learn of new citing documents meeting very specific criteria.

KeyCite plays an important role in case research, where it is used to determine that a decision is still "good law," and will be discussed more fully in Chapter 4.

b.   LexisNexis

Using LexisNexis is quite similar to using Westlaw, with just enough differences to make either a challenge for someone familiar only with one system. The first step in using LexisNexis is to choose an appropriate database from the menu on the screen. Exhibit 1–4 on page 35 shows a LexisNexis database list, with ''i'' icons linking to information about the scope of each database.

LexisNexis offers both natural language and terms and connectors searching. Natural language searching is similar to Westlaw's. The researcher can specify the number of documents retrieved, from as few as ten to as many as 250. ''Mandatory terms'' that *must* appear in all documents can be added and may produce a smaller result.

LexisNexis terminology for terms and connectors searching is slightly different than Westlaw's. Most connectors are similar, although the word *or* must be included between synonyms or related terms. Because an *or* is not understood between adjacent words, phrases in LexisNexis do not have to be entered in quotations. Proximity connectors begin with *w/* (as in *w/10*, *w/s*, or *w/p*), although each system is forgiving enough to understand the other's format. Like Westlaw, LexisNexis uses the *!* and * characters to truncate terms and find word variations. Exhibit 1–5 on page 36 shows a basic terms and connectors search screen.

LexisNexis includes a ''suggest terms for my search'' feature that is broader than a thesaurus. It lists not only synonyms and related concepts but terms that regularly appear in close proximity to the term. *Handgun*, for example, leads to such terms as *arrest*, *possession*, *probable cause*, *search warrant*, and *victim*. These may suggest further search terms or other lines of inquiry.

The LexisNexis counterpart to Westlaw's *fields* are called *segments*. Segments are added to a terms and connectors search by clicking on ''Restrict by Segment,'' and to a natural language search as ''mandatory terms.''

LexisNexis has three basic display formats. *Cite* provides a list of citations, including the overview and core terms; the researcher can choose *Show hits* to display the search terms as well. *Full* displays an entire document, and *KWIC*, short for "key words in context," shows an individual case with a window of twenty-five words around the occurrence of the search terms. Exhibit 1–6 on page 37 shows the full display for *City of New York v. Beretta U.S.A. Corp.*

LexisNexis also provides hyperlinks to cases, statutes, law review articles, and other documents available in its databases. Like Westlaw's *locate*, the *focus* feature provides a way to examine a retrieved set of documents for specific terms without incurring additional charges.

Two LexisNexis features providing other ways to focus or expand research are *More Like This* and *More Like Selected Text. More Like This* finds either cases that cite the same authorities (*Core Cites*) or cases that use similar terms (*Core Terms*). Choosing this feature when viewing the *Bell* case, for example, leads to options to retrieve documents citing the same cases *Bell* cites or to find similar cases by selecting from a list of core terms in *Bell* (including *affirmative defense, misuse, products liability,* and *superseding cause*).

A feature that may be useful when beginning a research project is *Search Advisor*. This provides a way to explore legal topics, such as Torts—Strict Liability—Abnormally Dangerous Activities, and then to search for cases within this specific subject area.

LexisNexis offers a service, *Alerts*, that automatically runs a search on a daily or weekly basis to monitor new developments. Along with *Focus, More Like This*, and *More Like Selected Text, Save as Alert* is listed at the top of a document display. These searches can be retrieved by clicking on the *Alerts* tab at the top of the screen. To the right of the *Alerts* tab, a *History* link allows you to return to any search performed within the past four weeks without incurring additional search costs.

LexisNexis also provides a way to bring research forward by finding later citations to a given document. The LexisNexis feature, *Shepard's*, is represented at the top of a document display by a "Shepardize" link and (in some database) by graphic symbols such as red or yellow signs. *Restrictions* on Shepard's can be used to see negative or positive citing references, or to run a *Focus* search within the text of the citing documents to find specific terms. *Shepard's Alerts* are a means to receive automatic notice of new citing documents.

Unlike Westlaw's KeyCite, which exists only electronically, *Shepard's Citations* is also available in a series of printed volumes. The printed version of *Shepard's* will be discussed, along with a fuller explanation of *Shepard's* online features, in Chapter 4.

More in-depth knowledge of Westlaw and LexisNexis comes from experience, training classes, and guides prepared for specific tools. It is easy to learn the basics of online research, but the expertise gained from practice and study will dramatically improve search effectiveness. Anyone can run an online search, but only a competent researcher can be confident that the results are accurate and complete.

§ 1–8. Completing a Research Project

Knowing when to stop researching can be just as difficult as knowing where to begin. To every research situation, however, comes a time when it is necessary to synthesize the information found and produce the required memorandum, brief, or opinion letter.

Sometimes the limits to research are set by the nature of the project. An assignment may be limited to a specified number of hours or a certain amount of money. If so, the ability to find information quickly and accurately is essential.

A more difficult decision must be made when there is no clear limit to the amount of research to be done. In such cases you must do enough research to be confident that your work is based on information that is complete and accurate. The surest way to achieve this confidence is to try several different approaches to the research problem. If a review of the secondary literature, a digest search, and online queries produce different conclusions, more research is necessary. When these various approaches lead to the same primary sources and a single conclusion, chances are better that a key piece of information has not eluded you.

No matter what criteria are used in determining when to stop researching, it is essential to verify that sources to be relied upon are still in force and "good law." No research is complete unless the latest supplements have been checked, current-awareness sources have been searched for new developments, and the status of cases to be relied upon has been determined.

Confidence in your research results is more likely when you have confidence generally in your research skills. Familiarity with legal resources and experience in their use will produce the assurance that your research is complete and accurate.

§ 1–9. Conclusion

As we will see in the following chapters, the law has a voluminous literature and a wide range of highly developed research tools. Many of these are unfamiliar even to experienced scholars in other disciplines. Learning to use these tools requires patience and effort, but in time you should become aware of the different functions they serve, their strengths and weaknesses, and the ways they fit together.

Too many practitioners of legal research understand little about the tools they use. As a result, they spin their wheels and overlook aids and shortcuts designed to help them. If you learn how legal resources work as you encounter them, and hone your skills through practice, this mastery will save you valuable time and effort.

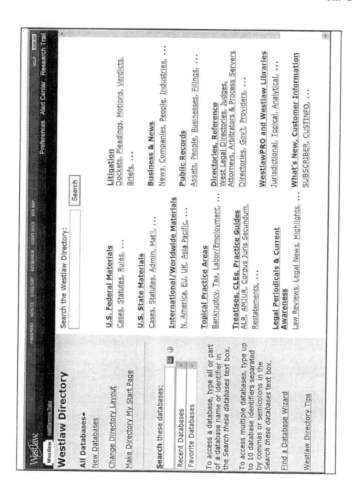

Exhibit 1–1. Westlaw directory screen.

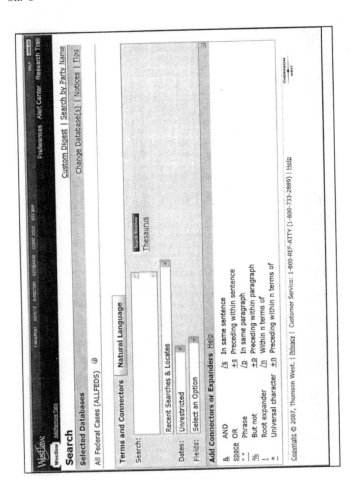

Exhibit 1–2. Westlaw terms and connectors search screen.

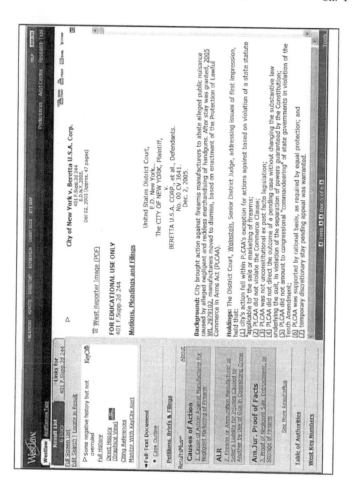

Exhibit 1–3. *City of New York v. Beretta U.S.A. Corp.*, 401 F.Supp.2d 244 (E.D.N.Y. 2005) on Westlaw.

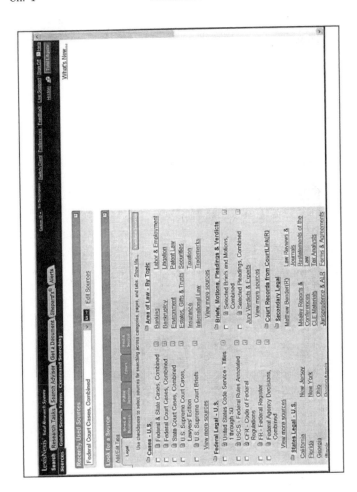

Exhibit 1–4. LexisNexis directory screen.

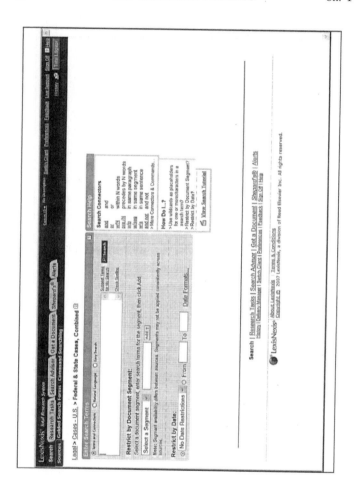

Exhibit 1–5. LexisNexis terms and connectors search screen.

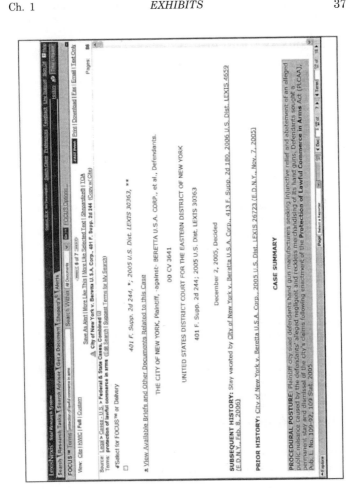

Exhibit 1–6. *City of New York U.S.A. Corp.,* 401 F.Supp.2d 244 (E.D.N.Y. 2005) on LexisNexis.

CHAPTER 2

BACKGROUND AND ANALYSIS

---

§ 2–1. Introduction

While it is the primary sources of law—such as constitutional provisions, legislative enactments, and judicial decisions—that determine legal rights and govern procedures, these primary sources can be notoriously difficult places in which to find answers. Certainly they are not the easiest places to begin a research project. The prudent researcher looks first for an explanation and analysis of the governing legal doctrines.

One of the most important purposes of the sources discussed in this chapter is to set forth and analyze established legal doctrine, explaining its nuances and leading researchers to understand how a problem fits into this doctrinal structure. They provide the context necessary to see how a particular issue relates to other concerns. They can also serve as an introduction to a new area of law or refresh a reader's recollection of a familiar area.

Some secondary sources, particularly treatises and law review articles, contain influential insights that can shape law reform or stimulate new legislation. Others are more practical, providing a straightforward overview of the law without advocating changes. Some sources are written primarily for law students and spell out basic doctrines, while others are designed for practicing lawyers and provide guidelines and forms to simplify common procedures.

One function that most secondary sources share is that they provide references to the primary sources needed for further research. Most texts and articles discuss the leading cases and major statutes, and contain extensive footnotes leading directly to these and numerous other sources. For the reader these footnote references may be among the more mundane aspects of a secondary source, but for the researcher they can be invaluable.

§ 2–2. Overviews

Even basic resources such as legal encyclopedias can be daunting to someone new to legal literature. For a start in understanding a legal problem, it may be helpful to begin with resources written for a more general audience.

Several works explain the nature of the American legal system and provide a broad outline of basic institutions and doctrines. Two recent publications are William Burnham, *Introduction to the Law and Legal System of the United States* (4th ed. 2006), and Peter Hay, *Law of the United States: An Overview* (2002). They explain common legal concepts and procedures, survey doctrinal areas such as contracts, torts, and family law, and provide references to major cases and other sources. At the beginning of each chapter, both books list or discuss texts with more extensive coverage of the specific subject area.

Several encyclopedias provide basic coverage of legal issues. One of the broadest and most accessible for general readers is *West's Encyclopedia of American Law* (2d ed., 13 vols. 2005), with nearly 5,000 entries including articles on basic legal doctrines and terminology, major court decisions, government agencies, and influential jurists and lawyers. Its articles are a mix of legal theory, history, and politics. Volume five, for example, includes biographies of Al Gore and Jesse Helms as well as overviews of Gun Control, Hate Crime, and Hunting.

Other reference works cover more specific topics in greater depth. Some, such as Joshua Dressler, ed., *Encyclopedia of Crime and Justice* (4 vols., 2d ed. 2002), or Leonard W. Levy & Kenneth L. Karst, eds., *Encyclopedia of the American Constitution* (6 vols., 2d ed. 2000), are well-respected interdisciplinary treatments with contributions from legal scholars as well as historians and political scientists. Kermit L. Hall, ed., *Oxford Companion to American Law* (2002), is a one-volume work covering a broad range of major legal concepts, institutions, cases, and historical figures, with most articles accompanied by references for further reading. David M. Walker, *Oxford Companion to Law* (1980), focuses on British institutions and legal history, but it also covers American topics and contains a great deal of useful information on our common law heritage.

Works such as these provide a broad perspective on legal issues, and can place these issues in the context of other political or societal concerns. They generally will not, however, answer more specific questions about particular legal situations, and they contain references to relatively few primary sources. For more detailed coverage, we must turn to works designed specifically for lawyers and law students.

§ 2–3. Legal Encyclopedias

Legal encyclopedias are not simply general encyclopedias about legal topics, but works that attempt to describe systematically the entire body of legal doctrine. Articles are arranged alphabetically by subject, with many covering very broad areas such as constitutional law or criminal law.

Encyclopedias are relatively easy to use and provide straightforward summaries of the law, and thus they are among the first law library resources used by new law students. In most instances, however, their perspective is quite limited. Legal encyclopedias tend to emphasize case law and neglect statutes and regulations, and they rarely examine the historical or societal aspects of the rules they discuss. Encyclopedias are relatively slow to reflect subtle changes in the law or to cover significant trends in developing areas. Unlike law review articles or scholarly treatises, they simply summarize legal doctrine without criticism or suggestions for improvement. They are generally not viewed as persuasive secondary authority, but rather as introductory surveys and as case-finding tools. Their extensive citations to judicial decisions give encyclopedias their major legal research value.

a. *American Jurisprudence 2d* and *Corpus Juris Secundum*

Two national legal encyclopedias were once competing works but are now both published by Thomson West: *American Jurisprudence 2d* (*Am. Jur. 2d*) and *Corpus Juris Secundum* (*C.J.S.*). Each of these sets contains more than 140 volumes, with articles on more than 400 broad legal topics. Some articles, such as "Cemeteries" or "Dead Bodies," are narrowly defined and cover just a few dozen pages, but more extensive articles such as "Corporations" or "Evidence" can occupy two or three volumes. Each article begins with a topical outline of its contents and an explanation of its scope. This is followed by an exhaustive text divided into numbered sections, explaining concepts and providing references to cases and other sources.

While *Am. Jur. 2d* and *C.J.S.* are quite similar, there are differences between these two works. Exhibits 2–1 and 2–2 on pages 62–63 show pages from the *Am. Jur.* Weapons and Firearms article and the *C.J.S.* Weapons article, discussing the potential liability of gun manufacturers. Note that they approach the same issue from somewhat different perspectives. *Am. Jur. 2d* says that firearm manufacturers generally "will not be held liable on a strict products liability theory," while *C.J.S.* states that "products liability may ... provide a cause of action." While both encyclopedias list numerous cases to support their text, there is very little overlap in the cases they choose to cite.

In *C.J.S.*, but not *Am. Jur. 2d*, each section or subsection begins with a concise statement of the general legal principle. This "black letter" summary is followed by text elaborating on the topic. Generally, the discussion in *Am. Jur. 2d* tends to focus a bit more on federal law, while *C.J.S.* seeks to provide an overall synthesis of state law. The discussion in both works is accompanied by copious footnotes to court decisions and occasional references to federal statutes, but neither work cites any state statutes.

Am. Jur. 2d and *C.J.S.* also contain references to other case finding materials. Both encyclopedias provide relevant *key numbers*, classifications that can be used to find cases in West digests. *Am. Jur. 2d* also includes references to *American Law Reports* (*ALR*) annotations, which describe and analyze cases on specific topics. Digests and *ALR* will be discussed in Chapter 4 with other case-finding tools.

Volumes in both sets are updated annually with pocket part supplements providing notes of new developments, and each encyclopedia publishes several revised volumes each year. In the instance of Exhibits 2–1 and 2–2 on pages 62–63, the *Am. Jur. 2d* volume was published in 2002 while the *C.J.S.* volume dates back to 2001. Researchers always need to be aware of the date of the work they are using, and careful not to rely on obsolete information. Even with a pocket part supplement, an older encyclopedia volume may neglect recent trends or cite cases that are no longer good law.

The basic means of access to the encyclopedias are the multivolume softcover indexes published annually for each set. It might be possible to browse through an article outline and find a relevant issue, but legal encyclopedia articles are very lengthy and cover extensive areas of legal doctrine. A pinpoint reference from the index usually saves considerable time. The indexes are very detailed and extensive, but finding the right section may require patience and flexibility. It may be necessary to rethink the terms used or to follow leads in cross-references. Each encyclopedia also includes a tables volume listing the federal statutes, regulations, court rules, and uniform laws discussed in the set, and C.J.S. has a multivolume table of cases it cites.

Westlaw provides access to both encyclopedias, while *Am. Jur. 2d* is also available through LexisNexis and on CD–ROM. The online versions include tables of contents, making it easier to see how a particular section fits in a broader context. Because neither system includes the encyclopedias' indexes, however, it might be best to limit a keyword search to terms used in topic and section headings. This can be done on Westlaw by using the fields PRELIM (for terms in the titles of the topic or subtopic) and TITLE (for terms in the title of the specific section), or in Lexis by using the segments HEADING and SECTION for these same categories. Natural language searches, which show the most relevant documents first, are also effective with resources such as encyclopedias, because there is no concern that important recent documents might rank lower than older documents and thus escape notice.

Am. Jur. 2d is often shelved with several related publications. The *Am. Jur. Deskbook* provides a variety of reference information about the legal system, including outlines of government structure, standards of the legal profession, financial tables, and demographic data of legal interest. Multivolume adjunct sets to *Am. Jur. 2d* include two focusing on trial preparation and practice (*Am. Jur. Proof of Facts* and *Am. Jur. Trials*) and two providing legal forms (*Am. Jur. Legal Forms 2d* and *Am. Jur. Pleading and Practice Forms*). These sets are all available on Westlaw, and all but *Am. Jur. Trials* are also published on CD–ROM.

b. Jurisdictional Encyclopedias

Several states have multivolume encyclopedias specifically focusing on the law of those jurisdictions. These state encyclopedias often do a better job of tying together statutory and case law than the national encyclopedias. While not generally viewed as authoritative, they can provide both a good general overview of state law and extensive footnotes to primary sources. As with the national encyclopedias, annual supplements update these sets.

Fewer than half of the states have their own legal encyclopedias, but these include ten of the twelve most populous jurisdictions. Several of the state encyclopedias are available online through Westlaw (California, Florida, Illinois, Indiana, Maryland, Michigan, North Carolina, Ohio, South Carolina, Texas) or LexisNexis (Florida, Illinois, Michigan, Minnesota, New York, Ohio, Pennsylvania, Tennessee, Texas, Virginia, West Virginia), as well as in print. Confusingly, these are not always called *Jurisprudence* or *Encyclopedia*; some have titles like *Dunnell Minnesota Digest* or *Strong's North Carolina Index 4th*, but their formats and functions are all quite similar. These can be found by browsing the Westlaw or Lexis directory by state and then looking for "Forms, Treatises, CLEs and Other Practice Materials" on Westlaw or "Restatements & Jurisprudences" on Lexis.

Many states have other reference works that provide extensive coverage of their law, although not necessarily made up of alphabetically arranged articles like the national encyclopedias. Sets such as *Kentucky Jurisprudence* and *Massachusetts Practice*, for example, contain separate volumes for doctrinal areas such as criminal procedure, domestic relations, and evidence. They may not cover all legal topics comprehensively, but they do address most major areas.

The *Martindale-Hubbell Law Digest* provides a sort of mini-encyclopedia for each of the fifty states, as well as for the District of Columbia, Puerto Rico, and the Virgin Islands. This annual publication summarizes each jurisdiction's law on more than a hundred legal topics, with citations to both statutory code sections and court decisions. The *Digest* is available both in print and through LexisNexis.

West Group also publishes an encyclopedia focusing specifically on federal law, *Federal Procedure, Lawyers' Edition*. It emphasizes procedural issues in civil, criminal and administrative proceedings, but many of its eighty chapters also discuss matters of substantive federal law. Because it deals exclusively with federal law rather than attempting to generalize about fifty state jurisdictions, it is often more precise and useful than *C.J.S.* or *Am. Jur. 2d* and includes helpful pointers for federal practice.

§ 2–4. Texts and Treatises

Thousands of texts and treatises written by legal scholars and practitioners address topics of substantive and procedural law. These range from multivolume specialized treatises and detailed surveys to short monographs on specific issues or limited aspects of practice in particular jurisdictions.

For centuries, legal treatises have played a vital role in legal research. They analyze the developing common law and contribute their own influence to this development. By synthesizing decisions and statutes, texts and treatises help to impose order on the chaos of individual precedents. Although they lack legal authority and effect, some are written by scholars of outstanding reputation and are well respected by the courts. Other texts offer convenient guides by which practitioners can familiarize themselves with specialized fields of law. Often these texts contain practice checklists and sample forms.

While there is no clear demarcation between different types of texts, they can be grouped into several general categories:

• Multivolume scholarly treatises surveying particular fields in depth (e.g., *Moore's Federal Practice*, *Wigmore on Evidence*) provide exhaustive coverage of specific subjects. Many of the original multivolume treatises were written by leading scholars (such as James William Moore or John H. Wigmore), but a number of titles are now produced by editorial staffs at publishing companies. While these are not accorded the same level of deference as the work of a respected scholar, they nonetheless provide extensive commentaries and numerous references to primary sources.

• Hornbooks and law school texts are written primarily for a student audience but can also be of value to anyone seeking an overview of a doctrinal area. These are distinct from the *casebooks* designed as teaching tools, which reprint cases for discussion and tend to provide a less straightforward summary of legal doctrine. Law school texts vary widely in their reputation and in the extent of citations they provide to cases and other sources. Some hornbooks, such as *McCormick on Evidence* or *Wright on Federal Courts*, can be viewed as one-volume treatises; they are highly respected and are frequently cited as authority in court decisions and law review articles. Other works, such as Thomson West's Nutshell Series, are meant primarily as law school study guides and are rarely cited by judges or scholars.

• Practitioners' handbooks and manuals, many published by groups such as the American Law Institute–American Bar Association (ALI–ABA) Joint Committee on Continuing Legal Education or the Practising Law Institute (PLI), are less useful for students but can be invaluable to practicing lawyers. They tend to address practical concerns, and many provide useful features designed to simplify routine aspects of law practice. Works focusing on the law of a specific state may be particularly useful for quickly determining the laws in force and finding relevant primary sources.

• Scholarly monographs on relatively narrow topics, such as Michael J. Klarman's *From Jim Crow to Civil Rights: The Supreme Court and the Struggle for Racial Equality* (2004) or Richard A. Posner's *Not a Suicide Pact: The Constitution in a Time of National Emergency* (2006), can help provide an understanding of the history or policy background of a particular area. They are often published by university presses and are similar to scholarly works in other disciplines. Because they are generally not exhaustive in their coverage of doctrinal issues and are rarely updated on a regular basis, such works are usually not the best sources for current research leads.

● Self-help publications, such as those published by Nolo Press (e.g., *Patent It Yourself* and *Your Rights in the Workplace*), can be useful starting points and often provide clear introductions to areas of law. They may oversimplify complex issues, however, and they tend to provide fewer leads to primary sources than works designed specifically for lawyers.

For any of these publications to be reliable for coverage of current legal issues, they must reflect changes in the law promptly and accurately. Some form of updating, whether by looseleaf inserts, pocket parts or periodic revision, is usually essential to preserve a treatise or text's value. An outdated text may be of historical or intellectual interest, but it cannot be relied upon as a statement of today's law.

Although printed texts remain the norm, an increasing number are available electronically. Westlaw provides access to more than 200 treatises, including major works such as LaFave & Scott's *Substantive Criminal Law*, *McCarthy on Trademarks and Unfair Competition*, Rotunda & Nowak's *Treatise on Constitutional Law*, and Wright & Miller's *Federal Practice and Procedure*. LexisNexis has a number of Matthew Bender treatises, including *Chisum on Patents*, *Collier on Bankruptcy*, *Immigration Law and Procedure*, and *Nimmer on Copyright*. Electronic texts are not necessarily updated more frequently than their print counterparts, but full-text keyword searching and desktop access provide greater flexibility and convenience.

Exhibit 2–3 on page 64 shows a page from a hornbook, *Products Liability Law*, by Professor David G. Owen of the University of South Carolina School of Law. Owen goes into much greater detail than the encyclopedias on the development of litigation against gun manufacturers and possible theories of recovery. This hornbook is only published in print, but the author's three-volume treatise, *Madden & Owen on Products Liability* (2000), is available on Westlaw as the MOPL database.

There are several ways to find relevant and useful texts and treatises. A basic starting place is a law library's online catalog. A simple subject or title keyword search may turn up too many results, but most catalogs allow searches to be limited to focus on recent publications or to books kept in a reserve collection.

Following research leads provided by other sources is usually a reliable way to find useful works. Treatises are often cited in cases and law review articles, and such references are likely to lead to works which are considered well-reasoned and reputable. Recommendations from professors or reference librarians may also be effective in identifying the most reliable and influential sources.

The subscription service IndexMaster <www. indexmaster.com> has a searchable database of the tables of contents and indexes from more than a thousand legal texts and treatises. It doesn't provide access to the texts themselves, but the PDFs of the tables of contents and indexes highlight the search terms and may indicate whether a particular title is worth tracking down (in the library online catalog or by other means).

Several printed guides list legal publications by subject. Most, unfortunately, do not differentiate between major treatises and obscure monographs, and few are updated regularly. The most extensive and current guide is found in Kendall Svengalis's annual *Legal Information Buyer's Guide and Reference Manual*. A 300–page chapter on treatises provides annotated listings in about sixty subject areas. Its annotations are more descriptive than critical, but they provide useful information about the scope and expense of the works listed. Most state legal research guides (listed in Appendix B at page 454) describe or list the treatises and practice materials focusing on the law of particular jurisdictions.

It may be difficult to evaluate texts without extensive use and expertise in the subject area, but several considerations may aid in deciding whether a particular work has research value. Questions to ask may include:

- a text's purpose and intended audience;

- its organization and scope;

- the reputation of the author and publisher, based on such factors as the importance of their previous publications;

- the clarity, comprehensiveness and usefulness of its footnotes, bibliography, and index; and

- the adequacy and timeliness of supplementation.

With growing familiarity in a particular area of law comes a sense of which sources are useful for providing background information, for working through a complicated legal issue, or for providing references to further research sources. Having access to a reliable treatise can allow you to explore an unfamiliar area in the company of an experienced and insightful guide.

§ 2–5.   Restatements of the Law

Some of the most important commentaries on American law are found in the series called *Restatements of the*

Law. These American Law Institute (ALI) texts attempt to organize and articulate the rules in selected subject fields. The reporters and advisors who have drafted *Restatements* are respected scholars and jurists, and their work is perhaps more persuasive in the courts than any other secondary material. Courts may sometimes even adopt *Restatement* provisions as correct statements of the law. The *Restatements* provide excellent summaries of basic doctrines, useful both for students learning an area of law and for lawyers seeking to apply the law to novel issues arising in practice. The current editions of all *Restatements* are also accessible online through both Westlaw and LexisNexis.

Each *Restatement* covers a distinct area of law. The first series of nine *Restatements* (*Agency, Conflict of Laws, Contracts, Judgments, Property, Restitution, Security, Torts,* and *Trusts*) was published between 1932 and 1946, and after several years a second series (of all the original topics except restitution and security, as well as *Foreign Relations Law*) was issued to reflect new developments or later thinking. Several components of the *Restatement of the Law (Third)* have been published: *Foreign Relations Law* (1987), *Trusts–Prudent Investor Rule* (1992), *Unfair Competition* (1995), *Suretyship and Guaranty* (1996), *Property–Mortgages* (1997), *Torts–Products Liability* (1998), *Property–Wills and Other Donative Transfers* (vols. 1–2, 1999–2003), *The Law Governing Lawyers* (2000), *Property–Servitudes* (2000), *Torts–Apportionment of Liability* (2000), *Trusts* (vols. 1–2, 2003), and *Agency* (2006). The ALI has also published two works as *Principles* (rather than *Restatements*): *Principles of Corporate Governance: Analysis and Recommendations* (1994), and *Principles of the Law of Family Dissolution: Analysis and Recommendations* (2002).

The process of drafting a *Restatement* or *Principles* is a long one, usually involving the publication of several preliminary and tentative drafts. Projects in the drafting process (in addition to the partially completed *Property– Wills and Other Donative Transfers* and *Trusts*) include *Restatements* covering *Employment Law, Restitution and Unjust Enrichment*, and *Torts: Liability for Physical Harm*; as well as *Principles of the Law of Aggregate Litigation* and *Principles of the Law of Nonprofit Organizations*. The American Law Institute website <www.ali. org> has information on publications and pending projects, but does not provide free access to full texts.

The *Restatements* are divided into sections, each of which contains a concise "black letter" statement of law, followed by explanatory comments and illustrations of particular examples and variations on the general proposition. Exhibit 2–4 on page 65 shows a page from the recent *Restatement* on products liability and its use of black-letter rule, comment, and illustration.

The comments and illustrations are followed in recent *Restatements* by Reporter's Notes providing background information on the section's development. In the three earliest *Restatements* in the second series (*Agency, Torts, and Trusts*), the Reporter's Notes are not printed after each section but appear in separate appendix volumes. The appendices for these and the other *Restatements* in the second and third series also contain annotations of court decisions which have applied or interpreted each section. Cases and law review articles citing *Restatements* can also be found through KeyCite and Shepard's (both on LexisNexis and in the printed *Shepard's Restatement of the Law Citations*).

§ 2–6. Law Reviews

The academic legal journals known as law reviews contain much of the most important scholarly commentary in American law. The law review is a form of scholarly publication unknown to most disciplines. It is usually edited by law students rather than established scholars, and serves as an educational tool for its editors as well as a forum for discussion of legal developments and theories. Most reviews follow a fairly standard format, containing lengthy *articles* and shorter *essays* by professors and lawyers, as well as *comments* or *notes* by students. Articles and essays by established scholars are more influential, but the student contributions can also be very useful in research. Like the articles, they are usually accompanied by extensive footnotes citing to primary sources and to other secondary sources. These footnotes help make law reviews an invaluable part of the research process.

Law review articles differ from more general works such as legal encyclopedias in several ways. Article authors often advocate changes in the legal system instead of presenting issues in a neutral manner. A number of influential articles have led directly to major changes in legal doctrine. Because articles are often written on novel legal topics, law reviews can be very helpful in researching developing areas of the law. And unlike works such as encyclopedias or treatises, law review articles are generally not updated once they are published.

In addition to general law reviews covering a variety of subjects, an ever growing number of specialized academic journals are published on topics from agricultural law to telecommunications. Some law schools publish a dozen or more general and specialized journals. Most specialized journals are student-edited, but a few, such as *Florida Tax Review* and *Supreme Court Review*, are edited by law school faculty members. The term "law review" generally encompasses all of these academic legal journals, whether or not those words appear in the title.

Bar associations and commercial publishers also publish legal journals. Articles in these journals tend to be shorter and more practical than those found in academic law reviews, often focusing on current developments of interest to practicing lawyers. Specialized practice sections of the American Bar Association publish some of the most respected bar journals, and state and local bar association journals may provide the best insights into practice concerns in specific jurisdictions.

Exhibit 2–5 on page 66 shows a page from a student comment in a recent law review issue, on the same topic as the encyclopedia and treatise pages shown earlier in this chapter. Note that the footnotes, which occupy more than half the page, provide references to several cases, the *Restatement (Second) of Torts*, and another law review note.

Thousands of law review articles are published every year, and effective research may require learning several means of access. For many researchers, the most frequently used approach is keyword searching in full-text databases. In addition, indexes available online and in print can expand retrieval and focus it more specifically on a topic.

a. Westlaw and LexisNexis

Both Westlaw and LexisNexis have full-text coverage of several hundred law reviews, with coverage for some reviews extending back to the early 1980s and many more beginning in the 1990s. It is possible to search in a specific law review or in databases combining the hundreds of available titles. LexisNexis law review coverage is available both through lexis.com (for most legal professionals and law students) and through LexisNexis Academic <web.lexis-nexis.com/universe/> (for university faculty and students).

Both major search methods, natural language and Boolean, can be useful when searching for law review articles. A natural language search finds articles that discuss search concepts at greatest length and are therefore most likely to be relevant. A Boolean keyword search can be used to find any article using any particular combination of words, including phrases, case names, or titles of other articles or books. Law review articles can be lengthy and discursive, so limiting a search to words in article titles may focus retrieval to those articles directly on point. Even if an article retrieved is not directly on point, its footnotes may provide references to other, more relevant sources—including treatises or journal volumes that are not themselves in the online database.

Another way to find law review articles on Westlaw or LexisNexis can be used once one relevant article is found. The display of the article indicates whether the system includes any later articles or other documents that cite it. Clicking on the KeyCite "citing references" symbol or "Shepardize" produces a list of subsequent articles. (In print, *Shepard's Law Review Citations* performs this same function.) Even if the first article you find is several years old, KeyCite and Shepard's provide an easy way to find related articles and bring your research up to date.

b. HeinOnline

Westlaw and LexisNexis provide the full text of articles, including footnotes, but the notes are generally grouped together at the end of the article. This can make it difficult to scan back and forth between the text and the notes looking for useful research leads. Another electronic service, HeinOnline <www.heinonline.org>, provides digitized page images from the original printed journal issues, thus placing the notes at the bottom of each page. HeinOnline covers more than a thousand journals, and its retrospective coverage extends back in most instances to the very first volumes of the journals in its database. The *University of Pennsylvania Law Review*, for example, is included back to 1852, when it began publication as the *American Law Register*. This full-text access to older law reviews makes HeinOnline particularly valuable in legal history research. For most titles its coverage extends nearly, but not quite, to the most recent issues.

HeinOnline offers two basic search options, an Author/Title Search and a Full Text Word and Phrase Search. The title search is a speedy way to finding articles on particular topics, assuming that they use the appropriate terms in their titles. The word search simply finds articles where the specified words all appear on the same page, and does not yet have the flexibility or convenience of Westlaw or LexisNexis full-text searching. HeinOnline also provides a Citation Navigator, allowing for direct retrieval of known documents. Westlaw and LexisNexis generally have more powerful search options to find recent law review articles, and HeinOnline is best used for historical research or document retrieval.

c. Periodical Indexes

Full-text searching is a powerful tool, but it does have limitations. Searching for particular terms can retrieve too many extraneous articles that only mention these terms in passing, not just those that focus specifically on a particular subject. Some law review articles are not available electronically and might never be found through online searches. For these reasons, periodical indexes remain valuable resources.

Two general indexes to English-language legal periodical literature are available. Both are issued in printed volumes with monthly pamphlets, but online searching is usually the most convenient form of access. *Index to Legal Periodicals and Books* (*ILP*) is available through WilsonWeb <www.hwwilson.com>, and to some subscribers through LexisNexis, Westlaw and other database systems. *LegalTrac* is available as part of the Gale Group's *InfoTrac* system <www.gale.com>, and is known as *Legal Resource Index* (*LRI*) on Westlaw and LexisNexis.

Each of these indexes covers more than 800 law reviews and periodicals, with more than twenty-five years of online coverage. *LegalTrac* coverage begins in 1980, and *ILP* in 1981. WilsonWeb also offers an *Index to Legal Periodicals Retrospective* database, cumulating entries from older index volumes from 1908 to 1981, and allows the historical and modern indexes to be combined for a truly comprehensive historical search.

Both *LegalTrac* and *ILP* offer keyword and natural language searching as well as extensive subject indexing, making it easy to find articles on related topics. *LegalTrac* uses detailed Library of Congress subject headings with extensive subheadings and cross-references, while *ILP* generally has fewer, broader headings. Articles on gun manufacturer liability, for example, might be indexed under "Firearms industry—Cases" in *LegalTrac* and "Weapons" in *ILP*.

Depending on the means of access, the indexes may also offer direct links to the full text of articles indexed. This method combines the best of both research worlds: expert indexing to ensure that relevant articles aren't missed, and immediate online access to the relevant texts.

Exhibit 2–6 on page 67 shows records for several articles found by searching for the keywords "firearm or handgun and products liability" in *LegalTrac*. Note that the first three articles retrieved all include links to the full text, and that one includes a PDF of the printed version. The full record for most articles includes links to the subject headings to which they are assigned, making it easy to use one relevant work to find others.

The printed version of *Index to Legal Periodicals and Books (ILP)* began publication in 1908, and indexes articles by subject and author, with a book review section and tables listing cases and statutes that are the focus of articles. (Earlier articles are covered by the Jones–Chipman *Index to Legal Periodical Literature*, with indexing back to 1770.) The printed counterpart to LegalTrac, known as the *Current Law Index (CLI)*, has been published since 1980. It has separate subject and author indexes, as well as case and statute tables. *LegalTrac* and *LRI* are somewhat broader in scope than *CLI*, with citations to several legal newspapers and to relevant articles in non-law periodicals.

d. Other Sources

The law review literature is also covered in several more general research databases. JSTOR <www.jstor.

org>, for example, includes more than three dozen legal journals in its interdisciplinary, retrospective coverage of more than 600 scholarly journals. Articles can be found through keyword searches and downloaded or printed as PDFs. JSTOR does not include issues from the most recent five to seven years, but it includes some titles not available through HeinOnline, such as *Journal of Law and Economics* and *Journal of Legal Studies.*

Google Scholar <scholar.google.com> provides a free way to search scholarly literature, including law reviews. Access to the full text of some articles is free, but for others it depends on whether your institution subscribes to databases such as JSTOR. In any event, clicking on the link to an article provides the citation necessary to find it by other means. Google Scholar listings also provide ways to expand research with links to more recent works citing the listed article ("Cited by") and articles with similar terms ("Related Articles").

Other free Internet sites also provide some access to recent law review literature. Some law review websites feature only tables of contents or abstracts, but a growing number make the full text of recent articles available. A few law reviews are published only electronically. The University of Southern California Law Library maintains list of links to law review websites <law.usc.edu/library/resources/journals.cfm>, noting which sites provide the full text of articles.

References to law review articles are often found in the process of researching primary sources such as case law or statutes. Annotated statutory codes often contain law review article citations, and the KeyCite and Shepard's displays for cases and statutes include references to any citing articles. These approaches will be discussed, along with other aspects of case and statutory research, in Chapters 4 and 5.

A useful source for identifying publications in a particular specialty is the LexisNexis Directory of Law Reviews <www.lexisnexis.com/lawschool/prodev/lawreview/>, which lists more than 600 journals by subject. It provides separate listing of student-edited journals and non-student-edited peer review and trade journals.

Law reviews and journals are not the only types of legal periodicals. More specialized and practice-oriented sources such as legal newspapers and newsletters, as well as tools providing notice of recent articles and new scholarship, are considered in Chapter 9.

§ 2–7. Conclusion

This brief survey of major secondary sources focuses on general resources that are likely to be the most helpful to beginning researchers. Encyclopedias, texts, *Restatements*, and law review articles are essential tools for someone starting out in analyzing a legal problem. They provide a broad introductory overview of legal doctrine as well as references to primary sources.

Secondary legal literature is much more extensive than these few materials, and additional resources will be discussed in later chapters. These general tools, however, can provide a solid basis for successful research of most legal issues.

third person, he and his employer, if any, can be found liable for the resulting injuries.[2] So long as he acts as a reasonably prudent man would act in a similar situation, he is not liable.[3]

§ 43 Liability of manufacturer or seller of firearm or ammunition

Research References

West's Key Number Digest, Weapons ⬅18(.5) to (2)

Products Liability: Firearms, Ammunition, and Chemical Weapons, 96 A.L.R. 5th 239

Firearm or ammunition manufacturer or seller's liability for injuries caused to another by use of gun in committing crime, 88 A.L.R. 5th 1

Liability of one who provides, by sale or otherwise, firearm or ammunition to adult who shoots another, 39 A.L.R. 4th 517

Products liability: air guns and BB guns, 94 A.L.R. 3d 291

Manufacturer's duty to test or inspect as affecting his liability for product-caused injury, 6 A.L.R. 3d 91

Privity of contract as essential to recovery in negligence action against manufacturer or seller of product alleged to have caused injury, 74 A.L.R. 2d 1111

Complaint, petition, or declaration—Injury due to negligent manufacture of ammunition or firearm, 25 Am. Jur. Pleading and Practice Forms, Weapons and Firearms § 5

Gun manufacturers are under no legal duty to protect citizens from the deliberate and unlawful use of their products.[1] The "ultra hazardous activity doctrine" does not apply to the manufacture or sale of firearms, as opposed to their use, and thus manufacturers and dealers cannot be held strictly liable under that doctrine for damages resulting from the use of those firearms.[2] Handgun manufacturers are held to the most exacting duty of care in the design of their product.[3] A manufacturer's negligence may arise from the failure to test and inspect its product.[4] Generally, firearm manufacturers and sellers will not be held liable on a strict products liability theory when sued by victims of firearms incidents, usually because the plaintiffs cannot establish that there was a defect in the weapon.[5]

---

[2]Cerri v. U.S., 80 F. Supp. 831 (N.D. Cal. 1948); Giant Food, Inc. v. Scherry, 51 Md. App. 586, 444 A.2d 483, 29 A.L.R.4th 134 (1982); Atchison v. Procise, 24 S.W.2d 187 (Mo. Ct. App. 1930); Cook v. Hunt, 1936 OK 672, 178 Okla. 477, 63 P.2d 693 (1936); Goodrich v. Morgan, 40 Tenn. App. 342, 291 S.W.2d 610 (1956).

[3]Shaw v. Lord, 1914 OK 32, 41 Okla. 347, 137 P. 885 (1914); Hatfield v. Gracen, 279 Or. 303, 567 P.2d 546 (1977); Goodrich v. Morgan, 40 Tenn. App. 342, 291 S.W.2d 610 (1956).

[Section 43]

[1]City of Philadelphia v. Beretta U.S.A. Corp., 277 F.3d 415 (3d Cir. 2002) (applying Pennsylvania law).

[2]Penelas v. Arms Technology, Inc., 778 So. 2d 1042 (Fla. Dist. Ct. App. 3d Dist. 2001), review denied, 799 So. 2d 218 (Fla. 2001).

[3]Endresen v. Scheels Hardware and Sports Shop, Inc., 1997 ND 38, 560 N.W.2d 225 (N.D. 1997).

[4]Herman v. Markham Air Rifle Co., 258 F. 475 (E.D. Mich. 1918); Sears, Roebuck & Co. v. Davis, 234 So. 2d 695 (Fla. Dist. Ct. App. 3d Dist. 1970); McLain v. Hodge, 474 S.W.2d 772 (Tex. Civ. App. Waco 1971), writ refused n.r.e., (Apr. 19, 1972).

[5]Merrill v. Navegar, Inc., 26 Cal. 4th 465, 110 Cal. Rptr. 2d 370, 28 P.3d 116 (2001); Penelas v. Arms Technology, Inc., 778 So. 2d 1042 (Fla. Dist. Ct. App. 3d Dist. 2001),

42

Exhibit 2–1.   79 Am. Jur. 2d *Weapons and Firearms* § 43 (2002).

misuse of the firearm or the injury inflicted, since a firearm is an inherently dangerous instrumentality.[16] However, negligent entrustment is available as a theory of liability only where the defendant had unrestricted control over the firearm.[17]

Theft.

Although the owner of a dangerous instrumentality such as a firearm is required to exercise a high degree of care when using a firearm or authorizing its use,[18] a firearm liability may not generally be imposed against the owner of a firearm for criminal use of firearm following theft, either based on negligence,[19] or on the theory of strict liability.[20]

§ 61 Manufacture and sale

The manufacturer and the seller of a weapon may be liable to one injured as the result of negligence. Strict or products liability may also provide a cause of action against such persons.

Research References

West's Key Number Digest: Weapons ⟨⟩1

A firearm, in the use for which it is intended, is a dangerous instrument within the scope of the principle that, under the ordinary rules of negligence, a manufacturer of such an instrument is liable in damages for an injury resulting from the negligent use of defective materials or from want of proper care and skill in either design[1] or the manufacturing process.[2] The most that is required, however, is the production of a weapon suitable for use under the conditions existing at the time it is put on the market,[3] and the manufacturer is not liable where the weapon is not used in an ordinary and reasonably foreseeable manner.[4] Under general rules, the complaint, declaration, or petition must be sufficient to state a cause of action,[5] and a want of proper care and skill in the manufacture must be alleged and proved[6] by sufficient evidence.[7] The mere bursting of a firearm does not alone suffice to make the manufacturer liable.[8]

Manufacturers have been held strictly liable for some injuries caused by firearms on a product liability basis,[9] though there is authority to the effect that the manufacture of fire-

[16]Ohio—Byers v. Hubbard, 107 Ohio App. 3d 677, 669 N.E.2d 320 (8th Dist. Cuyahoga County 1995).

[17]Colo.—Payberg v. Harris, 931 P.2d 544 (Colo. Ct. App. 1996).

[18]Mich.—Resteiner v. Sturm, Ruger & Co., Inc., 223 Mich. App. 374, 566 N.W.2d 53, Prod. Liab. Rep. (CCH) ¶ 14945 (1997).

[19]Md.—Valentine v. On Target, Inc., 112 Md. App. 679, 686 A.2d 636 (1996), cert. granted, 344 Md. 719, 690 A.2d 525 (1997) and judgment aff'd, 353 Md. 544, 727 A.2d 947 (1999).

Wash.—McGrane v. Cline, 94 Wash. App. 925, 973 P.2d 1092 (Div. 1 1999), review denied, 138 Wash. 2d 1018, 989 P.2d 1141 (1999).

Negligent entrustment

Father's estate was not liable for negligently entrusting juvenile with dangerous instrument, based upon juvenile's theft of pistol from father, where father was not aware that juvenile possessed pistol and therefore had no opportunity to prevent or control juvenile's use of it.

N.Y.—Brahm v. Hatch, 203 A.D.2d 640, 609 N.Y.S.2d 956 (3d Dep't 1994).

[20]Mich.—Resteiner v. Sturm, Ruger & Co., Inc., 223 Mich. App. 374, 566 N.W.2d 53, Prod. Liab. Rep. (CCH) ¶ 14945 (1997).

[Section 61]

[1]U.S.—Rodriguez v. Glock, Inc., 28 F. Supp. 2d 1064 (N.D. Ill. 1998).

La.—Cappo v. Savage Industries, Inc., 691 So. 2d 876, Prod. Liab. Rep. (CCH) ¶ 15042 (La. Ct. App. 2d Cir. 1997), writ denied, 700 So. 2d 509 (La. 1997).

N.D.—Endresen v. Scheels Hardware and Sports Shop, Inc., 1997 ND 38, 560 N.W.2d 225, Prod. Liab. Rep. (CCH) ¶ 14902 (N.D. 1997).

[2]N.Y.—Favo v. Remington Arms Co., 67 A.D. 414, 73 N.Y.S. 788 (3d Dep't 1901).

[3]N.Y.—Favo v. Remington Arms Co., 67 A.D. 414, 73 N.Y.S. 788 (3d Dep't 1901).

[4]N.Y.—Favo v. Remington Arms Co., 67 A.D. 414, 73 N.Y.S. 788 (3d Dep't 1901).

Pleading held insufficient

Pa.—Scurfield v. Federal Laboratories, 335 Pa. 145, 6 A.2d 559 (1939).

[6]Ill.—Miller v. Sears, Roebuck & Co. of Illinois, 250 Ill. App. 340, 1928 WL 4151 (1st Dist. 1928), cert. denied.

N.Y.—Favo v. Remington Arms Co., 67 A.D. 414, 73 N.Y.S. 788 (3d Dep't 1901).

[7]Conn.—Welshausen v. Charles Parker Co., 83 Conn. 231, 76 A. 271 (1910).

[8]Conn.—Welshausen v. Charles Parker Co., 83 Conn. 231, 76 A. 271 (1910).

[9]U.S.—Bell v. Glock, Inc. (USA), 92 F. Supp. 2d 1067 (D. Mont. 2000).

Pa.—DiFrancesco v. Excam, Inc., 434 Pa. Super. 173, 642 A.2d 529 (1994), appeal granted, 540 Pa. 599, 655 A.2d 988 (1995) and appeal dismissed as improvidently granted, 543 Pa. 627, 674 A.2d 214 (1996).

Exhibit 2–2. 94 C.J.S. *Weapons* § 61 (2001).

ties brought by most states of the Republic of Colombia, the European Community, and most of its member states.[109] After the district court dismissed most of their claims on the basis of *Canada*, the plaintiffs in *European Community* refiled with an emphasis on the defendants' money laundering, racketeering, and various tortious activities, but once again the case was dismissed, and the dismissal affirmed,[110] albeit with a small window for the plaintiffs to file another lawsuit on their money laundering claims.[111] Apparently the window was big enough, for one defendant settled with the EU soon thereafter for $1.25 billion.[112]

Firearms

Background. The menace of guns in American society, particularly handguns but also various assault rifles, has spawned a morass of litigation and debate.[113] Each year, tens of thousands of Americans are killed by guns—roughly the same number as are killed in car accidents.[114] While initially startling, this statistic reflects the fact that there are almost as many firearms in this nation as people.[115] While some

---

109. See European Cmty. v. Japan Tobacco, Inc., 186 F.Supp.2d 231 (E.D.N.Y. 2002) (holding that revenue rule required dismissal of smuggling claims seeking lost tax revenue but that money laundering claims . seeking other types of damages might proceed), aff'd in part, vacated in part, 355 F.3d 123 (2d Cir. 2004).

110. European Community v. RJR Nabisco, Inc., 355 F.3d 123 (2d Cir. 2004).

111. See id. at 138.

112. See, e.g., EU Signs $1.25B Deal with Philip Morris, nytimes.com (AP, July 9, 2004).

113. See Ausness, Tort Liability For the Sale of Non–Defective Products: An Analysis and Critique of the Concept of Negligent Marketing, 53 S.C. L. Rev. 907 (2002); Culhane and Eggan, Gun Torts: Defining a Cause of Action for Victims in Suits Against Gun Manufacturers, 81 N.C. L. Rev. 115 (2002); Lytton, Lawsuits Against the Gun Industry: A Comparative Institutional Analysis, 32 Conn. L. Rev. 1247 (2000); Lowry, Litigating Against Gun Manufacturers, 36 Trial 42 (Nov. 2000); Lytton, Tort Claims Against Gun Manufacturers for Crime-Related Injuries: Defining a Suitable Role for the Tort System in Regulating the Firearms Industry, 65 Mo. L. Rev. 1 (2000); Twerski and Sebok, Liability Without Cause? Further Ruminations on Cause-in-Fact as Applied to Handgun Liability, 32 Conn. L. Rev. 1379 (2000); Bhowik, et al., A Sense of Duty: Retiring the "Special Relationship" Rule and Holding Gun Manufacturers Liable for Negligently Distributing Guns, 4 J. Health Care L. & Pol'y 42 (2000); Kairys, Legal Claims of Cities Against the Manufacturers of Handguns, 71 Temp. L. Rev. 1

(1998); Bogus, Pistols, Politics and Products Liability, 59 U. Cin. L. Rev. 1103, 1145–48 (1991); Hardy, Product Liability and Weapons Manufacture, 20 Wake Forest L. Rev. 541 (1984); Turley, Manufacturers' and Suppliers' Liability to Handgun Victims, 10 N. Ky. L. Rev. 41 (1982). See also Notes, a Good Predictor of What the Future Holds for Gun Manufacturers?, 34 Ind. L. Rev. 419 (2001) (noting Hamilton v. Accu–Tek); 60 Md. L. Rev. 441 (2001) (noting Valentine v. On Target); 9 Harv. J. L. and Pub. Pol'y 764 (1986) (noting Kelley v. R.G. Indus.); 97 Harv. L. Rev. 1912 (1984); 49 Mo. L. Rev. 834 (1984) (noting Richman v. Charter Arms); 24 Wm. & Mary L. Rev. 467 (1983) (noting *Barker*); 1 Frumer and Friedman, Products Liability §§ 3.05, 12.07. Compare Notes, 108 Harv. L. Rev. 1679 (1995) (proposing statute imposing absolute liability for manufacture of ammunition), with 97 Harv. L. Rev. 1912, 1928 (1984) (role of handguns in society is properly for legislatures, and courts should not use products liability law to usurp control over issue of handgun control).

114. Gun fatalities divide as follows: 48% suicides, 47% homicides, 4% accidents, and 1% legal justice system. In addition, another 125,000 people are injured by guns each year. Lytton, Tort Claims Against Gun Manufacturers for Crime–Related Injuries: Defining a Suitable Role for the Tort System in Regulating the Firearms Industry, 65 Mo. L. Rev. 1, 1 (2000).

115. See Barnes, Taking Aim: The Impetus Driving Suits Against Gun Manufacturers, 27 Pepp. L. Rev. 735, 736 (2000) (noting, also that about half of all American households possess at least one gun).

Exhibit 2–3.   David G. Owen, Products Liability Law 661 (2005).

§ **11.** Liability of Commercial Product Seller or Distributor for Harm Caused by Post–Sale Failure to Recall Product

One engaged in the business of selling or otherwise distributing products is subject to liability for harm to persons or property caused by the seller's failure to recall a product after the time of sale or distribution if:

(a)(1) a governmental directive issued pursuant to a statute or administrative regulation specifically requires the seller or distributor to recall the product; or

(2) the seller or distributor, in the absence of a recall requirement under Subsection (a)(1), undertakes to recall the product; and

(b) the seller or distributor fails to act as a reasonable person in recalling the product.

Comment:

a. Rationale. Duties to recall products impose significant burdens on manufacturers. Many product lines are periodically redesigned so that they become safer over time. If every improvement in product safety were to trigger a common-law duty to recall, manufacturers would face incalculable costs every time they sought to make their product lines better and safer. Moreover, even when a product is defective within the meaning of § 2, § 3, or § 4, an involuntary duty to recall should be imposed on the seller only by a governmental directive issued pursuant to statute or regulation. Issues relating to product recalls are best evaluated by governmental agencies capable of gathering adequate data regarding the ramifications of such undertakings. The duty to recall or repair should be distinguished from a post-sale duty to warn about product hazards discovered after sale. See §§ 10 and 13.

Illustration:

1. MNO Corp. has manufactured and distributed washing machines for five years. MNO develops an improved model that includes a safety device that reduces the risk of harm to users. The washing machines sold previously conformed to the best technology available at time of sale and were not defective when sold. MNO is under no common-law obligation to recall previously-distributed machines in order to retrofit them with the new safety device.

b. Failure to recall when recall is specifically required by a governmental directive issued pursuant to statute or other governmental regulation. When a product recall is specifically required by a governmental directive issued pursuant to a statute or regulation, failure reasonably to comply with the relevant directive subjects the seller or other distributor to liability for harm caused by such failure. For the product seller or other distributor to be subject to liability

Exhibit 2–4. RESTATEMENT (THIRD) OF TORTS—PRODUCTS LIABILITY § 11 (1998).

C. City Suits and the Emergence of the Public Nuisance Claim

In 1998, New Orleans became the first city to bring suit against gun manufacturers for such abuses.[47] Over the next five years, thirty-two more cities and municipalities followed suit in a common attempt to recoup their financial losses and force the industry to adopt safer standards.[48] To achieve this end, various cities tried various traditional torts, with little success.[49]

The City of Chicago, however, took a new approach[50] in November of 1998 by bringing a public nuisance[51] claim against the gun industry.[52] The city claimed that, by irresponsibly marketing and distributing their products, the industry had created and maintained an illegal market for gun trafficking in Chicago.[53] The claim was dismissed in circuit court. The appellate court reversed only to have the Illinois Supreme Court reverse

---

aforementioned case); DOJ v. City of Chicago, 537 U.S. 1229 (2003) (vacating the Seventh Circuit opinion and remanding the matter to be reconsidered at the lower court levels, in light of the last-minute appropriations bill); City of Chicago v. United States Dep't of Treasury, 384 F.3d 429, 435 (7th Cir. 2005) (holding that the appropriations bill created no repeal by implication, and that the ATF must divulge the data in question); City of Chicago v. United States Dep't of Treasury, 2004 U.S. App. Lexis 28002, No. 01-2167 (7th Cir. Dec. 21, 2004) (granting the ATF's petition for rehearing en banc, in light of the Consolidated Appropriations Act of 2005).

47. Annie Tai Kao, Note, *A More Powerful Plaintiff: State Public Nuisance Lawsuits Against the Gun Industry*, 70 GEO. WASH. L. REV. 212, 213 (2002). *See also* BROWN & ABEL, *supra* note 9, at 1-6 (describing how the New Orleans suit was set into motion by the murder of gospel singer Raymond Miles).

48. Kao, *supra* note 47, at 213.

49. *See* Eggen & Culhane, *supra* note 9, at 136-41 (stating that plaintiffs bringing product liability suits argued that handguns were inherently defective, but the courts dismissed such claims, finding that weapons used in crimes operate exactly ss intended). City plaintiffs brought strict liability suits as well, in which they argued that the manufacture and marketing of handguns is an abnormally dangerous activity. *Id.* at 150. These, too, were dismissed, because the courts found that the third party criminal use of the weapons was what made them abnormally dangerous, not the industry's manufacture and marketing practices. *Id.* at 150-54. Likewise, claims against manufacturers for negligent marketing and negligent entrustment foundered on the element of proximate cause, because the relationship between gun manufacturers and criminals was deemed too remote. *Id.* at 142-50.

50. Kao, *supra* note 47, at 214.

51. *See* RESTATEMENT (SECOND) OF TORTS § 821B(1) (1979) (defining a public nuisance as "an unreasonable interference with a right common to the general public"). This interference must be of a continuing or long-lasting nature, and the actor must know or have reason to know of it. *Id. See also* Kao, *supra* note 47, at 214 (clarifying that the right implicated in the governmental lawsuits is the public's right to health and safety). The interference is the gun industry's irresponsible design, marketing, and distribution of firearms to the public. *Id.*

52. *City of Chicago v. Beretta U.S.A. Corp.*, 785 N.E.2d at 20.

53. *Id.* at 20-21.

Exhibit 2–5. James L. Daniels, Comment, *Violating the Inviolable: Firearm Industry Retroactive Exemptions and the Need for a New Test for Overreaching Federal Prohibitions*, 38 J. MARSHALL L. REV. 955, 962 (2005).

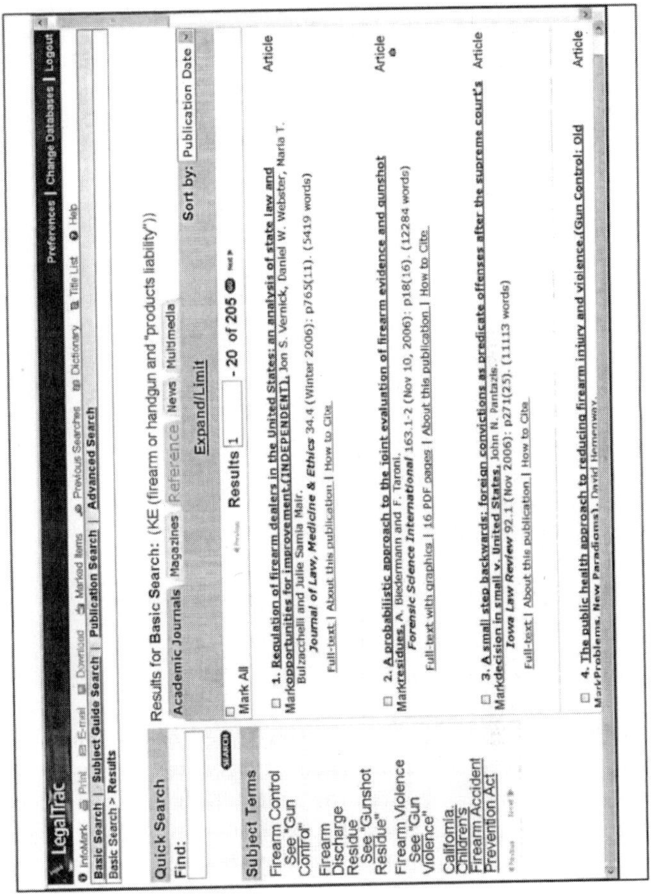

Exhibit 2–6. LegalTrac search results list.

CHAPTER 3

CASE LAW SOURCES

---

§ 3–1. Introduction

Reports of judicial decisions are among the most important sources of legal authority in the common law system. Over the course of time, judges shape legal doctrines to address the complex issues of changing society. Legislative enactments now cover an ever broader range of issues, but case law continues to retain its vitality. Even a statute that may appear straightforward must be read in light of the court decisions which construe and apply its provisions.

Court reports are the subject of this chapter and Chapter 4. This chapter describes the court reports and online databases in which cases are found, while the following chapter discusses ways to use these resources to find relevant cases. Together, the two chapters provide an introduction to case law research.

To use court reports effectively, it is necessary to understand the hierarchical structure of the American judicial system. Litigation usually begins in a *trial court*. The jurisdiction of these courts may be based on geography (the U.S. District Courts in the federal system, or county courts in many states) or subject (the U.S. Tax Court, or state family courts and probate courts). In the trial court, *issues of fact* (such as which of two cars entered an intersection first) are decided by the fact finder, either the judge or a jury. These findings are binding on the parties and cannot be appealed. *Issues of law* (such as whether a witness's statement is admissible at trial) are decided by the judge, and a party who disagrees with these rulings can appeal them to a higher court.

Appeals from trial court decisions are generally taken to an *intermediate appellate court* (the U.S. Courts of Appeals and similar state tribunals). An appellate court usually consists of a panel of three or more judges, who typically confer and vote on the issues after considering written briefs and oral argument for each side. One of the judges writes an opinion summarizing the question and stating the court's holding. Dissenting judges may write separate opinions outlining their views.

The *court of last resort* in each jurisdiction (called the Supreme Court in the federal system and in most states) usually reviews cases from the intermediate appellate courts, but may take appeals directly from trial courts. Unlike other appellate courts, most courts of last resort have discretion in deciding which cases they will hear. Their role in the judicial system is not to resolve every individual dispute, but rather to establish rules, review legislative and administrative acts, and resolve differences among intermediate appellate courts. A court of last resort's decisions on issues of law are binding on all courts within its jurisdiction.

Numerous works provide more extensive discussions of the role of judges in deciding cases and creating legal doctrine. Daniel John Meador's *American Courts* (2d ed. 2000) is one of the more concise introductory works. Longer treatments designed as course texts but useful for background reading and references to other sources include Lawrence Baum, *American Courts: Process and Policy* (5th ed. 2001) and Robert A. Carp et al., *Judicial Process in America* (6th ed. 2004).

Most court reports consist of the decisions of courts of last resort and intermediate appellate courts on issues of law. Very few trial court decisions are published. Trial court decisions on issues of fact have no precedential effect and usually do not even result in written judicial opinions. A jury verdict at the end of a trial, for example, produces no published decision unless the judge must rule on a motion challenging the verdict on legal grounds. Some trial court decisions on issues of law are published, but they are generally less important than appellate court decisions. Selected intermediate appellate court decisions and nearly all decisions from courts of last resort are published both in printed volumes and electronically.

A bit of history may help in understanding court reports. The American colonies inherited the English legal system and its common law tradition. Colonial lawyers and judges relied on English precedents, as no decisions of American courts were published until *Kirby's Reports*, in Connecticut, in 1789. Reports from other states and from the new federal courts soon followed. *Official* series of court reports (published pursuant to statutory direction or court authorization) began in several states in the early 1800s. Many of these early reports were cited by the names of their reporters and are known as *nominative reports*.

As the country grew in the 19th century, the number of reported decisions increased dramatically and official reporting systems began to lag further and further behind. The need for timely access to cases was met by commercial publishers. In 1876, John B. West began publishing selected decisions of the Minnesota Supreme Court in a weekly leaflet, the *Syllabi*. Three years later he launched the *North Western Reporter*, covering five surrounding states as well as Minnesota. By 1887, West published cases from every state and the federal system, in what became known as the National Reporter System. These reporters are now the most widely accepted source for citations to court opinions. Exhibit 3–1 on page 94 shows the beginning of a case in *West's Atlantic Reporter*.

New decisions are now available electronically much sooner than they are published in print. The most widespread electronic resources are the commercial databases Westlaw and LexisNexis, but a number of smaller companies and court websites also provide access to court decisions. Even though many researchers find and read cases online instead of in printed reports, cases are still identified by citations to the published volumes. Generally, only cases unavailable in print are cited to electronic sources.

The first print appearance of a new decision is the official *slip opinion* issued by the court itself, usually an individually paginated copy of a single decision. Slip opinions provide the text of new cases and are often available free from official court websites, but they have two major drawbacks for research purposes. They rarely provide editorial enhancements summarizing the court's decision and facilitating the research process, and because their page numbering is not final they must be cited by docket number and date rather than to a permanent published source. Several jurisdictions have ameliorated this second problem by assigning public domain citations to their recent cases. Such opinions are numbered sequentially as they are issued, and each paragraph is numbered so that a particular point in an opinion can be identified. The public domain citation for the case in Exhibit 3–1 on page 94, *State v. Cleaves*, is 2005 ME 67, indicating that this is the 67th decision delivered in 2005 by the Supreme Judicial Court of Maine. The page shown includes the first numbered paragraph of the court's opinion and the beginning of the second paragraph.

The next form of printed court reports provides the editorial summaries and page citations lacking in slip opinions. Cases usually appear first in weekly or biweekly pamphlets known as *advance sheets*, containing a number of decisions paginated in a continuous sequence, and then in bound volumes. The volumes consolidate the contents of several advance sheets, and most contain alphabetical tables of the cases reported as well as subject indexes or digests. They are numbered consecutively, often in more than one successive series. When the volumes of a reporter reach an arbitrary number (such as 100 or 300), publishers frequently start over with volume

1, second series. Some reporters are now in their third or fourth series. If a reporter is in a second or later series, that must be indicated in its citation in order to distinguish it from the same volume number in the first series. The case in Exhibit 3–1, for example, is on page 872 of volume 874 of the second series of the *Atlantic Reporter*, and is cited as *State v. Cleaves*, 874 A.2d 872 (Me. 2005).

Most court reports include editorial features which make it easier to find and understand the decisions. In West's National Reporter System series, each case is prefaced with a brief summary of its holding, called a *synopsis*, and with numbered editorial abstracts, or *headnotes*, of the specific legal issues. Each headnote is assigned a legal topic and a number indicating a particular subdivision of that topic. This classification plan, known as the *key number system*, consists of over four hundred broad topics and tens of thousands of subtopics. The headnotes are reprinted by subject in *digests*, which allow uniform subject access to the cases of different jurisdictions and will be discussed in Chapter 4. *State v. Cleaves* in Exhibit 3–1 has three numbered headnotes, in the Criminal Law and Weapons topics.

Exhibit 3–1 includes other standard features of court reports. In the middle of the right column is a list of the lawyers representing the parties. Below this are the names of the judges who heard the case, and that of the judge writing the majority opinion.

LexisNexis adds its own editorial material, including a case summary outlining the procedural posture, overview and outcome, as well as headnotes and computer-generated "Core Terms." Exhibit 3–2 on page 95 shows the LexisNexis version of *State v. Cleaves*, including the beginning of the case summary. In this instance the Lexis display also includes the docket number, located immediately below the names of the parties, useful for tracking down briefs and other information.

§ 3–2. Supreme Court of the United States

The Supreme Court of the United States stands at the head of the judicial branch of government, and provides the definitive interpretation of the U.S. Constitution and federal statutes. Its decisions are studied not only by lawyers but by political scientists, historians, and citizens interested in the development of social and legal policy.

The Supreme Court is the court of last resort in the federal court system. It also has the final word on federal issues raised in state courts, and it hears cases arising between states. The Court exercises a tight control over its docket and has wide discretion to decline review, or to *deny a writ of certiorari* as it is called in almost all cases. The Supreme Court usually accepts for consideration only those cases that raise significant policy issues. In recent years it has issued opinions in fewer than ninety cases during its annual term, which begins on the first Monday of October and ends in late June or early July.

Numerous reference works explain the history and role of the Supreme Court in the American political and legal system. Two of the more highly esteemed are Leonard W. Levy et al., eds., *Encyclopedia of the American Constitution* (6 vols., 2d ed. 2000), and Kermit L. Hall, ed., *Oxford Companion to the Supreme Court of the United States* (2d ed. 2005), which both provide encyclopedic coverage of the Court and include articles on major cases, doctrinal areas, and individual justices. David G. Savage, *Guide to the U.S. Supreme Court* (2 vols., 4th ed.

2004) is arranged thematically rather than alphabetically, but it too explains major doctrines and provides historical background. A wide range of statistical and historical information is available in Lee Epstein et al., eds., *The Supreme Court Compendium: Data, Decisions, and Developments* (4th ed. 2007). The major practical guide for lawyers bringing a case before the Court is Robert L. Stern et al., *Supreme Court Practice* (8th ed. 2002).

Of websites providing background information on the Court, one of the most useful is from the Supreme Court Historical Society <www.supremecourthistory.org>. It includes sections on the Court's history and how it works, as well as a guide to researching various Supreme Court topics. The Supreme Court's own website <www.supremecourtus.gov> also includes a variety of information in its "About the Supreme Court" section.

Reference sources are useful for historical and general background, but they cannot cover the latest developments and they are no substitute for reading the opinions of the Supreme Court. The Court makes law through its decisions in individual cases. These decisions are available in a variety of printed and electronic means. They are published in three permanent bound reporters and in a weekly newsletter providing access to new decisions, and they can be searched and retrieved through several commercial databases and free Internet sites.

a. The *United States Reports*

Begun in 1790 as a private venture, the *United States Reports* (cited as U.S.) became official in 1817 and continues today as the official edition of United States Supreme Court decisions. The government publishes several volumes of *U.S. Reports* every year. The decisions appear first in slip opinion form, followed by an official advance sheet (called the "preliminary print"), and finally the bound *U.S. Reports* volume. Unfortunately, as with many government publications, the *U.S. Reports* tends to be published rather slowly. More than a year passes before a decision appears in the preliminary print, and another year before its inclusion in a bound volume. (In contrast, the decisions are available electronically within minutes of their issuance.)

The early volumes of Supreme Court decisions are now numbered sequentially as part of the *U.S. Reports* series, but for many years they were cited only by the names of the individual reporters. *Bluebook* citations to these early cases include a parenthetical reference to the nominative reporter volume, as in *Marbury v. Madison*, 5 U.S. (1 Cranch) 137 (1803), while *ALWD* rules use the *U.S. Reports* citation only. Older cases and articles, however, tended to cite only the nominative reports, so a familiarity with the early reporters' names and their periods of coverage will make it easier to read and understand these citations:

1–4 Dallas (Dall.)	1–4 U.S. (1790–1800)
1–9 Cranch	5–13 U.S. (1801–15)
1–12 Wheaton (Wheat.)	14–25 U.S. (1816–27)
1–16 Peters (Pet.)	26–41 U.S. (1828–42)
1–24 Howard (How.)	42–65 U.S. (1843–61)
1–2 Black	66–67 U.S. (1861–63)
1–23 Wallace (Wall.)	68–90 U.S. (1863–75)

Beginning with volume 91 (October Term 1875), *U.S. Reports* volumes are cited only by number and not by the name of the reporter. Thus the official citation of the Supreme Court's decision in *Muscarello v. United States* is 524 U.S. 125 (1998), meaning the case beginning on page 125 of volume 524 of the *U.S. Reports*. The opening pages of the official report of *Muscarello* appear in Exhibits 3–3 and 3–4 on pages 96–97. This version does not include numbered headnotes, but the Court's reporter of decisions prefaces the text of each decision with a *syllabus* summarizing the case and the Court's holding. Following the syllabus, Exhibit 3–4 identifies the attorneys in the case and shows the beginning of the majority opinion by Justice Breyer.

The Supreme Court website <www.supremecourtus. gov> has new slip opinions as soon as they are announced, in PDF to replicate the appearance of the printed slip opinions. The site has slip opinions from recent terms, although these lack the pagination necessary for citing purposes. Under the heading "Opinions— Bound Volumes," the site also has PDF files containing the bound volumes of *U.S. Reports* beginning with volume 502 (October Term 1991). With each volume of a thousand pages or more, these are large and rather cumbersome files but they do provide access to the official text.

Much more extensive online coverage is provided by the subscription site HeinOnline <www.heinonline. org>, which provides searchable and browseable access to page images of the *U.S. Reports* all the way from volume one through the preliminary prints to the most recent slip opinions. Cornell Law School's Legal Information Institute <supct.law.cornell.edu/supct/> provides a free source for PDF images of current and recent slip opinions. Image files begin in 1997, although Cornell also has all cases since 1990 and several hundred historic decisions. Cornell also offers a notification service for new decisions, providing the official syllabus by e-mail with links to the full text.

b. *Supreme Court Reporter* and *Lawyers' Edition*

Supreme Court opinions are also printed in two commercially published series, Thomson West's *Supreme Court Reporter* (cited as S. Ct.) and LexisNexis's *United States Supreme Court Reports, Lawyers' Edition* (known simply as *Lawyers' Edition*, and cited as L. Ed.). These reporters are valuable because they contain editorial features not available in the official *U.S. Reports*, and they are the versions found in Westlaw and LexisNexis respectively.

Because the *U.S. Reports* are published so slowly, the *Bluebook* and the *ALWD Citation Manual* specify that a recent opinion that does not yet have a *U.S.* citation should be cited to the *Supreme Court Reporter* or *Lawyers' Edition*. Both of these sources are published in paperback advance sheets within a few weeks of decision. The permanent bound volumes are not published until the cases appear in the *U.S. Reports* volumes, so that the commercial editions can include *star paging* with references to the official *U.S. Reports* page numbers. Star paging allows the researcher to use the commercial volumes while citing directly to the official text.

The *Supreme Court Reporter* began in 1882, with cases from volume 106 of the *U.S. Reports*. As a component of West's National Reporter System, it includes the publisher's editorial synopses and headnotes. The opening page of *Muscarello v. United States* as it appears in the *Supreme Court Reporter* at 118 S. Ct. 1911 is shown in Exhibit 3–5 on page 98, including the synopsis and first

West headnote. Note the star paging before the petitioner's name at the beginning of the case.

Westlaw provides the text of the *Supreme Court Reporter*, but its database of Supreme Court cases extends beyond the Supreme Court Reporter's coverage in both directions. The database has complete historical coverage of the Court's decisions since 1790, and new decisions are available within minutes of their release. For cases since 1918 that have been published in bound *Supreme Court Reporter* volumes, Westlaw provides the option to view and print a PDF file of the printed version.

Lawyers' Edition contains all Supreme Court decisions since the Court's inception in 1790. It is now in a second series, and its version of *Muscarello* is cited as 141 L. Ed. 2d 111 (1998). Like the *Supreme Court Reporter*, *Lawyers' Edition* contains editorial summaries and headnotes for each case. The early *Lawyers' Edition* volumes are particularly valuable, because the editors worked from the original manuscripts rather than the sometimes erroneous versions in the *U.S. Reports*. For some cases they include information, such as the exact date of decisions, not found in the official reports.

Like Westlaw, LexisNexis has Supreme Court cases since the Court's inception in 1790, as well as the most recent decisions the same morning that they are announced. The online cases include the *Lawyers' Edition* editorial treatment, including star paging references to the official *U.S. Reports*.

c.   Other Sources

While *Supreme Court Reporter* and *Lawyers' Edition* are published much sooner than the official *U.S. Reports*, there is still a lag of several weeks while editors prepare their synopses and headnotes. Another publication provides access to Supreme Court cases much sooner in a newsletter format, reproducing the official slip opinions and mailing them to subscribers the week they are announced. This service, *The United States Law Week* (cited as U.S.L.W.), published by the Bureau of National Affairs, is the preferred *Bluebook* and *ALWD* citation for very recent Supreme Court decisions. As will be discussed in Chapter 8, *U.S. Law Week* also provides extensive information about the Supreme Court's docket, arguments, and other developments.

Researchers without Westlaw or LexisNexis access can find Supreme Court opinions at several free Internet sites, in addition to the Court's own website and Cornell's Legal Information Institute. Two sites for free access to the entire retrospective Supreme Court collection back to 1790 are Justia.com <supreme.justia.com> and lexisONE <www.lexisone.com>, LexisNexis's website for small law firms. FindLaw <www.findlaw.com/casecode/supreme.html> has all opinions since 1893. Both Justia.com and FindLaw provide hypertext links in opinions to other Supreme Court cases cited.

Subscription sites such as Loislaw <www.loislaw.com> and VersusLaw <www.versuslaw.com> also have more than a century of older decisions. A number of publishers offer CD–ROM versions of Supreme Court opinions; some of these include only recent cases, while others provide complete coverage since 1790.

§ 3–3. Lower Federal Courts

The federal court system has grown extensively from the thirteen District Courts and three Circuit Courts created by the Judiciary Act of 1789. The intermediate appellate courts in the federal system, the United States Courts of Appeals, are divided into thirteen circuits, consisting of the First through Eleventh Circuits (each covering several states), the District of Columbia Circuit, and the Federal Circuit. The general trial courts, the United States District Courts, are divided into ninety-four districts, with one or more in each state. In addition, there are several specialized trial courts, such as the Bankruptcy Courts, the Court of Federal Claims, and the Court of International Trade. The map in Exhibit 3–6 on page 99 show the boundaries of the circuits and districts. The U.S. Courts website has a color version of this map with links to individual court sites <www.uscourts.gov/courtlinks/>.

The most comprehensive and most frequently used sources for federal court opinions are the databases of Westlaw and LexisNexis, which have complete coverage back to the beginning of the court system in 1789. The *Bluebook* and *ALWD Citation Manual*, however, require that cases be cited to printed reporters if available there.

There is no counterpart to the *U.S. Reports* for the decisions of the U.S. Courts of Appeals and District Courts. The only officially published sources are the individual slip decisions the courts issue and post on their websites. The only comprehensive printed sources for lower federal court decisions are reporters published by Thomson West. In 1880 West's *Federal Reporter* began covering decisions of both the district and circuit courts. More than 1,700 volumes later it is now in its third series (cited as F.3d). In 1932, with the increasing volume of litigation in the federal courts, West began another series called *Federal Supplement* (F. Supp.) for selected U.S. District Court decisions, leaving the *Federal*

Reporter to cover U.S. Courts of Appeals decisions. *Federal Supplement* is now in its second series (F. Supp. 2d), and also includes decisions of the U.S. Court of International Trade and rulings from the Judicial Panel on Multidistrict Litigation. Like the *Supreme Court Reporter*, both of these reporters contain editorial synopses and headnotes with key numbers, allowing researchers to find cases through West's series of digest publications.

Because these reporters cover so many different courts (unlike the *U.S. Reports*), citations to the *Federal Reporter* or *Federal Supplement* must identify the specific circuit or district in parentheses. The lower court's ruling in the *Muscarello* case, for example, is cited as *United States v. Muscarello*, 106 F.3d 636 (5th Cir. 1997). This is vital information in evaluating the scope and precedential value of a decision, but beginning researchers often omit this detail.

The *Federal Reporter* and *Federal Supplement* publish thousands of new decisions each year, but not every case the lower federal courts consider is represented by a decision published in one of these reporter series. Some matters are settled or tried to a jury verdict and do not result in any written opinions. Decisions in many cases are issued as slip opinions but are not published in the reporters. In an attempt to limit the proliferation of reported cases, each circuit has local court rules establishing criteria to determine whether decisions are published (e.g., establishing a new rule of law, resolving a conflict in the law, or involving issues of continuing public interest). Under a new Federal Rule of Appellate Procedure, "unpublished" or "non-precedential" decisions issued after January 1, 2007, can be cited as persuasive authority, but the handling of earlier decisions varies from circuit to circuit. Some courts prohibit citation of these decisions; some allow citation, but with restrictions; and some simply limit their precedential value.

Some "unpublished" decisions are available in printed sources. In 2001, West began publishing *Federal Appendix*, a series limited to Court of Appeals decisions "not selected for publication in the *Federal Reporter*." These decisions are published with headnotes and are indexed in West's digests, but it remains necessary to determine to what extent they can be cited as precedent. More unreported decisions can be found online from Westlaw, LexisNexis, and court websites. For some unreported decisions, particularly in older cases, it may be necessary to contact the clerk of the court.

Before the inception of the *Federal Reporter* in 1880, federal court decisions were issued in more than a hundred different series of nominative reports. West gathered these cases in the 1890s into a thirty-volume series called *Federal Cases*. This set incorporates over 20,000 early decisions, arranged in alphabetical sequence by case name.

Another West series, *Federal Rules Decisions* (F.R.D.), began publication in 1940 and contains a limited number of U.S. District Court decisions dealing with procedural issues under the Federal Rules of Civil Procedure and the Federal Rules of Criminal Procedure. *Federal Rules Decisions* also includes judicial conference proceedings and occasional speeches or articles dealing with procedural law in the federal courts.

Thomson West also issues a number of other reporters in specialized subject fields of federal law. These selective reporters include: *Military Justice Reporter* (1978–date), containing decisions of the U.S. Court of Appeals for the Armed Forces (formerly the U.S. Court of Military Appeals), as well as selected decisions of the Court of Criminal Appeals for each military branch; *Bankruptcy Reporter* (1980–date), containing Bankruptcy Court decisions and bankruptcy decisions from the U.S. District Courts; *Federal Claims Reporter* (1982–date), containing U.S. Court of Federal Claims (formerly U.S. Claims Court) decisions; and *Veterans Appeals Reporter* (1991–date), containing U.S. Court of Veterans Appeals decisions. These last three reporters also reprint decisions from the Courts of Appeals and Supreme Court in their subject areas. West's National Reporter System does not include decisions from the U.S. Tax Court, which are published by the government, in *Reports of the United States Tax Court* (1942–date), and by the major commercial tax publishers.

Federal court decisions are also printed in a variety of other sources, including commercial topical reporters designed for practitioners in specialized subject areas. Some cases appearing in these sources are not available in the *Federal Reporter* or *Federal Supplement*, although there is extensive duplication. In addition to *Federal Rules Decisions*, West publishes two more series of cases on procedural issues which are *not* part of its National Reporter System, *Federal Rules Service* (1939–date) and *Federal Rules of Evidence Service* (1979–date). Other reporters in specialized areas include *American Maritime Cases* (1923–date), *Environment Reporter Cases* (1970–date), and *U.S. Patents Quarterly* (1929–date). Several topical reporters, such as BNA's *Fair Employment Practice Cases* (1969–date) and CCH's *Trade Cases* (1948–date), are published as adjuncts to looseleaf services on those topics.

Westlaw and LexisNexis provide full-text coverage of all federal court cases that appear in print in these various reporters, back to the earliest decisions in *Federal Cases*, and new decisions are available online well before they are published. Once the final printed version of a case is published in a bound volume, Westlaw makes the page images available online. In addition, the electronic services also provide access to many decisions which never appear in the reporters, making them the most comprehensive sources for current decisions. Databases in both services include thousands of decisions not available in any other form, except as slip opinions. As a result many case citations are to the online databases. Exhibit 3–7 on page 100 shows a case available on Westlaw but not in print, *City of New York v. Beretta U.S.A. Corp.*, 2005 WL 1279183 (E.D.N.Y. May 26, 2005). The same case is available from LexisNexis, where its citation is 2005 U.S. Dist. LEXIS 10313.

Recent decisions from the Courts of Appeals are also available from free Internet sites. LexisONE provides five years of free coverage, and in most instances sites for individual circuits have opinions going back to about 1995. Sources such as the U.S. Courts homepage <www.uscourts.gov/courtlinks/> provide quick access to specific circuit court sites.

District and bankruptcy courts are also represented on the Internet, but most of these sites focus on local rules and procedures rather than the text of decisions. The U.S. Courts homepage provides links to each court's site, and FindLaw has a list of websites <www.findlaw.com/10fedgov/judicial/district_courts.html> with brief descriptions of their contents.

Commercial services such as Loislaw and VersusLaw provide more extensive Internet access to Court of Appeals decisions. Loislaw coverage generally begins in 1924, while VersusLaw has coverage from 1930 for most circuits. District court coverage varies, with selected cases from 1921 on Loislaw and 1932 on VersusLaw. Lower federal court decisions are published on CD–ROM as well, in most instances in separate products for individual circuits.

§ 3–4. State Courts

Although federal law governs an increasing range of activities, state courts have a vital lawmaking role on many issues, including important areas such as family law, contracts, insurance, and substantive criminal law. A state's court of last resort has the final say in interpreting the state's constitution and statutes.

The structure of most state court systems roughly follows the federal paradigm, with various trial courts, intermediate appellate courts, and a court of last resort. There are, however, wide variations. A few states have no intermediate appellate courts, with appeals going directly from the trial court to the state supreme court. Other states have more complicated systems, with more than one appellate court for different subject areas. Some states even have separate courts of last resort for civil and criminal matters.

A good way to develop a quick familiarity with a state court system is to examine a chart of its structure, such as those found in the U.S. Bureau of Justice Statistics publication *State Court Organization 2004* or the National Center for State Courts' annual *State Court Caseload Statistics*. Both organizations have these publications online in PDF (<www.ojp.usdoj.gov/bjs/abstract/sco04. htm> and <www.ncsconline.org/D_Research/csp/ CSP_Main_Page.html>). The tables are reprinted in several other sources, including the annual issues of *BNA's Directory of State and Federal Courts, Judges, and Clerks* and CQ Press's *Federal-State Court Directory*.

Just as Supreme Court decisions are published both in the official *U.S. Reports* and in commercial reporters, so decisions from state appellate courts are traditionally published both in official reports, issued by or under the auspices of the courts themselves, and in West's series of National Reporter System volumes.

The computer systems of LexisNexis and Westlaw are virtually comprehensive sources for state court decisions, lacking only a very few early reports from some states. The online systems include some opinions not available in print, but coverage is generally limited to the same courts for which reports are published. Very few state trial court decisions are available either in print or in online case databases. It may be necessary to contact the court for copies of opinions and other documents.

a. Official Reports

Like the *U.S. Reports*, state official reports are the authoritative version of a court's decisions and must be cited in briefs before that court. They are generally less widely available than commercial reporters, which are usually published more quickly and are more useful in research. In fact, twenty-one states have ceased publishing official reports series and have designated a West reporter as the authoritative source of state case law. Appendix A of this book, on page 427, gives information

on the current status of the published reports in each
state.

Forms of publication vary from state to state. Some
states publish just one series of reports, containing decisions of the state supreme court and in some instances of
intermediate appellate courts as well. More than a dozen
states issue two or more series of reports, with separate
series for decisions of the supreme court, for intermediate appellate decisions, and in a few states for selected
trial court decisions. New York, for example, has three
official series: *New York Reports*, covering the Court of
Appeals, the state's court of last resort; *Appellate Division Reports*, covering the Appellate Divisions of the
Supreme Court; and *Miscellaneous Reports*, with decisions of various lower courts. Some states publish official
slip decisions and advance sheets, but not every state.
Exhibit 3–8 on page 101 shows the first page of *Commonwealth v. Wilkerson*, an opinion of the Supreme Judicial
Court of Massachusetts, in *Massachusetts Reports*. Instead of numbered headnotes, note that it simply has an
introductory paragraph summarizing the decision.

Even though official reports do not generally include
links to a comprehensive digest system like West's, they
can still provide a valuable perspective on a state's appellate court decisions. If the summaries or headnotes are
written by court staff or by lawyers practicing in that
state, they may be more attuned to local judicial developments than headnotes written by commercial editors.
Some official reports include research leads not found in
the West reporters, and others provide their own classification and digest systems. Although official reports are
less widely used than West's, in some jurisdictions they
maintain an important research role.

As with the early *U.S. Reports* volumes, the early reports of several of the older states were once cited as nominative reports (identified by the names of their reporters). Many of these volumes have now been incorporated into the numbered series, but it may still be necessary to use an abbreviations dictionary or other reference work to understand some case citations. Westlaw and LexisNexis generally recognize the nominative reporter citations, so there may be no need to decipher the citation before retrieving a case online.

b. National Reporter System

West's National Reporter System includes a series of *regional reporters* publishing the decisions of the appellate courts of the fifty states and the District of Columbia. The National Reporter System divides the country into seven regions, and publishes the decisions of the appellate courts of the states in each region together in one series of volumes. Five of these sets are now in their second series (*Atlantic* (A.2d), *North Eastern* (N.E.2d), *North Western* (N.W.2d), *South Eastern* (S.E.2d), *Southern* (So. 2d); and two have started their third series (*Pacific* (P.3d) and *South Western* (S.W.3d)). These sets are supplemented by separate reporters for the two most populous states, *California Reporter* (Cal. Rptr. 3d) and *New York Supplement* (N.Y.S.2d). (Cases from the highest courts of California and New York appear in both the regional and the state reporter, while lower court cases are not published in the *Pacific* or *North Eastern Reporter*.) These nine reporters, together with West's federal court reporters, comprise a uniform system tied together by the key number headnote and digest scheme. The map in Exhibit 3–9 on page 102 shows which states are included in each region of the reporter system; it is

available in color online <lawschool.westlaw.com/
federalcourt/NationalReporterPage.asp>. Appendix A, on
page 427, indicates the scope of coverage for each state
appellate court in the regional reporters.

West also publishes individual reporters for over thirty
additional states. Unlike the *California Reporter* and
New York Supplement, however, most of these other
series simply reprint a state's cases from its regional
reporter, including the original regional reporter pagination. These "offprint" reporters are published for
practitioners who need their own state courts' decisions
but not cases from other states.

Exhibit 3–10 on page 103 shows the first page of the
Massachusetts Supreme Judicial Court decision in *Commonwealth v. Wilkerson*, as printed in West's *North
Eastern Reporter*. Note that this version includes an
introductory synopsis and three numbered headnotes. In
addition, the *North Eastern Reporter* version includes
star paging indicating the exact page breaks in the official *Massachusetts Reports*.

In most states, cases appear in both official and National Reporter System editions. Cases are traditionally
cited to both of these sources, with the official reports
cited first. Note in Exhibit 3–10 that the official citation
is printed above the name of the case. The two citations
for the same decision are known as *parallel citations*. In
Commonwealth v. Wilkerson, 436 Mass. 137, 763 N.E.2d
508 (2002), for example, the citation to the official *Massachusetts Reports* precedes the citation to the unofficial
North Eastern Reporter.

The *Bluebook* and *ALWD Citation Manual* require
parallel citations *only* for cases cited in documents submitted to that state's courts; in other documents such as

law review articles and memoranda, only the National Reporter System citation is used. (If Massachusetts had a public domain citation system like Utah's, that citation would be included along with the West citation.) If the cited reporter does not clearly identify the deciding court (as does *Massachusetts Reports*), remember to include this information in parentheses with the date: *Commonwealth v. Wilkerson*, 763 N.E.2d 508 (Mass. 2002).

If you have a citation to only one report of a case, there are several ways to find its parallel citation. The simplest is usually to retrieve the case in an online database, which will generally provide both citations. The parallel citation is sometimes, but not always, printed at the beginning of the case, as it is in Exhibit 3–10 on page 103. Thomson West publishes a series of volumes called the *National Reporter Blue Book*, which is updated annually and lists the starting page of each case in the official reports and provides cross-references to National Reporter System citations.

Not all cases have parallel citations. Only the official reports exist for older state cases, before West created the National Reporter System in the 1880s. On the other hand, in those states that have discontinued their official reports and have not institute public domain citation systems, only the West reporter citation will exist for recent cases.

c. Other Sources

In addition to Westlaw and LexisNexis, other commercial online databases also provide access to state court decisions; Loislaw, for example, has more than eighty years of case law for most states. Numerous state CD–ROM publications are available as well, many combining court decisions with current statutory codes and other materials.

Free Internet sites provide convenient access to court decisions beginning in the mid- to late–1990s, although some states maintain only the most recent three months of decisions on their official websites. A few states lead the way with much more extensive databases; the Oklahoma State Courts Network <www.oscn.net> has the entire history of the state's appellate courts, back to 1890. As it does with the U.S. Courts of Appeals, lexisONE provides a five-year collection of state appellate decisions.

The easiest way to find websites for state court decisions is through a general legal resources site such as FindLaw. Its State Resources page <www.findlaw.com/11stategov/> provides links to official and commercial sites for each state under "Primary Materials." Several law school sites, including Cornell's Legal Information Institute <www.law.cornell.edu/opinions.html>, have similar links, and the National Center for State Courts has a "Court Web Sites" list <www.ncsconline.org/D_KIS/info_court_web_sites.html> with links to state judiciary systems and individual courts.

§ 3–5. Conclusion

This chapter has introduced case law as it is published in the United States today, both in print and through a variety of electronic means. While publication methods have changed dramatically, the structure of court systems and the inherent nature of judicial decisions remain relatively constant. This chapter's focus has been on the cases themselves, leaving to subsequent chapters the methods of finding case law relevant to a research problem. Chapter 4 will discuss several of the most important means of case research.

In addition to their value as legal precedent and their importance in legal research, court reports constitute a literary form with other values as well. They describe human problems and predicaments—domestic crises, moral failings, economic troubles. They reflect the larger social, political and economic trends and conditions of life in particular periods and places. And they frequently have a unique literary quality which adds to the tone and substance of the prose of their time. Judicial decisions have always been an influential part of our literature.

2005 ME 67

STATE of Maine

v.

William R. CLEAVES Jr.

Supreme Judicial Court of Maine.

Submitted On Briefs: May 17, 2005.

Decided: June 10, 2005.

Background: Defendant was convicted in the Superior Court, Washington County, Gorman, J., of reckless conduct with a firearm. Defendant appealed.

Holdings: The Supreme Judicial Court, Alexander, J., held that:

(1) trial court's failure to instruct jury on the justifications of competing harms and self-defense was not obvious error, and

(2) evidence was sufficient to support conviction.

Affirmed.

1. Criminal Law ⬅1038.2

Trial court's failure to instruct jury, with respect to charge of the reckless conduct with a firearm, on the justifications of competing harms and self-defense was not obvious error; defense made a choice to waive justification instructions, as presenting justification issue to jury could have suggested an inference that defense was conceding that the crime may have been committed but may have had a justification, and such would have been inconsistent with defense trial strategy. 17-A M.R.S.A. §§ 101, subd. 1, 103, 108, subd. 1.

2. Criminal Law ⬅1030(1)

For obvious error to require the reversal of a judgment, the error must deprive the party of a fair trial or resulted in such a serious injustice that, in good conscience, the judgment cannot be allowed to stand.

3. Weapons ⬅17(4)

Evidence was sufficient to support reckless conduct with a firearm conviction; evidence indicated that defendant grabbed a loaded firearm, introduced it into an altercation, and then waived it around for up to twenty minutes of struggling, and no loose shells were found on defendant's person or in the vicinity of the struggle to support defendant's claim that he was unloading firearm during the struggle. 17-A M.R.S.A. §§ 211, 1252, subds. 4, 5.

_____

Michael E. Povich, District Attorney, Paul F. Cavanaugh, 1st Asst. Dist. Atty., Calais, for State.

Christopher James Whalley, Esq., Ellsworth, for defendant.

Panel: SAUFLEY, C.J., and CLIFFORD, RUDMAN, ALEXANDER, CALKINS, and LEVY, JJ.

ALEXANDER, J.

[¶ 1] William R. Cleaves Jr. appeals from a judgment of the Superior Court (Washington County, *Gorman J.*) finding him guilty, after a jury trial, of reckless conduct with a firearm (Class C), 17-A M.R.S.A. §§ 211(1), 1252(4), (5) (1983 & Supp.2004). Cleaves asserts that the court committed obvious error in failing to instruct the jury on the justifications of competing harms, 17-A M.R.S.A. § 103 (1983), and self-defense, 17-A M.R.S.A. § 108(1) (1983). Because trial counsel did not request the instructions at issue and no obvious error is demonstrated in the court not giving the instructions *sua sponte,* we affirm the conviction.

I. CASE HISTORY

[¶ 2] William R. Cleaves Jr. and his fiancée, now his wife, were living with her two

Exhibit 3–1.   *State v. Cleaves*, 2005 ME 67, 874 A.2d 872.

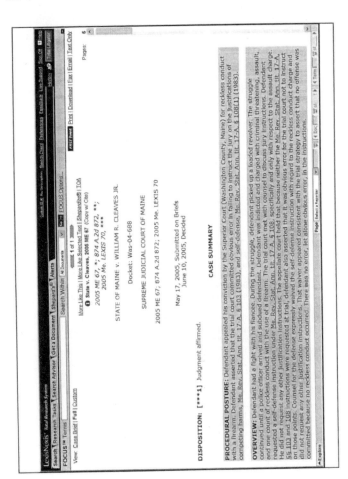

Exhibit 3–2. *State v. Cleaves*, 2005 ME 67, on LexisNexis.

Syllabus

MUSCARELLO *v.* UNITED STATES

CERTIORARI TO THE UNITED STATES COURT OF APPEALS FOR THE FIFTH CIRCUIT

No. 96–1654.　Argued March 23, 1998—Decided June 8, 1998*

A person who "uses or carries a firearm" "during and in relation to" a "drug trafficking crime" is subject to a 5-year mandatory prison term. 18 U. S. C. § 924(c)(1).　In the first case, police officers found a handgun locked in the glove compartment of petitioner Muscarello's truck, which he was using to transport marijuana for sale.　In the second case, federal agents at a drug-sale point found drugs and guns in the trunk of petitioners' car.　In both cases, the Courts of Appeals found that petitioners had carried firearms in violation of § 924(c)(1).

Held: The phrase "carries a firearm" applies to a person who knowingly possesses and conveys firearms in a vehicle, including in the locked glove compartment or trunk of a car, which the person accompanies. Pp. 127–139.

　(a) As a matter of ordinary English, one can "carry firearms" in a wagon, car, truck, or other vehicle which one accompanies.　The word's first, or basic, meaning in dictionaries and the word's origin make clear that "carry" includes conveying in a vehicle.　The greatest of writers have used "carry" with this meaning, as has the modern press.　Contrary to the arguments of petitioners and the dissent, there is no linguistic reason to think that Congress intended to limit the word to its secondary meaning, which suggests support rather than movement or transportation, as when, for example, a column "carries" the weight of an arch.　Given the word's ordinary meaning, it is not surprising that the Federal Courts of Appeals have unanimously concluded that "carry" is not limited to the carrying of weapons directly on the person but can include their carriage in a car.　Pp. 127–132.

　(b) Neither the statute's basic purpose—to combat the "dangerous combination" of "drugs and guns," *Smith* v. *United States,* 508 U. S. 223, 240—nor its legislative history supports circumscribing the scope of the word "carry" by applying an "on the person" limitation.　Pp. 132–134.

　(c) Petitioners' remaining arguments to the contrary—that the definition adopted here obliterates the statutory distinction between "carry" and "transport," a word used in other provisions of the "fire-

*Together with No. 96–8837, *Cleveland et al.* v. *United States,* on certiorari to the United States Court of Appeals for the First Circuit.

Exhibit 3–3.　*Muscarello v. United States,* 524 U.S. 125 (1998).

126 MUSCARELLO *v.* UNITED STATES

Opinion of the Court

arms" section of the United States Code; that it would be anomalous to construe "carry" broadly when the related phrase "uses . . . a firearm," 18 U. S. C. § 924(c)(1), has been construed narrowly to include only the "active employment" of a firearm, *Bailey* v. *United States*, 516 U. S. 137, 144; that this Court's reading of the statute would extend its coverage to passengers on buses, trains, or ships, who have placed a firearm, say, in checked luggage; and that the "rule of lenity" should apply because of statutory ambiguity—are unconvincing. Pp. 134–139.

No. 96–1654, 106 F. 3d 636, and No. 96–8837, 106 F. 3d 1056, affirmed.

BREYER, J., delivered the opinion of the Court, in which STEVENS, O'CONNOR, KENNEDY, and THOMAS, JJ., joined. GINSBURG, J., filed a dissenting opinion, in which REHNQUIST, C. J., and SCALIA and SOUTER, JJ., joined, *post*, p. 139.

Robert H. Klonoff argued the cause for petitioner in No. 96–1654. With him on the briefs were *Gregory A. Castanias, Paul R. Reichert,* and *Ron S. Macaluso. Norman S. Zalkind,* by appointment of the Court, 522 U. S. 1074, argued the cause for petitioners in No. 96–8837. With him on the briefs were *Elizabeth A. Lunt, David Duncan,* and *John H. Cunha, Jr.,* by appointment of the Court, 522 U. S. 1074.

James A. Feldman argued the cause for the United States in both cases. With him on the brief were *Solicitor General Waxman, Acting Assistant Attorney General Keeney,* and *Deputy Solicitor General Dreeben.*†

JUSTICE BREYER delivered the opinion of the Court.

A provision in the firearms chapter of the federal criminal code imposes a 5-year mandatory prison term upon a person who "uses or carries a firearm" "during and in relation to" a "drug trafficking crime." 18 U. S. C. § 924(c)(1). The question before us is whether the phrase "carries a firearm" is limited to the carrying of firearms on the person. We hold that it is not so limited. Rather, it also applies to a person

†*Daniel Kanstroom, David Porter,* and *Kyle O'Dowd* filed a brief for the National Association of Criminal Defense Lawyers et al. as *amici curiae* urging reversal.

Exhibit 3–4. *Muscarello*, 524 U.S. at 126.

Arg. 9.[5]

* * *

[8] When Congress makes Indian reservation land freely alienable, it manifests an unmistakably clear intent to render such land subject to state and local taxation. The repurchase of such land by an Indian tribe does not cause the land to reassume tax-exempt status. The eight parcels at issue here were therefore taxable unless and until they were restored to federal trust protection under § 465. The judgment of the Court of Appeals with respect to those lands is reversed.

It is so ordered.

524 U.S. 125, 141 L.Ed.2d 111

|₁₂₆Frank J. MUSCARELLO, Petitioner,

v.

UNITED STATES.

Donald E. CLEVELAND and Enrique Gray–Santana, Petitioners,

v.

UNITED STATES.

Nos. 96–1654, 96–8837.

Argued March 23, 1998.

Decided June 8, 1998.

The United States District Court for the Eastern District of Louisiana, Marcel Livaudais, Jr., J., granted motion to quash de-

fendant's conviction of carrying firearm during and in relation to drug trafficking crime in light of intervening case law. The Fifth Circuit Court of Appeals, 106 F.3d 636, reversed and remanded. In second case, defendant was convicted of same firearms offense following jury trial before the United States District Court for the District of Massachusetts, Robert E. Keeton, J. The First Circuit Court of Appeals, 106 F.3d 1056, affirmed. Both defendants petitioned for certiorari. The Supreme Court, Justice Breyer, held that: (1) phrase "carries a firearm" is not limited to carrying of firearms on person, but also applies to person who knowingly possesses and conveys firearms in a vehicle, which person accompanies, and (2) both carrying drugs and weapons in truck of vehicle to drug-sale location and carrying firearm in locked glove compartment of vehicle while transporting drugs were "carrying firearm" within statute.

Affirmed.

Justice Ginsburg filed dissenting opinion, in which Chief Justice Rehnquist, and Justices Scalia and Souter joined.

1. Weapons ⟜10

Phrase "carries a firearm" as used in statute imposing mandatory prison term upon person who uses or carries firearm during and in relation to drug trafficking crime, is not limited to carrying of firearms on person, but also applies to person who knowingly possesses and conveys firearms in a vehicle, including in the locked compartment or trunk of a car, which the person accompanies. 18 U.S.C.A. § 924(c)(1).

See publication Words and Phrases for other judicial constructions and definitions.

---

5. The Leech Lake Band and the United States, as *amicus,* also argue that the parcels at issue here are not alienable—and therefore not taxable—under the terms of the Indian Nonintercourse Act, which provides: "No purchase, grant, lease, or other conveyance of lands … from any Indian nation or tribe … shall be of any validity in law or equity, unless the same be made by treaty or convention entered into pursuant to the Constitution." 25 U.S.C. § 177.

This Court has never determined whether the Indian Nonintercourse Act, which was enacted in 1834, applies to land that has been rendered

alienable by Congress and later reacquired by an Indian tribe. Because the parcels at issue here are not alienable—and therefore not taxable—under the terms of the Indian Nonintercourse Act, which provides: "No taxation if it remains freely alienable", and because it was not addressed by the Court of Appeals, we decline to consider it for the first time in this Court. See, e.g., *Matsushita Elec. Indus. Co. v. Epstein,* 516 U.S. 367, 379, n. 5, 116 S.Ct. 873, 880, n. 5, 134 L.Ed.2d 6 (1996) (declining to address issue both because it was "outside the scope of the question presented in this Court" and because "we gener-

---

Exhibit 3–5.   *Muscarello v. United States,* 118 S.Ct. 1911 (1998).

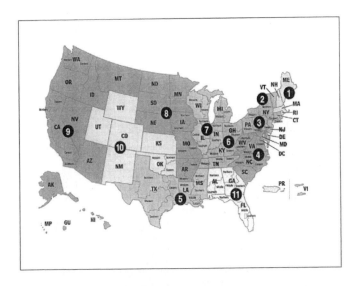

Exhibit 3–6. Map of the United States Courts of Appeals and District Courts, <www.uscourts.gov/courtlinks/>.

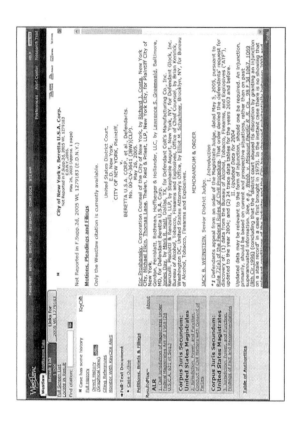

Exhibit 3–7. *City of New York v. Beretta U.S.A. Corp.*, 2005 WL 1279183 (E.D.N.Y. May 26, 2005).

Commonwealth *v.* Wilkerson.

COMMONWEALTH *vs.* RON P. WILKERSON.

Barnstable. January 10, 2002. - February 25, 2002.

Present: MARSHALL, C.J., GREANEY, IRELAND, SPINA, COWIN, SOSMAN, & CORDY, JJ.

Probable Cause. Arrest. Search and Seizure, Arrest, Probable cause. *Constitutional Law,* Search and seizure, Probable cause. *Registrar of Motor Vehicles,* Records.

On a criminal defendant's motion to suppress certain physical evidence on the ground that his arrest was constitutionally invalid because probable cause was based on what was later disclosed to be erroneous information provided to the arresting officer by the registry of motor vehicles about the status of the defendant's license, the motion was properly denied, where, since the arresting officer relied on records of an independent State agency rather than police records to make the otherwise proper arrest, there was no unlawful conduct to be deterred by exclusion of the evidence, and nothing to encourage the police to maintain current and accurate computer records. [139-143]

An issue whether Miranda warnings were necessary at the time of a criminal defendant's arrest was not present, where no contention as to the need for, and lack of, the warnings was raised at the hearing on the defendant's motion to suppress evidence or at trial, and where nothing was raised at the trial to require the judge to inquire sua sponte into the voluntariness of the defendant's postarrest statements. [143]

COMPLAINT received and sworn to in the Barnstable Division of the District Court Department on May 15, 2000.

A pretrial motion to suppress evidence was heard by *Joan E. Lynch,* J., and the case was tried before her.

The Supreme Judicial Court on its own initiative transferred the case from the Appeals Court.

Harris Krinsky for the defendant.

Julia K. Holler, Assistant District Attorney, for the Commonwealth.

GREANEY, J. A jury in the District Court convicted the defendant of possession of a firearm (a rifle) without a firearms identification card, G. L. c. 269, § 10G. The defendant argues

---

Exhibit 3–8. *Commonwealth v. Wilkerson*, 436 Mass. 137 (2002).

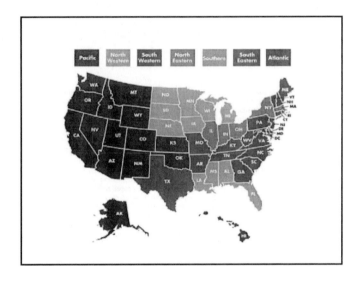

Exhibit 3–9. Map of West National Reporter System, <lawschool.
westlaw.com/federalcourt/NationalReporterPage.asp>.

508 Mass.   **763 NORTH EASTERN REPORTER, 2d SERIES**

436 Mass. 137

⌐₁₃₇COMMONWEALTH

v.

Ron P. WILKERSON.

Supreme Judicial Court of Massachusetts, Barnstable.

Submitted Jan. 10, 2002.

Decided Feb. 25, 2002.

Defendant was convicted, in the District Court Department, Barnstable Division, Joan E. Lynch, J., of possession of a firearm without a firearms identification card. Defendant appealed, and the appeal was transferred. The Supreme Judicial Court, Greaney, J., held that erroneous information from registry of motor vehicles provided probable cause for defendant's arrest.

Affirmed.

1. Automobiles ⬅️**349(4)**

Information furnished to police officer by registry of motor vehicles, that motorist's license to drive had been suspended, provided probable cause to arrest motorist for operating a vehicle after license suspension, though the information was later determined to be erroneous, where the police were not responsible for the error; the error was in the records of the registry of motor vehicles, and the registry of motor vehicles was an independent State agency. U.S.C.A. Const.Amend. 4; M.G.L.A. Const. Pt. 1, Art. 14; M.G.L.A. c. 16, § 9; c. 90, §§ 8, 22, 30.

2. Arrest ⬅️**63.4(4)**

Probable cause to arrest is not vitiated when the basis on which the police officer acted is shown after the fact to have been erroneous, because the existence of probable cause is determined at the moment of arrest, not in light of subsequent events. M.G.L.A. Const. Pt. 1, Art. 14.

3. Criminal Law ⬅️**394.4(4)**

The interest in deterring unlawful police conduct, which is the foundation of the exclusionary rule, is not implicated where police rely on erroneous records of an independent State agency to make an otherwise proper arrest. U.S.C.A. Const. Amend. 4; M.G.L.A. Const. Pt. 1, Art. 14.

———

Harris Krinsky, Boston, for the defendant.

Julia K. Holler, Assistant District Attorney, for the Commonwealth.

Present: MARSHALL, C.J., GREANEY, IRELAND, SPINA, COWIN, SOSMAN, & CORDY, JJ.

GREANEY, J.

A jury in the District Court convicted the defendant of possession of a firearm (a rifle) without a firearms identification card, G.L. c. 269, § 10G. The defendant argues ⌐₁₃₈that his pretrial motion to suppress the rifle (seized from the trunk of the automobile he was driving after the arrest and the impoundment of the vehicle) should have been granted. He asserts that his arrest for operating the automobile after his license had been suspended was constitutionally invalid because, in making the arrest, the police officer relied on erroneous information furnished by the registry of motor vehicles (registry) regarding the status of the defendant's driver's license. The defendant also argues that his statements made to the police after his arrest should have been suppressed because he was not afforded the Miranda warnings. Finally, the defendant claims that the trial

Exhibit 3–10. *Commonwealth v. Wilkerson*, 763 N.E.2d 508 (Mass. 2002).

CHAPTER 4

CASE LAW RESEARCH

§ 4–1. Introduction

For the doctrine of precedent to operate effectively, lawyers must be able to find cases which control or influence a court's decisionmaking. This requires locating "cases on point," earlier decisions with factual and legal issues similar to a dispute at hand. It is then necessary to determine that these decisions are valid law and have not been reversed, overruled, or otherwise discredited.

This chapter discusses several major tools which perform these functions, but it is not exhaustive. Several resources discussed in other chapters—such as legal encyclopedias, law reviews, annotated codes, and looseleaf services—are also valuable in case research. Much of legal research revolves around finding cases, a pursuit that is not confined to the methods introduced in this one chapter.

We start with an overview of electronic case research, the approach most widely used in legal practice today. We then introduce printed tools such as West digests and *ALR* annotations. These are complex resources that may at first seem more confusing than helpful, but skill in their use can yield more thorough, accurate results than online searching alone. The assistance of editors who have analyzed and classified related cases can lead to insights that a researcher using only full-text databases might never reach.

§ 4–2. Electronic Research

Chapter 1 provided a brief overview of basic online research techniques that can be applied in any database. This section will focus more specifically on ways to use case databases effectively.

This section focuses on Westlaw and LexisNexis procedures, but for researchers without access to these databases other alternatives are available. Several lower-cost case databases, such as Loislaw and VersusLaw, include extensive coverage of case law, and many college and university libraries subscribe to LexisNexis Academic, which incorporates many of LexisNexis's features. Some researchers may have access to their state's case law on CD–ROM rather than online. Generally these services and products provide access to the same cases as Westlaw and LexisNexis, but without the sophisticated editorial materials those systems provide.

Free Internet sites may be a starting point in case research, but they rarely provide a comprehensive result. They may offer a searchable database of a particular court's opinions, but most are limited in coverage to the past few years (or months), and opportunities to search multiple jurisdictions are limited. (There are exceptions. LexisONE permits searching the most recent five years of cases from all state courts or all federal appellate courts. The Legal Information Institute provides an engine <www.law.cornell.edu/usca/search/> that searches recent opinions from all of the U.S. Courts of Appeals, but the results are incomplete and can be difficult to decipher.)

Although free sites are most useful for obtaining copies of new decisions and monitoring recent developments, they may provide one or two cases that can lead to other documents. It is essential, however, not to overlook important precedent just because it is too old for a limited database.

a. Westlaw

The first decision in online case research is whether to limit a search to a specific jurisdiction. For some issues, it may not matter what courts in other states have decided. The only relevant cases are those from a particular state or within a narrow doctrinal area. For some research questions, however, other cases may be persuasive authority or may provide useful analogies.

Westlaw's most extensive case databases cover the entire country (ALLCASES for federal and state cases, ALLFEDS for just federal cases, and ALLSTATES for just state cases). For most research questions, however, it may be more productive to begin in a database limited to a specific state (XX–CS, using the postal abbreviation for the state). Because federal courts often are required to interpret state laws, another option is to search a database, XX–CS–ALL, that combines those state cases with the relevant federal jurisdictions (the U.S. Supreme Court, the particular U.S. Court of Appeals, and the U.S. District Courts within the state). This approach may yield too many results, as it includes *all* Supreme Court cases and *all* cases from the Court of Appeals, whether or not they arose in that state. These have precedential value in the state's federal district courts but usually have no relevance on issues of state law. It is usually best to start with just that state's courts and then expand to check federal case law once a more specific search can be crafted. Finding a small number of cases directly on point is better than finding a large number of vaguely relevant cases.

While searching the full text of opinions can often find relevant cases, the most effective Westlaw searches take advantage of the editorial synopsis and headnotes that precede each case (as shown in the several exhibits in Chapter 3). This focuses retrieval to cases that turn on the specific research issues, rather than any and all cases that may only mention the terms in passing.

There are two basic ways to search the synopsis and headnotes in Westlaw cases. Westlaw considers these parts of the case document as "fields," or portions of a document to which a search can be limited. Most fields can be entered into a search by using a two-letter abbreviation. The introductory summary is the *synopsis (sy)* field. (In cases added to Westlaw since December 2003, the synopsis is divided into *background* and *holding* fields, as shown in *State v. Cleaves* in Exhibit 3–1 on page 94. In earlier cases, as shown in *Muscarello v. United States* and *Commonwealth v. Wilkerson* in Exhibits 3–5 and 3–10 on pages 98 and 103, the synopsis is just one paragraph.) The background and holding can also be searched separately, but the synopsis field combines the two and searches earlier cases as well.

Following the synopsis are the numbered headnotes, which make up the *digest (di)* field. The digest field combines the *topic (to)* field, consisting of the subject heading and key number, and the *headnote (he)* field, containing the text of the note itself. While each of these fields can be searched separately, often the strongest search is one that encompasses the synopsis and digest by using both fields at once. A search for *sy,di(handgun)* will retrieve a smaller body of cases more precisely on point than a simple full-text search for *handgun*.

The other way to search the headnotes on Westlaw is to use the digest topics and key numbers assigned to each headnote. The West digest system consists of over 400 topics, arranged alphabetically from Abandoned and Lost Property to Zoning and Planning. *State v. Cleaves*, for example, has headnotes assigned to the topics Criminal Law and Weapons.

Each topic is then divided into numbered sections, called *key numbers*, designating specific points of law for that topic. This classification system serves the same purpose for legal topics that call numbers do for library books, in that it allows related items to be classed together whether or not they use the same keywords. The same legal issue may arise, for example, in cases involving handgun manufacturers and cigarette companies, but it may not occur to you to search for both "tobacco" and "firearms." The key numbers provide a way to make sure that all relevant cases on a single subject are being retrieved.

Some narrow topics like Party Walls employ relatively few key numbers, while broader ones such as Taxation or Trade Regulation may have thousands. The first headnote in *Muscarello v. United States*, shown in print in Exhibit 3–5 on page 98 and on Westlaw in Exhibit 4–1 on page 138, is Weapons 10, dealing with the manner of carrying or concealment of weapons.

For use in Westlaw, each of the topics has been assigned a number between 1 and 414. Weapons is topic 406, for example, and a search for Weapons ⌐═ 10 is *406k10*. This key number can used in combination with other terms to create a very precise and effective search.

Obviously you are not going to begin a research project with a search like *406k10*. The trick, though, is to assess the cases you retrieve through a keyword search or a synopsis and digest search; if a retrieved headnote is particularly relevant, then its key number can be used to find other cases. One way to do this is to click on the appropriate hyperlinked heading or key number. This brings up a Custom Digest search screen, on which you specify the courts to search and add keyword search terms if desired. The subsequent search finds similar headnotes, with links to the full text of the cases. Exhibit

4–2 on page 139 shows the search screen for *406k10* linked from the *Muscarello* headnote.

To make key number use more accessible, Westlaw also has a feature it calls Keysearch. To use Keysearch, you scan a list of forty-five broad topics and numerous more detailed subtopics until you reach the specific focus of your inquiry. Clicking on this term leads to a search screen on which you can specify a database and add additional search terms if you wish. Westlaw automatically creates a search to match the legal topic. Its search does not appear on the initial screen, but is revealed by clicking on *View/Edit Full Query.* For Criminal Justice— Particular Crimes—Weapons—Elements of Offenses, it creates the quite elaborate search: *406k4 406k5 406k14 406k15 220k5265 (258Ak790 /p (unlawful! unauthoriz! illegal! wrongful! /p use used using possess! sale sell purchas! buy! dispos!) (conceal! carry carries carried carrying) /p weapon gun pistol revolver shotgun handgun silencer rifle fire-arm grenade bomb bayonet).* (For cases without West headnotes, it prepares an even longer terms and connectors search.)

In addition to the synopsis and digest, other fields can be used to search particular parts of case documents. Thus searches can be limited to the names of the parties (*ti* or *title*), the judge writing the opinion (*ju* or *judge*), or a particular court (*co* or *court*). The easiest way to use these fields is to select one from the drop-down menu on the search screen; this enters the field abbreviation into the search with the cursor between the parentheses symbols.

Some fields allow research that is virtually impossible by other means. It would be a lengthy and tedious process manually to find all opinions written by a particular judge, but online case databases can easily retrieve a complete list of a judge's opinions with searches such as *ju(molloy)*. You can examine a judge's decisions on a particular topic by combining this request with other search terms.

As part of the screen display of a case, Westlaw provides citations to published versions, whether in official reports, West's National Reporter System, or looseleaf topical reporters, as well as to public domain citations. It also provides *star paging* references showing the exact reporter page on which particular text is printed, so that a quotation or reference can be cited to the appropriate page.

Westlaw's KeyCite feature is an integral part of case display. It shows whether a case is still good law, and provides a convenient way to find cases on related topics. KeyCite performs several valuable functions in the research process, and will be discussed later in the chapter with other citators, in § 4–5 beginning on page 127.

b. LexisNexis

For years a major difference between case research on Westlaw and LexisNexis was that Westlaw included editorial summaries of cases while LexisNexis had only the court opinions. LexisNexis, however, now has Case Summaries and headnotes for cases back to the 1930s, so its databases can be searched in several ways similar to those used in Westlaw. The Case Summaries and headnotes are accompanied by computer-generated "core terms" listing several of the major keywords found in the opinion. Exhibit 4–3 on page 140 shows these features as part of its display of *Muscarello v. United States*.

A LexisNexis Case Summary consists of three parts, a Procedural Posture explaining the nature and status of the litigation, an Overview summarizing the facts of the case, and an Outcome providing a brief description of the court's decision. For effective use of segment searching (the LexisNexis counterpart to Westlaw's fields), it is necessary to recognize that each of these is a distinct segment of the case document and must be searched separately. LexisNexis has no segment combining the parts of the Case Summary (no counterpart to Westlaw's *sy,di* search), but limiting a search to the Overview segment usually produces the most relevant results.

LexisNexis headnotes do not employ a numerical classification system like West's key numbers, but they can also be useful in case research. The terms in headnotes can be searched as a distinct segment. Once a relevant case is found, its headnotes can be incorporated into further searching in several ways. Clicking on "More Like This Headnote" runs a natural language search using the terminology of the headnote. Clicking on the hyperlinked topic headings for a headnote opens up a Search Advisor window displaying a topical outline of the subject area. Once you verify that the specific topic is relevant and click on it again, you can run a search retrieving other cases assigned to the same heading.

The LexisNexis headnotes are also valuable when expanding research using Shepard's Citations, which will be discussed separately in section§ 4–5.

LexisNexis includes star paging references to official reports, West's National Reporter System, and various topical reporters. Note at the top of the display of *Muscarello* in Exhibit 4–3 on page 140 that the U.S., S. Ct., and L. Ed. 2d cites are given followed by one, two, and three asterisks respectively. These asterisks in the body of the opinion show exactly where new pages in each reporter begin.

While many LexisNexis search features are also available to users of LexisNexis Academic and lexisONE, case display is not the same through these systems. Neither Academic nor lexisONE includes the case summaries or other editorial additions provided by lexis.com, and neither includes hypertext links to other documents cited in retrieved cases.

§ 4–3. West Digests

Digests are publications reprinting in a subject arrangement the headnotes from court reports; they are among the most powerful methods of case-finding. Despite the ease and flexibility of online access, keyword searching may miss relevant cases that can be found in the digests. Editorial analysis in organizing and classifying cases may lead to analogous cases that use different words from those that might occur to a researcher.

The most comprehensive digest system is Thomson West's key number system, covering every case in the publisher's National Reporter System. As explained earlier in this chapter, headnotes are written for each case and are assigned to a legal topic and a specific key number classification within that topic. A digest is simply a publication that reprints these headnotes in classified order.

All headnotes for cases in an advance sheet or reporter volume are reprinted in a Key Number Digest in the front of the advance sheet or at the back of the bound reporter volume. These digests serve as subject indexes to the cases in the advance sheet or volume. West then reprints these headnotes, arranged by key number, in multivolume digest series to provide subject access to the cases in hundreds of reporter volumes. Exhibit 4–4 on page 141 shows a page from West's Supreme Court Digest reprinting several headnotes from *Muscarello v. United States* under Weapons ⟜ 10.

The Thomson West key number system is not the only digest classification system used in legal research. Some looseleaf services and topical reporters use digests for cases in specific subject areas and will be discussed briefly in Chapter 9. *United States Supreme Court Reports, Lawyers' Edition* is accompanied by a digest arranging its cases' headnotes by subject, but the *Lawyers' Edition* classification system does not appear in other reports and is useful only for Supreme Court research.

Digests are valuable case-finders, but they do have several shortcomings. They consist simply of case abstracts, with no explanatory text, and it is often necessary to wade through many irrelevant entries to find citations to significant authorities. Headnotes may reflect dicta and may even misstate points of law in the cases they abstract. Digests generally don't indicate that a case may no longer be good law, unless it has been directly reversed or modified. It is essential to locate and read the cases themselves in order to find those which are actually pertinent, and then to verify their status using KeyCite or Shepard's Citations.

a. Finding Cases in Digests

To use a digest, you must identify a topic and key number relevant to the problem. Digest topics and key numbers can be found in several ways: (1) by using a

Descriptive–Word Index after analyzing the factual and legal issues involved in a problem; (2) by surveying the outline of a relevant legal topic; or (3) by using the headnotes of a case known to be on point. In addition, digests provide alphabetical tables of cases, so you can use the name of a known case to find its citations and the topics and key numbers to which its headnotes have been assigned.

Descriptive-Word Method. To find the appropriate key number under which relevant cases are digested, it is usually most productive to begin with the Descriptive–Word Index shelved either at the beginning or the end of each digest set. This detailed index lists thousands of factual and legal terms, and provides references to key numbers.

You can approach a Descriptive–Word Index either by looking up legal issues, such as causes of action, defenses, or relief sought; or, usually more efficiently, by looking up factual elements in an action, such as parties, places, or objects involved. For example, in a products liability case involving handgun manufacturers, you might use the index to investigate some of the legal issues or facts involved in the case (weapons, strict liability, proximate cause, standing). Exhibit 4–5 on page 142 shows a page from a Descriptive–Word Index, including a reference under the Weapons subheading "Carrying–Manner of carrying" to Weapons ⌦ 10. Besides numerous references to the Weapons topic, entries on the page also lead to the Constitutional Law and Criminal Law topics and provide cross-references to other digest entries such as Assault and Battery and Robbery.

Finding appropriate key numbers in the index can sometimes be a simple step. A researcher using any legal index, however, should be prepared for some frustration. Even the most thorough index cannot list every possible approach to a legal or factual issue. It is often necessary to rethink issues, reframe questions, check synonyms and alternate terms, and follow leads in cross-references.

When turning from the index to the volume of digest abstracts, it is often helpful to look first at the outline of the topic to verify that the legal context is indeed appropriate. You may be looking for cases on substantive negligence issues, for example, but find that a key number that appeared relevant actually deals with some other issue such as the standard of review for summary judgment. Exhibit 4–6 on page 143 contains the outline for the Weapons topic, showing how ⟜⟝ 10 fits with other issues involving the regulation and use of firearms.

Topic Approach. It is also possible to bypass the Descriptive–Word Index and go directly to the West digest topic that seems most relevant to a problem. Each topic begins with a scope note, indicating which subjects it includes and which are covered in related topics. The Weapons topic, for example, covers issues such as the right to bear arms and offenses involving concealed weapons, but it does not incorporate matters such as the regulation of militias (covered in the Militia topic) or specific crimes committed using weapons (covered in topics such as Homicide or Assault and Battery).

Once the correct topic is found, analyze the outline to select the appropriate key number for a specific issue. An advantage of this method is that it provides the context of the individual key numbers; reading through the outline may help clarify issues or raise concerns you had not yet considered. This can be a very time-consuming approach, however, and beginning researchers may not have the legal background to choose the right topic and determine the appropriate issues. In most instances, the index is a faster and more reliable starting point.

Case Headnotes. The easiest and most foolproof way to use a digest is to begin with the headnotes of a case on point. When you already know of a relevant case, you can find it in the National Reporter System volume or on Westlaw, scan its headnotes for relevant issues, and then use the key numbers accompanying these headnotes to search the digest. This eliminates the need to search through indexes or to analyze the digest's classification system, and reduces the likelihood of turning to the wrong issue or getting stuck in a dead end. This method, of course, requires that at least one initial case be found through other means, but several other case-finding resources—from legal encyclopedias to online full-text searches—have already been discussed.

b. *Decennial* and *General Digests*

West digests are available for the entire country, for some regions, for individual states, and for a few specific subjects. Choosing the right digest depends on the scope of the inquiry. For some research you may want to find cases from only one jurisdiction, but for other projects you may be interested in developments throughout the country. A more focused digest obviously covers fewer cases but is usually easier to use.

The most comprehensive series of digests is known as the American Digest System. Its most current component, the *General Digest*, collects and publishes headnotes from all West advance sheets. The *General Digest* is published about every three weeks, with each volume covering the entire range of more than 400 digest topics.

One *General Digest* volume cumulates entries from about twenty reporter volumes from federal and state courts.

The entries in the *General Digest* do not cumulate, so one may have to look through several dozen volumes to search for recent cases. This search is eased somewhat by tables listing the key numbers found in each volume. These tables cumulate every tenth volume. If twenty-seven *General Digest* volumes have been published, for example, it would be necessary to check the tables in volumes 10, 20, and 27. An excerpt from one of these tables is shown in Exhibit 4–7 on page 144.

Every few years, West recompiles the headnotes from the *General Digest* and publishes them in a multivolume set called a *Decennial Digest*. The name *Decennial* comes from the fact that these sets used to be published every ten years. The *Eighth Decennial*, for example, covers cases decided between 1966 and 1976. Due to the increased volume of case law, West now compiles these digests after every sixty volumes of the *General Digest*. The *Eleventh Decennial Digest, Part 2* is the most recent set, covering 2001–04.

The first unit of the American Digest System, called the *Century Digest*, covers the long period from 1658 to 1896. It was followed by a *First Decennial Digest* for 1897 to 1906, and subsequent *Decennials* for each decade since. The topics and key numbers used for points of law are generally the same in each unit of the digest system, from the most recent back to the *First Decennial*. The *Century Digest* employs a slightly different system, but the *First Decennial* provides cross-references between the two units. Thus research using a digest key number can turn up cases from the seventeenth century to the present.

The law, of course, has not remained static over these centuries. West attempts to reflect new developments by revising and expanding old topics and by establishing new topics. When they are introduced, new or revised topics are accompanied by tables converting older topics and key numbers into those newly adopted and vice versa. In 2001, for example, West created the new topics Child Custody and Child Support, with subject matter formerly found in Divorce, Parent and Child, and other topics. The new topics include conversion tables so that you can find related cases whether they are using the older *Decennials* or the newest *General Digest* volumes.

The digest changes slowly, however, and it may take several years for new areas of legal doctrine to be recognized and to receive adequate coverage. Until 2004, for example, cases involving products liability claims about firearms were classified in the Weapons topic under "Liabilities for injuries from illegal or negligent manufacture, sale, or use." As the amount of firearms litigation grew, weapons were given their own key number, 60.5, within the Products Liability topic. Because cases in newly developing areas of the law are often assigned to general key numbers, digest research may not be the best way to find cases in these areas.

c. Jurisdictional and Regional Digests

The American Digest System covers cases in all of West's reporters, and is therefore a massive, sometimes unwieldy finding tool. West also publishes digests covering the decisions of smaller geographical or jurisdictional units. There are digests for four of the regional reporter series (*Atlantic*, *North Western*, *Pacific*, and *South Eastern*), and for every state but Delaware, Nevada and Utah. The state digests include references to all the cases West publishes from the state's courts, as well as federal cases arising from the U.S. District Courts in that state. (Federal courts often interpret and apply state law, sometimes addressing issues with which the state courts have not yet dealt.)

One advantage of using a state digest instead of the American Digest System is that a single volume can contain all relevant headnotes from a century or more. (For about a dozen states, the current digest only provides coverage of cases back to 1930 or later, and an earlier digest must be consulted for complete retrospective coverage to the earliest court decisions. Most research, however, requires consulting only the current set for cases on point.) Instead of being issued in ten-year installments, state digests cumulate and are kept up to date by annual pocket parts in the back of each volume, by quarterly pamphlets between annual supplements, and by occasional replacement volumes incorporating the newer material.

Another significant advantage to state digests arises when classifications change, as happened with the Child Custody and Child Support topics in 2001. As part of the process, West editors reclassified the headnotes in thousands of older relevant cases, but this change is reflected only on Westlaw and in newly recompiled state digest volumes. *Decennial Digests* are closed sets, and conversion tables are needed to find relevant cases under the older classifications.

West also publishes a separate series of digests for federal court decisions, containing headnotes reprinted from the *Supreme Court Reporter*, *Federal Reporter*, *Federal Appendix*, *Federal Supplement*, *Federal Rules Decisions*, and the reporters for specialized federal courts.

The current set is known as the *Federal Practice Digest 4th*. Its volumes are supplemented by annual pocket parts, and the entire set is further updated with bi-monthly pamphlets. Earlier cases are covered by four previous sets, the *Federal Digest* (1754–1939), *Modern Federal Practice Digest* (1939–61), *Federal Practice Digest 2d* (1961–75), and *Federal Practice Digest 3d* (1975 to mid–1980s).

The decisions of the Supreme Court of the United States are also covered by a West digest devoted solely to its decisions, the *United States Supreme Court Digest*. (Note that *Lawyers' Edition* is also accompanied by its own digest, *United States Supreme Court Digest, Lawyers' Edition*, which uses a different classification system.) Other digests for specialized federal courts include *West's Bankruptcy Digest*, *Military Justice Digest*, *Federal Claims Digest*, and *Veterans Appeals Digest*.

Regional and jurisdictional digests include Tables of Cases which can be used to find decisions by name. These tables are usually more convenient than the *Decennial Digest* tables since they cover longer time periods and are updated by pocket parts. If a case's jurisdiction is unknown, of course, it may be necessary to consult the tables in the *Decennial* or *General Digests*.

d. *Words and Phrases*

West reprints some headnote abstracts in a separate multivolume set, *Words and Phrases*. Headnotes are included in *Words and Phrases* if a court defines or interprets a legally significant term. *Words and Phrases* is arranged alphabetically rather than by key number, and it can be a useful tool when the meaning of a specific term is at issue.

The *Words and Phrases* set covers the entire National Reporter System. Shorter "Words and Phrases" lists also appear in many West digests and in West reporter volumes and advance sheets. Exhibit 4–8 on page 145 shows a page from *Words and Phrases* including the first headnote from *Muscarello v. United States*, interpreting the meaning of the phrase "carries a firearm."

Judicial definitions from *Words and Phrases* can also be found on Westlaw by searching the *wp* field. For example, a search in the ALLCASES database for *wp(carr! /2 firearm)* will retrieve *Muscarello* and several other cases defining "carry a firearm" or "carrying a firearm."

§ 4–4. *American Law Reports* Annotations

At the same time that West was developing its National Reporter System in the late 19th century, other publishers were attempting a different approach to case reporting. They selected "leading cases" for full-text publication, and provided commentaries, or *annotations*, which surveyed the law on the subject of the selected case and in the process described other decisions with similar facts, holdings, or procedures. Selective publication was not a successful alternative to comprehensive reporting, but the annotations have proved to be valuable case research tools.

Among the early sets of annotated reporters were the "Trinity series" (*American Decisions*, *American Reports* and *American State Reports*) (1871–1911) and *Lawyers Reports Annotated* (*LRA*) (1888–1918). *LRA*'s successor, *American Law Reports* (*ALR*), began in 1919 and is now published in two current series: *ALR6th* for general and state legal issues, and *ALR Federal 2d* for issues of federal law. A few annotations limited to Supreme Court cases are also published in *United States Supreme Court Reports, Lawyers' Edition*.

Annotations summarize the cases on a specific topic and classify decisions that have reached conflicting results. The coverage of *ALR* is not encyclopedic, and not every research issue is covered by its annotations. An annotation directly on point, however, can save considerable research time. It does the initial time-consuming work of finding relevant cases, and arranges them according to specific fact patterns and holdings. Because it synthesizes the cases into a narrative discussion, rather than simply offering a collection of headnotes, an annotation is usually easier to understand than a digest.

Annotations differ significantly from other narrative resources such as treatises and law review articles. Their main purpose is to organize the varied judicial decisions from around the country into a coherent body of law. They generally do not criticize these decisions or analyze legal problems, nor do they attempt to integrate case law into a broader view of society as the better secondary sources do. They are best viewed as research tools rather than as secondary authority which may persuade a tribunal, and are cited as convenient compilations of prevailing judicial doctrine.

ALR annotations are available on both Westlaw and LexisNexis. Westlaw coverage goes all the way back to the beginning of *ALR1st*, and is updated weekly. It even includes new annotations that have not yet been released for publication in the print *ALR*. LexisNexis coverage begins with *ALR2d* and is not updated as frequently, but it also includes *Lawyers' Edition 2d* annotations. Annotations beginning with *ALR3d* are also published on CD–ROM.

a. Format and Content

An *ALR* volume usually contains from ten to twenty annotations, each analyzing decisions on an issue raised in an illustrative recent case, which is printed in full either before the annotation or at the end of the volume. Each annotation begins with a table of contents, a detailed subject index, and a table listing the jurisdictions of the cases discussed. In volumes published since 1992 (the beginning of *ALR5th*), this introductory material has also included a Research References section providing leads to encyclopedias, practice aids, digests, and other sources, as well as sample electronic search queries and relevant West digest key numbers. Exhibits 4–9 and 4–10 on pages 146–147 show pages from the beginning of an *ALR5th* annotation on the liability of firearm manufacturers for injuries caused by the use of guns in committing crimes. Exhibit 4–9 shows the table of contents, organizing the annotation's sections according to theories of liability and whether or not liability was established. Exhibit 4–10 shows parts of the index, listing specific factual scenarios and legal issues arising in the cases discussed, and the jurisdictional table, a state-by-state listing of the cases.

The first two sections of an annotation are an introduction describing its scope and a summary providing a general overview and giving practice pointers. For annotations before *ALR6th* and *ALR Fed 2d*, § 1[b] provides a list of related *ALR* annotations; these are now included in the Research References section. From the firearm manufacturer annotation, Exhibit 4–11 on page 148 shows the list of related annotations in § 1[b] and the beginning of the § 2 summary. The remaining sections of the annotation then summarize cases on point from throughout the country, arranged according to their facts and holdings.

The annotation in Exhibits 4–9 through 4–11 on pages 146–148 was originally published in 2001, but its annual supplement also provides references to more recent developments (including the effect of the Protection of Lawful Commerce in Arms Act, passed in 2005). *ALR3d–6th*, *ALR Fed*, and *ALR Fed 2d* are updated with pocket parts in each volume, but *ALR1st* and *ALR2d* use other methods. These older annotations are not used as often as those in the newer series, but many remain current and continue to be updated. *ALR2d* volumes have no pocket parts, so instead new cases are summarized in a separate set of blue *Later Case Service* volumes, which *do* have annual pocket parts. Annotations in *ALR1st* are updated through a set called *ALR1st Blue Book of Supplemental Decisions*, which simply lists relevant new case citations. The electronic versions incorporate supplementary material into the appropriate sections of the annotation.

If later cases substantially change the law on a subject covered by an annotation, a new annotation may either supplement or completely supersede the older annotation. The older volume's pocket part or other supplement alerts you to the existence of the newer treatment (another good reason to *always* check the pocket part). Online, a notice and a link to the newer annotation simply replaces the older work. Another way to determine whether an annotation has been superseded is to check the "Annotation History Table" in the back of each volume of the *ALR Index*, which lists all superseding and supplementing annotations.

b.   Finding Annotations

The online versions of *ALR* annotations are searchable by keyword, just like cases or law review articles. Annotations describe the facts of the cases discussed, including aspects unrelated to the subject of the annotation, so a full-text search often turns up numerous documents on unrelated topics. Because annotations have descriptive titles and introductory summaries, it may be useful to limit a search to the *title* or *summary* portions of the document. A natural language search, which automatically ranks documents by relevance, may also be a way to focus in on the most useful annotations.

The basic tool for subject access to the printed version of *ALR* is the seven-volume *ALR Index*, which is kept current by quarterly pocket parts. (The annotations in the first series of *ALR* are indexed in a separate *ALR First Series Quick Index*, and *Lawyers' Edition* annotations are listed in its *Quick Case Table with Annotation References*.) A less comprehensive *ALR Quick Index* covers only *ALR3d-6th*, and is published as an annual softcover volume; a separate *ALR Federal Quick Index* is limited to *ALR Fed* and *ALR Fed 2d* annotations. Exhibit 4–12 on page 149 shows a page from the *ALR Index*, including references under "Weapons and Firearms" to the annotation illustrated and to other annotations on firearm manufacturing.

Remember that in almost all *ALR* annotations, either section 1[b] or the Research References section provides a list of other annotations on related topics. If a quick check of the index does not turn up an annotation directly on point but does lead to one on a related issue, the most productive next step may be to turn to that annotation and read through its list of related annotations. This list could lead to analogies or concepts you may not have thought to check in the index. The section 1[b] list shown in Exhibit 4–11 on page 148, for example, includes a dozen cross-references to annotations on topics such as the validity of "assault weapon" prohibitions and liability for selling guns to children.

Another means of access to annotations is through the *ALR Digest*, a multivolume set classifying *ALR*'s annotations and cases in West's key number system. Older digests using a different classification system may be found in some libraries, but these are no longer being updated.

One can also find relevant annotations by using a particular cited case or statute. The citators to be discussed in the next section, KeyCite and Shepard's Citations, both include coverage of annotations citing cases, and KeyCite also lists annotations citing statutes. In print, the *ALR Index* is accompanied by a volume listing the statutes, rules and regulations cited in *ALR2d* to *5th* and *ALR Federal*, and the more recent series have multivolume tables of cases listing the decisions cited in their annotations.

Several other sources, including some annotated codes and encyclopedias, provide references to relevant *ALR* annotations. Note, for example, the *ALR* references in *Am. Jur. 2d* in Exhibit 2–1 on page 62.

§ 4–5. Citators

The body of published American case law is filled with decisions which have long since been overruled or limited to specific facts. Before relying on any case, an attorney must verify its current validity. This process of updating cases was traditionally performed by checking printed volumes known as *Shepard's Citations*, and as a result it is sometimes known as *Shepardizing*. Shepard's information is now available electronically on LexisNexis as well as in print, and Westlaw has a competing electronic resource, KeyCite, that provides a similar service.

Citators perform three major functions, whether they are used electronically or in print:

• Providing parallel citations for the decision and references to other proceedings in the same case, allowing you to trace a case's judicial history;

• Indicating if subsequent cases have overruled, limited, or otherwise diminished a case's precedent, providing the information you need to determine whether it is still good law; and

• Listing research leads to later citing cases, as well as periodical articles, attorney general opinions, *ALR* annotations, and other resources, enabling you to find related cases and to trace the development of a legal doctrine forward from a known case to the present.

KeyCite and Shepard's are invaluable resources not only because they validate research already done and ensure that cases are still "good law." They also serve as powerful links from one document to others on related issues, providing one of the most effective ways to find sources for further research. They analyze and sort these cases, providing information about their impact on the cited case and their relevance to a particular research issue.

While KeyCite and Shepard's provide the most systematic and thorough methods for verifying the status of a case, it is also possible to find citing references by doing a full-text search in later documents for a case's name or citation. Automating this process is in effect what is done by Loislaw's GlobalCite or the Oklahoma State Courts Network's "Citationizer" <www.oscn.net>.

a. KeyCite

Westlaw's citator service, KeyCite, is incorporated fully into its case research system. Any case display on Westlaw provides several links to KeyCite information. Links on the left side of the screen include *Full History* (decisions which may bear a direct impact on a case's validity) and *Citing References* (the full list of citing documents). In addition, a small symbol at the top of the case display indicates what citator information is available. A red flag generally indicates that a case is not good law on some point, and a yellow flag that there is some negative history. If neither of these flags is applicable, a blue "H" indicates that there is some case history information available or a green "C" shows that there are citing references. Clicking on one of these symbols leads directly to the case's KeyCite display. KeyCite information can also be accessed by typing a citation into a form on Westlaw's welcome screen, or by clicking on the KeyCite link at the top of any Westlaw screen.

Full History includes prior and subsequent decisions in the same litigation, so that the case can be traced through the appellate process, and "negative indirect history" cases, those decisions involving different litigants that may have an adverse impact on the precedential value of the cited case. Be aware, however, that "negative" history is broadly construed. A lower court decision that declines to extend a Supreme Court precedent to an unrelated area is listed as "distinguishing" its holding. This is considered a negative citation, even though it has no impact on the Supreme Court decision's precedent. Another option, Direct History (Graphical View), shows the course of the litigation with arrows and separate sections for trial courts, intermediate appellate courts, and courts of last resort.

Citing References lists negative citing cases first, and then the remaining cases by the extent to which they discuss the cited case, with rankings from four stars (an extended discussion) to one star (mentioned in a list with other citations). KeyCite also indicates those cases that quote directly from the cited case, by adding quotation marks to the display. Secondary sources such as law review articles and *ALR* annotations are listed next, followed by briefs and other appellate and trial court documents. The court documents, but not the secondary sources, include star rankings and quotation marks. Links provide access to the full text of any of these citing documents.

KeyCite provides several ways to focus your retrieval. *Limits* can be used to see only those references from specific jurisdictions, or those that cite the point of law in particular headnotes. KeyCite can also limit by depth of treatment (number of stars) or by type of citing document (e.g., cases, law review articles, treatises and encyclopedias). One of the most powerful KeyCite tools is the ability to use the *Locate* feature to run a keyword search within the citing documents. This can focus immediately on those documents applying a precedent to a particular set of facts.

Another way to move directly from a displayed case to a KeyCite result is to use the *KeyCite Notes* link preceding each headnote. This takes you directly to a screen on which you choose what type of citing documents you wish to see (or to a notice that there are no *KeyCite Notes* references for the headnote), and then to a list of KeyCite references limited to those discussing this particular legal issue.

Exhibit 4–13 on page 150 shows KeyCite results for *Muscarello v. United States*, 524 U.S. 125 (1998), the text of which has already been shown in several Exhibits. *Muscarello* has been cited in more than a thousand documents, but the first screen shows the "negative cases," those later decisions that have distinguished its holding or recognized its limitations. Note that the citing cases are all from lower courts, so none of them are "negative" references in that they don't overrule *Muscarello* or question its status as controlling precedent.

b. Shepard's Citations Online

Shepard's Citations is an integral part of LexisNexis case research. One of the choices at the top of a case display is "Shepardize," and in most instances a signal to the left of the case name indicates the nature of citing documents. A red stop sign indicates strong negative treatment (e.g., the case has been reversed or overruled), while a yellow caution sign indicates possible negative treatment (e.g., its holding has been criticized or limited). A green plus sign indicates positive history or treatment, and a blue circle indicates other citing references. Like KeyCite, Shepard's has a broad definition of "negative" treatment.

One can also choose *Shepard's* from the menu at the top of the LexisNexis screen, and then type in a citation. When choosing this approach, one has the option of retrieving a list of decisions which may have a direct impact on a case's validity ("Shepard's for Validation," limited to proceedings in the same litigation and any negative citing cases) or the full list of citing documents ("Shepard's for Research").

Shepard's does not rank documents as Westlaw does, but instead provides a broader range of treatment codes. Some, but not all, positive cases are given treatment codes such as "followed" or "explained" to indicate the nature of their citations. Citing cases are displayed by jurisdiction, beginning with cases from the home jurisdiction of the cited case. *Restrictions* in Shepard's can be used to see only those references with particular treatments (negative only, positive only, or your choice of specific codes), as well as cases from specific jurisdictions or those that cite the point of law in particular headnotes. It is also possible to run a "focus" search within the text of the citing cases to find specific fact patterns or terminology.

Exhibit 4–14 on page 151 shows a Shepard's screen from LexisNexis, displaying the result for *Muscarello v. United States*. Note that the display begins with a Summary listing the number of negative, positive, and neutral citing cases, with links to those using specific treatment codes, and to citing secondary sources as well.

Although their editorial treatment and arrangement differ, KeyCite and Shepard's generally provide coverage of the same citing cases. Both include cases that are designated as unpublished but are available through the online databases, as well as cases published in the official reports, West reporters, and other topical reporters. Occasionally one service includes a reference to an unpublished decision available through its database but not the other, but the differences in case coverage are slight. Both provide thorough coverage and timely notice of new developments.

Coverage of secondary sources in the two services does differ. Both have references to *ALR* annotations and to law reviews available online. Shepard's also lists citing references in selected law reviews back as far as 1957, even though most of the earlier articles are not available online in full text. KeyCite is limited to materials available on Westlaw, but it generally provides more extensive coverage of recent law reviews as well as legal encyclopedias and treatises. For *Muscarello*, for example, KeyCite lists about twenty more law review articles than Shepard's.

It is important when using either KeyCite or Shepard's Citations to understand that their signals and editorial signposts are just tools for the researcher, not authoritative statements of the law. Relying on a red flag or a stop sign is no substitute for reading a citing document and determining for yourself its scope and effect. A case that has been overruled on one point may still be good law on other issues, but learning this requires reading the overruling case itself and perhaps examining *its* subsequent history.

c. *Shepard's Citations* in Print

While the electronic versions of KeyCite and Shepard's compete for customers, *Shepard's Citations* is the only choice for researchers using print resources. There is no print version of KeyCite, but sets of *Shepard's Citations* are published for the Supreme Court, the lower federal courts, every state, the District of Columbia, Puerto Rico, and each region of the National Reporter System.

In order to convey a large amount of information in a small space, the print versions of *Shepard's* use a system of one-letter symbols to indicate the treatment of citing cases. The letter *c*, for example, stands for *criticized*; *d* for *distinguished*, and *j* for *citing in dissenting opinion*. In addition, the abbreviations used to identify citing sources are usually shorter than the citations commonly used in the *Bluebook* and other sources. *California Reporter 2d* becomes *CaR2d* in a *Shepard's* volume. These symbols and abbreviations may be confusing at first, but they are listed in tables at the front of each volume.

Printed *Shepard's Citations* can never be quite as current as the electronic resources, but most sets are supplemented biweekly or monthly. Each contains one or more maroon bound volumes, and supplementary pamphlets of varying colors. To help you know which volumes or supplements they need to use, the cover of each supplement includes a list, "What Your Library Should Contain," of the current volumes and pamphlets for the set.

Exhibit 4–15 on page 152 shows a page from *Shepard's United States Citations* containing references to the *Muscarello* case. After the page number (the large bold "125") and the name and date of the case, the first references are the parallel citations in *Lawyers' Edition* and the *Supreme Court Reporter*, listed in parentheses. These are followed by references to other documents in the *Muscarello* litigation (indicated by the code *s*), and then subsequent citing cases. Note that several of the citing cases either explain (*e*) or follow (*f*) the Muscarello holding.

The citing cases are listed by jurisdiction, first subsequent Supreme Court cases, then the lower federal courts by circuit, and finally state court cases. These references indicate the exact pages on which *Muscarello* is cited, rather than the first page of the citing decisions. The final column includes references to *Muscarello* in more than a dozen law review articles.

Shepardizing state cases in print adds one wrinkle not apparent from the *Muscarello* exhibit. References in law review articles are noted in the state *Shepard's* set, but not in the regional *Shepard's*. On the other hand, citing cases from other states appear only in the regional series and not in the state *Shepard's*. Both state citators and regional citators list citing cases from the home jurisdiction and in federal courts, but neither provides a complete list of all citing documents.

Supplementary *Shepard's* pamphlets also include recent citing cases, listed by their Lexis citations if reporter citations are not yet available. LexisNexis subscribers can use these citations to find the cases online, while other *Shepard's* users can learn the names of the cases by entering the citation in lexisONE or calling a toll-free customer service number.

Electronic citators have numerous advantages over printed *Shepard's Citations*. New cases are added within hours or days. Coverage is not divided into separate state and regional citators, with each displaying only some of the citing documents. Citing entries are compiled into a single online listing, eliminating the need to search through multiple volumes and pamphlets. Because page space is not a concern, case treatments and names of publications are spelled out rather than abbreviated. One can easily narrow retrieval to specific treatments or headnote numbers, without scanning a lengthy list of citations. Finally, hypertext links make it possible to go directly from the online citator to the text of citing cases. For some researchers, however, the printed version of *Shepard's Citations* remains the primary means to verify the validity of decisions and to find research leads.

§ 4–6. Conclusion

This chapter has introduced both electronic and print resources for case research. Many students tend to rely very heavily on keyword searching, and only when they leave law school do they learn that computerized research can be very expensive. Yet financial constraints are only one reason not to rely exclusively on methods that depend on your ability to phrase an effective search request. If the language of a decision does not precisely match the request, it will remain undiscovered unless other research methods are also used. Full-text keyword searches are most effective as part of a research strategy that integrates a number of different approaches.

Often the author or editor's work in organizing and analyzing cases is indispensable. Treatises and law review articles analyze the leading cases in a subject area, while digests and annotations sort and index cases by precise facts or issues. Keyword searches may not identify the most important cases or distinguish easily between holding and dictum. There are times when editorial assistance can achieve results with greater speed and precision than electronic means alone.

No single case-finder is the best for all purposes. Research involving the interpretation of a statute leads to an annotated code for case-finding, while a problem requiring general background knowledge of a topic suggests that you begin with a treatise. You must analyze each research problem separately and choose appropriate approaches. Experimentation and the development of skill in using various case-finding methods will enable you to make the most effective choices for each problem encountered.

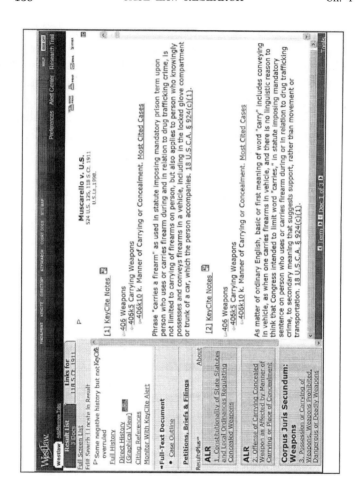

Exhibit 4–1. Westlaw headnotes for *Muscarello v. United States*, 524 U.S. 125 (1998).

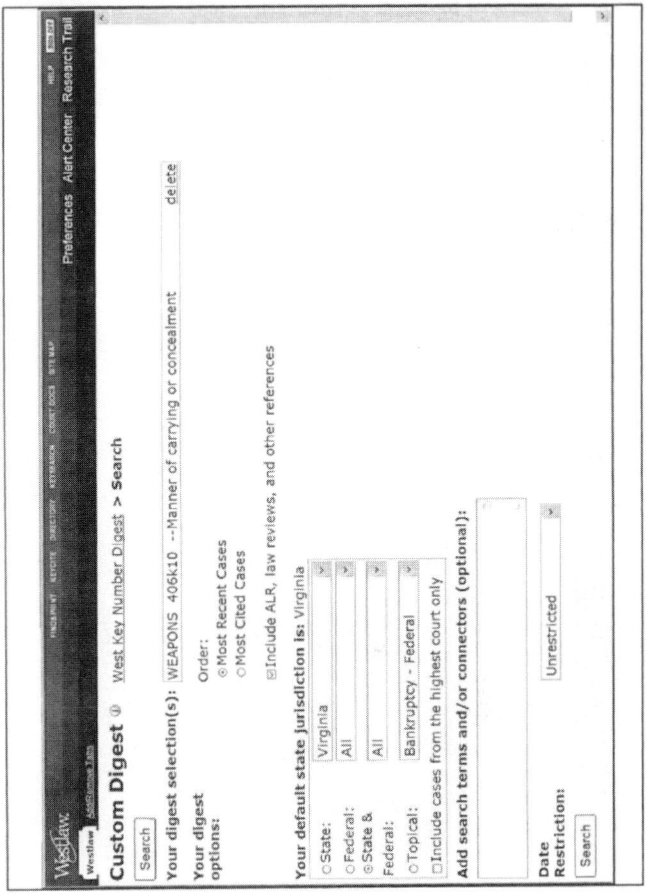

Exhibit 4–2. Westlaw Custom Digest search screen for *406k10*.

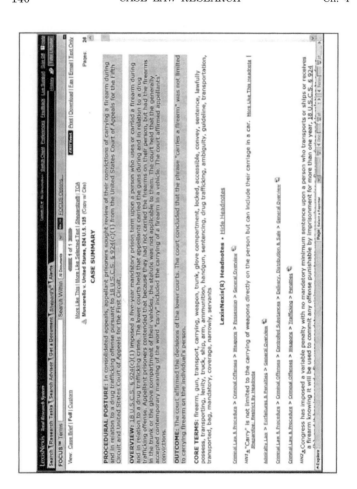

Exhibit 4–3. Lexis display of *Muscarello v. United States*, 524 U.S. 125 (1998).

◎6   WEAPONS

For later cases, see same Topic and Key Number in Pocket Part

"carrying," as opposed to "using," his gun. 18 U.S.C.A. §§ 2, 111, 924(c), (c)(1, 2).

> Busic v. U. S., 100 S.Ct. 1747, 446 U.S. 398, 64 L.Ed 2d 381, on remand 639 F.2d 940, certiorari denied 101 S.Ct. 3055, 452 U.S. 918, 69 L.Ed.2d 422.

◎7. —— Intent or purpose.

U.S.Fla. 1993. Phrase "in relation to," within meaning of statute requiring imposition of specified penalties if defendant, during and in relation to drug trafficking crime, uses or carries firearm, while expansive, clarifies, at minimum, that firearm must have some purpose or effect with respect to drug trafficking crime; its presence or involvement cannot be result of accident or coincidence. 18 U.S.C.A. § 924(c)(1).

> Smith v. U.S., 113 S.Ct. 2050, 508 U.S. 223, 124 L.Ed.2d 138, rehearing denied 114 S.Ct. 13, 509 U.S. 940, 125 L.Ed 2d 765.

◎8. —— Weapons prohibited.

U.S.Tex. 2000. Statute prohibiting the use or carrying of a "firearm" in relation to a crime of violence, which increased the penalty when weapon used or carried was a "machinegun," used the word "machinegun" and similar words to state an element of a separate, aggravated crime; while statute's literal language, taken alone, appeared neutral, its overall structure strongly favored the "new crime" interpretation. 18 U.S.C.A. § 924(c)(1).

> Castillo v. U.S., 120 S.Ct. 2090, 530 U.S. 120, 147 L.Ed 2d 94, on remand 220 F.3d 648.

◎9. —— Places prohibited.

For other cases see the Decennial Digests and WESTLAW.

◎10. —— Manner of carrying or concealment.

U.S.La. 1998. Phrase "carries a firearm" as used in statute imposing mandatory prison term upon person who uses or carries firearm during and in relation to drug trafficking crime, is not limited to carrying of firearms on person, but also applies to person who knowingly possesses and conveys firearms in a vehicle, including in the locked glove compartment or trunk of a car, which the person accompanies. 18 U.S.C.A. § 924(c)(1).

> Muscarello v. U.S., 118 S.Ct. 1911, 524 U.S. 125, 141 L.Ed.2d 111.

As matter of ordinary English, basic or first meaning of word "carry" includes conveying in vehicle, as when one carries firearms in vehicle, and there is no linguistic reason to think that Congress intended to limit word "carries," in statute imposing mandatory sentence on person who uses or carries firearm during or in relation to drug trafficking crime, to secondary meaning that suggests support, rather than movement or transportation. 18 U.S.C.A. § 924(c)(1).

> Muscarello v. U.S., 118 S.Ct. 1911, 524 U.S. 125, 141 L.Ed.2d 111

Neither basic purpose nor legislative history of statute prohibiting use or carrying of firearm during and in relation to drug trafficking crime support circumscribing scope of word "carries" by applying "on the person" limitation 18 U.S.C.A. § 924(c)(1).

> Muscarello v. U.S., 118 S.Ct. 1911, 524 U.S. 125, 141 L.Ed.2d 111.

Term "transport" as used in firearms statutes is broader than term "carrying" in that it includes "carry" but encompasses other activity, and thus, definition of term "carry" in statute prohibiting carrying of firearm during and in relation to drug trafficking crime, which includes possessing and conveying firearms in vehicle that person accompanies, does not equate terms "carry" and "transport." 18 U.S.C.A § 924(c)(1)

> Muscarello v. U.S., 118 S.Ct. 1911, 524 U.S. 125, 141 L.Ed.2d 111.

Narrow construction of word "use" to include only "active employment" of firearm for purpose of statute imposing mandatory sentence on person who "uses" or "carries" firearm during and in relation to drug trafficking crime does not make anomalous broader construction of word "carries" to include conveying firearms in vehicle, which person accompanies, as narrow interpretation of word "carries" would remove act of carrying a gun in car entirely from the statute's reach, leaving a gap in coverage Congress did not intend. 18 U.S.C.A. § 924(c)(1).

> Muscarello v. U.S., 118 S.Ct. 1911, 524 U.S. 125, 141 L.Ed.2d 111.

Giving term "carries" broad interpretation that includes possessing and conveying firearm in vehicle which one accompanies does not unfairly extend coverage of statute imposing mandatory sentence for using or carrying firearm "during and in relation to" drug trafficking crime to passengers on buses, trains or ships who have placed firearm in their checked luggage, beyond scope of what Congress likely intended, as carrying must occur "during and in relation to" a drug crime. 18 U.S.C.A. § 924(c)(1).

> Muscarello v. U.S., 118 S.Ct. 1911, 524 U.S. 125, 141 L.Ed.2d 111.

◎11–15. *For other cases see the Decennial Digests and WESTLAW.*

Library references
  C.J.S. Weapons.

Exhibit 4–4.   Weapons ◎ 10, 13A United States Supreme Court Digest 470 (2005).

WEAPONS

References are to Digest Topics and Key Numbers

WEALTH

Generally. See heading **PECUNIARY CONDITION**, generally.

EQUAL protection, status as suspect classification, **Const Law** ⬅ 213.1(1)

WEAPONS

ACTIONS for injuries, **Weap** ⬅ 18(2)

APPEAL and error in criminal proceedings. See heading **CRIMINAL APPEALS**, generally.

ARMED robbery. See heading **ROBBERY**, ARMED robbery.

ASSAULT with dangerous or deadly weapon. See heading **ASSAULT AND BATTERY**, WEAPONS.

BEARING, right to,
Generally, **Weap** ⬅ 1
Ninth Amendment, **Const Law** ⬅ 82(6.1)
Second Amendment, incorporation through due process clause, **Const Law** ⬅ 274(2)

BRANDISHING, **Weap** ⬅ 14

BURDEN of proof,
Civil proceedings, **Weap** ⬅ 18(2)
Criminal proceedings, **Weap** ⬅ 17(2)

CARRYING,
Generally, **Weapons** ⬅ 5-13
Concealment, manner of, **Weapons** ⬅ 10
Defenses in general, **Weapons** ⬅ 12
See also heading **CRIMINAL LAW, DEFENSES**.
Elements in general, **Weapons** ⬅ 6
Excuse or justification, **Weapons** ⬅ 12
Intent or purpose, **Weapons** ⬅ 7
Licenses, **Weapons** ⬅ 12
Manner of carrying, **Weapons** ⬅ 10
Necessity, defense of, **Crim Law** ⬅ 38
Occasions exempted from prohibition, **Weapons** ⬅ 11
Permits, **Weapons** ⬅ 12
Persons exempted from prohibition,
Generally, **Weapons** ⬅ 11
Mail carriers, **Weapons** ⬅ 11(3)
Officers, **Weapons** ⬅ 11(1)
Travelers, **Weapons** ⬅ 11(2)
Places within scope of prohibition, **Weapons** ⬅ 9
Weapons within scope of prohibition, **Weapons** ⬅ 8

CHILDREN and minors,
Civil liability for acts of minor, **Weap** ⬅ 18

WEAPONS—Cont'd
CHILDREN and minors—Cont'd

Possession by minor, offense, **Weap** ⬅ 4
Sale or transfer to minor, offense, **Weap** ⬅ 4

CIVIL liability, sale or use, **Weap** ⬅ 18

COMMERCE power, regulation under, **Commerce** ⬅ 82.50

CONCEALMENT, **Weap** ⬅ 10

CONSTITUTIONAL law,
Generally, **Weap** ⬅ 3
Bearing, right to. See subheading BEARING, right to, under this heading.
Due process. See subheading DUE process under this heading.
Equal protection. See heading EQUAL protection under this heading.
Ninth Amendment,
Bearing, right to, **Const Law** ⬅ 82(6.1)
Regulation under commerce power, **Commerce** ⬅ 82.50
Second Amendment. See heading SECOND Amendment under this heading.

CONSUMER protection, **Cons Prot** ⬅ 11

CONVICTS, rights with respect to weapons,
Generally, **Weap** ⬅ 4
Carrying, **Weap** ⬅ 6

CORRECTIONAL facilities,
Bringing weapons into facility by non-inmate, **Prisons** ⬅ 17.5
Offenses by inmates, **Convicts** ⬅ 5

CRIMINAL proceedings in general, **Weap** ⬅ 17

DANGEROUS weapons. See heading **DANGEROUS AND DEADLY WEAPONS**, generally.

DEFENSES in actions for injuries, **Weap** ⬅ 18(1)

DEMONSTRATIVE evidence, **Crim Law** ⬅ 404(3, 4)

DIFFERENT offenses in same transaction, **Crim Law** ⬅ 29(15)

DOUBLE jeopardy
See also heading **DOUBLE JEOPARDY**, generally.
Weapons offense and other offense, identity, **Double J** ⬅ 140

DUE process,
Registration, **Const Law** ⬅ 274(2)
Second Amendment right to bear arms,
Incorporation through due process clause, **Const Law** ⬅ 274(2)

Exhibit 4–5. Descriptive-Word Index, 1F UNITED STATES SUPREME COURT DIGEST 517 (2001).

WEAPONS

SUBJECTS INCLUDED

Right to bear arms in self-defense or in defense of the state

Regulation of manufacture, dealing in, and use of weapons

Liabilities for injuries therefrom caused by negligence

Offenses of having or carrying weapons concealed or in any other manner prohibited, pointing or shooting firearms, etc., not constituting any other distinct offense

SUBJECTS EXCLUDED AND COVERED BY OTHER TOPICS

Militia, matters relating to, see MILITIA

Premises liability cases involving injuries caused by shooting, where the alleged negligence is not directly related to the weapon itself, see NEGLIGENCE ☞1160 and related lines in that topic

Specific injuries or crimes committed by use of weapons, see ASSAULT AND BATTERY, HOMICIDE, and other specific topics

Tort liability of manufacturers, distributors, and others for defects or dangers in weapons or parts thereof, see PRODUCTS LIABILITY

For detailed references to other topics, see Descriptive-Word Index

---

Analysis

Exhibit 4–6.   Weapons, 13A United States Supreme Court Digest 460 (2005).

WEAPONS

☞

1—22, 23, 27
3—21, 22, 23, 24, 25, 26, 27, 28,
    29, 30
4—21, 22, 23, 24, 25, 26, 27, 28,
    29, 30
5.1—24
6—21, 23, 24, 25, 26
8—22, 27
9—24
10—24, 28, 29
11(1)—30
12—22, 23, 24, 25, 26, 27, 28, 29,
    30
13—23, 27, 28
15—24, 26, 29
17(1)—21, 22, 24, 25, 27, 28, 29
17(2)—21, 22, 23, 24, 26, 27, 29
17(3)—21, 22, 23, 24, 25
17(4)—21, 22, 23, 24, 25, 26, 27,
    28, 29, 30
17(5)—23, 24, 25, 27, 30
17(6)—21, 22, 23, 24, 25, 26, 27,
    28, 29, 30
17(8)—21, 23, 24, 25, 26, 27, 28,
    29, 30
19—27
22—24

Exhibit 4–7.   Table of Key Numbers, 30 GENERAL DIGEST 1026 (2006).

CARRIES

Ill.App.3d 680, appeal denied 162 Ill.Dec. 495, 580 N.E.2d 121, 141 Ill.2d 547.—Kidnap 17.

CARRIES A FIREARM

U.S.La. 1998. Phrase "carries a firearm" as used in statute imposing mandatory prison term upon person who uses or carries firearm during and in relation to drug trafficking crime, is not limited to carrying of firearms on person, but also applies to person who knowingly possesses and conveys firearms in a vehicle, including in the locked glove compartment or trunk of a car, which the person accompanies. 18 U.S.C.A. § 924(c)(1).—Muscarello v. U.S., 118 S.Ct. 1911, 524 U.S. 125, 141 L.Ed.2d 111.—Weap 10.

CARRIES ANOTHER FROM ONE PLACE TO ANOTHER

Wis.App. 1995. Forced movement of person from one room to another in same building satisfies "carries another from one place to another" element of kidnapping statute. W.S.A. 940.31(1)(a).—State v. Wagner, 528 N.W.2d 85, 191 Wis.2d 322, review denied 531 N.W.2d 328.—Kidnap 17.

CARROLL ISSUE

C.A.D.C. 1965. A "Carroll issue" exists, and television licensee has standing to contest grant of competitive license for reason that economic injury to existing television station, while not in and of itself a matter of moment, becomes important when on the facts it spells diminution or destruction of service. Communications Act of 1934, § 309 as amended 47 U.S.C.A. § 309.—Southwestern Operating Co. v. F.C.C., 351 F.2d 834, 122 U.S.App.D.C. 137, opinion after remand In re Applications of K-SIX TELEVISION, INC. , LAREDO, TEX. For Construction Permit for New Television Broadcast Station, 1965 WL 12124, reconsideration granted in part 1966 WL 14240, issued 1966 WL 13612, reconsideration granted 1966 WL 13681.—Tel 1110.

CARRY

U.S.La. 1998. Term "transport" as used in firearms statutes is broader than term "carrying" in that it includes "carry" but encompasses other activity, and thus, definition of term "carry" in statute prohibiting carrying of firearm during and in relation to drug trafficking crime, which includes possessing and conveying firearms in vehicle that person accompanies, does not equate terms "carry" and "transport." 18 U.S.C.A. § 924(c)(1).—Muscarello v. U.S., 118 S.Ct. 1911, 524 U.S. 125, 141 L.Ed.2d 111.—Weap 4, 10.

C.A.D.C. 1989. Instruction on meaning of using or carrying firearm during and in relation to drug trafficking offense was not plainly erroneous; judge defined term "carry" as meaning to bear on or about one's person or to be convenient of access or within reach, and defendant claimed the

instruction impermissibly broadened meaning of term carrying in case in which defendant had been found in one bedroom and guns in another. 18 U.S.C.A. § 924(c)(1).—U.S. v. Anderson, 881 F.2d 1128, 279 U.S.App.D.C. 413.—Crim Law 1038.1(4).

C.A.9 (Cal.) 1980. For purposes of statute prohibiting conveying dangerous weapons from place to place in a prison, "convey" can properly be used interchangeably with "transport" or "carry." 18 U.S.C.A. § 1792.—U.S. v. Kirkland, 637 F.2d 654.—Convicts 5.

C.A.11 (Fla.) 1998. Defendant did not "carry" revolver found hidden with 1.3 pounds of powder cocaine in compartment under stairwell in his residence, and he thus did not commit offense of carrying a firearm during and in relation to a drug trafficking crime, absent direct evidence or sufficient circumstantial evidence that defendant, rather than another person such as his female companion who was in residence at time of search, was the one who carried the firearm to its place in compartment. 18 U.S.C.A. § 924(c).—U.S. v. Mount, 161 F.3d 675.—Weap 17(4).

C.A.11 (Fla.) 1998. Transporting firearms in trunk of car satisfied "carry" prong of statute proscribing using or carrying firearm during and in relation to drug trafficking crime. 18 U.S.C.A. § 924(c).—U.S. v. Sanchez, 138 F.3d 1410, certiorari denied Diaz v. U.S., 119 S.Ct. 211, 525 U.S. 892, 142 L.Ed.2d 174, certiorari denied 119 S.Ct. 414, 525 U.S. 967, 142 L.Ed.2d 336.—Weap 10.

C.A.11 (Fla.) 1997. In order to sustain conviction under "use" prong of statute dealing with using or carrying firearm during and in relation to drug trafficking crime, government must show active employment of firearm, such as firing, attempted firing, brandishing, displaying, bartering, or striking; to sustain conviction under "carry" prong, government must show actual transporting of firearm during and in relation to drug trafficking offense, i.e., that defendant carried firearm on his person or carried firearm in vehicle used for drug distribution during and in relation to drug trafficking offense. 18 U.S.C.A. § 924(c)(1).—U.S. v. Chirinos, 112 F.3d 1089, certiorari denied Martinez v. U.S., 118 S.Ct. 701, 522 U.S. 1052, 139 L.Ed.2d 644, certiorari denied Gonzalez v. U.S., 118 S.Ct. 701, 522 U.S. 1052, 139 L.Ed.2d 644.—Weap 4, 6.

C.A.11 (Ga.) 1998. "Carry," for purposes of offense of using or carrying firearm during and in relation to drug trafficking crime, means to move while supporting. 18 U.S.C.A. § 924(c).—Bazemore v. U.S., 138 F.3d 947.—Weap 6.

C.A.11 (Ga.) 1998. For purpose of charge of carrying or using firearm during and in relation to drug trafficking offense, "carry" requires more than proof of mere possession; government must prove that defendant actually transported firearm as well. 18 U.S.C.A. § 924(c).—U.S. v. Leonard,

Exhibit 4–8. "Carries a Firearm," 6 WORDS AND PHRASES 162 (Supp. 2006).

TABLE OF CONTENTS

Research References

Index

Jurisdictional Table of Cited Statutes and Cases

ARTICLE OUTLINE

I. PRELIMINARY MATTERS

II. FIREARM MANUFACTURER OR SELLER

A. ACTION BROUGHT BY VICTIM OR THE LIKE

B. ACTIONS BROUGHT BY GOVERNMENTAL ENTITIES

III. AMMUNITION MANUFACTURER OR SELLER

Exhibit 4–9. George L. Blum, Annotation, *Firearm or Ammunition Manufacturer or Seller's Liability for Injuries by Use of Gun in Committing Crime*, 88 A.L.R.5th 1, 2 (2001).

Jurisdictional Table of Cited Statutes and Cases*

UNITED STATES

ALASKA

---

* Statutes, rules, regulations, and constitutional provisions bearing on the subject of the annotation are included in this table only to the extent that they are reflected in the court opinions discussed in this annotation. The reader should consult the appropriate statutory or regulatory compilations to ascertain the current status of relevant statutes, rules, regulations, and constitutional provisions.

For federal cases involving state law, see state headings.

Exhibit 4–10. 88 A.L.R.5th at 6.

[b] Related annotations

Validity, construction, and application of state or local law prohibiting manufacture, possession, or transfer of "assault weapon," 29 A.L.R.5th 664. 29 ALR5th 664.

Validity of state gun control legislation under state constitutional provisions securing the right to bear arms. 86 ALR4th 931.

Products liability: sufficiency of evidence to support product misuse defense in actions concerning weapons and ammunition. 59 ALR4th 102.

Liability of one who provides, by sale or otherwise, firearm or ammunition to adult who shoots another. 39 ALR4th 517.

Liability of private citizen or his employer for injury or damage to third person resulting from firing of shots at fleeing criminal. 29 ALR4th 144.

Products liability: blasting materials and supplies. 18 ALR4th 206.

Liability of one who sells gun to child for injury to third party. 4 ALR4th 331.

Products liability: air guns and BB guns. 94 ALR3d 291.

Liability for injury or death of minor or other incompetent inflicted upon himself by gun made available by defendant. 75 ALR3d 825.

Right of member of Armed Forces to recover from manufacturer or seller for injury caused by defective military material, equipment, supplies, or components thereof. 38 ALR3d 1247.

Res ipsa loquitur doctrine with respect to firearms accident. 46 ALR2d 1216.

Liability of manufacturer or wholesaler for injury caused by third person's use of explosives or other dangerous article sold to retailer in violation of law. 11 ALR2d 1028.

§ 2. Summary and comment

[a] Generally

Some courts apply strict rules of accountability for injuries resulting from the discharge of a firearm. It has been held that one is liable civilly for damages for injuries inflicted by an unintentional discharge of a firearm unless one shows that the injury was unavoidable. In several cases courts held that the test of liability is not whether the injury was accidentally inflicted, but whether the defendant was free from all blame. According to the theory of these cases, it is no defense that the act occurred by misadventure, and without the wrongdoer's intending it. The defendant must show such circumstances as would appear to the court that the injury done to the plaintiff was inevitable, and the defendant was not chargeable

12

Exhibit 4–11. 88 A.L.R.5th at 12.

ALR INDEX

WEAPONS AND FIREARMS—Cont'd

Labor and employment—Cont'd
  forbidding carrying of weapons, as
  to person on his own premises or at
  his place of business, **57 ALR3d
  938**

Lesser offenses, propriety of lesser-
  included-offense charge to jury in
  federal prosecution for crime involving
  property rights, **105 ALR Fed 669**

Liability of one who provides firearm, **39
  ALR4th 517**

Licenses and permits
  Ammunition (this index)
  concealed weapons, who is entitled to
    permit to carry concealed weapons,
    51 ALR3d 504
  dealers, validity, construction, and
    application of provisions of Gun
    Control Act of 1968 (18 U.S.C.A.
    § 922(m) and 923(g)) and
    implementing regulations relating to
    firearms registration and recording
    requirements imposed upon feder-
    ally licensed firearms dealers, **33
    ALR Fed 824**
  engaging business under 18 U.S.C.A.
    § 923(a), providing that no person
    shall engage in business as a fire-
    arms or ammunition importer,
    manufacturer, or dealer without a
    federal license, **53 ALR Fed 932**
  possession, see group Possession in
    this topic
  revocation or denial of application for
    license to import, manufacture, or
    deal in firearms or ammunition, **61
    ALR Fed 511**
  transient nonresidents, application of
    statute or regulation dealing with
    registration or carrying of weapons
    to transient nonresident, **68 ALR3d
    1253**
  willfully, when has applicant for
    license under Gun Control Act of
    1968 willfully violated statute or
    regulations within meaning of 18
    U.S.C.A. § 923(d)(1)(C), **59 ALR
    Fed 254**

Mace (this index)

WEAPONS AND FIREARMS—Cont'd

Manufacturers and manufacturing
  assault weapons: validity, construction,
    and application of state or local law
    prohibiting manufacture, possession,
    or transfer of "assault weapon," **?^
    ALR5th 664**
  crime, firearm or ammunition
    manufacturer or seller's liability for
    injuries caused to another by use of
    gun in committing crime, **88
    ALR5th 1**
  engage in business under 18 U.S.C.A.
    § 923(a), providing that no person
    shall engage in business as a fire-
    arms or ammunition importer,
    manufacturer, or dealer without a
    federal license, **53 ALR Fed 932**
  judicial review, under 18 U.S.C.A.
    § 923(f)(3), of revocation or denial
    of application for license to import,
    manufacture, or deal in firearms or
    ammunition, **61 ALR Fed 511**
  products liability, firearms, ammuni-
    tion, and chemical weapons, **15
    ALR4th 909**

Military equipment, right of member of
  armed forces to recover from
  manufacturer or seller for injury caused
  by defective military material, equipment, supplies, or components thereof,
  38 ALR3d 1247

Minors, see group Children in this topic

Misuse defense, sufficiency of evidence to
  support, see group Products liability in
  this topic

Motive, see group Intent or motive in this
  topic

Motor vehicles, see group Automobiles
  and highway traffic in this topic

Multiple offenses, receipt, possession, or
  transportation of multiple firearms as
  single or multiple offense under 18
  U.S.C.A. App. 1 § 1202(a)(1), making it
  federal offense for convicted felon to
  receive, possess, or transport any
  firearm, **62 ALR Fed 829**

Multiple victims, single act affecting
  multiple victims as constituting multiple
  assaults or homicides, **8 ALR4th 960**

Consult POCKET PART for Later Annotations

Exhibit 4–12.   Weapons and Firearms, T-Z ALR INDEX 654 (2001).

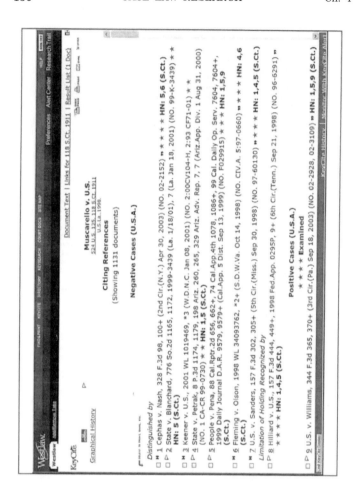

Exhibit 4–13. KeyCite results for *Muscarello v. United States*, 524 U.S. 125 (1998).

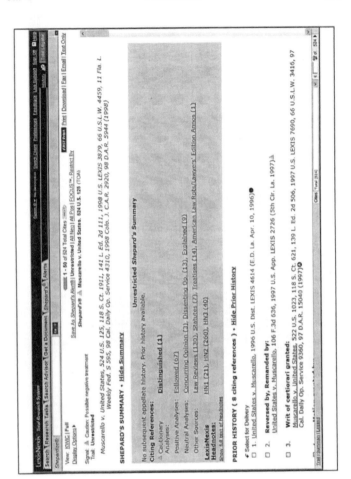

Exhibit 4–14. Shepard's results for *Muscarello v. United States*, 524 U.S. 125 (1998).

Vol. 524   **UNITED STATES REPORTS**

Cir. 11	201F3d220	56Fed Appx	53Fed Appx	Ind
f) 155F3d1343	f) 219F3d287	[638	[827	715NE835
Calif	256F3d180	83Fed Appx	73Fed Appx	La
85CA4th1067	f) 286F3d658	[114	73Fed Appx	776So2d1172
f) 85CA4th1074	294F3d473	84Fed Appx	10FS2d1139	Md
102CaR2d757	f) 344F3d370	[574	14FS2d1204	362Md713
f) 102CaR2d762	39Fed Appx	f) 84Fed Appx	76FS2d1037	j) 145MdA454
La	[787	[575	Cir. 10	155MdA408
f) 789So2d720	40Fed Appx	86Fed Appx	162F3d1287	766A2d645
Mass	[697	[891	204F3d1294	j) 805A2d1140
441Mas15	2003USDist	99Fed Appx	237F3d1190	843A2d248
802NE1035	[LX21091	[670	323F3d852	Tex
—125—	10FS2d505	46FS2d697	340F3d1188	f) 998SW723
Muscarello v	30FS2d808	69FS2d942	f) 369F3d1149	j) 70SW838
United States	f) 30FS2d810	198FS2d930	f) 3Fed Appx	66ChL676
1998	150FS2d812	Cir. 7	[965	70ChL519
(141LE111)	f) 187FS2d423	150F3d786	79Fed Appx	101CR1
(118SC1911)	Cir. 4	f) 183F3d708	[367	87Geo1124
s) 522US1023	183F3d315	j) 201F3d877	83Fed Appx	87Geo1231
s) 522US1074	f) 183F3d318	209F3d989	[303	88Geo1021
s) 523US1002	186F3d455	211F3d390	f) 83Fed Appx	89Geo1084
s) 106F3d636	259F3d249	274F3d451	[304	89Geo1193
s) 106F3d1056	293F3d706	305F3d657	f) 37FS2d1209	90Geo1099
f) 525US801	296F3d223	e) 305F3d658	44FS2d1236	90Geo1130
526US12	4Fed Appx153	354F3d692	Cir. 11	90Geo1240
j) 526US283	14Fed Appx	9Fed Appx553	144F3d755	116HLR2387
Cir. 1	[191	Cir. 8	148F3d1263	117HLR459
149F3d69	15Fed Appx69	f) 147F3d784	f) 161F3d679	2001ILR1025
162F3d9	92FS2d482	149F3d828	183F3d1295	100McL505
162F3d23	95FS2d599	153F3d706	j) 183F3d1302	75NYL139
181F3d171	f) 302FS2d630	154F3d787	283F3d1249	148PaL1213
181F3d206	Cir. 5	157F3d556	28FS2d1341	112YLJ1577
205F3d484	145F3d752	f) 160F3d501	Cir. DC	—151—
225F3d27	j) 152F3d358	174F3d937	153F3d771	New Mexico ex
230F3d5	j) 157F3d298	193F3d924	f) 161F3d70	rel. Ortiz v
305F3d35	f) 157F3d305	234F3d1051	169F3d10	Reed
137FS2d23	f) 161F3d258	235F3d1073	e) 169F3d14	1998
Cir. 2	163F3d912	Cir. 9	216F3d1165	(141LE131)
164F3d734	172F3d384	f) 147F3d1162	254F3d171	(118SC1860)
164F3d803	179F3d350	153F3d946	332ADC96	s) 124NM129
214F3d120	197F3d739	157F3d1185	f) 333ADC171	s) 947P2d86
j) 215F3d265	270F3d232	162F3d1025	335ADC94	cc) 236F3d588
245F3d132	278F3d505	f) 165F3d690	e) 335ADC94	Cir. 1
266F3d106	314F3d798	182F3d1048	342ADC322	244FS2d3
287F3d180	Cir. 6	f) 185F3d1021	349ADC94	Cir. 5
324F3d82	2004USApp	195F3d547	18FS2d33	2004USDist
328F3d100	[LX8663	203F3d1147	55FS2d8	[LX2317
e) 328F3d106	149F3d463	206F3d1341	223FS2d210	Calif
~) 354F3d152	156F3d712	223F3d953	Cir. Fed.	99CA4th945
368F3d199	157F3d430	f) 223F3d956	284F3d1348	f) 99CA4th946
5Fed Appx33	f) 157F3d449	226F3d1045	ClCt	j) 99CA4th959
47Fed Appx	f) 159F3d959	237F3d1033	44FedCl 88	122CaR2d94
[593	e) 159F3d961	j) 237F3d1035	121TCt15	f) 122CaR2d95
2003USDist	174F3d780	244F3d740	j) 121TCt33	j) 122CaR2d105
[LX18268	176F3d889	292F3d654	Ariz	D C
f) 18FS2d230	182F3d426	f) 301F3d1106	198Az265	775A2d1109
76FS2d193	182F3d465	303F3d1151	8P3d1179	N M
181FS2d215	f) 192F3d570	10Fed Appx	Calif	127NM337
f) 181FS2d216	209F3d478	[427	f) 74CA4th1086	980P2d1071
204FS2d673	f) 293F3d968	24Fed Appx	f) 88CaR2d662	Utah
207FS2d146	f) 357F3d628	[721	Colo	989P2d1106
f) 207FS2d149	369F3d932	36Fed Appx	30P3d818	
e) 207FS2d149	9Fed Appx290	[266	70P3d1198	
234FS2d349	13Fed Appx	f) 43Fed Appx	Haw	
Cir. 3	[286	[87	93Haw112	
147F3d283	f) 40Fed Appx	43Fed Appx	997P2d38	
169F3d790	[65	[157		

Exhibit 4–15.   1.11 SHEPARD'S UNITED STATES CITATIONS 1342 (2004).

CHAPTER 5

CONSTITUTIONS AND STATUTES

---

§ 5–1. Introduction

The preceding chapters focused on case law because of the importance of appellate decisions in the common law system and in American legal education. The legislature, however, is the branch of government charged with making laws, and legislative enactments play just as vital a role as decisions in today's legal system. Most appellate court decisions, in fact, involve the application or interpretation of statutes rather than the consideration of common law principles.

This chapter considers constitutions, which establish the form and limitations of government power, as well as legislation. These forms of law are discussed in one chapter because they are often published together, and because research methods are similar. In considering constitutional provisions or statutes, it is important to find not only the relevant text but also cases that interpret this text and define its terms. The most common research sources for both constitutions and statutes are *annotated codes*, which provide the text of public laws in force accompanied by notes of court decisions.

The nature of legal authority assigned to constitutions and legislation is different from that of case law. These sources have binding or mandatory authority within their own jurisdiction, but in other jurisdictions they have no effect and are not even persuasive authority. One state's laws may influence another state's legislature considering similar legislation, and judicial decisions applying or construing a statute may persuade other courts confronting similar issues, but the statutory language itself carries no authority outside its own jurisdiction.

Determining early in the research process whether a problem involves constitutional or statutory provisions can save considerable time, as this significantly affects the direction of your research. Experienced researchers develop a sense of which issues are likely to be governed by constitution or statute, and whether these issues are matters of federal or state law. Substantive criminal law, for example, is generally defined by the enactments of a state legislature, while defendants' procedural rights are determined by both federal and state constitutional law. As legislatures continue to enact statutes to govern traditional common law areas such as contract and tort, more and more questions involve some statutory research. Secondary sources and cases generally provide references to the relevant provisions, so it should soon become apparent from your introductory research whether statutory research is warranted.

§ 5–2. The U.S. Constitution

The United States Constitution is the basic law of the country, defining political relationships, enumerating the rights and liberties of citizens, and creating the framework of national government. Unlike statutes, which are often written in extreme detail and specificity, the Constitution contains concise statements of broad principles. It entered into force in March 1789, and it has only been amended twenty-seven times in more than two centuries. Among the most important of these amendments are the Bill of Rights, guaranteeing personal liberties, and the Fourteenth Amendment, applying these protections to the states.

Although its text has changed little, courts have applied the Constitution to numerous situations which its drafters could not have foreseen. In interpreting constitutional provisions, it is particularly important to examine relevant Supreme Court decisions and those of the lower federal courts. Judicial interpretations of constitutional principles are no less important to legal research than the language of the Constitution.

The text of the Constitution appears in numerous publications ranging from simple pamphlets to standard reference works such as *Black's Law Dictionary*. It is included in online and CD–ROM collections of federal statutes and is available at dozens of government and private Internet sites. The Constitution Society provides an annotated listing of several online sources <www. constitution.org/cs_found.htm>.

The Constitution is also printed at the beginning of the *United States Code*, the official publication of federal statutes. However, two annotated statutory publications, *United States Code Annotated (USCA)* and *United States Code Service (USCS)*, are more useful in legal research. (*USCA* and *USCS* are the versions of the Constitution available through Westlaw and LexisNexis, respectively.) These publications provide much more than just the text of the Constitution. Each clause is accompanied by abstracts of cases, arranged by subject and thoroughly indexed. Some major provisions have thousands of case abstracts in several hundred subject divisions. The Constitution is so heavily annotated that it occupies twenty-four volumes in *USCA* and ten volumes in *USCS*. The annotations are regularly updated in annual pocket parts for each volume and interim pamphlets throughout the year. These exhaustive annotations make the annotated codes essential resources in determining how the Constitution's broad principles have been applied to specific circumstances.

Of the many commentaries on the Constitution, one of the most extensive and authoritative is *The Constitution of the United States of America: Analysis and Interpretation*, published every ten years by the Congressional Research Service of the Library of Congress. This text is a useful starting point for constitutional research, with a thorough analysis of Supreme Court decisions applying each provision of the Constitution. The current version, edited by Johnny H. Killian, George A. Costello, and Kenneth R. Thomas, was published in 2004 and covers cases through June 2002. The volume is updated by a biennial pocket part, the coverage of which generally lags a year or two behind current developments. This edition of the Constitution is available online in PDF at GPO Access <www.gpoaccess.gov/constitution/>. The previous edition is available on FindLaw <www.findlaw.com/casecode/constitution/>, with hypertext links to footnotes and to Supreme Court cases discussed. Both sites include full-text search capabilities. Exhibit 5–1 on page 187 shows the beginning of this work's discussion of the Second Amendment, with footnotes citing several scholarly monographs, law review articles, and Supreme Court decisions.

Another helpful background source is Leonard W. Levy et al., eds., *Encyclopedia of the American Constitution* (6 vols., 2d ed. 2000), which includes articles on constitutional doctrines as well as on specific court decisions, people, and historical periods. Shorter works providing similar treatment of constitutional issues include Kermit L. Hall, ed., *The Oxford Companion to the Supreme Court of the United States* (2d ed. 2005), and Jethro K. Lieberman, *A Practical Companion to the Constitution* (1999).

For further historical research, you can turn to the documents prepared by those who drafted, adopted, and ratified the Constitution. There was no official record of the debates in the constitutional convention, but Max Farrand's *The Records of the Federal Convention of 1787* (3 vols. 1911 & supp. 1987) is considered the most authoritative source. The traditional source for the state ratification debates is Jonathan Elliot, *The Debates in the*

Several State Conventions on the Adoption of the Federal Constitution (2d ed., 5 vols. 1836–45). A much more comprehensive modern treatment originally edited by Merrill Jensen and now by John P. Kaminski et al., *The Documentary History of the Ratification of the Constitution* (18 vols. to date, 1976–date), is still in the process of publication and contains debates, commentaries and other documents. The Library of Congress website provides full-text access to both Farrand's *Records* and Elliot's *Debates* <memory.loc.gov/ammem/amlaw/>. Philip B. Kurland & Ralph Lerner, eds., *The Founders' Constitution* (5 vols. 1987) <press-pubs.uchicago.edu/founders/>, and Neil H. Cogan, ed., *The Complete Bill of Rights: The Drafts, Debates, Sources, and Origins* (1997) are useful collections of excerpts from source documents arranged by the constitutional provision to which they apply.

§ 5–3. State Constitutions

Each state is governed by its own constitution, which establishes the structure of government and guarantees fundamental rights. While state constitutions are roughly comparable to their federal counterpart, they tend to be much more detailed and generally are amended far more frequently. Some states have revised and replaced their constitutions several times.

State constitutions can be important sources in cases involving individual rights. While a state cannot deprive citizens of federal constitutional rights, its constitution can guarantee rights beyond those provided under the U.S. Constitution. Just as the U.S. Supreme Court is the arbiter of the scope of protections offered by the federal constitution, the state court of last resort determines the scope of its constitution.

The best source for a state constitution is usually the annotated state code, which provides both the latest text and notes of court decisions interpreting and construing constitutional provisions. Pamphlet texts are also published in many states, and state constitutions are available through online databases, as part of state CD–ROM products, and on the Internet from state government sites. Of several sites providing multistate access to primary sources, the most convenient for the text of constitutions may be FindLaw's listing <www.findlaw.com/11stategov/indexconst.html>.

Current state constitutions are compiled in *Constitutions of the United States: National and State* (7 vols., 2d ed. 1974–date). William F. Swindler, ed., *Sources and Documents of United States Constitutions* (11 vols., 1973–79) also includes superseded state constitutions and other historical documents, with background notes, editorial comments, and a selected bibliography for each state. Swindler's work is based in part on the classic compilation edited by Benjamin Perley Poore, *The Federal and State Constitutions, Colonial Charters, and Other Organic Laws of the United States* (2 vols., 2d ed. 1878), still available in many libraries.

For research into a particular state's constitution, one of the best starting places may be a volume in the series *Reference Guides to the State Constitutions of the United States*. This monograph series began with Robert F. Williams, *The New Jersey State Constitution: A Reference Guide* (1990), and now covers more than forty states. Each volume includes a summary of the state's constitutional history, a detailed section-by-section analysis of the constitution with background information and discussion of judicial interpretations, and a brief bibliographical essay providing references for further research.

Journals and proceedings of state constitutional conventions can provide insight into framers' intent, although the lack of indexing in many older volumes can make for difficult research. These documents are available on microfiche in *State Constitutional Conventions, Commissions, and Amendments*, covering all fifty states from 1776 through 1988, and are listed in a series of bibliographies beginning with Cynthia E. Browne's *State Constitutional Conventions from Independence to the Completion of the Present Union, 1776–1959: A Bibliography* (1973).

§ 5–4. Publication of Statutes

American statutes are published in three basic versions, whether in print or electronic form. The first version of a newly enacted statute is the *slip law*. Each law is issued by itself on a single sheet or as a pamphlet with separate pagination. Neither federal nor state slip laws are widely distributed in print, but government websites generally provide convenient access to the texts of new laws.

Next are the *session laws*. The statutes are arranged by date of passage and published in separate volumes for each legislative term. Official session laws are generally published only in bound volumes after a session has ended, but commercial *advance session law services* provide the texts of new laws in pamphlet form on a more timely basis. Session law volumes are generally indexed, but these indexes rarely cumulate and subject access to more than one session can be difficult. For most jurisdictions the *Bluebook* and the *ALWD Citation Manual* require citation to session law volume and page numbers, but this information is not always available online.

In most jurisdictions, the session laws constitute the *positive law* form of legislation, *i.e.*, the authoritative, binding text of the laws. Other forms (such as codes) are only *prima facie* evidence of the statutory language, unless they have been designated as positive law by the legislature.

Although the chronologically arranged session laws contain the official text of legislative enactments, they have limited use as research tools. Researchers usually need the laws currently in force, rather than the laws passed during a specific legislative term. They also need convenient access to amendments and related legislation. For this they turn to the third and most useful form of statutory publication, the *statutory compilation* or *code*.

Codes collect current statutes of general and permanent application and arrange them by subject. The statutes are grouped into broad subject topics, usually called *titles*, and within each title they are divided into chapters and then numbered sections. The parts of a single legislative act may be printed together or may be scattered by subject through several different titles. A detailed index for the entire code provides access to the sections dealing with particular problems or topics.

Some jurisdictions have official code publications containing the text of the statutes in force. If an official edition is published, it is usually the authoritative text and should be cited in briefs and pleadings. Almost every jurisdiction provides online access to its code, but the official status of these online versions varies considerably.

Most official codes, whether in print or online, are *unannotated*; that is, they do not include references to judicial decisions which have applied or construed the statutes. Finding relevant cases is such an important part of statutory research that the most useful sources are annotated codes with these notes of decisions, issued by commercial publishers and available through Westlaw or LexisNexis. Most annotated codes also provide historical comments and cross references to legal encyclopedias and other publications.

Codes, whether annotated or unannotated, must be updated regularly to include the numerous statutory changes which occur every time a legislature meets. An outdated code is virtually useless for current research. Some officially published codes are updated only by the issuance of a new edition every few years, and some government websites are not updated very regularly. Most annotated code publications, on the other hand, are supplemented by annual pocket parts and quarterly pamphlets, and their online counterparts may be even more up to date.

Printed resources are particularly well suited for statutory research, because code volumes make it easy to find related provisions and to place a section in its context. To understand the language in a specific section, it's often necessary to see an entire code chapter or title. An essential part of statutory research, whether in print or online, is surveying the surrounding sections to determine the scope and meaning of a particular statutory provision.

Getting a sense of a section's context is easier to do in a printed book, but Westlaw and LexisNexis both provide ways to see nearby sections. Westlaw users can click on

"Previous Section" or "Next Section" links at the top of the display to move from section to section, or click on the highlighted title of the chapter to open a new window displaying all of its sections. Clicking on "Table of Contents" on the left side of the screen will display the list of title, chapter and section headings. LexisNexis users can either select "Book Browse" to move between sections or click on the TOC links at the top of the screen to see the list of titles, chapters, and sections.

Westlaw also provides online access to the indexes that accompany Thomson West's printed codes. A search in the index may give a more complete picture of the law than a keyword search and may find related sections that would otherwise be missed. The indexes are available from the database directory ("Statutes Indexes") or from links at the top of code database search screens.

§ 5–5. Federal Statutes

The United States Congress meets in two-year terms, consisting of two annual sessions, and enacts several hundred statutes each term. These statutes range from simple designations of commemorative days to complex environmental or tax legislation spanning hundreds of pages. Each act is designated as either a *public law* or a *private law*, and assigned a number indicating the order in which it was passed. Pub. L. 110–1, for example, is the first public law passed during the 110th Congress (2007–08).

Public laws are designed to affect the general public, while private laws are passed to meet special needs of an individual or small group. The distinction between the two is sometimes blurred, as when a special interest group promotes "public" legislation that actually affects very few people. Both types are passed in the same way and both appear in the session laws, but in separate numerical series. Only public laws, however, become part of the statutory code.

a.   Slip Laws and Session Laws

The slip law, an individually paginated pamphlet, is the first official text of a new statute and is available from Congress itself or from the U.S. Government Printing Office. Beginning with the 104th Congress in 1995, the Government Printing Office's GPO Access provides PDF files of public laws through the Internet <www. gpoaccess.gov/plaws/>. For current legislation this is one of the quickest and most effective sources, with new laws appearing online within a few days or weeks of enactment. For the very latest laws, it may be necessary to check the legislative site THOMAS <thomas.loc.gov> for the *enrolled bill*, or the version that was passed by both houses and sent to the President. THOMAS has enrolled bills back to the 101st Congress (1989–90).

After the end of each session of Congress, the public and private slip laws are cumulated, corrected, and issued in bound volumes as the official *Statutes at Large* for the session. These are cited by volume and page number. The Brady Handgun Violence Prevention Act, Pub. L. 103–159, 107 Stat. 1536 (1993), shown in Exhibit 5–2 on page 188, begins on page 1536 of volume 107 of the *Statutes at Large*.

Although the *Statutes at Large* is not the most convenient source for federal legislation, it maintains a vital role in legal research. In most instances it is the official statement of the law, and it is a necessary source for determining the specific language Congress enacted at any given time. This is important for lawyers as well as historians. It is often necessary to determine when a particular provision took effect or was repealed, or to reconstruct the precise text as it was enacted. Sections of a Public Law may be distributed among several titles in the code, but the *Statutes at Large* provides each act of Congress in its entirety.

There is a delay of about two years before *Statutes at Large* volumes are published, but slip laws on GPO Access include the *Statutes at Large* pagination within weeks of enactment. Westlaw and LexisNexis provide the official pagination even more quickly. Westlaw's US–PL database has only laws from the current term of Congress, with older laws back to 1973 in a separate US–PL–OLD database. The USCS Public Laws file on Lexis has laws back to 1988. The full texts of these acts are searchable by keyword.

Westlaw and LexisNexis also have retrospective coverage of the *Statutes at Large* back to 1789, but earlier acts are available as image-based PDFs and only citations, dates, and summary information are searchable. Westlaw's US–STATLRG file covers 1789–1972, and on Lexis-Nexis the United States Statutes at Large file provides pre–1988 coverage. (Under law school subscriptions, older acts can be retrieved only by citation.)

Retrospective PDF coverage of the *Statutes at Large* back to 1789 is provided by other subscription databases as well. Potomac Publishing <www.potomacpub.com> adds features such as hypertext links between acts and lists of subsequent and pending amendments, and it presents each act as a single PDF file (unlike Westlaw and LexisNexis, which divide larger acts into smaller units of 10 to 50 pages). HeinOnline <www.heinonline. org> is not quite as up-to-date as the other databases, covering only the bound *Statutes at Large* volumes, but it makes the first fifteen pages of each act searchable.

The Library of Congress provides free access to the first eighteen volumes of the *Statutes at Large*, through 1875, as part of its "A Century of Lawmaking for a New Nation: U.S. Congressional Documents and Debates, 1774–1875" collection <memory.loc.gov/ammem/amlaw/ lwsl.html>.

In print, the first appearance of federal statutes after the slip laws is in two advance session law services, Thomson West's *United States Code Congressional and Administrative News* (*USCCAN*) and LexisNexis's *Advance* pamphlets to the *United States Code Service* (*USCS*). Both services issue monthly pamphlets, publishing new federal statutes within two or three months of enactment. Like the slip laws, each page of text in *USCCAN* and *USCS Advance* indicates the location at which it will eventually appear in the official *Statutes at Large*.

USCCAN and *USCS Advance* include other materials such as new court rules, presidential documents, and selected administrative regulations. *USCCAN* (but not *USCS Advance*) has two additional features. It reprints selected congressional committee reports (usually considered the most important sources of legislative history, as will be discussed in Chapter 6), and it is recompiled into bound volumes at the end of each session. It provides a permanent source for federal session laws back to 1941, although it did not follow the official *Statutes at Large* pagination until 1975.

b. The *United States Code*

The first official subject compilations of federal legislation were the *Revised Statutes of the United States* of 1873, and its second edition of 1878. Congress enacted the first edition of the *Revised Statutes* as positive law in its entirety, expressly repealing the original *Statutes at Large* versions of its contents. It is therefore the authoritative text for most laws enacted before 1873, and is still needed occasionally in modern research.

Although the *Revised Statutes* rapidly became outdated, no other official compilation was prepared for almost fifty years. Finally, in 1926, the first edition of the *United States Code* was published, arranging the laws by subject into fifty titles. The *U.S. Code* is published in a completely revised edition of about thirty-five volumes every six years, with an annual supplement of one or more bound volumes. These supplements are cumulative, so it is necessary only to consult the main set and its latest supplement.

The *U.S. Code* is available free online from several sites, but none of the free sources is more current than the official printed version. Neither do any of them offer a PDF replica of the official print edition, which is the citation source required by the *Bluebook* and the *ALWD Citation Manual*. Cornell Law School's Legal Information Institute <www.law.cornell.edu/uscode/> is the most user-friendly of the free sites, with flexible search options and hyperlinked cross-references between code sections. The government makes the code available through the House of Representatives Office of the Law Revision Counsel <uscode.house.gov> and GPO Access <www. gpoaccess.gov/uscode/>.

Updating a code section found on any of these free Internet site requires using the House Office of the Law Revision Counsel's site. "United States Code Classification Tables" page <uscode.house.gov/classification/tables.shtml> provide references to newly enacted laws, and searching by section number will retrieve an "UPDATE" link if there is a recent amendment to the section. Hypertext links to the amendments are not provided, so updating on free sites can be a laborious process.

Nearly half of the *U.S. Code* titles have been reenacted as positive law, and for them the code has become the authoritative text. For the others, the *Statutes at Large* is authoritative and the *U.S. Code* is *prima facie* evidence of the law. A list of all code titles, indicating which titles have been reenacted, appears in the front of each *U.S. Code* volume and is reproduced here as Exhibit 5–3 on page 189.

Unlike citations to the *Statutes at Large* or to cases, citations to the *U.S. Code* refer to title and section rather than to volume and page. For example, 18 U.S.C. § 925A (2000), shown in Exhibit 5–4 on page 190, is the citation for section 925A of Title 18 (Crimes and Criminal Procedure). This provision was added to the *U.S. Code* as part of the Brady Act, as shown by the parenthetical reference following its text to Pub. L. No. 103–119, title I, § 104(a).

In addition to the text of statutes, the *U.S. Code* also includes historical notes, cross references, and other research aids. Parenthetical references indicate the *Statutes at Large* or *Revised Statutes* sources of each section, including any amendments. These references lead to the version that may be the authoritative text, and from there to legislative history documents relating to the law's enactment. In Exhibit 5–4 on page 190, note that § 926 was originally enacted in 1968 and was then amended later the same year and again in 1986 and 1994. The "Amendments" note following the section indicates the precise nature of each of these changes.

Even when discussing statutes currently in force, decisions and other documents sometimes refer to provisions by session law citation rather than by code section. It is then necessary to determine where a law is codified, as well as whether it is still in force. A simple way to do this is to use a *parallel reference table* found in three volumes at the end of the *U.S. Code*. The example shown in Exhibit 5–5 on page 191 provides *U.S. Code* references for laws enacted in 1993, including the Brady Act shown in Exhibit 5–2 on page 188. Note that it is possible to work from the year (1993), the term of Congress (103d), or *Statutes at Large* volume (107); and that some sections listed under Pub. L. 103–160 in this exhibit are not in the current *U.S. Code* because they have been repealed (Rep.). Other parallel reference tables provide access from the former numbering of revised titles to current section numbers, and from the *Revised Statutes* to the *U.S. Code*.

Another table, "Acts Cited by Popular Name," can be used to find an act if its citation is not known. This table lists laws alphabetically under either short titles assigned by Congress or names by which they have become commonly known, and provides citations to the laws in both the *Statutes at Large* and the *U.S. Code*. Exhibit 5–6 on page 192 shows a page from this table in the 2000 *U.S. Code*, with a reference under the heading "Brady Handgun Violence Prevention Act." Note that this law is listed under its official name, rather than under "Brady

Act" or "Brady Bill," by which it may be more commonly known. "Popular names" are not necessarily the ones that appear in newspapers and on television.

Without a reference to a specific statute, the general index is the place to begin research in the *U.S. Code*. This basic tool for finding federal statutes by subject consists of several volumes, and it is updated in each annual supplement. Exhibit 5–7 on page 193 shows a page from the index providing references to a variety of provisions under the heading "Weapons," including numerous references under "Manufacturers and manufacturing" and other subheadings to federal firearms provisions in 18 U.S.C. §§ 921–930. Statutory indexes are often full of cross-references (such as the "Juvenile Delinquents and Dependents" entry in Exhibit 5–7) and long lists of subheadings and sub-subheadings. Indexes can be unwieldy and confusing, but they remain essential resources in statutory research. Statutes may be easier to find through indexes than through full-text keyword searches, which often yield too many irrelevant results.

c. Annotated Codes

The *United States Code* has the text of federal laws, but two major shortcomings limit its value to legal researchers. It is not updated on a timely basis, and there is no information about court decisions applying or interpreting code sections. These decisions are so important that most researchers turn instead to one of two commercially published, annotated editions of the code, *United States Code Annotated* (*USCA*), published by West Group and available on Westlaw, or *United States Code Service* (*USCS*), published by and available on LexisNexis. Beyond the text of the law and notes of court decisions, they also provide references to legislative history, administrative regulations, and various secondary sources. These features have made the annotated codes the most widely used sources of federal statutes.

Unlike the official *U.S. Code*, which is published in a new edition every six years, *USCA* and *USCS* consist of volumes of varying ages, all updated with annual pocket parts or pamphlet supplements. Replacement volumes are published when supplements get too unwieldy. In the case of the illustrations in Exhibits 5–8 to 5–10 on pages 194–196, showing firearms sections of Title 18, the *USCA* volume was published in 2000 and the *USCS* volume in 2005. For other provisions, the *USCA* volume may well be the more current of the two.

Exhibit 5–8 on page 194 shows the beginning of § 921, the definitions section, in *USCA*. Note that these are the legal definitions for terms "as used in this chapter," one reason it is essential to be aware of context and neighboring sections. These definitions may affect interpretation of other sections in the chapter, but they are not applicable to matters elsewhere in the code.

Exhibit 5–9 on page 195 shows a *USCA* page containing annotations for § 925, including references to *Am. Jur. 2d* and two law review articles, as well as the beginning of the notes of decisions. These notes are preceded by an alphabetical subject index. Exhibit 5–10 on page 196 shows a similar page of § 925 annotations in *USCS*, with references to case notes arranged by topic.

Either annotated code will serve admirably for most research purposes, but for extensive analysis of a particular statute it maybe necessary to check both *USCA* and *USCS*. Each provides selective annotations of court decisions, and some cases may be found in one but not in the other. *USCA*'s annotations are generally the more extensive of the two, but numerous cases appear only in *USCS*. The excerpted notes shown in Exhibits 5–9 and 5–10 on pages 195–196, for example, have only one case in common. These two exhibits cover the same code section and some of the same issues, but the annotations are arranged differently and each version cites cases not found in the other.

It is also worth noting that notes of decisions do not follow every code section. Every single section of the *U.S. Code* has not been the subject of judicial interpretation. Some sections are uncontroversial and have not led to litigation, while others may be too new for any reported cases. The absence of annotations means that a section must be interpreted without the assistance of court decisions directly on point.

When using a *USCA* or *USCS* volume, *always* check its pocket part for recent amendments and notes of new decisions. Exhibit 5–11 on page 197 shows both of these features in a *USCA* pocket part, showing 2001 amendments to 18 U.S.C. § 930 and reference to a case decided since the publication of the 2000 volume.

The annotated codes also include extensive indexes, parallel reference tables, and popular name tables similar to those in the *U.S. Code*. Like the code sections, these features are updated in the annual supplements and interim pamphlets.

As noted earlier, both annotated editions of the code are available online (*USCA* on Westlaw and *USCS* on LexisNexis). Exhibits 5–12 and 5–13 on pages 198–199 show 18 U.S.C. § 931, a section added to the code in 2002, as it appears in its Westlaw and LexisNexis versions.

Westlaw has the code in both unannotated (USC) and annotated (USCA) forms, allowing you to decide whether or not to include the extensive case annotations in a search. In some instances searching keywords in the annotations may retrieve far too many documents, but the wording of the annotations may lead to relevant sections that might not have been found otherwise. LexisNexis does not have a separate unannotated database, but a *text* or *unanno* segment search will limit queries to the statutory language. Because statutory language often includes cross-references and exceptions which may result in retrieval of irrelevant documents, it may help to use fields or segments to limit a search further to words in the title, chapter, and section headings. Westlaw uses the field *prelim* or *pr* for title, subtitle and chapter designations, and *caption* or *ca* for the section number and description. LexisNexis uses the segment *heading* for titles, subtitles and chapters, and *section* for individual sections.

The online code databases are updated to include laws from the current session of Congress; notes above the heading on LexisNexis and at the bottom of the Westlaw display indicate the latest public law to be included in code coverage. If a section has been amended by a public law too recent to be incorporated, both services provide notices to check for more current legislative action. A significant advantage of accessing a code section online is that amendments and new case notes are incorporated into the main document rather than found in a separate pocket supplement.

The database systems also provide access to the parallel reference and popular name tables in the annotated codes. Westlaw, which has the *USCA* index as well

(USCA–IDX), has convenient links from the tables and index to the text of listed code sections.

Specialized online and looseleaf services provide another source for current, annotated statutes in some subject fields. Most services include federal statutes affecting their fields, accompanied by abstracts of judicial and administrative decisions, relevant administrative regulations, and explanatory text. Major tax services such as the *Standard Federal Tax Reporter* (CCH) and *United States Tax Reporter* (RIA) are basically heavily annotated editions of title 26 of the *U.S. Code*, also known as the Internal Revenue Code.

d. KeyCite and Shepard's Citations

While *USCA* and *USCS* provide notice of statutory amendments and citing cases, more extensive research leads can be found by using KeyCite or Shepard's Citations. Westlaw's KeyCite is available only electronically, while Shepard's information can be found online through LexisNexis and in the printed *Shepard's Federal Statute Citations*. A major advantage of KeyCite and Shepard's is that they provide much more current information than the annotations in the codes. The latest decisions can be found in the citators months before case annotations are written and published.

KeyCite's coverage of statutes includes the cases summarized in *USCA*'s annotations, but it expands on these by listing other citing cases and articles as well as recent and pending legislation. The cases in the annotations are listed under the index headings used in *USCA*, but without the annotation abstracts. These are followed by "additional citations," other cases listed by jurisdiction in descending chronological order. These cases are not indexed by subject, but they represent references that cannot be found through the annotated code. The older "additional citations" cases listed may not be very important, but this section also includes the most recent court decisions. (Another way to find these is to click on the Cases–Last 60 Days link.) KeyCite also provides references to pending legislation and to any law review articles and other secondary sources available through Westlaw.

Westlaw's statutory display includes KeyCite symbols similar to those used for cases. A red flag indicates that a section has been amended or repealed, or that it's been ruled unconstitutional or otherwise invalid. A yellow flag indicates that pending legislation affecting the section is available, or that court decisions may have limited its scope or validity. The section in Exhibit 5–12 on page 198 has a green C symbol, indicating that it has citing references.

LexisNexis statutory displays include a *Shepardize* link. Clicking on this link may retrieve a number of separate documents because Shepard's, online or in print, lists citing sources under the exact provision or provisions cited. A case citing a specific subsection is listed under that subsection, while one citing a range of sections is listed under an entry for the entire range. It may therefore be necessary to scan a number of entries to find relevant citations. Shepard's has separate listings, for example, for "18 U.S.C. sec. 925" and for subsections such as "18 U.S.C. sec. 925(a)(1)" and "18 U.S.C. sec. 925(a)(2)(b)." Still other documents citing several sections are listed under "18 U.S.C. §§ 921 et seq." or "18 U.S.C. 922 to 925." This approach makes it more difficult to get a comprehensive listing of all relevant documents, but it is ideal for research needing to focus in on a very specific subsection. Shepard's coverage of citations in law reviews, both in print and online, is generally somewhat less extensive than KeyCite's.

The printed *Shepard's Federal Statute Citations* provides broader coverage of sources than the LexisNexis online version, with lists of federal court citations to repealed provisions of older *United States Code* editions and to acts in the *Statutes at Large* which have not been incorporated into the code. *Shepard's Federal Statute Citations* does not include state court decisions and law review articles citing federal laws; these are listed instead in Shepard's individual state citators and in *Shepard's Federal Law Citations in Selected Law Reviews*.

§ 5–6. State Statutes

State statutes appear in many of the same forms as their federal counterparts, with slip laws, session laws, codes, and annotated codes. Current session laws and codes are available from government Internet sites, and annotated codes are published both electronically and in print.

a. Slip Laws and Session Laws

State slip laws are rarely distributed widely in paper, but every state legislature provides Internet access to recently enacted laws. Many state legislative websites, however, do not have a separate collection of enactments but instead present these texts as bills, mixed in with others that are still pending or that did not become law. Two easy ways to find legislative websites are to start with the state homepage (usually <www.[state].gov>), or to check a site with multistate links such as the National Conference of State Legislatures <www.ncsl.org/public/leglinks.cfm>.

Every state has a session law publication similar to the *U.S. Statutes at Large*, containing the laws enacted at each sitting of its legislature. The names of these publications vary from state to state (*e.g.*, *Acts of Alabama*, *Statutes of California*, *Laws of Delaware*). In most states the session laws are the authoritative positive law text of the statutes, and they may be needed to examine legislative changes or to reconstruct the language in force at a particular date.

Westlaw and LexisNexis provide the texts of new legislation from every state, with retrospective files going back to at least 1991. These are known on Westlaw as "Legislative Services" and on Lexis as "Advance Legislative Services" or ALS. The major difference between the two systems is that Westlaw has two separate databases for each state, one for the current legislative sessions (XX–LEGIS) and a "historical" database with the older session laws back to the late 1980s or early 1990s (XX–LEGIS–OLD). Lexis has just one database for each state combining older and newer sessions.

In print, commercially published session law services for most states contain laws from a current legislative session, very much as *USCCAN* and *USCS Advance* do for congressional enactments. Most larger law libraries have older state session laws in microform. HeinOnline <www.heinonline.org> is in the process of providing retrospective online coverage of these older session law collections.

b. Codes

All states have subject compilations of their statutes similar to the *U.S. Code*. Some states publish unannotated official codes, regularly revised on an annual or biennial basis. In the states with regularly published official codes, this is usually the authoritative text which should be cited according to the *Bluebook* and the *ALWD Citation Manual*.

Almost every state provides access to its code through a government website. The official status of these codes varies, and the statutes are rarely accompanied by very extensive notes. Most codes can be accessed through browsing the table of contents or searching by keyword. Several convenient compilations of links are available, including the list of state legal materials at Cornell's Legal Information Institute <www.law.cornell.edu/ states/listing.html> and "Full–Text State Statutes and Legislation on the Internet" <www.prairienet.org/ ∽scruffy/f.htm>, which is updated regularly and includes helpful search tips.

Most researchers rely on annotated codes containing summaries of relevant court decisions and other references, published in most instances by either Thomson West or LexisNexis. Several states have competing codes from both publishers. The authority of annotated codes varies from state to state, but they are usually accepted as at least *prima facie* evidence of the statutory law.

Annotated state codes are edited and supplemented in much the same way as federal statutes, although there are variations from state to state. Some codes are more thorough and comprehensive than others. Supplementation is generally by annual pocket parts, updated in many states by quarterly interim pamphlets. A few state codes are published in binders or in annual softcover editions, rather than as bound volumes with pocket parts.

Westlaw and LexisNexis provide access to annotated codes from all fifty states, as well as the District of Columbia, Guam, Puerto Rico, and the Virgin Islands. (In non-law libraries, LexisNexis Academic provides access to individual codes; another product, LexisNexis State Capital, also permits retrieval by citation and keyword searching of multiple states.) Westlaw even offers two different publishers' versions of annotated codes in thirteen states and the District of Columbia, and *three* different versions for Nevada. As in the federal databases, Westlaw users can choose between annotated and unannotated versions of codes, and LexisNexis users can search in the *text* or *unanno* segment to avoid cases where relevant terms appear only in the annotations. The fields and segments for limiting searches to captions and section headings, discussed in the federal section, are also available. Both systems add notices to statutes that have been amended by slip laws not yet incorporated into the code database. Lexis has a "Legislative Alert" with links to new acts, and the Westlaw display has a red flag linking to legislative action.

The outline and arrangement of code material varies from state to state. While most codes are divided into titles and sections, in a format similar to the *U.S. Code*, several states have individual codes designated by name rather than title number (e.g., commercial code, penal code, tax code). Exhibit 5–14 on page 200 shows a section of the California Penal Code, as published in *West's Annotated California Codes*. Note that it provides not only the text of the statute, but historical notes tracing its development, references to regulations and encyclopedias, and annotations of a court decision and a California Attorney General opinion.

State codes usually provide references to the original session laws in parenthetical notes following each section, as shown in Exhibit 5–14 on page 200, but only some include notes indicating the changes made by each amendment. Most also include tables with cross references from session law citations and earlier codifications to the current code. Each state code has a substantial general index of one or more volumes. Westlaw includes indexes (XX–ST–IDX) for forty-one states and the District of Columbia.

At least one annotated code from every state is in each ABA-approved law school library. The *Bluebook* and *ALWD Citation Manual* provide listings by state of the names and citations of current official and commercially published codes. State legal research guides (listed in Appendix B on page 454) provide information about earlier codes and statutory revisions, official and unofficial editions, and statutory indexes for individual states.

c.   KeyCite and Shepard's Citations

State code sections can also be checked in KeyCite or Shepard's Citations, which may retrieve cases and articles not mentioned in the annotated code. The online coverage of both citators is limited to current code sections. Shepard's print state citators also cover earlier codifications and session laws. Shepard's generally lists statutes as cited, so it may be necessary to check references under both a current code section and its predecessors to find relevant material.

Another Shepard's publication, *Shepard's Acts and Cases by Popular Names: Federal and State*, lists statutes by title and provides references to code citations. This set is most useful when the name of an act is known but not its state, or when similar acts from several states are sought.

d. Multistate Research Sources

Most state statutory research situations require finding the law in one particular state, for which that state's code is the primary research tool. Sometimes, however, it is necessary to compare statutory provisions among states or to survey legislation throughout the country. Multistate surveys of state laws can be frustrating and time-consuming, since different state codes may not use the same terminology for similar issues.

Several resources can help to make multistate statutory research a bit easier. Both Westlaw and Lexis have databases containing the codes of all fifty states; Westlaw offers either annotated (STAT–ANN–ALL) or unannotated (STAT–ALL) versions. These databases can save considerable time, although it is important to remember that any single search may not retrieve all relevant laws. It may be necessary to verify search results by checking the printed state code indexes.

The Internet provides convenient multistate access to code provisions in some subject areas. One of the most comprehensive sites is Cornell Legal Information Institute's topical index to state statutes on the Internet <www.law.cornell.edu/topics/state_statutes.html>, with links to code sites in several dozen broad categories. Sites collecting statutes on specific topics are also available, but it is important that verify that these are regularly and reliably updated.

Topical looseleaf services often collect state laws in their subject areas, making it easy to compare state provisions in areas such as taxation or employment law.

More general coverage is provided by two publications, the annual *Martindale-Hubbell Law Digest* (available on LexisNexis) and Richard A. Leiter, *National Survey of State Laws* (5th ed. 2005) (available on Westlaw). These works are arranged in very different ways.

Martindale-Hubbell is arranged by state and summarizes each jurisdiction's law on more than a hundred legal topics. It focuses on commercial and procedural information most likely to be needed by lawyers in other states, and provides citations to both code sections and court decisions. A search in the online version for a topic heading can retrieve the relevant summary for each state. Exhibit 5–15 on page 201 shows the Lexis version of the Massachusetts criminal law digest, one of fifty-three documents retrieved (fifty states, the District of Columbia, Puerto Rico, and the Virgin Islands) with the search *topic(criminal law)*. Note that it includes citations to several Massachusetts statutes, as well as a link in the second paragraph to a court decision.

The *National Survey of State Laws* is arranged by topic rather than by state, with tables summarizing state laws in forty-six areas and providing citations to codes. Its "Gun Control" section, for example, includes information on illegal arms, waiting periods, ownership restrictions, and laws prohibiting firearms on or near school grounds. The *National Survey* focuses more on social and political issues than *Martindale-Hubbell*, with sections on topics such as capital punishment, prayer in public schools, right to die, and stalking. The *National Survey of State Laws* is part of Westlaw's 50 State Surveys (SURVEYS) database, which also includes surveys prepared by West editors consisting of links to states code provisions. A topical listing of Westlaw's surveys is available by clicking on the "50 State Surveys" link at the top of any state statute search screen.

Numerous other online and print resources summarize or reprint state laws on specific topics. The National Conference of State Legislatures, for example, has an extensive online collection of surveys and compilations <www.ncsl.org/programs/lis/lrl/50statetracking.htm> on topics ranging from criminal justice to health care. Some sources omit the code references that are essential for verifying and updating their information, but those that do can be invaluable time-savers.

A valuable series of bibliographies called *Subject Compilations of State Laws* (1981–date) describes collections and lists of state statutes. This set does not itself summarize or cite the statutes, but it provides annotated descriptions of sources that do so. These include books, compendia, websites, and law review articles, which often have footnotes with extensive listings of state code citations. Exhibit 5–16 on page 202 shows a page from this publication, with entries under the heading "Firearms" for two law review articles and a U.S. Department of Justice publication.

e. Uniform Laws

Most multistate research requires finding a wide variety of legislative approaches to a particular topic. In a growing number of areas, however, states have adopted virtually identical acts. This can dramatically reduce the confusion caused by the application of conflicting state statutes. The National Conference of Commissioners on Uniform State Laws (NCCUSL), created in 1892 to prepare legislation which would decrease unnecessary conflicts, has drafted more than two hundred laws. Most of these are in force in at least one state, and some (such as the Uniform Commercial Code or Uniform Child Custody Jurisdiction Act) have been enacted in virtually every jurisdiction.

Uniform Laws Annotated, a multivolume set published by Thomson West (and available online from Westlaw), contains every uniform law approved by the NCCUSL, lists of adopting states, Commissioners' notes, and annotations to court decisions from adopting jurisdictions. These annotations allow researchers in one state to study the case law developed in other states with the same uniform law. A decision from another state is not binding authority, but its interpretation of similar language may be quite persuasive. The set is supplemented annually by pocket parts and by the pamphlet *Directory of Uniform Acts and Codes; Tables–Index*, which lists the acts alphabetically and includes a table of jurisdictions indicating the acts adopted in each state. LexisNexis has several dozen uniform laws, unannotated, in the Model Acts and Uniform Laws section of its Secondary Legal folder.

The text of a uniform law can also be found, of course, in the statutory code of each adopting state, accompanied by annotations from that state's courts. The state code contains the law as actually adopted and in force, rather than the text as proposed by the Commissioners. The NCCUSL version is merely a proposal, but the state code version is the law.

NCCUSL uniform laws, as well as drafts of its current projects, are available on the Internet <www.law. upenn.edu/library/ulc/ulc.htm>. Cornell's Legal Information Institute provides "Uniform Law Locators" <www. law.cornell.edu/uniform/>, listing links to official sites where the text as adopted in particular states can be found.

The NCCUSL is not the only organization drafting legislation for consideration by state legislatures. The American Law Institute has produced the Model Penal Code and other model acts; the American Bar Association has promulgated and revised the Model Business Corporation Act; and the Council of State Governments publishes an annual volume of *Suggested State Legislation*.

f. Interstate Compacts

An interstate compact is an agreement between two or more states, which under the Constitution requires approval by Congress. Compacts generally appear in the *U.S. Statutes at Large* and in the session laws and codes for the states that are parties. The National Center for Interstate Compacts <www.csg.org/programs/ncic/> provides a variety of useful resources on the subject, including a searchable database of more than 1,500 compacts in state codes. Compacts are also listed alphabetically in an appendix to Caroline N. Broun et al., *The Evolving Use and the Changing Role of Interstate Compacts: A Practitioner's Guide* (2006), with citations to the enabling federal and state legislation.

§ 5–7. Conclusion

In some ways statutory research is easier than case research, because the major resources are more accessible and more regularly updated. In many situations a good annotated code provides most of the necessary research leads. This convenience is undercut, however, by the opacity of statutory language. Judicial prose can be a model of clarity when compared to the texts of many federal and state statutes.

Researching statutory or constitutional law is rarely limited to finding a relevant provision and making sure that it remains in force. It is usually necessary to search for judicial decisions applying or construing its language. Administrative regulations may provide more specific requirements, and attorney general opinions on the meaning of the provision may also be available. A further understanding can be gained from treatises or law review articles.

Ambiguities and vagueness in statutes often lead to difficulties in interpretation. Some statutory ambiguities stem from poor draftsmanship, but many are the inevitable result of negotiation and compromise in the legislative process. Lawyers frequently study legislative documents in order to determine the meaning of the statutory text. This research in legislative history is the focus of the next chapter.

BEARING ARMS

SECOND AMENDMENT

A well regulated Militia, being necessary to the security of a free State, the right of the people to keep and bear Arms shall not be infringed.

IN GENERAL

In spite of extensive recent discussion and much legislative action with respect to regulation of the purchase, possession, and transportation of firearms, as well as proposals to substantially curtail ownership of firearms, there is no definitive resolution by the courts of just what right the Second Amendment protects. The opposing theories, perhaps oversimplified, are an "individual rights" thesis whereby individuals are protected in ownership, possession, and transportation, and a "states' rights" thesis whereby it is said the purpose of the clause is to protect the States in their authority to maintain formal, organized militia units. [1] Whatever the Amendment may mean, it is a bar only to federal action, not extending to state [2] or private [3] restraints. The Supreme Court has given effect to the dependent clause of the Amendment in the only case in which it has tested a congressional enactment against the constitutional prohibition, seeming to affirm individual protection

---

[1] A sampling of the diverse literature in which the same historical, linguistic, and case law background is the basis for strikingly different conclusions is: Staff of Subcom. on the Constitution, Senate Committee on the Judiciary, 97th Congress, 2d Sess., The Right to Keep and Bear Arms (Comm. Print 1982); DON B. KATES, HAND-GUN PROHIBITION AND THE ORIGINAL MEANING OF THE SECOND AMENDMENT (1984); GUN CONTROL AND THE CONSTITUTION: SOURCES AND EXPLORATIONS ON THE SECOND AMENDMENT (Robert J. Cottrol ed., 1993); STEPHEN P. HALBROOK, THAT EVERY MAN BE ARMED: THE EVOLUTION OF A CONSTITUTIONAL RIGHT (1984); Symposium, *Gun Control*, 49 LAW & CONTEMP. PROBS. 1 (1986); Sanford Levinson, *The Embarrassing Second Amendment*, 99 YALE L.J. 637 (1989); JOYCE LEE MALCOLM, TO KEEP AND BEAR ARMS: THE ORIGINS OF AN ANGLO-AMERICAN RIGHT (1994); Glenn Harlan Reynolds, *A Critical Guide to the Second Amendment*, 62 TENN. L. REV. 461 (1995); William Van Alystyne, *The Second Amendment and the Personal Right to Bear Arms*, 43 DUKE L.J. 1236 (1994).

[2] Presser v. Illinois, 116 U.S. 252, 265 (1886). *See also* Miller v. Texas, 153 U.S. 535 (1894); Robertson v. Baldwin, 165 U.S. 275, 281-282 (1897). The non-application of the Second Amendment to the States was more recently reaffirmed in Quilici v. Village of Morton Grove, 695 F. 2d 261 (7th Cir. 1982), *cert. denied*, 464 U.S. 863 (1983).

[3] United States v. Cruikshank, 92 U.S. 542 (1875).

1273

Exhibit 5–1. THE CONSTITUTION OF THE UNITED STATES OF AMERICA: ANALYSIS AND INTERPRETATION 1273, S. Doc. No. 108–17 (Johnny H. Killian et al. eds., 2004).

107 STAT. 1536   PUBLIC LAW 103–159—NOV. 30, 1993

Public Law 103–159
103d Congress

An Act

Nov. 30, 1993
[H.R. 1025]

To provide for a waiting period before the purchase of a handgun, and for the establishment of a national instant criminal background check system to be contacted by firearms dealers before the transfer of any firearm.

Be it enacted by the Senate and House of Representatives of the United States of America in Congress assembled,

Brady Handgun
Violence
Prevention
Act.
Inter-
governmental
relations.
Law
enforcement
and crime.
18 USC 921 note.

TITLE I—BRADY HANDGUN CONTROL

SEC. 101. SHORT TITLE.

This title may be cited as the "Brady Handgun Violence Prevention Act".

SEC. 102. FEDERAL FIREARMS LICENSEE REQUIRED TO CONDUCT CRIMINAL BACKGROUND CHECK BEFORE TRANSFER OF FIREARM TO NON-LICENSEE.

(a) INTERIM PROVISION.—

(1) IN GENERAL.—Section 922 of title 18, United States Code, is amended by adding at the end the following:

Effective date.
Termination
date.

"(s)(1) Beginning on the date that is 90 days after the date of enactment of this subsection and ending on the day before the date that is 60 months after such date of enactment, it shall be unlawful for any licensed importer, licensed manufacturer, or licensed dealer to sell, deliver, or transfer a handgun to an individual who is not licensed under section 923, unless—

"(A) after the most recent proposal of such transfer by the transferee—

"(i) the transferor has—

"(I) received from the transferee a statement of the transferee containing the information described in paragraph (3);

"(II) verified the identity of the transferee by examining the identification document presented;

"(III) within 1 day after the transferee furnishes the statement, provided notice of the contents of the statement to the chief law enforcement officer of the place of residence of the transferee; and

"(IV) within 1 day after the transferee furnishes the statement, transmitted a copy of the statement

Exhibit 5–2.   Brady Handgun Violence Prevention Act, Pub. L. 103–159, 107 Stat. 1536 (1993).

TITLES OF UNITED STATES CODE

*1. General Provisions.	27. Intoxicating Liquors.
2. The Congress.	*28. Judiciary and Judicial Procedure; and Appendix.
*3. The President.	
*4. Flag and Seal, Seat of Government, and the States.	29. Labor.
	30. Mineral Lands and Mining.
*5. Government Organization and Employees; and Appendix.	*31. Money and Finance.
	*32. National Guard.
6. Domestic Security.	33. Navigation and Navigable Waters.
7. Agriculture.	†34. [Navy.]
8. Aliens and Nationality.	*35. Patents.
*9. Arbitration.	*36. Patriotic and National Observances, Ceremonies, and Organizations.
*10. Armed Forces; and Appendix.	
*11. Bankruptcy; and Appendix.	*37. Pay and Allowances of the Uniformed Services.
12. Banks and Banking.	
*13. Census.	*38. Veterans' Benefits; and Appendix.
*14. Coast Guard.	*39. Postal Service.
15. Commerce and Trade.	*40. Public Buildings, Property, and Works.
16. Conservation.	41. Public Contracts.
*17. Copyrights.	42. The Public Health and Welfare.
*18. Crimes and Criminal Procedure; and Appendix.	43. Public Lands.
	*44. Public Printing and Documents.
19. Customs Duties.	45. Railroads.
20. Education.	*46. Shipping; and Appendix.
21. Food and Drugs.	47. Telegraphs, Telephones, and Radiotelegraphs.
22. Foreign Relations and Intercourse.	
*23. Highways.	48. Territories and Insular Possessions.
24. Hospitals and Asylums.	*49. Transportation.
25. Indians.	50. War and National Defense; and Appendix.
26. Internal Revenue Code; and Appendix.	

*This title has been enacted as positive law. However, any Appendix to this title has not been enacted as positive law.
†This title was eliminated by the enactment of Title 10.

Exhibit 5–3. Titles of United States Code, 1 UNITED STATES CODE iii (Supp. IV 2004).

in par. (4), and authorized the Secretary to permit the importation of ammunition for examination and testing in text following par. (4).

EFFECTIVE DATE OF 1996 AMENDMENT

Amendment by Pub. L. 104–106 effective on the earlier of the date on which the Secretary of the Army submits a certification in accordance with section 5523 of [former] Title 36, Patriotic Societies and Observances, or Oct. 1, 1996, see section 1624(c) of Pub. L. 104–106, set out as a note under section 4316 of Title 10, Armed Forces.

EFFECTIVE DATE OF 1988 AMENDMENT; SUNSET PROVISION

Amendment by section 2(c) of Pub. L. 100–649 effective 30th day beginning after Nov. 10, 1988, and amendment by section 2(f)(2)(C), (E) effective 15 years after such effective date, see section 2(f) of Pub. L. 100–649, as amended, set out as a note under section 922 of this title.

EFFECTIVE DATE OF 1986 AMENDMENT

Amendment by Pub. L. 99–308 applicable to any action, petition, or appellate proceeding pending on May 19, 1986, see section 110(b) of Pub. L. 99–308, set out as a note under section 921 of this title.

EFFECTIVE DATE OF 1984 AMENDMENT

Amendment by Pub. L. 98–573 effective 15th day after Oct. 30, 1984, see section 214(a), (b) of Pub. L. 98–573, set out as a note under section 1304 of Title 19, Customs Duties.

EFFECTIVE DATE OF 1968 AMENDMENT

Amendment by Pub. L. 90–618 effective Dec. 16, 1968, except subsecs. (a)(1) and (d) effective Oct. 22, 1968, see section 105 of Pub. L. 90–618, set out as a note under section 921 of this title.

SECTION REFERRED TO IN OTHER SECTIONS

This section is referred to in section 922 of this title; title 22 section 2778.

§ 925A. Remedy for erroneous denial of firearm

Any person denied a firearm pursuant to subsection (s) or (t) of section 922—

(1) due to the provision of erroneous information relating to the person by any State or political subdivision thereof, or by the national instant criminal background check system established under section 103 of the Brady Handgun Violence Prevention Act; or

(2) who was not prohibited from receipt of a firearm pursuant to subsection (g) or (n) of section 922,

may bring an action against the State or political subdivision responsible for providing the erroneous information, or responsible for denying the transfer, or against the United States, as the case may be, for an order directing that the erroneous information be corrected or that the transfer be approved, as the case may be. In any action under this section, the court, in its discretion, may allow the prevailing party a reasonable attorney's fee as part of the costs.

(Added Pub. L. 103–159, title I, § 104(a), Nov..30, 1993, 107 Stat. 1543.)

REFERENCES IN TEXT

Section 103 of the Brady Handgun Violence Prevention Act, referred to in par. (1), is section 103 of Pub. L. 103–159, which is set out as a note under section 922 of this title.

§ 926. Rules and regulations

(a) The Secretary may prescribe only such rules and regulations as are necessary to carry out the provisions of this chapter, including—

(1) regulations providing that a person licensed under this chapter, when dealing with another person so licensed, shall provide such other licensed person a certified copy of this license;

(2) regulations providing for the issuance, at a reasonable cost, to a person licensed under this chapter, of certified copies of his license for use as provided under regulations issued under paragraph (1) of this subsection; and

(3) regulations providing for effective receipt and secure storage of firearms relinquished by or seized from persons described in subsection (d)(8) or (g)(8) of section 922.

No such rule or regulation prescribed after the date of the enactment of the Firearms Owners' Protection Act may require that records required to be maintained under this chapter or any portion of the contents of such records, be recorded at or transferred to a facility owned, managed, or controlled by the United States or any State or any political subdivision thereof, nor that any system of registration of firearms, firearms owners, or firearms transactions or dispositions be established. Nothing in this section expands or restricts the Secretary's authority to inquire into the disposition of any firearm in the course of a criminal investigation.

(b) The Secretary shall give not less than ninety days public notice, and shall afford interested parties opportunity for hearing, before prescribing such rules and regulations.

(c) The Secretary shall not prescribe rules or regulations that require purchasers of black powder under the exemption provided in section 845(a)(5) of this title to complete affidavits or forms attesting to that exemption.

(Added Pub. L. 90–351, title IV, § 902, June 19, 1968, 82 Stat. 234; amended Pub. L. 90–618, title I, § 102, Oct. 22, 1968, 82 Stat. 1226; Pub. L. 99–308, § 106, May 19, 1986, 100 Stat. 459; Pub. L. 103–322, title XI, § 110401(d), Sept. 13, 1994, 108 Stat. 2015.)

REFERENCES IN TEXT

The date of the enactment of the Firearms Owners' Protection Act, referred to in subsec. (a), is the date of enactment of Pub. L. 99–308, which was approved May 19, 1986.

AMENDMENTS

1994—Subsec. (a)(3). Pub. L. 103–322 added par. (3).

1986—Subsec. (a). Pub. L. 99–308, § 106(1)–(4), designated existing provision as subsec. (a), and in subsec. (a) as so designated, in provision preceding par. (1) substituted "may prescribe only" for "may prescribe" and "as are" for "as he deems reasonably", and in closing provision substituted provision that no rule or regulation prescribed after May 19, 1986, require that records required under this chapter be recorded at or transferred to a facility owned, managed, or controlled by the United States or any State or political subdivision thereof, nor any system of registration of firearms, firearms owners, or firearms transactions or dispositions be established and that nothing in this section expands or restricts the authority of the Secretary to inquire into the disposition of any firearm in the course of a criminal investigation for provision that the Secretary give reasonable public notice, and afford an op-

Exhibit 5–4.   18 U.S.C. §§ 925A–926 (2000).

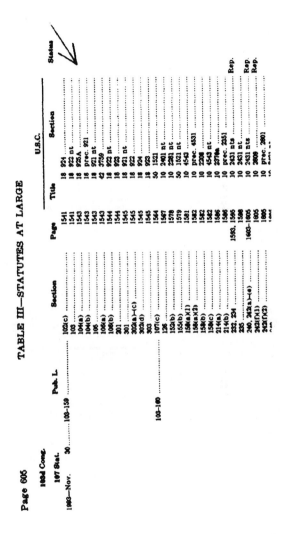

Exhibit 5–5. Table III—Statutes at Large, 29 UNITED STATES CODE 605 (2000).

ACTS CITED BY POPULAR NAME   Page 746

Blue Star Mothers of America Act
  Pub. L. 86-653, July 14, 1960, 74 Stat. 515

Board for International Broadcasting Act of 1973
  Pub. L. 93-129, Oct. 19, 1973, 87 Stat. 456 (22
  U.S.C. 2871 et seq.)
  Short title, see 22 U.S.C. 2871 note

**Board for International Broadcasting Authoriza-
tion Act, Fiscal Years 1980 and 1981**
  Pub. L. 96-60, title III, Aug. 15, 1979, 93 Stat.
  402

**Board for International Broadcasting Authoriza-
tion Act, Fiscal Years 1982 and 1983**
  Pub. L. 97-241, title IV, Aug. 24, 1982, 96 Stat.
  295

**Board for International Broadcasting Authoriza-
tion Act, Fiscal Years 1984 and 1985**
  Pub. L. 98-164, title III, Nov. 22, 1983, 97 Stat.
  1036

**Board of Veterans' Appeals Administrative Pro-
cedures Improvement Act of 1994**
  Pub. L. 103-271, July 1, 1994, 108 Stat. 740
  Short title, see 38 U.S.C. 301 note

Bodie Protection Act of 1994
  Pub. L. 103-433, title X, Oct. 31, 1994, 108 Stat.
  4509

Boggs Act
  Nov. 2, 1951, ch. 666, 65 Stat. 767 (21 U.S.C.
  174)

Boiler Inspection Act of the District of Columbia
  July 25, 1936, ch. 802, 49 Stat. 1917

Boise Laboratory Replacement Act of 2000
  Pub. L. 106-291, title III, § 351, Oct. 11, 2000,
  114 Stat. 1004

Bomb Threats Act
  Pub. L. 91-452, title XI, § 1102(a), Oct. 15, 1970,
  84 Stat. 956 (18 U.S.C. 844)

Bond Act (Public Officers)
  Mar. 2, 1895, ch. 177, § 5, 28 Stat. 807

Bond Limitation Act
  See Second Liberty Bond Act

**Bond Purchase Clause (Sundry Civil Appropria-
tion Act)**
  Mar. 3, 1881, ch. 133, § 2, 21 Stat. 457

Bonner Act
  See Federal Boating Act of 1958

Bonneville Project Act of 1937
  Aug. 20, 1937, ch. 720, 50 Stat. 731 (16 U.S.C.
  832 et seq.)
  Short title, see 16 U.S.C. 832 note

Bonus Act
  See World War Adjusted Compensation Act

Bonus Payment Act, 1936
  See Adjusted Compensation Payment Act,
  1936

Book Postage Act
  June 30, 1942, ch. 459, 56 Stat. 462

Booth Act (California School Lands)
  Mar. 1, 1877, ch. 81, 19 Stat. 267

Borah Act
  Aug. 25, 1937, ch. 777, 50 Stat. 810

Borah Resolution (Armament Conference)
  See Disarmament Conference Resolution

Border Smog Reduction Act of 1998
  Pub. L. 105-286, Oct. 27, 1998, 112 Stat. 2773
  Short title, see 42 U.S.C. 7401 note

**Borland Amendment (District of Columbia Im-
provements)**
  July 21, 1914, ch. 191, 38 Stat. 524

Bosque Redondo Memorial Act
  Pub. L. 106-511, title II, Nov. 13, 2000, 114
  Stat. 2369 (16 U.S.C. 431 note)

Boston National Historical Park Act of 1974
  Pub. L. 93-431, Oct. 1, 1974, 88 Stat. 1184 (16
  U.S.C. 410z et seq.)
  Short title, see 16 U.S.C. 410z note

Boulder Canyon Project Act
  Dec. 21, 1928, ch. 42, 45 Stat. 1057 (43 U.S.C.
  617 et seq.)
  Short title, see 43 U.S.C. 617t

Boulder Canyon Project Adjustment Act
  July 19, 1940, ch. 643, 54 Stat. 774 (43 U.S.C.
  618 et seq.)
  Short title, see 43 U.S.C. 618o

Boulder City Act of 1958
  Pub. L. 85-900, Sept. 2, 1958, 72 Stat. 1726 (43
  U.S.C. 617a note)

Bowman Act (Claims)
  Mar. 3, 1883, ch. 116, 22 Stat. 485

Boykin Merchant Marine Act
  June 6, 1939, ch. 186, 53 Stat. 810

Brady Handgun Violence Prevention Act
  Pub. L. 103-159, title I, Nov. 30, 1993, 107 Stat.
  1536
  Short title, see 18 U.S.C. 921 note

**Breast and Cervical Cancer Mortality Prevention
Act of 1990**
  Pub. L. 101-354, Aug. 10, 1990, 104 Stat. 409 (42
  U.S.C. 300k et seq.)
  Short title, see 42 U.S.C. 201 note

**Breast and Cervical Cancer Prevention and
Treatment Act of 2000**
  Pub. L. 106-354, Oct. 24, 2000, 114 Stat. 1381
  Short title, see 42 U.S.C. 1305 note

Bretton Woods Agreements Act
  July 31, 1945, ch. 339, 59 Stat. 512 (22 U.S.C.
  286 et seq.)
  Short title, see 22 U.S.C. 286 note

**Bretton Woods Agreements Act Amendments of
1978**
  Pub. L. 95-435, Oct. 10, 1978, 92 Stat. 1051

Bridge Act of 1906
  Also known as the General Bridge Act of 1906
  Mar. 23, 1906, ch. 1130, 34 Stat. 84 (33 U.S.C.
  491 et seq.)
  Short title, see 33 U.S.C. 491 note

Bring Them Home Alive Act of 2000
  Pub. L. 106-484, Nov. 9, 2000, 114 Stat. 2195 (8
  U.S.C. 1157 note)

Exhibit 5–6. Acts Cited by Popular Name, 27 UNITED STATES CODE 746
(2000).

GENERAL INDEX **Page 1188**

Exhibit 5–7. General Index, 35 UNITED STATES CODE 1188 (2000).

For more information on using WESTLAW to supplement your research, see the WESTLAW Electronic Research Guide, which follows the Explanation.

§ 921. Definitions

(a) As used in this chapter—

(1) The term "person" and the term "whoever" include any individual, corporation, company, association, firm, partnership, society, or joint stock company.

(2) The term "interstate or foreign commerce" includes commerce between any place in a State and any place outside of that State, or within any possession of the United States (not including the Canal Zone) or the District of Columbia, but such term does not include commerce between places within the same State but through any place outside of that State. The term "State" includes the District of Columbia, the Commonwealth of Puerto Rico, and the possessions of the United States (not including the Canal Zone).

(3) The term "firearm" means (A) any weapon (including a starter gun) which will or is designed to or may readily be converted to expel a projectile by the action of an explosive; (B) the frame or receiver of any such weapon; (C) any firearm muffler or firearm silencer; or (D) any destructive device. Such term does not include an antique firearm.

(4) The term "destructive device" means—

    (A) any explosive, incendiary, or poison gas—

        (i) bomb,

        (ii) grenade,

        (iii) rocket having a propellant charge of more than four ounces,

        (iv) missile having an explosive or incendiary charge of more than one-quarter ounce,

        (v) mine, or

        (vi) device similar to any of the devices described in the preceding clauses;

    (B) any type of weapon (other than a shotgun or a shotgun shell which the Secretary finds is generally recognized as particularly suitable for sporting purposes) by whatever name known which will, or which may be readily converted to, expel a projectile by the action of an explosive or other propellant, and which has any barrel with a bore of more than one-half inch in diameter; and

161

Exhibit 5–8.   18 U.S.C.A. § 921 (West 2000).

Ch. 44   FIREARMS

18 § 925
Note 3

Administrative Law, 1 Am Jur 2d § 650.
Weapons and Firearms, 79 Am Jur 2d § 33.

Forms

Weapons and Firearms, 20 Am Jur Legal Forms 2d §§ 262:1–5.

Law Review and Journal Commentaries

Congress paralyzes section 925(c) of the Gun Control Act. 49 Administrative
L.Rev. 501 (1997).
Hitting the mark: strict liability for defective handgun design. Michael Dillon, 24
Santa Clara L.Rev. 743 (1984).

WESTLAW ELECTRONIC RESEARCH

See WESTLAW guide following the Explanation pages of this volume.

Notes of Decisions

Appropriations   14
Civil rights restored   9
Constitutionality   1
Construction with other laws   2
Exhaustion of administrative remedies
    13
Importation   3
Interstate commerce   4
Licensed gun dealers   7
Pattern of behavior   11
Presumptions   10
Removal of prohibition   8
Review   15
Statement of reasons   12
States and political subdivisions   6
Use of United States   5

1. Constitutionality

Congress acted within its power under
the Commerce Clause in enacting statute
which barred domestic violence misde-
meanants from possessing firearms, including government-issued firearms, giv-
en requirement that government satisfy
statute's jurisdictional element in prosecuting violation by proving that defendant possessed firearm in or affecting
commerce. Fraternal Order of Police v.
U.S., C.A.D.C.1999, 173 F.3d 898, 335
U.S.App.D.C. 359, certiorari denied 120
S.Ct. 324.

2. Construction with other laws

Provision of this section affording a
procedure to secure relief from any firearms disability imposed on a convicted
felon applies not only to those disabilities
imposed by this chapter, but also to disabilities on possession imposed by sections 1201 and 1202 of the Appendix to
this title. U. S. v. Graves, C.A.3 (Pa.)
1977, 554 F.2d 65.

3. Importation

Secretary of Treasury's temporary suspension on importation of semiautomatic
assault weapons was not arbitrary or capricious, notwithstanding firearms dealer's contention that semiautomatic rifle
had not physically changed and that suspension was not based on any evidence;
Gun Control Act required consideration
of rifle's use in addition to its physical
structure, and there was sufficient evidence of dramatic proliferation in use of
assault-type rifles in criminal activity.
Gun South, Inc. v. Brady, C.A.11 (Ala.)
1989, 877 F.2d 858.

Authority of Bureau of Alcohol, Tobacco and Firearms to regulate importation
of assault rifles for official use of federal,
state and local governmental entities encompasses first domestic sale of rifle to
ensure that it is imported for official government use. U.S. v. Nevius, C.D.Ill.
1992, 792 F.Supp. 609.

Statute under which Secretary of Treasury was required to authorize importation of firearms generally recognized as
particularly suitable for or readily adapt-
able to sporting purposes precluded federal officials' interdiction of a gun dealer's imported semiautomatic weapons
purchased under permits validly issued
and valid when acted upon; weapons
were interdicted by Customs Service
upon their arrival in the United States
pursuant to intervening moratorium on
importation of semiautomatic weapons
formulated as part of national drug policy. Gun South, Inc. v. Brady, N.D.Ala.
1989, 711 F.Supp. 1054, reversed 877
F.2d 858.

597

Exhibit 5–9.   18 U.S.C.A. § 925 notes (West 2000).

18 USCS § 925

INTERPRETIVE NOTES AND DECISIONS

I. IN GENERAL

1. Generally
2. Constitutional matters
3. Relation to other laws
4. Exemption for government
5. Authorization to import particular items
6. Relief from disabilities
7. Search and seizure
8. Miscellaneous

II. JUDICIAL REVIEW

9. Scope and standard of review
10. Denial of application for relief from disabilities
11. Failure or refusal to act on application for relief from disabilities
12. Miscellaneous

I. IN GENERAL

1. Generally

18 USCS § 925(a) does not exempt any sale or delivery of firearms by its terms; it expressly covers only "transportation, shipment, receipt, or importation". United States v Brooks (1980, CA5 Fla) 611 F2d 614 (ovrld in part on other grounds by United States v Henry (1984, CA5 Tex) 749 F2d 203).

Neither 18 USCS § 925 nor any purported application of state statutes will exempt defendant from application of federal firearms laws where a defendant is convicted felon and seeks to individually purchase and own firearm. United States v Kozerski (1981, DC NH) 518 F Supp 1082, affd without op (1984, CA1 NH) 740 F2d 952, cert den (1984) 469 US 842, 83 L Ed 2d 86, 105 S Ct 147.

2. Constitutional matters

18 USCS § 925 was unconstitutional insofar as it purported to withhold public interest exception from those convicted of domestic violence misdemeanors; government may not bar such people from possessing firearms in public interest while imposing lesser restriction on those convicted of crimes that differ only in being more serious. FOP v United States (1998, App DC) 332 US App DC 49, 152 F3d 998.

Due process did not entitle felon to bearing to determine whether he was dangerous because results of such bearing would have had no bearing on whether he was subject to disability imposed by 18 USCS § 922(g)(1); and because substantive classification drawn by Congress—which kept firearms out of hands of all convicted felons, not just those who represent ongoing threat to society—was not so arbitrary or unreasonable as to violate Fifth Amendment, felon's constitutional challenge to effective suspension of 18 USCS § 925(c) was rejected. Black v Snow (2003, DC Dist Col) 272 F Supp 2d 21, affd (2004, App DC) 110 Fed Appx 130.

3. Relation to other laws

By means of 18 USCS § 925, person may obtain relief from 18 USCS Appx § 1202(a)(1), which makes it crime for any person who has been convicted of crime punishable by imprisonment for term exceeding one year to ship, transport or receive firearm. United States v Synnes (1971, CA8 Minn) 438 F2d 764, vacated on other grounds (1972) 404 US 1009, 30 L Ed 2d 657, 92 S Ct 687.

Relief provision, 18 USCS § 925, is applicable to 18 USCS Appx § 1202, since first provision speaks broadly, declaring that Secretary of Treasury [now Attorney General] could grant relief from disabilities imposed "by federal laws," and since it refers to "possession," activity largely within province of 18 USCS Appx § 1202. United States v Graves (1977, CA3 Pa) 554 F2d 65.

As matter of law, gun dealer who is winding down his operations under 18 USCS § 925(b) pursuant to valid license cannot be convicted of possession of firearms under 18 USCS § 922(g)(1). United States v Douglass (1992, CA9 Nev) 974 F2d 1046, 92 CDOS 7081, 92 Daily Journal DAR 11408, amd, reh den (1992, CA9 Nev) 92 Daily Journal DAR 14059.

18 USCS § 925(c) left court with no basis on which to determine that Attorney General's withholding of action on convict felon's application was unlawful and in these circumstances, court lacked power under Administrative Procedures Act to compel agency action. Black v Snow (2003, DC Dist Col) 272 F Supp 2d 21, affd (2004, App DC) 110 Fed Appx 130.

4. Exemption for government

Despite provisions of 18 USCS § 922(h) which restricts receipt of firearms by those convicted of felony, § 925(a)(1) allows convicted felon currently employed as adult corrections officer to carry weapon. Hyland v Fukuda (1978, CA9 Hawaii) 580 F2d 977.

18 USCS § 925 does not exempt sale of firearms through undisclosed under-cover agent of United States. Perri v Department of Treasury; Perri v Department of Treasury, BATF (1981, CA9 Ariz) 637 F2d 1332.

18 USCS § 925(a)(1) grants BATF authority to regulate transfer of firearm from importer to law enforcement agency for which firearm was imported, i.e., "first sales," since BATF must have authority to require truthful statements about purpose for purchase of weapons in order for § 925(a)(1), which excepts government agencies from prohibition of 18 USCS § 922(l), to have meaning. United States v F.J. Vollmer & Co. (1993, CA7 Ill) 1 F3d 1511, cert den (1994) 510 US 1043, 126 L Ed 2d 655, 114 S Ct 688.

Since right to possess firearm is not fundamental

Exhibit 5–10. 18 U.S.C.S. § 925 notes (LexisNexis 2005).

18 § 929   CRIMES AND CRIMINAL PROCEDURE

Treatises and Practice Aids

Wright & Miller: Federal Prac. & Proc. § 873, Proceedings to Which Rules Apply.

Wright & Miller: Federal Prac. & Proc. App. C, Appendix C. Advisory Committee Notes for the Federal Rules of Criminal Procedure for the United States District Courts.

§ 930. Possession of firearms and dangerous weapons in Federal facilities

[See main volume for text of (a) and (b)]

(c) A person who kills any person in the course of a violation of subsection (a) or (b), or in the course of an attack on a Federal facility involving the use of a firearm or other dangerous weapon, or attempts or conspires to do such an act, shall be punished as provided in sections 1111, 1112, 1113, and 1117.

[See main volume for text of (d) to (h)]

(Added Pub.L. 100–690, Title VI, § 6215(a), Nov. 18, 1988, 102 Stat. 4361, and amended Pub.L. 101–647, Title XXII, § 2205(a), Nov. 29, 1990, 104 Stat. 4857; Pub.L. 103–322, Title VI, § 60014, Sept. 13, 1994, 108 Stat. 1973; Pub.L. 104–294, Title VI, § 603(t), (u), Oct. 11, 1996, 110 Stat. 3506; Pub.L. 107–56, Title VIII, § 811(b), Oct. 26, 2001, 115 Stat. 381.)

HISTORICAL AND STATUTORY NOTES

Amendments

2001 Amendments. Subsec. (c). Pub.L. 107–56, § 811(b), struck out "or attempts to kill"

after "A person who kills", inserted "or attempts or conspires to do such an act," before "shall be punished", and substituted "1113, and 1117" for "and 1113".

LIBRARY REFERENCES

American Digest System

Weapons ⬤9, 17(8).

Research References

ALR Library

86 ALR 4th 931, Validity of State Gun Control Legislation Under State Constitutional Provisions Securing the Right to Bear Arms.

197 ALR, Fed. 1, Validity, Construction, and Application of 18 U.S.C.A. § 2339A, Proscribing Providing Material Support to Terrorists.

184 ALR, Fed. 485, Validity, Construction, and Application of Federal Brady Act, and Implementing Federal and State Regulations Thereunder.

Encyclopedias

84 Am. Jur. Trials 109, Litigating Against the Firearm Industry.

Forms

Am. Jur. Pl. & Pr. Forms Nuisances § 15.3, Complaint, Petition, or Declaration-By Political Subdivision-Public Nuisance and Unfair Business Practices-Negligent Design and Marketing of Guns.

Notes of Decisions

1. Conspicuous notice

Federal employee was properly disciplined for bringing a firearm into work even though there were no notices posted at front and rear exits of office where employee worked and federal criminal prohibition on possessing firearm in federal facility required proof of such posting or actual

notice of prohibition; government did not have to prove that employee violated a criminal law in order to discipline him, and in any event employee was found to have actual knowledge of agency's ban. Haver v. Department of Agriculture, C.A.Fed.2002, 53 Fed.Appx. 112, 2002 WL 31780960, Unreported. Officers And Public Employees ⬤ 69.7

§ 931. Prohibition on purchase, ownership, or possession of body armor by violent felons

(a) **In general.**—Except as provided in subsection (b), it shall be unlawful for a person to purchase, own, or possess body armor, if that person has been convicted of a felony that is—

(1) a crime of violence (as defined in section 16); or

(2) an offense under State law that would constitute a crime of violence under paragraph (1) if it occurred within the special maritime and territorial jurisdiction of the United States.

(b) **Affirmative defense.**—

(1) **In general.**—It shall be an affirmative defense under this section that—

(A) the defendant obtained prior written certification from his or her employer that the defendant's purchase, use, or possession of body armor was necessary for the safe performance of lawful business activity; and

156

Exhibit 5–11.   18 U.S.C.A. § 930 (West Supp. 2006).

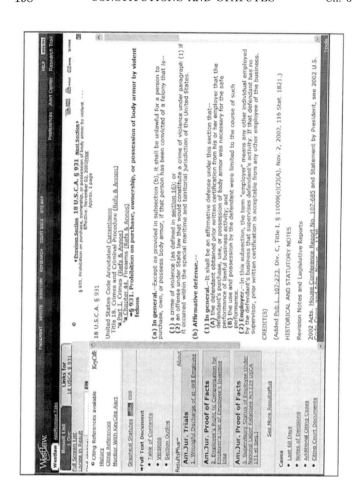

Exhibit 5–12.   18 U.S.C.A. § 925 (Westlaw through 2006 legislation).

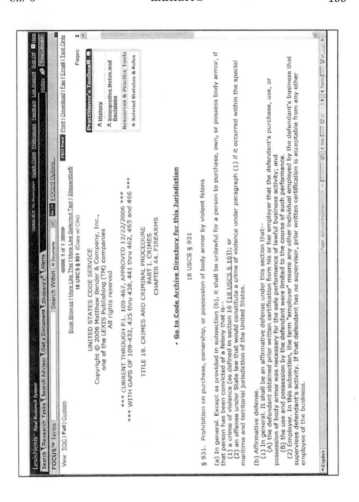

Exhibit 5–13. 18 U.S.C.S. § 925 (Lexis through 2006 legislation).

MACHINE GUNS § 12200
Title 2 Note 1

§ 12200. Definition

The term "machinegun" as used in this chapter means any weapon which shoots, or is designed to shoot, automatically, more than one shot, without manual reloading, by a single function of the trigger, and includes any frame or receiver which can only be used with that weapon. The term also includes any part or combination of parts designed and intended for use in converting a weapon into a machinegun. The term also includes any weapon deemed by the federal Bureau of Alcohol, Tobacco, and Firearms as readily convertible to a machinegun under Chapter 53 (commencing with Section 5801) of Title 26 of the United States Code.

(Added by Stats.1953, c. 36, p. 661, § 1. Amended by Stats.1965, c. 33, p. 913, § 1; Stats.1967, c. 1281, p. 3084, § 1; Stats.1969, c. 1003, p. 1974, § 1; Stats.1983, c. 101, § 148; Stats.1986, c. 1423, § 1.)

Historical and Statutory Notes

The 1965 amendment rewrote the section which read:

"The term machine gun as used in this chapter shall apply to and include all firearms known as machine rifles, machine guns, or submachine guns capable of discharging automatically and continuously loaded ammunition of any caliber in which the ammunition is fed to such gun from or by means of clips, disks, drums, belts or other separable mechanical device and all firearms which are automatically fed after each discharge from or by means of clips, disks, drums, belts or other separable mechanical device having a capacity greater than 10 cartridges."

The 1967 amendment deleted the words "or semiautomatically" following automatically and included frame or receiver.

The 1969 amendment added the last sentence relating to any combination of parts for use in converting a weapon into a machine gun.

The 1983 amendment made nonsubstantive changes.

The 1986 amendment substituted "also includes any part or" for "shall also include any" in the second sentence, and added the third sentence.

Derivation: Stats.1927, c. 552, p. 938, § 2; Stats.1933, c. 450, p. 1170, § 3.

Library References

Firearms control recommendation. Report of Assembly Interim Committee on Criminal Procedure, 1965 to 1967, Vol. 22, No. 12, p.49. Vol. 2 of Appendix to Journal of Assembly, Reg. Sess., 1967.

Regulation and control of firearms. Report of Assembly Interim Committee on Criminal Procedure, 1963 to 1965, Vol. 22, No. 6. Vol. 2 of Appendix to Journal of the Assembly, Reg.Sess., 1965.

Words and Phrases (Perm.Ed.)

Legal Jurisprudences

Cal Jur 3d Crim L § 1600.
Am Jur 2d Weapons and Firearms §§ 1, 2, 4, 32.

Treatises and Practice Aids

Witkin & Epstein, Criminal Law (2d ed) §§ 1090, 1107, 1501.

Notes of Decisions

In general 1

-----

1. In general

In prosecution for possession of a machine gun, evidence supported finding that the part of alleged 50-caliber machine gun found in search was a "frame" or "receiver" which could only be used with machine gun. People v. Tall-madge (App. 2 Dist. 1980) 163 Cal.Rptr. 372, 103 Cal.App.3d 980.

A U.S. model M1.30 caliber carbine was a machine gun under this section, as it read prior to 1965 amendment, when a clip with a capacity of more that 10 cartridges is attached to the gun or such a clip and gun are within the immediate possession of one person or corporation. 43 Ops.Atty.Gen. 314, 6–19–64.

419

Exhibit 5–14. Cal. Penal Code § 12200 (West 2000).

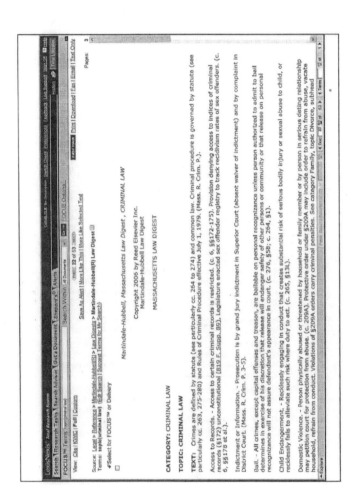

Exhibit 5–15. Massachusetts Law Digest: Criminal Law, MARTINDALE-HUBBELL LAW DIGEST (LexisNexis 2006).

Firearms

4471.01 Bhowmik, Rachana. "Aiming for Accountability: How City Lawsuits Can Help Reform an Irresponsible Gun Industry." *Journal of Law and Policy* 11 (2002):67-134.

Pp. 94-95, fns. 95 and 96. Summaries. Cites to codes. Covers the twenty-one states that have laws "prohibiting municipalities from bringing tort actions against" firearm manufacturers and dealers.

4471.02 Hartley, A. Nicole. "Business Owner Liability and Concealed Weapons Legislation: A Call for Legislative Guidance for Pennsylvania Business Owners." *Penn State Law Review* 108 (2003):637-56.

Pp. 648-49, fns. 71-82. Citations only. Cites to codes. Covers laws on permits to carry concealed weapons.

4471.03 Regional Justice Information Service. *Survey of State Procedures Related to Firearm Sales, Midyear 2002.* Washington: U.S. Department of Justice, Office of Justice Programs, Bureau of Justice Statistics, 2003. 90 pp. (NCJ 198830) HV7436.S87. J29.35. 96-174430, 98-641591.

Pp. 17-71. Summaries. Cites to codes. Covers persons not permitted to own handguns (alcoholics, aliens, drug addicts, felons, juvenile delinquents, the mentally ill, and minors); restoration of the right to own firearms; prohibited firearms (machine guns, short-barreled rifles or shotguns, and other firearms); regulated sales (gun shows, pawnbrokers, and private sales); permits to purchase, carry, or conceal; background checks; waiting periods; purchaser fees; record retention; and registration. Includes American Samoa, Guam, Puerto Rico, and the Virgin Islands. Current as of June 2002.

Pp. 74-84. Charts and tables. Cites to codes. Covers persons prohibited from owning firearms, background checks, permit procedures, fees, record retention, appeals, databases accessed for background checks, and regulated sales.

Note: Available on the Internet. URL: [www.ojp.usdoj.gov/bjs/pub/pdf/ssprfs02.pdf] and [purl.access.gpo.gov/GPO/LPS2865]. Previous editions published in 2002 (2001-2002 Nyberg 4230.04), 2000 (1999-2000 Nyberg 3279.14), 1997 (1998-99 Nyberg 3550.09), and 1996 (1995-96 Nyberg 2853.09).

90

Exhibit 5–16. Cheryl Rae Nyberg, Subject Compilations of State Laws 2002–2003: An Annotated Bibliography 90 (2004).

CHAPTER 6

LEGISLATIVE INFORMATION

---

§ 6–1. Introduction

The ambiguities so common in the language of statutes require lawyers and scholars to locate legislative documents from which they can try to discern the intended purpose of an act or the meaning of particular statutory language. Researchers also need to investigate the current progress of proposed laws under consideration by the legislature. These processes—determining the meaning or intent of an enacted law, and ascertaining the status of a pending bill—comprise legislative history research.

Legislative history is an area in which there is a strong dichotomy between federal and state research. Federal legislative history is thoroughly documented with numerous sources, while state legislative history research can be quite frustrating. On both the federal and state level, however, the Internet has made a significant contribution to the dissemination of information. Government websites make it quite easy to learn about the status of pending legislation and to obtain documents relating to recently passed acts. Research into the background of older laws, however, may still require access to printed sources.

§ 6–2. Federal Legislative History Sources

An understanding of the legislative process is essential for research in legislative history. Numerous background sources are available for understanding Congress and its work. One of the most extensive reference works is Donald C. Bacon, Roger H. Davidson & Morton Keller, eds., *Encyclopedia of the United States Congress* (4 vols. 1995), which provides a broad historical and political science perspective on the institution. *Congressional Quarterly's Guide to Congress* (2 vols., 5th ed. 2000) has a wide range of political, historical, and statistical information; Part III, Congressional Procedures, is particularly useful in understanding committee and floor action. Two shorter official documents prepared by the House and Senate parliamentarians, *How Our Laws Are Made* and *Enactment of a Law*, are available from the Library of Congress' THOMAS system <thomas.loc.gov>, under the heading "The Legislative Process."

Each stage in the enactment of a federal law may result in a significant legislative history document. The following are the most important potential steps in the legislative process and their related documents:

Action	Document
Preliminary inquiry	Transcripts of hearings on the general subject of the proposed legislation
Executive recommendation	Presidential message proposing an administration bill
Introduction of bill and referral to committee	Slip bill as introduced
Hearings on bill	Transcript of testimony and exhibits
Approval by committee	Committee report, including committee's version of bill
Legislative debates	*Congressional Record*, sometimes including texts of bill in amended forms
Passage by first house	Final House or Senate version of the proposed legislation
Other house	Generally same procedure and documents as above
Referral to conference committee (if texts passed by houses differ)	Conference committee version of bill; conference committee report
Passage by one or both houses of revised bill	Enrolled bill sent to President

Action	**Document**
Approval by President	Presidential signing statement; slip law, subsequently published in *Statutes at Large* and classified by subject in the *U.S. Code*

Of the many types of documents issued by Congress, a few are particularly important for legislative history research. *Bills* are the major source for the texts of pending or unenacted legislation. *Committee reports* analyze and describe bills and are usually considered the most authoritative sources of congressional intent. *Floor debates* may contain a sponsor's interpretation of a bill or the only explanation of last-minute amendments. *Hearings* can provide useful background on the purpose of an act.

This section introduces these various documents, with a brief explanation of how they are published and their availability in electronic sources including THOMAS <thomas.loc.gov>, the Library of Congress website for legislative information, and the Government Printing Office's GPO Access <www.gpoaccess.gov/legislative.html> as well as Westlaw and LexisNexis. Section 6–3 then looks in greater depth at these and other resources for legislative history research.

a. Bills

The texts of bills are needed by researchers interested in pending or failed legislation, and may also help in interpreting enacted laws. Variations among the bills and amendments can aid in determining the intended meaning of an act, as each deletion or addition made during the legislative process implies a deliberate choice of language by the legislators.

Bills are individually numbered in separate series for each house, and retain their identifying numbers through both sessions of a Congress. Pending bills lapse at the end of the two-year term, and a new bill must be reintroduced the following term if it is to be considered.

Some public laws arise from *joint resolutions* rather than bills. These usually, but not always, deal with matters of a limited or temporary nature. Joint resolutions and bills differ in form but have the same legal effect. There are two other forms of resolution that do not have the force of law: *concurrent resolutions* expressing the opinion of both houses of Congress, and *simple resolutions* concerning the procedures or expressions of just one house.

Often bills with similar or identical language, known as *companion bills*, are introduced in both the House and Senate so that each can begin consideration, but if each chamber passes its own bill there is no single bill that has passed both houses and can be presented to the President. A procedure that Congress frequently employs is called an *amendment in the nature of a substitute*. This is an amendment that deletes everything after the enacting clause (i.e., "Be it enacted by the Senate and House of Representatives of the United States of America in Congress assembled"), and inserts new text in its place. Sometimes this is done simply because it is more convenient to replace an entire bill than to make specific changes, but another reason is that the House and Senate must pass the same bill for it to go to the President and become law. The significance of this for researchers is that the number of the bill that becomes law is not necessarily the number of the version that was the subject of congressional hearings, committee reports, or perhaps even floor debates. The key language in an enacted law may have come from another bill with a different number and a different set of legislative history documents.

Bills are available electronically from several sources. THOMAS has the text of bills since 1989, and GPO Access begins coverage in 1993 <www.gpoaccess.gov/bills/> with PDF files replicating the printed bills. Texts of bills are also available online from commercial electronic services, including LexisNexis (1989–date) and Westlaw (1995–date). Older bills are available in microfiche in many larger law libraries.

Exhibit 6–1 on page 237 shows the bill S. 2268 as introduced in the Senate in 2002, printed from the GPO Access website. This is an early version of the legislation that three years later would become the Protection of Lawful Commerce in Arms Act, Pub. L. 109–92, 119 Stat. 2095 (2005).

b.   Committee Reports

Reports are generally considered the most important sources of legislative history. They are issued by the committees of each house on bills they approve and send to the whole house for consideration, and by conference committees of the two houses to reconcile differences between House and Senate versions of a bill. (Committees also issue reports on various investigations, nominations and hearings not related to pending legislation.) Reports usually include the text of the bill, describe its contents and purposes, and give reasons for the committee's recommendations, sometimes with minority views.

One of the most informative portions of a committee report is the section-by-section analysis of the bill, explaining the purpose and meaning of each provision.

Committee reports are published in numbered series which indicate house, Congress, and report number, with conference committee reports included in the series of House reports. Exhibit 6–2 on page 238 shows the first page of H.R. Rep. No. 107–727, pt. 2 (2002), reporting the House Committee on the Judiciary's views on a version of the Protection of Lawful Commerce in Arms Act. Note at the bottom of the page that the committee is amending the bill by deleting everything after the enacting clause and substituting new language.

Committee reports are issued by the Government Printing Office, and all the reports for a session are collected, along with House and Senate Documents, in an official compilation called the *Serial Set*. (Bound *Serial Set* volumes after 1996 are not widely distributed, but many libraries bind their sets of individual reports.) GPO Access <www.gpoaccess.gov/serialset/creports/> and THOMAS coverage begins in 1995, and the commercial databases have all committee reports beginning in 1990 as well as selected earlier coverage. Selected reports are also reprinted in *United States Code Congressional and Administrative News (USCCAN)*. *LexisNexis U.S. Serial Set Digital Collection*, <www.lexisnexis.com/academic/serialset/> covering 1789–1969, and Readex's *U.S. Congressional Serial Set (1817–1980) with American State Papers (1789–1838)* <www.readex.com> both provide retrospective, full-text digital coverage.

Reports are the final product of committee deliberation. The process by which committees reach consensus is through *markup sessions*, but transcripts of these are only rarely published. Newspapers and wire services reporting on Capitol Hill, however, often provide coverage of markup sessions, and these articles are available through online services including Westlaw and LexisNexis.

c. Debates

Debates in the House and Senate are generally not as influential as committee reports as sources of legislative intent. While reports represent the considered opinion of those legislators who have studied a bill most closely, floor statements are often political hyperbole and may not even represent the views of the proposed legislation's supporters. The most influential statements are those from a bill's sponsor or its floor managers (the committee members responsible for steering the bill through consideration). These may even correct errors in a committee report or explain aspects of a bill not discussed in the report.

In a few instances, floor debates are the best available legislative history source. Bills are often amended on the floor, sometimes with language that was not considered in committee and thus was not discussed in a committee report. If so, the record of floor debate may be the only available explanation of the intended purpose of the amendment.

The source for debates is the *Congressional Record*, a nearly verbatim transcript published each day that either house is in session. It is subject to revision only by members of Congress who wish to amend their own remarks. In addition, the *Record* includes extensions of floor remarks, exhibits from legislators, communications on pending legislation, and other material Senators and Representatives wish to have printed. Each daily issue has separately paginated "S" and "H" sections for Senate and House proceedings.

The *Congressional Record* never contains hearings and only rarely includes committee reports—although it does include the text of conference committee reports. Bills are sometimes read into the *Record*, particularly if they have been amended on the floor or in conference committee. The *Congressional Record*'s primary role, however, is as a report of debates and actions taken. An excerpt from the *Record*, showing Senate consideration of the Protection of Lawful Commerce in Arms Act, is shown in Exhibit 6–3 on page 239.

Each *Congressional Record* issue contains a Daily Digest summarizing the day's activities. The digest lists the bills introduced, reports filed, measures debated or passed, and committee meetings held. *Record* page references for floor activity are included, making the Daily Digest a good starting place if only the date of congressional action is known. An index to the *Record*, by subject, name of legislator, and title of legislation, is published every two weeks. The printed indexes do not cumulate during a session, but an online version on GPO Access <www.gpoaccess.gov/cri/> does cumulate. The indexes include a useful "History of Bills and Resolutions" table providing index references and status information by bill number. The printed table only lists references to bills that have been acted on during the two-week period, but the online version <www.gpoaccess.gov/hob/> has information for the entire session.

The *Congressional Record* can be searched electronically through several online sources. Coverage begins in 1989 on THOMAS, and in 1994 on GPO Access <www.gpoaccess.gov/crecord/>. THOMAS's version makes it easy to browse the Daily Digest by date and has links from the index and Daily Digest to *Record* pages and to bill texts. GPO Access only offers browsing back to 1998, but it provides the *Record* in PDF format replicating the printed version. Westlaw and LexisNexis coverage extends back to 1985.

Several years after each annual session, its proceedings are published in a bound *Congressional Record* edition of more than twenty volumes. This edition renumbers the separately paginated Senate and House sections into one sequence, and it includes a cumulative index, a compilation of the Daily Digest, and a cumulative "History of Bills and Resolutions" table listing all bills introduced during the session and summarizing their legislative history.

Once the permanent edition is published, it becomes the standard source to be cited for congressional debates. Converting a citation from the daily edition to the bound edition is unfortunately not an easy task. There is no correlation between the paginations, and no tables provide cross-references. To find the permanent edition citation, it is usually necessary to start over in the index or the Daily Digest looking for references to the topic or speaker, or to skim through the specific day's section looking for a specific passage.

Finding a citation in the permanent edition is not made easier by the fact that most libraries have this set only in microform. GPO Access is adding the permanent edition <www.gpoaccess.gov/crecordbound/>, but thus far only two volumes (1999 and 2000) are available. Other online sources for the *Congressional Record*, including Westlaw and LexisNexis, contain the daily edition and *not* the permanent edition that should be cited.

The predecessors of the *Congressional Record*, which began in 1873, are the *Annals of Congress* (1789–1824); the *Register of Debates* (1824–37); and the *Congressional Globe* (1833–73). All of these earlier publications, as well as the *Congressional Record* for 1873–77, are available online through the Library of Congress "A Century of Lawmaking for a New Nation" site <memory.loc.gov/ammem/amlaw/>.

House and *Senate Journals* are also published (and are, in fact, the only congressional publications required by the Constitution). Unlike the *Congressional Record*, however, these do not include the verbatim debates. The journals merely record the proceedings, indicate whether there was debate, and report the resulting action and votes taken. The *House Journal* is more voluminous and includes the texts of bills and amendments given floor consideration. Both journals include "History of Bills and Resolutions" tables and indexes.

d. Hearings

Senate and House committees hold hearings on proposed legislation and on other subjects under congressional investigation such as nominations or impeachments. Government officials, scholars, and interest group representatives deliver prepared statements and answer questions from committee members. The transcripts of most hearings are published, accompanied by material submitted by interested individuals and groups such as letters and article reprints.

Hearings are held to determine the need for new legislation or to bring before Congress information relevant to its preparation and enactment. Hearings provide useful background information, but they are not generally considered persuasive sources of legislative history on the meaning of an enacted bill. Their importance as evidence of legislative intent is limited because they focus more on the views of interested parties rather than those of the lawmakers themselves.

Hearings are generally identified by the title which appears on the cover, the bill number, the name of the subcommittee and committee, the term of Congress, and the year. Exhibit 6–4 on page 240 shows the first page of *Protection of Lawful Commerce in Arms Act: Hearing Before the Subcomm. on Commercial and Administrative Law of the H. Comm. on the Judiciary*, 109th Cong. (2005).

A search for relevant hearings should not be limited to the term in which a particular law is enacted, because consideration of an issue may extend over several years. Hearings on earlier versions of the Protection of Lawful Commerce in Arms Act, for example, were held in 2002 and 2003. Hearings are not held for every bill, however, and not all hearings are published.

Hearings are published by the Government Printing Office, and some beginning in 1995 are available through GPO Access <www.gpoaccess.gov/chearings/>. Westlaw and LexisNexis usually provide access to commercially prepared documentation well before the official transcripts are published. Westlaw has witnesses' prepared statements in the databases USTESTIMONY and CONGTMY, while Lexis has hearing transcripts in its "Legislation and Politics/U.S. Congress/Committee Hearing Transcripts" folder. Most committee websites (linked from the Senate <www.senate.gov> and House <www.house.gov> sites) provide access to material from current hearings, including prepared statements of legislators and witnesses.

e. Other Congressional Publications

Congress also produces a variety of other publications which are less frequently consulted in legislative history research. These publications can, however, be important sources of related information.

Committee prints contain a variety of material prepared specifically for committee use, ranging from studies by its staff or outside experts to compilations of earlier legislative history documents. Some prints contain statements by committee members on pending bills. Others can be useful analyses of laws under the jurisdiction of a committee, such as the House's biennial *Green Book: Background Material and Data on Major Programs Within the Jurisdiction of the Committee on Ways and Means*. Committee prints are distributed by the Government Printing Office, but they are not as widely available online as reports or hearings. Selective coverage through LexisNexis begins in 1994, and GPO Access <www.gpoaccess.gov/cprints/> has a limited number of prints beginning in 1997. The most comprehensive subscription source for committee prints is the *LexisNexis Congressional Research Digital Collection* <www.lexisnexis.com/crdc/>, which includes thousands of committee prints dating back to 1830.

The series of *House* and *Senate documents* are only occasionally useful as sources of legislative history. These include material such as the *Budget of the United States Government*, special studies or exhibits prepared for Congress, presidential messages, and communications from executive departments or agencies. They are published in a numbered series for each house, appear in the official *Serial Set*, and are available starting in 1995 on GPO Access and LexisNexis. Presidential messages accompanying proposed legislation and statements issued when signing or vetoing bills are also printed in the *Congressional Record*.

The Senate issues two series of publications in the process of treaty ratification. *Treaty documents* contain the texts of treaties before the Senate for its advice and consent, and *Senate executive reports* from the Foreign Relations Committee contain its recommendations on pending treaties. These publications are discussed more fully in Chapter 11.

Congress also supervises three major investigative and research agencies that produce a range of important analyses and reports. The Congressional Budget Office (CBO) <www.cbo.gov> produces cost estimates for bills reported out of committee as well as a variety of budget reports, analytical studies, and background papers. The Government Accountability Office (GAO) <www.gao.gov> studies the programs and expenditures of the federal government, and frequently recommends specific congressional actions. The CBO and GAO both provide extensive access to their reports and other documents through their websites, and GAO reports back to 1995 are available through Westlaw (GAO–RPTS database) and LexisNexis.

The third and most wide-ranging research arm of Congress is the Congressional Research Service (CRS). Each year it produces several thousand new or updated reports, including legal and policy analyses, economic studies, bibliographies, statistical reviews, and issue briefs that provide background information on major legislative issues. The CRS has no publicly accessible website and does not regularly publish its reports, but many reports have been made available by others. Several sites provide links to thousands of CRS reports available online; among the most extensive are Open CRS <www.opencrs.com> and the University of North Texas Libraries' Congressional Research Service Reports site <digital.library.unt.edu/govdocs/crs/index.tkl>. CRS reports back to 1916 are available online through the subscription-based *LexisNexis Congressional Research Digital Collection*, and LexisNexis publishes a microform edition of these reports as *Major Studies and Issue Briefs of the Congressional Research Service*. LLRX.com has a regularly updated guide to CRS reports <www.llrx.com/features/crsreports.htm> with links to numerous other sources for these documents.

§ 6–3. Congressional Research Resources

While researchers are interested in Congress for numerous reasons, this discussion focuses on tools useful for two basic legal research tasks: investigating the meaning of an enacted law, and tracking the status of pending legislation. You can use a number of approaches for these purposes. For recently enacted laws and pending legislation, electronic resources provide current and thorough coverage. For older bills, the choices dwindle to a few tools that provide retrospective coverage.

Although the ability to compile legislative histories is an important skill, you should be aware that it can be a frustrating endeavor. Even after finding all the relevant legislative materials on a statute, you may find that the legislature never explained or discussed the particular language at issue. Another frustration comes from the increasing use of omnibus legislation and unorthodox procedures. Numerous bills are often combined into mammoth enactments of several hundred pages, and materials addressing a particular provision within a huge omnibus bill can be far more difficult to locate than those on a bill with one discrete subject. In other instances there may be no relevant committee reports or hearings, as some bills bypass the committee process and go directly to the floor for consideration.

The bill number is usually the key to finding congressional documents or tracing legislative action. It appears on an enacted law both in its slip form and in the *Statutes at Large.* In the enacted Protection of Lawful Commerce in Arms Act, shown in Exhibit 6–5 on page 241, note that the bill number (S. 397) is included in brackets in the right margin. Bill numbers have been included in *Statutes at Large* since 1903; earlier numbers can be found in Eugene Nabors, *Legislative Reference Checklist* (1982, available in HeinOnline's U.S. Federal Legislative History Library). Bill numbers do not appear, unfortunately, in the *United States Code* or in either of its annotated editions.

Bill numbers lead easily to printed or electronic status tables, which indicate actions taken and provide references to relevant documents. These tables can be used both for pending bill searches and for retrospective research on enacted laws.

A quick head start in legislative history research can come from the Public Law itself. At the end of each act, in either slip law or *Statutes at Large*, there appears a brief legislative history summary with citations of committee reports, dates of consideration and passage in each house, and references to presidential statements. The summary for the PLCAA is shown in Exhibit 6–6 on page 242. In this instance, the summary provides references to the *Congressional Record* debate shown in earlier exhibits, but not to the House report on a different but related bill. References to hearings or to reports from earlier Congresses are never included. Summaries have appeared at the end of each law passed since 1975, and *Statutes at Large* volumes from 1963 to 1974 include separate "Guide to Legislative History" tables.

Gathering a complete legislative history can be a very time-consuming process, as the necessary documents are scattered among many publications and may be difficult to obtain. For some major enactments, however, convenient access is provided by publications reprinting the important bills, debates, committee reports, and hearings. These compiled histories can save the considerable time and trouble involved in finding relevant references and documents, although it is important to be aware that they may not necessarily have *every* relevant document. They are published both by government agencies (particularly the Congressional Research Service of the Library of Congress) and by commercial publishers. Online compiled legislative histories, including bills and committee reports, are available on HeinOnline, LexisNexis, and Westlaw for several dozen major acts in areas such as bankruptcy, tax, and environmental law.

The basic tool for identifying and locating published compiled legislative histories is Nancy P. Johnson, *Sources of Compiled Legislative Histories* (1979–date, available in HeinOnline's U.S. Federal Legislative History Library). Arranged chronologically by Congress and

Public Law number, it provides a checklist of available compiled legislative histories for acts as far back as 1789 and includes an index by name of act. It covers not only compilations which reprint the legislative history documents in full, but also law review articles and other sources that list and discuss relevant documents but do not reprint them. Another source listing compilations issued by the government is Bernard D. Reams, Jr., *Federal Legislative Histories: An Annotated Bibliography and Index to Officially Published Sources* (1994).

One of the most useful resources in legislative history research is the Law Librarians' Society of Washington, D.C.'s *Legislative Source Book* <www.llsdc.org/sourcebook/>. This site includes a number of useful features, including quick links to congressional committee publications, questions and answers on legislative research, and a practitioner's guide to compiling a federal legislative history (which in turn includes links to dozens of other Internet guides on the topic).

a. THOMAS and Other Congressional Websites

For current legislation or laws enacted since 1973, one of the easiest places to begin research is with Congress itself. THOMAS <thomas.loc.gov> is the website introduced in 1995 by the Library of Congress to make legislative information freely available to the public. The scope of THOMAS has grown considerably since its debut, and it now provides access to a wide range of information and documents.

THOMAS provides both the text of bills and summaries of their status or legislative history. It is possible to search either bill text or bill summaries by keyword or bill number. Legislative history summaries are available in THOMAS for laws enacted since 1973, but summaries for older laws lack some of the features included for more recent legislation. Links to the text of legislation, for example, are available beginning in 1989, and *Congressional Record* page references and links have been added beginning in 1993. A portion of the THOMAS summary for H.R. 800, the House version of the PLCAA, is shown in Exhibit 6–7 on page 243. This excerpt is the "All Actions" status section, with links to the *Congressional Record* and to the House report on the bill as well as a cross-reference to S. 397 for further action.

THOMAS has the text of many congressional documents, and it also includes links to the Government Printing Office's GPO Access <www.gpoaccess.gov/legislative.html>, which provides these documents as PDF files. GPO Access is the more comprehensive source for documents, but it is a less user-friendly and informative site than THOMAS. Its search functions are more limited, and there are no links between its congressional documents.

THOMAS and GPO Access are the major comprehensive websites for congressional information. In addition, each chamber maintains a website (<www.senate.gov> and <www.house.gov>) with information on its procedures as well as links to pages for individual members and committees. Most committee homepages have summaries of major pending legislation, background information, hearing statements, and schedules of upcoming meetings.

Numerous other government, educational, and commercial websites have congressional information. THOMAS's "Resources for Legislative Researchers" page

<thomas.loc.gov/home/legbranch/otherleg.html>   has
links to many of these sites.

b. LexisNexis Congressional and CIS

Congressional Information Service, Inc. (CIS), a subsidiary of LexisNexis, is one of the most important pro-
viders of congressional documentation. CIS indexes cover
virtually all congressional publications since 1789, except
the *Congressional Record* and its predecessors, and CIS
provides full-text copies of the documents either in microform or online. CIS databases are offered in different
ways to academic institutions and to other subscribers.
In most markets CIS information is available as part of
regular Lexis subscriptions, but universities, colleges and
law schools have access through LexisNexis Congressional <web.lexis-nexis.com/congcomp/>. Law students can
use their Lexis accounts for some legislative history
research, but they need to turn instead to LexisNexis
Congressional for more extensive resources.

CIS first began indexing congressional materials in
1970, and its coverage is divided into two basic time
periods. For the period before 1970, it publishes several
retrospective indexes covering the Serial Set, executive
documents and reports, hearings, and committee prints.
These printed indexes are cumulated online as "Congressional Indexes, 1789–1969." Keyword searching is the
general form of access, but specific fields such as bill
numbers can be searched and retrieval can be limited to
designated years in order to focus on particular legislation.

The pre–1970 documents are available in microform,
and CIS is currently adding digital collections as subscription components of LexisNexis Congressional. Re-

ports and documents are now available as the *LexisNexis U.S. Serial Set Digital Collection*, and committee prints (as well as CRS reports) are available as part of the *LexisNexis Congressional Research Digital Collection*. CIS is in the process of digitizing its retrospective collections of committee hearings.

For the period beginning in 1970, CIS publishes extensive abstracts and subject indexes covering all congressional publications except the *Congressional Record* in a monthly *CIS Index* which is cumulated into annual bound volumes. The online, subscription-based LexisNexis Congressional provides all the information in *CIS Index*, with several enhancements including keyword searching and links from legislative histories to the documents described. Other online features include bill-tracking summaries; full-text access to bills, reports, the *Congressional Record*, and other congressional documents beginning in the 1980s; transcripts of hearing testimony; and information on committees and legislators.

Online or in the print *CIS Index*, reports, hearings, prints, and documents are indexed by subject, title, and bill number; the indexes provide references to abstracts summarizing the contents of these documents. Exhibit 6–8 on page 244 shows the CIS abstract for the hearing shown in Exhibit 6–4 on page 240, indicating the names and affiliations of the witnesses and the focus of their testimony. The number beginning with "Y4.J89/1" below the title of the hearing is the Superintendent of Documents classification, which is used in most libraries for locating government publications. The "H521–35" in the heading for the abstract is the CIS accession number for the publication, and is the number used to find this hearing in CIS's microfiche collection of documents. To experienced legislative researchers, both "Y4.J89/1" and "H521" identify this hearing as a publication of the House Committee on the Judiciary.

For laws passed since 1984, LexisNexis Congressional and *CIS Index Legislative Histories* volumes provide summaries of relevant bills, hearings, reports, debates, presidential documents and any other legislative actions. Rather than limiting coverage to a single term of Congress, these include references to earlier hearings and other documents on related bills from prior Congressional sessions. They are generally considered the most complete and descriptive summaries of the legislative history of federal enactments. Exhibit 6–9 on page 245 shows the beginning of the CIS legislative history for the Protection of Lawful Commerce in Arms Act. This summary includes all of the documents shown in this chapter's exhibits, even if they were not directly related to the bill that was eventually passed in 2005.

From 1970 to 1983, LexisNexis Congressional and *CIS Index Abstracts* volumes include legislative histories of enacted laws, but these are less convenient to use because they simply list the CIS numbers for the reports, hearings and other materials listed. It is necessary to turn to the abstracts for more information. These summaries, nonetheless, are among the most thorough sources available for their period.

c. *USCCAN*

United States Code Congressional and Administrative News (*USCCAN*) was mentioned in Chapter 5 as a source for the texts of enacted laws. For major acts it also reprints one or more committee reports, making it a convenient compilation for basic legislative research. The scope of coverage varies, but *USCCAN* generally prints either a House or Senate report and the conference committee report, if one was issued. It also provides references to some of the committee reports it does not reprint, and to the dates of consideration in the *Congressional Record*. *USCCAN* has been printing committee reports since it began in 1941, and may be one of the most convenient sources for reports predating online access.

The LH database on Westlaw includes the reports reprinted in *USCCAN* beginning in 1948, and from 1990 onward it contains all congressional committee reports, including reports on bills that did not become law. As noted earlier, Westlaw also has databases with congressional bills, the *Congressional Record*, and hearing testimony. Access to these resources is available through the Westlaw directory (U.S. Federal Materials—Legislative History), and also by setting up a tabbed "Legislative History—Fed" page. This page shows the congressional lawmaking process in graphical format, and clicking on any of the twelve steps in the diagram leads to a menu of possible databases to search for information.

In the printed *USCCAN*, the public laws and committee reports are published in separate "Laws" and "Legislative History" sections. Each section prints material in order by public law number, and cross-references are provided between the laws and reports. The report is preceded by references to steps in the passage of the legislation, including dates of consideration and passage in each house. The report is reprinted in full, except for the portion printing the text of the act.

Both monthly advance sheets and annual bound volumes of *USCCAN* also include tables with basic legislative history information, listing each public law's date of approval, *Statutes at Large* citation, bill and report numbers, committees, and dates of passage in each house. Monthly issues also include a "Major Bills Pending" table, arranged by subject and showing the progress of current legislation.

One reason that *USCCAN* legislative histories are easy to find is that references to them are provided in the notes in the *United States Code Annotated*. Westlaw's online version of *USCA* includes links from the statutory notes to the *USCCAN* summary and reports, making it particularly easy to locate the reports from the code section. Note, however, that a reference after a specific section means only that legislative history on the act is available, not that pertinent material on that section will be found.

USCCAN provides only selective coverage of committee reports, and further research is often required. There are no references to hearings, prints, documents, or materials from previous Congresses, so anyone preparing a complete legislative history will need to use other resources. But it does provide a handy starting point and is easily accessible in most law libraries. For a researcher looking for general background or a quick section-by-section analysis, *USCCAN* may be all that is needed.

d. CQ Resources

Congressional Quarterly (CQ) is a news service and publisher of several sources of information on congressional activity. Its most widely read publication is *CQ Weekly* (formerly *Congressional Quarterly Weekly Report*), which provides background information on pending legislation and news of current developments. *CQ Weekly* does not include the texts of documents or comprehensive bill-tracking, but it does provide valuable analysis and background discussion of laws and legislative issues. Exhibit 6–10 on page 246 shows a page from a 2005 issue discussing the final passage of the PLCAA.

CQ Weekly contains tables of House and Senate votes, a status table for major legislation, and a legislative history table for new public laws. An annual *CQ Almanac Plus* cumulates much of the information in the *Weekly Report* into a useful summary of the congressional session. More frequent publications for current congressional news include *CQDaily* and *CQ Midday Update*, which is available free by e-mail. These resources are primarily useful for people needing quick day-to-day information on legislative activity.

CQ publications are available through LexisNexis in the legal, government and business markets. For academic and public libraries, CQ Library <library.cqpress.com> provides a subscription-based Web version of *CQ Weekly* and free access to its index, which is updated weekly. For researchers whose primary focus is legislative research, CQ's online service CQ.com <www.cq.com> provides customized bill-tracking information including a Bill Comparison feature that makes it easier to find changes between two versions of proposed legislation. It also has the text of documents, including bills, committee reports, and the *Congressional Record*, as well as extensive information about committee meetings and floor activity.

Numerous other newspapers and magazines also focus on developments in Washington. In addition to general news sources, specialized publications include *National Journal* (weekly) and *Roll Call* (twice weekly). National

Journal Group Inc. also publishes a *CongressDaily* newsletter, and all three of these publications are available through both Westlaw and LexisNexis.

Other online subscription services, such as Gallery-Watch.com <gallerywatch.com>, also provide information on Congress, including bill tracking and committee markup reports. Designed for specialists in current congressional information, these services may offer a range of sophisticated tracking and notification services unavailable from free government sites and more general database systems.

e. Printed Status Tables

For the purpose of tracking current legislation and researching recently enacted laws, online resources provide advantages of convenience and speed that are unmatched by printed resources. For earlier bills and laws, however, printed resources may be the best available sources of information.

CCH's *Congressional Index* is issued in two looseleaf volumes for each Congress, with weekly updates. Its extensive coverage of pending legislation includes an index of bills by subject and author, a digest of each bill, and a status table of actions taken on each bill (but not the documents themselves). This status table contains references to hearings, a feature lacking in many other legislative research aids. *Congressional Index*, published since 1938, is one of the most valuable sources of information on bills predating the coverage of electronic bill-tracking services.

Often several bills are introduced on related topics, and it can be difficult to tell from electronic sources which of these bills (if any) is being acted upon. In such cases, using a printed index and status table may be a quicker way to compare bills than a series of electronic queries. *Congressional Index* does not contain the texts of bills or reports, but it does provide a wide range of other information on Congress, including lists of members and committee assignments; an index of enactments and vetoes; lists of pending treaties, reorganization plans, and nominations; a table of voting records; and a weekly newsletter.

As noted earlier, the *Congressional Record* includes status tables which can be useful for both current and retrospective research. A "History of Bills and Resolutions" table is published in the biweekly index, cumulated for each session in the bound index volume, and available online going back to 1993 <www.gpoaccess.gov/hob/>. It includes report and public law numbers, but no references to hearings. This is one of the best sources of page citations for debates within the *Record*. The entries provide dates and page references, but do not have hypertext links from these references to the documents. (GPO Access coverage appears to extend back to 1983, but the tables before 1993 have no page references.)

The final cumulative table is not issued for several years after the end of a session. It is published after the bound edition of the *Record* and uses the final pagination instead of the separate "S" and "H" pages in the daily edition. Although this table is less complete than commercial sources such as *CIS/Index* or *Congressional Index*, it remains one of the best sources available for older laws. These tables have been published annually since the 1867 volume of the *Congressional Globe*, long before the earliest coverage of most commercial publications.

For even earlier acts, the House and Senate Journals all the way back to the First Congress (1789–91) include tables or lists of bills indicating when they were reported, passed, or received other floor action. Most of these are found in the subject index under "Bills." These early journals are all available online through the Library of Congress's "A Century of Lawmaking for a New Nation" site <memory.loc.gov/ammem/amlaw/>.

f. Directories

One of the fastest and simplest ways to find out about the status of pending legislation is to call congressional staff members responsible for drafting or monitoring the bill. They may be able to provide information or insights that would never appear in published status tables or reports. The best sources for detailed information on staff members are two competing commercial directories, *Congressional Staff Directory* (three times per year) and *Congressional Yellow Book* (quarterly). Internet versions of both directories (<www.csd.cq.com>, <www. leadershipdirectories.com>) are updated weekly but are available to subscribers only.

The *Official Congressional Directory* (biennial) is not as detailed as the commercial directories, but it provides information about individuals, offices and the organizational structure of Congress. This directory is available through GPO Access <www.gpoaccess.gov/cdirectory/>; the Internet version, unlike its print counterpart, is modified during the term to reflect changes.

Two useful sources for background information on members of Congress, both published biennially, are National Journal's *Almanac of American Politics* and *CQ's Politics in America*. These provide in-depth biographical portraits with information on voting records and ratings from interest groups, as well as a brief narrative and statistical overview of each congressional district.

A retrospective *Biographical Directory of the United States Congress, 1774–Present* (including coverage of the Continental Congress) is available online <bioguide. congress.gov>, and provides basic information on the more than 13,000 persons who have served in Congress. A printed version of the same resource, under the title *Biographical Directory of the American Congress, 1774–1996* (1997), covers the 1st through 104th Congresses and includes a Congress-by-Congress listing of congressional leaders and state delegations.

§ 6–4. State Legislative Information

Legislative history on the state level is a research area of sharp contrasts. Information on current legislation is widely available on the Internet, but documents that might aid in the interpretation of enacted laws can be difficult or impossible to find.

First the good news: Most state legislatures do excellent jobs of providing Internet access to current status information and to the text of pending bills. The better websites have several means of searching for bills, and some offer e-mail notification services when particular bills are acted upon. Some states offer other features such as bill summaries, committee minutes, and staff analyses.

Legislative websites can be found by using a search engine to find "[state] legislature," from state homepages (usually <www.[state].gov>), or from one of the many general starting points. The National Conference of State Legislatures has a convenient "State Legislatures Internet Links" site <www.ncsl.org/public/leglinks.cfm>, which allows you either to go directly to a specific site or to create a customized list of links for specific content (such as bill information or legislator biographies) from all states or a selected list of states.

A valuable feature found on many legislative websites is an introductory guide to the state's lawmaking procedures. State legislatures generally follow the federal paradigm, but there can be significant differences from state to state and an important first step in studying legislative action in a particular state is to learn about its procedures. Guides and other resources, such as charts showing how bills become law, can save considerable time and confusion.

The commercial databases also provide text and status information for pending legislation. Both Westlaw and LexisNexis have databases for each state, as well as multistate databases useful for monitoring developments in legislatures throughout the country. Historical bill text and tracking databases extend on both systems back to the early 1990s. Researchers in university and public libraries may have access to LexisNexis's bill-tracking and other legislative information through its State Capital website <web.lexis-nexis.com/stcapuniv/>.

For thirty-six states, Westlaw also provides legislative history databases containing documents such as reports, bill analyses, legislative journals, and committee reports. Contents vary from state to state depending on the materials available. These documents are tied to the display of specific state code sections. If a code section is derived from an act for which legislative history documents are available, "Reports and Related Materials" appears as one of the links on the left of the screen. As with federal statutes, however, a link does not necessarily mean that there is relevant information on the particular section. Dates of coverage vary between states but generally begin in the late 1990s or early 2000s.

Researchers needing to interpret statutes enacted before the late 1990s face a more difficult task. Bills from older sessions can be hard to locate. Almost every state has a legislative journal, but very few of these actually include transcripts of the debates. Only a few states publish committee reports, and even fewer publish hearings.

The materials that are available vary widely from state to state. Often they are not published in either print or electronic form, but are only available at the state capitol. Some states have "bill jackets" with legislative information, and some have microform records or tape recordings of sessions. In many instances, contemporary newspaper accounts may be the best available source of information about a sponsor's statements or proceedings.

Two useful books identify the resources available for each state. Lynn Hellebust, *State Legislative Sourcebook: A Resource Guide to Legislative Information in the Fifty States* (annual) provides information on the legislative processes and include references to available published and online sources. References include a "best initial contact" for each state, as well as information on websites, introductory guides, telephone numbers for ascertaining bill status, bill tracking services, and legislative documents such as session laws and summaries of legislation. William H. Manz, *Guide to State Legislative and Administrative Materials* (2002 ed.) covers a broader range of printed and online sources for bills, legislative history materials, and numerous other sources of state law.

A guide to legislative research processes in a specific state can be invaluable. Most of the state legal research guides listed in Appendix B, on page 454, include discussion of available legislative history resources for their states. Law library websites in the jurisdiction you are researching, particularly the state legislative library if there is one, may have posted guides to doing legislative history research in their state. The Indiana University School of Law's "State Legislative History Research Guides and State Legislatures on the Web" <www.law.indiana.edu/library/services/sta_leg.shtml> provides links to nearly a hundred online guides, and some are listed in Manz's *Guide to State Legislative and Administrative Materials*. State bar journals frequently publish articles describing legislative history research in the state.

Many states have official agencies responsible for recommending and drafting new legislation. These groups, including law revision commissions, judicial councils, and legislative councils, often publish annual or topical reports summarizing their work. For recommendations enacted into law, these reports may be valuable legislative history documentation.

Directory information on state legislatures, including organization, members, committees, and staffs, is contained in official state manuals (sometimes called *Bluebooks* or *Redbooks*), published annually or biennially by most states. The directory for a specific state is likely to provide the most detailed information, but several multistate directories are also published. General multistate government directories such as *State Yellow Book* (quarterly) include extensive coverage of the legislative branches, with information on both individual members and committees. The Council of State Governments publishes an annual *CSG State Directory*, which covers legislatures in *Directory I: Elective Officials* and *Directory II: Legislative Leadership, Committees and Staff*.

§ 6–5. Conclusion

Researchers sometimes view legislative history as an arcane and complex field, rather than as a basic legal research process. Every lawyer should have a grasp of the major resources. Legislative materials are essential tools both in interpreting statutes and in monitoring current legal developments.

The electronic resources available from the online databases and from the government itself have made information on pending legislation easily accessible, while research into the history of enacted laws requires more refined skill. For federal statutes, a review of material reprinted in *USCCAN* may be sufficient to determine whether a further inquiry in legislative resources is necessary; from there a fuller picture may be obtained from LexisNexis Congressional or other tools. The materials for state statutes vary dramatically between jurisdictions, but no state has resources comparable to those available for federal statutes.

Legislative history documents can be useful in statutory research, but they are just one of several important resources in understanding statutes. The court decisions found through annotated codes and other means may provide authoritative judicial interpretations. Even secondary sources may be persuasive in determining the scope and meaning of an act. Many statutes are implemented by more detailed regulations and decisions from administrative agencies, and these materials may be essential for fully understanding the underlying statute.

107TH CONGRESS
2D SESSION

S. 2268

To amend the Act establishing the Department of Commerce to protect manufacturers and sellers in the firearms and ammunition industry from restrictions on interstate or foreign commerce.

_____

IN THE SENATE OF THE UNITED STATES

APRIL 25, 2002

Mr. MILLER (for himself and Mr. CRAIG) introduced the following bill; which was read twice and referred to the Committee on Commerce, Science, and Transportation

_____

A BILL

To amend the Act establishing the Department of Commerce to protect manufacturers and sellers in the firearms and ammunition industry from restrictions on interstate or foreign commerce.

1   *Be it enacted by the Senate and House of Representa-*

2 *tives of the United States of America in Congress assembled,*

3 **SECTION 1. SHORT TITLE.**

4   This Act may be cited as the "Protection of Lawful

5 Commerce in Arms Act".

6 **SEC 2. AMENDMENT TO ORGANIC ACT.**

7   The Act entitled "An Act to establish the Department

8 of Commerce and Labor", approved February 14, 1903

Exhibit 6–1.   S. 2268 (107th Cong. 2002).

| 107TH CONGRESS
2d Session | HOUSE OF REPRESENTATIVES | REPT. 107–727
Part 2 |

PROTECTION OF LAWFUL COMMERCE IN ARMS ACT

OCTOBER 8, 2002.—Committed to the Committee of the Whole House on the State
of the Union and ordered to be printed

Mr. SENSENBRENNER, from the Committee on the Judiciary,
submitted the following

R E P O R T

[To accompany H.R. 2037]

[Including cost estimate of the Congressional Budget Office]

The Committee on the Judiciary, to whom was referred the bill
(H.R. 2037) to amend the Act establishing the Department of Commerce to protect manufacturers and sellers in the firearms and ammunition industry from restrictions on interstate or foreign commerce, having considered the same, reports favorably thereon with
amendments and recommends that the bill as amended do pass.

CONTENTS

The amendments are as follows:

Strike all after the enacting clause and insert the following:

SECTION 1. SHORT TITLE.

This Act may be cited as the "Protection of Lawful Commerce in Arms Act".

SEC. 2. FINDINGS; PURPOSES.

(a) FINDINGS.—The Congress finds the following:

(1) Citizens have a right, under the Second Amendment to the United
States Constitution, to keep and bear arms.

82–218

Exhibit 6–2.　H.R. Rep. No. 107–727, pt. 2 (2002).

Congressional Record

United States
of America

PROCEEDINGS AND DEBATES OF THE *109th* CONGRESS, FIRST SESSION

Vol. 151	WASHINGTON, WEDNESDAY, JULY 27, 2005	*No. 104—Book II*

Senate

PROTECTION OF LAWFUL COMMERCE IN ARMS ACT

The PRESIDING OFFICER. The Senate will now proceed to the consideration of S. 397, which the clerk will report.

The assistant legislative clerk read as follows:

A bill (S. 397) to prohibit civil liability actions from being brought or continued against manufacturers, distributors, dealers, or importers of firearms or ammunition for damages, injunctive or other relief resulting from the misuse of their products by others.

The PRESIDING OFFICER. The majority leader.

CLOTURE MOTION

Mr. FRIST. Mr. President, yesterday, as everyone knows, we invoked cloture on the motion to proceed to this underlying legislation with a vote of 66 to 32. Although we are now proceeding to the substance of the bill, it has been made clear that the bill will be subjected to a filibuster. While we respect a Senator's right to debate this liability, it is apparent that a cloture vote will be needed to ultimately bring this very bipartisan bill to a final vote. For that reason, I send a cloture motion to the desk.

The PRESIDING OFFICER. The cloture motion having been presented under rule XXII, the Chair directs the clerk to read the motion.

The legislative clerk read as follows:

CLOTURE MOTION

We the undersigned Senators, in accordance with the provisions of rule XXII of the Standing Rules of the Senate, do hereby move to bring to a close, debate on the motion to proceed to Calendar No. 15, S. 397: A bill to prohibit civil liability actions from being brought or continued against manufacturers, distributors, dealers, or importers of firearms or ammunition for damages, injunctive or other relief resulting from the misuse of their products by others.

Bill Frist, George Allen, Larry E. Craig, Craig Thomas, Michael B. Earl, Jeff Sessions, Kit Bond, Lamar Alexander, Mitch McConnell, Sam Brownback, Tom Coburn, Richard Burr, John McCain, Richard Shelby, Saxby Chambliss, John Ensign, Chuck Hagel.

Mr. FRIST. Mr. President, this vote can technically ripen as early as 1 a.m., not tomorrow but the next day, Friday morning. I am not certain at this point if we will vote then or later that morning. I will continue and want to continue to consult with my colleagues on the schedule.

As we just discussed on the Senate floor, we have a lot of business to accomplish over the next several days. We have the energy conference report, the highway conference report, the Interior bill, the veterans health money attached, a number of nominations. Therefore, I hope that when cloture is invoked, we can find a way to bring this bill to a final vote so that we can expedite some of these other very important issues.

AMENDMENT NO. 1605

Having said that, I now send an amendment to the desk and ask for its consideration.

The PRESIDING OFFICER. The clerk will report the amendment.

The legislative clerk read as follows:

The Senator from Tennessee [Mr. FRIST], for Mr. CRAIG, proposes an amendment numbered 1605.

Mr. FRIST. Mr. President, I ask unanimous consent that the reading of the amendment be dispensed with.

The PRESIDING OFFICER. Without objection, it is so ordered.

The amendment is as follows:

(Purpose: To amend the exceptions)

On page 10, line 5, strike "or" and all that follows through line 16 and insert the following:

(v) an action for death, physical injuries or property damage resulting directly from a defect in design or manufacture of the product, when used as intended or in a reasonably foreseeable manner, except that where the discharge of the product was caused by a volitional act that constituted a criminal offense then such act shall be considered the sole proximate cause of any resulting death, personal injuries or property damage; or

Mr. FRIST. I ask for the yeas and nays.

The PRESIDING OFFICER. Is there a sufficient second?

There appears to be a sufficient second.

The yeas and nays were ordered.

AMENDMENT NO. 1606 TO AMENDMENT NO. 1605

Mr. FRIST. I now send a second-degree amendment to the desk.

The PRESIDING OFFICER. The clerk will report.

The legislative clerk read as follows:

The Senator from Tennessee [Mr. FRIST] proposes an amendment numbered 1606 to amendment No. 1605.

Mr. FRIST. Mr. President, I ask unanimous consent that the reading of the amendment be dispensed with.

Mr. KENNEDY. I object.

The PRESIDING OFFICER. Objection is heard. The clerk will read the amendment.

The legislative clerk read as follows:

(Purpose: To make clear that the bill does not apply to actions commenced by the Attorney General pursuant to the Gun Control Act and National Firearms Act)

At the end, insert the following:

(vi) an action or proceeding commenced by the Attorney General to enforce the provisions of chapter 44 of title 18, United States Code, or chapter 53 of the Internal Revenue Code of 1986.

The PRESIDING OFFICER. The Senator from Idaho.

Mr. CRAIG. Mr. President, the actions that have just taken place have put us on S. 397, the Protection of Lawful Commerce in Arms Act. Earlier this morning, I submitted for the RECORD some now 67 cosponsors, which demonstrates that this bill is clearly very bipartisan legislation, supported by a Republican and Democrat majority in the Senate.

The actions the leader has just taken to file cloture would allow the cloture motion to ripen by as early as 1 a.m. Friday morning. Amendments have just been filed by the leader, and we will begin the process of debate on this important legislation.

With that in mind, if this bill and this debate seem familiar to any of us,

Exhibit 6–3.   151 Cong. Rec. S9087 (daily ed. July 27, 2005).

PROTECTION OF LAWFUL
COMMERCE IN ARMS ACT

TUESDAY, MARCH 15, 2005

HOUSE OF REPRESENTATIVES,
SUBCOMMITTEE ON COMMERCIAL
AND ADMINISTRATIVE LAW,
COMMITTEE ON THE JUDICIARY,
Washington, DC.

The Subcommittee met, pursuant to notice, at 10:10 a.m., in Room 2141, Rayburn House Office Building, Hon. Chris Cannon (Chair of the Subcommittee) presiding.

Mr. CANNON. Good morning, ladies and gentlemen. This hearing of the Subcommittee on Commercial and Administrative Law will now come to order to consider today H.R. 800, the "Protection of Lawful Commerce in Arms Act," which was introduced on February 15 by our colleague from Florida, Mr. Stearns. It currently has 157 cosponsors, including me.

H.R. 800 addresses abusive lawsuits aimed at the firearms industry. It provides that a qualified civil liability action cannot be brought in any State or Federal court. Qualified civil liability action is defined as a civil action or proceeding brought by any person against a manufacturer or seller of firearms or ammunition for damages resulting from the criminal or unlawful misuse of such products.

There are exceptions, however. The bill does not prohibit an action against a person who transfers a firearm or ammunition knowing that it will be used to commit a crime of violence or a drug trafficking crime or to commit an identical or a comparable State felony offense. It also does not prohibit an action brought against a seller for negligent entrustment or negligence per se.

The bill also includes several additional exceptions, including one for actions in which a manufacturer or seller of a qualified product knowingly and willfully violates a State or Federal statute applicable to sales or marketing when such violation was a proximate cause of the harm for which relief is sought. Other exceptions under the bill include one for actions for breach of contract or warranty in connection with the purchase of a firearm or ammunition and an exception for actions for damages resulting directly from a defect in design or manufacture of a firearm or ammunition when used as intended. The bill also makes clear that only licensed manufacturers and sellers are covered by the bill.

Tort law rests on a foundation of personal responsibility. A product may not be defined as defective unless there is something wrong with the product rather than with the product's use. How-

(1)

Exhibit 6–4. *Protection of Lawful Commerce in Arms Act: Hearing Before the Subcomm. on Commercial and Administrative Law of the H. Comm. on the Judiciary,* 109th Cong. 1 (2005).

PUBLIC LAW 109–92—OCT. 26, 2005   119 STAT. 2095

Public Law 109–92
109th Congress

An Act

To prohibit civil liability actions from being brought or continued against manufacturers, distributors, dealers, or importers of firearms or ammunition for damages, injunctive or other relief resulting from the misuse of their products by others.

Oct. 26, 2005
[S. 397]

Be it enacted by the Senate and House of Representatives of the United States of America in Congress assembled,

Protection of
Lawful
Commerce in
Arms Act.
15 USC 7901
note.

SECTION 1. SHORT TITLE.

This Act may be cited as the "Protection of Lawful Commerce in Arms Act".

SEC. 2. FINDINGS; PURPOSES.

15 USC 7901.

(a) FINDINGS.—Congress finds the following:

(1) The Second Amendment to the United States Constitution provides that the right of the people to keep and bear arms shall not be infringed.

(2) The Second Amendment to the United States Constitution protects the rights of individuals, including those who are not members of a militia or engaged in military service or training, to keep and bear arms.

(3) Lawsuits have been commenced against manufacturers, distributors, dealers, and importers of firearms that operate as designed and intended, which seek money damages and other relief for the harm caused by the misuse of firearms by third parties, including criminals.

(4) The manufacture, importation, possession, sale, and use of firearms and ammunition in the United States are heavily regulated by Federal, State, and local laws. Such Federal laws include the Gun Control Act of 1968, the National Firearms Act, and the Arms Export Control Act.

(5) Businesses in the United States that are engaged in interstate and foreign commerce through the lawful design, manufacture, marketing, distribution, importation, or sale to the public of firearms or ammunition products that have been shipped or transported in interstate or foreign commerce are not, and should not, be liable for the harm caused by those who criminally or unlawfully misuse firearm products or ammunition products that function as designed and intended.

(6) The possibility of imposing liability on an entire industry for harm that is solely caused by others is an abuse of the legal system, erodes public confidence in our Nation's laws, threatens the diminution of a basic constitutional right and civil liberty, invites the disassembly and destabilization of other industries and economic sectors lawfully competing

Exhibit 6–5. Protection of Lawful Commerce in Arms Act, Pub. L. No. 109–92, 119 Stat. 2095 (2005).

LEGISLATIVE HISTORY—S. 397:

CONGRESSIONAL RECORD, Vol. 151 (2005):
 July 27–29, considered and passed Senate.
 Oct. 20, considered and passed House.
WEEKLY COMPILATION OF PRESIDENTIAL DOCUMENTS, Vol. 41 (2005):
 Oct. 26, Presidential statement.

Exhibit 6–6. Legislative History, Pub. L. No. 109–92, 119 Stat. 2096 (2005).

The LIBRARY of CONGRESS THOMAS

The Library of Congress > THOMAS Home > Bills, Resolutions > Search Results

Item 1 of 1

PREVIOUS:BILL STATUS | NEXT:BILL STATUS
NEW SEARCH | HOME | HELP | ABOUT STATUS

H.R.800
Title: To prohibit civil liability actions from being brought or continued against manufacturers, distributors, dealers, or importers of firearms or ammunition for damages or injunctive or other relief resulting from the misuse of their products by others.
Sponsor: Rep Stearns, Cliff [FL-6] (introduced 2/15/2005)   Cosponsors (257)
Related Bills: S.397
Latest Major Action: 6/14/2005 Placed on the Union Calendar, Calendar No. 70.
House Reports: 109-124
Note: For further action, see S.397, which became Public Law 109-92 on 10/26/2005.

ALL ACTIONS:

2/15/2005:
    Introductory remarks on measure. (CR H590)
2/15/2005:
    Referred to the House Committee on the Judiciary.
3/10/2005:
    Referred to the Subcommittee on Commercial and Administrative Law.
3/15/2005:
        Subcommittee Hearings Held.
4/11/2005:
    Subcommittee on Commercial and Administrative Law Discharged.
4/20/2005:
        Committee Consideration and Mark-up Session Held.

Exhibit 6–7.   THOMAS Bill Summary and Status, H.R. 800 (109th Cong. 2005) <thomas.loc.gov>.

H521-35 **PROTECTION OF LAWFUL**
COMMERCE IN ARMS ACT.
Mar. 15, 2005. 109-1. 150 p.
•Item 1020-A (Paper).
•Item 1020-B (Microfiche).
°Y4.J89/1:109-21.
Committee Serial No. 109-21.

Hearing before the *Subcom on Commercial and Administrative Law* to consider H.R. 800, the Protection of Lawful Commerce in Arms Act, to prohibit certain civil liability actions against licensed firearms and ammunitions manufacturers, sellers, and trade associations for damages resulting from the criminal or unlawful third party use of a firearm or ammunition product.

Bill applies to all Federal and State courts and is intended to negate allegedly frivolous individual and municipal lawsuits against the firearms industry.

Supplementary material (p. 53-146) includes submitted statements, articles, a witness's written replies to Subcom questions, correspondence, and:

a. H.R. 1225, the Terrorist Apprehension and Record Retention Act of 2005, to provide that if a criminal background check for prospective firearm purchasers indicates that the applicant is a known or suspected member of a terrorist organization that the information should be transmitted to the appropriate State and Federal officials, and that all records generated in the course of the check be retained for ten years, text (p. 57-59).

b. GAO, "Gun Control and Terrorism: FBI Could Better Manage Firearm-Related Background Checks Involving Terrorist Watch List Records," Jan. 2005 (p. 60-102).

c. H.R. 1136, the Protect Law Enforcement Armor Act, to direct the Department of Justice to promulgate standards for the testing of armor-piercing ammunition, and to prohibit the manufacture, sale, possession or transfer of the Five-SeveN Pistol or any other handgun that uses armor-piercing ammunition, text (p. 106-110).

H521-35.1: Mar. 15, 2005. p. 10-52. .

Witnesses: **WALTON, Rodd C.,** Secretary and General Counsel, Sigarms, Inc.

HENIGAN, Dennis A., Director, Legal Action Project, Brady Center To Prevent Gun Violence.

BECKMAN, Bradley T., Counsel, North American Arms.

KEANE, Lawrence G., Senior Vice President, National Shooting Sports Foundation.

Statements and Discussion: Differing views on H.R. 800; support for H.R. 800, citing need to prevent frivolous lawsuits against firearms industry (related correspondence, p. 32-45); opposition to H.R. 800, citing rights of gun violence victims to file civil suits against the firearm industry arising from crimes committed by purchasers.

Exhibit 6–8. 2005 CIS INDEX ANNUAL: ABSTRACTS OF CONGRESSIONAL PUBLICATIONS 204.

Public Law 109-92   **119 Stat. 2095**

Protection of Lawful Commerce in Arms Act

October 26, 2005

Public Law

1.1   **Public Law 109-92, approved Oct. 26, 2005. (S. 397)**

(CIS05:PL109-92   9 p.)

"To prohibit civil liability actions from being brought or continued against manufacturers, distributors, dealers, or importers of firearms or ammunition for damages, injunctive or other relief resulting from the misuse of their products by others."

Prohibits certain civil liability actions in Federal or State courts against licensed firearms or ammunitions manufacturers, sellers, or trade associations for damages resulting from unlawful third party use of a firearm or ammunition product.

Requires dismissal of such lawsuits that are pending on the date of enactment of this act.

Prohibits importers, manufacturers or dealers from selling or delivering handguns, unless the transferees are provided with secure gun storage or safety devices, and establishes civil penalties for violations.

Establishes immunity from certain civil liability actions for persons who use secure gun storage or safety devices.

Revises criminal code provisions relating to the manufacture, importation and use of armor-piercing ammunition, and establishes additional criminal penalties.

Requires the Department of Justice to report to Congress on the feasibility of a uniform standard for the testing of armor-piercing ammunition.

Title 5 is cited as the Child Safety Lock Act of 2005.

P.L. 109-92 Reports

107th Congress

2.1   **H. Rpt. 107-727, pt. 1 on H.R. 2037, "Protection of Lawful Commerce in Arms Act," Oct. 7, 2002.**

(CIS02:H363-28   17 p.)
(Y1.1/8:107-727/PT.1.)

Recommends passage, with an amendment in the nature of a substitute, of H.R. 2037, the Protection of Lawful Commerce in Arms Act, to require the Department of Commerce to establish a voluntary list of manufacturers and sellers of guns and ammunition and the associations that represent them, and to limit the civil liability of listed entities in the event of harm caused by the criminal, suicidal, or negligent use of a firearm or ammunition by a third party.

Bill is intended to curb allegedly frivolous individual and municipal lawsuits against firearms manufacturers and dealers.

Includes dissenting views (p. 16-17).

2.2   **H. Rpt. 107-727, pt. 2 on H.R. 2037, "Protection of Lawful Commerce in Arms Act," Oct. 8, 2002.**

(CIS02:H523-50   62 p.)
(Y1.1/8:107-727/PT.2.)

Recommends passage, with an amendment in the nature of a substitute, of H.R. 2037, the Protection of Lawful Commerce in Arms Act, to prohibit certain civil liability actions against licensed firearms and ammunitions manufacturers, sellers, and trade associations for damages resulting from the criminal or unlawful third party use of a firearm or ammunition product.

Bill applies to all Federal and State courts and is intended to negate allegedly frivolous individual and municipal lawsuits against the firearms industry.

H.R. 2037 is related to H.R. 123 and H.R. 1966.

Includes transcript (p. 32-62) of Committee Oct. 2, 2002 markup session on H.R. 2037 (text, p. 33-40; amendment, p. 42-49).

108th Congress

2.3   **H. Rpt. 108-59 on H.R. 1036, "Protection of Lawful Commerce in Arms Act," Apr. 7, 2003.**

(CIS03:H523-8   109 p.)
(Y1.1/8:108-59.)

Recommends passage, with an amendment in the nature of a substitute, of H.R. 1036, the Protection of Lawful Commerce in Arms Act, to prohibit certain civil liability actions against licensed firearms and ammunitions manufacturers, sellers, and trade associations for damages resulting from the criminal or unlawful third party use of a firearm or ammunition product.

Bill applies to all Federal and State courts and is intended to negate allegedly frivolous individual and municipal lawsuits against the firearms industry.

Includes transcript (p. 33-96) of Committee Apr. 3, 2003 markup session on H.R. 1036 (text, amendment, p. 34-53).

Includes dissenting views (p. 97-109).

109th Congress

2.4   **H. Rpt. 109-124 on H.R. 800, "Protection of Lawful Commerce in Arms Act," June 14, 2005.**

(CIS05:H523-20   151 p.)
(Y1.1/8:109-124.)

Recommends passage, with an amendment in the nature of a substitute, of H.R. 800, the Protection of Lawful Commerce in Arms Act, to prohibit certain civil liability actions against licensed firearms and ammunitions manufacturers, sellers, and trade associations for damages resulting from the criminal or unlawful third party use of a firearm or ammunition product.

Bill applies to all Federal and State courts and is intended to negate allegedly frivolous individual and municipal lawsuits against the firearms industry.

Includes transcript (p. 42-138) of Committee Apr. 20, May 18, and May 25, 2005, markup sessions on H.R. 800 (text, p. 43-55; amendments, p. 62-125 passim).

Includes dissenting views (p. 139-151).

H.R. 800 is related to 108th Congress H.R. 1036, 107th Congress H.R. 123, and 107th Congress H.R. 2037.

Exhibit 6–9.   2005 CIS INDEX ANNUAL: LEGISLATIVE HISTORIES OF US PUBLIC LAWS 229.

WEEKLY REPORT OCT. 17-21

[LEGAL AFFAIRS]

Bill on Gun Liability Completed
House clears measure for president

BOX SCORE

BILL: S 397 — To provide civil liability protection for makers, dealers and importers of firearms and ammunition.

LATEST ACTION: House cleared, 283-144, on Oct. 20.

NEXT LIKELY ACTION: President signs into law.

REFERENCE: House passage, CQ Weekly p. 2118; House Judiciary Committee approval, p. 1454; Senate bill last Congress, 2004 Almanac, p. 12-13; House bill last Congress, 2003 Almanac, p. 13-14.

■ GO TO **WWW.CQ.COM** FOR MORE ■

By SETH STERN

THE HOUSE CLEARED LEGISLATION last week that would shield gun manufacturers and dealers from being sued when third parties misuse their products.

The Oct. 20 vote on the bill (S 397) — 283-144 — is a victory for the National Rifle Association and Republican efforts to overhaul the civil justice system by limiting liability lawsuits. The Senate passed the bill, sponsored by Larry E. Craig, R-Idaho, with bipartisan support July 29. President Bush has said he will sign it into law. *(House vote 534, p. 2862)*

Craig's measure would prohibit civil liability actions in any state or federal court against manufacturers, distributors, dealers and importers of firearms and ammunition. Trade groups also would be protected. All pending actions would be dismissed.

Supporters say allowing such lawsuits is like

taking car manufacturers to court when people drive drunk. They say the liability suits are often filed by anti-gun critics hoping to drive manufacturers out of business with exorbitant legal fees. House Judiciary Committee Chairman F. James Sensenbrenner Jr., R-Wis., said such litigation threatens to "bankrupt the national firearms industry and deny all Americans their fundamental, constitutionally guaranteed right to bear arms."

Maryland Democrat Chris Van Hollen complained that "what it actually does is protect those gun dealers who are engaged in wrongful, negligent sales of weapons to criminals."

The bill would not preclude lawsuits against those who knowingly sell or transfer firearms intended to be used for a crime, or cases in which proper use resulted in physical injury, death or property damage because of a defect in the firearm.

The debate over firearm industry lawsuits began in 1998, when New Orleans led several cities in an effort to sue handgun manufacturers to pay for the cost of urban violence. Gun-rights lobbyists succeeded in enacting protections for the industry in states, but the federal law took much longer because of Senate resistance; that was softened by the gain of four Republican seats last year. ■

[LEGAL AFFAIRS]

House Passes 'Cheeseburger Bill'
Obesity lawsuits on food firms barred

BOX SCORE

BILL: HR 554 — To limit the civil liability of the food industry.

LATEST ACTION: House passed, 306-120, on Oct. 19.

NEXT LIKELY ACTION: Senate consideration not expected this year.

REFERENCE: House committee passage, CQ Weekly, p. 1454; background, 2004 CQ Weekly, p. 290.

■ GO TO **WWW.CQ.COM** FOR MORE ■

By SETH STERN

LEGISLATION THAT WOULD BAR lawsuits by plaintiffs claiming a food company's high-calorie offerings were to blame for their obesity won House passage Oct. 19, but the measure faces an overloaded agenda in the Senate.

Lawmakers passed the bill (HR 554) by a vote of 306-120 after they rejected four Democratic amendments and adopted a manager's amendment by Judiciary Chairman F. James Sensenbrenner Jr., R-Wis. *(House vote 533, p. 2862)*

But, as in the last Congress, the bill stands little chance of winning Senate passage this year. That chamber has little floor time, and the Senate Judiciary Committee is occupied by the Supreme Court nomination of Harriet Miers.

While tort reform advocates acknowledge the bill is unlikely to be taken up in the Senate this year, they are hopeful about increasing support next year. "I see that one growing," said Sen. Larry E. Craig, R-Idaho.

The House measure, sponsored by Ric Keller, R-Fla., and dubbed "the cheeseburger bill," seeks to block civil lawsuits against food manufacturers, sellers or trade associations in federal or state courts when a claim is based on an individual's weight gain, obesity or any weight-related health condition.

Plaintiffs still could sue for breach of contract or warranty, or when a food manufacturer or seller "knowingly" violated a federal or state law regarding the manufacture or marketing of a product.

The House adopted Sensenbrenner's manager's amendment by voice vote. It changed the section of the bill that sets out the types of information a plaintiff must provide to a judge to determine whether the lawsuit should proceed or be dismissed.

Lawmakers rejected Democratic amendments that would have blocked food industry trade associations, food manufacturers and

sellers from suing individuals; permitted obesity-related lawsuits against large chains (those with 20 or more outlets) to be filed on behalf of minors age 8 and younger; exempted from the bill's provisions actions by state attorneys general and state agencies enforcing state consumer protection laws concerning mislabeling or other unfair and deceptive trade practices; and allowed lawsuits involving a dietary supplement relating to a person's weight gain, obesity or any health condition associated with weight gain or obesity. *(House votes 529, 530, 531 and 532, p. 2862)* ■

Exhibit 6–10. Seth Stern, *Bill on Gun Liability Completed: House Clears Measure for President*, 63 CQ WKLY. 2856 (2005).

CHAPTER 7

ADMINISTRATIVE LAW

---

§ 7–1.   Introduction

The executive is one of the three coordinate branches of government, but historically its lawmaking role was limited to orders and regulations needed to carry out the legislature's mandates. With the modern growth of government bureaucracy, however, the rules created by executive agencies can be legal sources with immediate and pervasive impact.

Administrative law takes several forms, as agencies can act both somewhat like legislatures and somewhat like courts. They may promulgate binding regulations governing activities within their jurisdiction, or they may decide matters involving particular litigants on a case-by-case basis. Approaches vary from agency to agency.

Although executive agencies have existed in this country since its creation, the real growth of administrative law began in the late nineteenth century as the government sought to deal with the increasingly complex problems of industrialized society. In the 1930s, Congress created new independent regulatory agencies such as the Federal Communications Commission and the Securities and Exchange Commission to administer its New Deal programs. A third boom in administrative law occurred around 1970, as agencies such as the Environmental Protection Agency, the Consumer Product Safety Commission, and the Occupational Safety and Health Administration were created to address growing environmental and health concerns. The regulatory landscape is still evolving, as the Homeland Security Act of 2002 created a new cabinet department and several new agencies. Administrative regulations and decisions continue to proliferate.

Most of this chapter focuses on federal administrative law, but state agencies can play an important a role in many areas of activity. States also delegate lawmaking responsibilities to counties and cities, which enact ordinances and have their own local agencies. While federal administrative law is relatively easy to research, state and local sources may be difficult to locate and even harder to update.

§ 7–2.   Background Reference Sources

When researching administrative law, it is important to determine what agency has jurisdiction and develop a preliminary understanding of its structure and functions. In some situations the relevant agency is obvious, but in others it may require background analysis or a close reading of statutory and judicial sources to determine an agency's role.

a.   Agency Websites

There are many different agency organizations and models. Most agencies are formed by legislation which defines their purpose and limits their parameters. It is important to understand an agency's organizational structure, legal mandates and information sources before delving into the documents it produces.

An agency's website often provides a convenient source of information on its history and current activities. Here, depending on the agency, it is usually possible to find introductory overviews, organization charts, speeches, policy documents, directories, and other useful resources. The online information should be the most current available, and may include press releases and other resources not available in print.

Under the Electronic Freedom of Information Act Amendments of 1996, agency websites are required to include "statements of policy and interpretations that have been adopted by the agency," as well as "administrative staff manuals and instructions to staff that affect a member of the public." Congress further defined the scope of agency websites in the E–Government Act of 2002, mandating that they provide descriptions of the agency's mission and information about its organizational structure.

In part as a result of this legislation, agency websites are increasingly the first place to look for information and documents. Website organization and ease of access, however, vary considerably from agency to agency. Some have well organized "Reference Rooms" clearly accessible from their homepages, while others may hide documents under obscure Freedom of Information Act links. A site map, if available, may help in understanding a website's structure and organization.

Researchers can find several lists of government websites on the Internet. One of the most thorough and reliable of these lists is Louisiana State University's Federal Agencies Directory <www.lib.lsu.edu/gov/fedgov.html>. It lists agencies both alphabetically and by departmental hierarchy. The site links to more than 1000 executive branch and agency sites. Washburn School of Law's WashLaw site has an "Agency Guidance Table" <www.washlaw.edu/doclaw/executive5m.html> which covers only about seventy major agencies, but for each it provides direct links (if available) to publications, organization charts, forms, opinions, manuals, libraries, and directories. USA.gov <www.usa.gov>, the federal government's public portal, also provides an A–Z Agency Index with links to websites.

b. Guides and Directories

In order to know which agency website to visit, it may be necessary to do a bit of background research in order to determine which agency has jurisdiction over a particular area. Sometimes information that is unavailable from the agency site is needed, such as contact information for specific personnel. For purposes such as these, federal government guides and directories may be valuable resources.

Determining the appropriate agency can be done in several ways. Statutes or cases found during the research process may lead to the relevant agency's regulations or decisions. A useful source for identifying federal agencies is CQ Press's annual *Washington Information Directory*, which is organized by subject and provides descriptions and access information for federal agencies as well as congressional committees and nongovernmental organizations. Exhibit 7–1 on page 280 shows a page from this directory for the topic "Sentencing and Corrections," with information about the Bureau of Prisons (BOP), several other offices in the Department of Justice, and the U.S. Sentencing Commission.

Once a relevant agency has been identified, one of the most convenient sources for general information about its structure, authority, and functions is the *United States Government Manual*. This annual federal government directory, available both in print and on the Internet <www.gpoaccess.gov/gmanual/>, provides descriptive listings of each executive department and more than fifty independent agencies and commissions. It includes references to statutes under which the agencies operate and explains the agencies' functions and major operating units. Organizational charts are provided for most major agencies, and sources of information (including publications, telephone numbers, and websites) are listed. The *Government Manual* provides quick answers to questions which might otherwise require extensive research.

The *United States Government Manual* provides an overview of the entire federal government, focusing on the executive branch. CQ Press's *Federal Regulatory Directory* (12th ed. 2006) has a more extensive analysis of thirteen major regulatory agencies, with shorter treatment of more than a hundred other agencies and offices. Historical background can be found in George T. Kurian, ed., *A Historical Guide to the U.S. Government* (1998), with alphabetically arranged entries on departments and agencies, as well as major concepts and issues in administrative law.

Agency websites and resources such as the *U.S. Government Manual* and the *Federal Regulatory Directory* provide general information and the names of major agency officials, but they rarely have extensive listings of other staffers. To learn about the status of a particular regulation or enforcement activity, it is often necessary to contact agency staff directly by phone or e-mail. The most productive inquiries are directed as specifically as possible to the responsible division and official. Several directories provide more detailed information about personnel, including telephone numbers and e-mail addresses. Three with comparable coverage are *Carroll's Federal Directory* (quarterly), CQ Press's *Federal Staff Directory* (three times a year) and Leadership Directories' *Federal Yellow Book* (quarterly). Carroll Publishing and Leadership Directories also produce companion volumes covering federal regional offices outside the Washington, D.C. area. All of these directories are also available through their publishers' subscription websites (<www. govsearch.com>, <fsd.cq.com>, and <www.leadership directories.com>). Exhibit 7–2 on page 281 shows a portion of the Bureau of Prisons entry in the *Federal*

Yellow Book. Note that it provides direct extensions for officials such as the general counsel and deputy general counsel.

§ 7–3. Federal Regulations

The basic mechanism by which most agencies govern their areas of expertise is the *regulation*, a detailed administrative order similar in form to a statute. Regulations are also known as *rules*; these terms are used interchangeably in U.S. administrative law. The publication of regulations follows a standard procedure: they are first issued chronologically in a daily gazette, the *Federal Register*; and then the rules in force are arranged by subject in the *Code of Federal Regulations*. These two publications are the central official resources in federal administrative law research.

a. *Federal Register*

As the federal government promulgated more and more executive and administrative orders and regulations in the early New Deal period, locating regulations and determining which were in force became increasingly difficult. There was no requirement that regulations be published or centrally filed, and two cases reached the U.S. Supreme Court before it was discovered that the administrative orders on which they were based were no longer in effect. This embarrassment, and the resulting criticism, led Congress in 1935 to establish a daily publication of executive and administrative promulgations. The *Federal Register* began publication in March 1936 as a chronological source for administrative documents, similar to a session law text.

In 1946, the Administrative Procedure Act expanded the scope of the *Federal Register* considerably by creating a rulemaking system requiring the publication of proposed regulations for public comment. Judicial decisions in the 1960s and 1970s, overturning regulations seen as arbitrary or capricious, led agencies to provide fuller explanations of their actions and greater evidence of public involvement in the decisionmaking process. In addition to the text of proposed and final rules, the *Register* now includes extensive preambles describing the need for the regulatory changes and responding to comments on proposed rules.

These preambles make the *Federal Register* much more than a simple "session regulation" text, because the explanatory information never appears in the *Code of Federal Regulations*. Exhibit 7–3 on page 282 shows a final rule of the Bureau of Prisons as published in the *Federal Register*, implementing regulations on suspending rules in emergencies. The page shown contains a summary, contact information, and responses to comments on the proposed rule.

The *Federal Register* is published in print, but the most convenient access is usually through the Internet. Issues since volume 59 (1994) are available free from GPO Access <www.gpoaccess.gov/fr/>, with each new issue added the morning of its publication. Regulations can be found by browsing the daily tables of contents or through keyword searches, and documents can be viewed as PDF files replicating the printed page.

The *Federal Register* is also available online through several commercial services. Westlaw's FR–ALL database has coverage extending all the way back to 1936. (Documents before 1980 are searchable, but they display only in PDF form. The FR database begins coverage in 1981 and does not have PDF images.) LexisNexis begins coverage in the summer of 1980, and CQ.com in 1990. These services also generally have new issues online the day they are published. HeinOnline does not have the most recent issues, but like Westlaw it provides retrospective coverage back to the first volume in 1936. Most large law libraries also have complete runs of the *Federal Register* back to 1936 in microform.

The Unified Agenda <www.gpoaccess.gov/ua/> is a useful feature published twice a year in the *Federal Register*, in April and October. The Unified Agenda lists regulatory actions under development and provides information on their status and projected dates of completion. This can be a good way to learn about areas of agency activity that have not yet reached the proposed rulemaking stage.

Each daily *Federal Register* begins with a table of contents and a list of the *Code of Federal Regulations* citations for new or proposed regulations in the issue. The table of contents is organized alphabetically by agency, so researchers can easily monitor a particular agency's activity. (A monthly index to the *Federal Register* is arranged like the daily table of contents, with entries by agency rather than by subject.) Skimming the *Register*'s table of contents is part of many lawyers' daily routine, and from the GPO Access search page you can sign up to have it delivered each morning by e-mail. Exhibit 7–4 on page 283 shows the list of *CFR* parts affected in the *Federal Register* issue in which the BOP emergency regulations were published, with a reference to these regulations at 28 C.F.R. Part 501.

Several readers' aids are provided in the back of each issue, including telephone numbers for information and assistance, a list of new public laws, and a listing of *Federal Register* pages and dates for the month (so that someone with a page reference can determine which issue to consult). The most important of these readers' aids is a cumulative list of *CFR* parts affected since the beginning of the month, similar to the one shown in Exhibit 7–4.

An index to the *Federal Register* is published monthly. The index is arranged like the daily table of contents, with entries by agency rather than by subject. Each month's index cumulates those earlier in the year, so the January–February index replaces the January index, and the January–December index serves as the final annual index. The index is available back to 1994 on the Office of the Federal Register's website <www.archives.gov/ federal-register/>, and back to 1936 on HeinOnline.

The Office of the Federal Register website provides additional information, including a tutorial *The Federal Register: What It Is and How to Use It* <www.archives. gov/federal-register/tutorial/> that has a detailed explanation of the publication of federal regulations.

The *Register* has permanent reference value because it contains material which never appears in the *Code of Federal Regulations*. Not only does it provide the agency preambles explaining regulatory actions, but it may also be the only available source for temporary changes occurring between annual *CFR* revisions. Researching the histories of administrative agency regulations would be impossible without access to the *Federal Register*.

b. *Code of Federal Regulations*

As with statutes, chronological publication of regulations is insufficient for most legal research. It is necessary to know what regulations are in force, regardless of when they were first promulgated. In 1937 the Federal

Register Act was amended to create the *Code of Federal Regulations*, the first edition of which was published in 1938. The set now consists of more than two hundred paperback volumes, revised on an annual basis.

The regulations in the *CFR* are collected from the *Federal Register* and arranged in a subject scheme of fifty titles, similar to that of the *U.S. Code*. (Some *CFR* titles cover the same topics as the *U.S. Code* title with the same number, but others focus on completely different subjects.) Titles are divided into chapters, each containing the regulations of a specific agency. The back of every *CFR* volume contains an alphabetical list of federal agencies indicating the title and chapter (or chapters) of each agency's regulations.

CFR chapters are divided into parts, each of which covers a particular topic, and finally parts are divided into sections. Exhibits 7–5 and 7–6 on pages 284–285 show sample pages of the *CFR* from Title 28 (Judicial Administration), Chapter V (Bureau of Prisons), Parts 500 (General Definitions) and 501 (Scope of Rules). A citation to the *CFR* provides the title, part, section, and year of publication. The section on Bureau of Prisons emergencies, for example, is cited as 28 C.F.R. § 501.1 (2006). (The section is a distinct number, not a decimal; § 501.12 would follow § 501.11 and not fall between § 501.1 and § 501.2.)

At the beginning of each *CFR* part is an *authority note* showing the statutory authority under which the regulations have been issued. After this note, or at the end of each section, is a *source note* providing the citation and date of the *Federal Register* in which the regulation was last published in full. This reference is the key to finding background information and comments explaining the regulations. In Exhibit 7–5 on page 284, note that the regulations are issued under the authority of several sections of the *United States Code*, and that the source for § 500.1 is 44 Fed. Reg. 38,244, June 29, 1979, as amended on four subsequent occasions. The source for § 501.1, as shown in Exhibit 7–6 on page 285, is the Federal Register regulation shown in Exhibit 7–3 on page 282.

The *Bluebook* mandates citation to the official, annually revised edition of the *CFR*. (The *ALWD Citation Manual* permits citation to an online source, if that information is noted parenthetically.) The official volumes are updated and replaced on a rotating cycle throughout the year. The revisions of the various titles are issued on a quarterly basis: Titles 1–16 with regulations in force as of January 1; titles 17–27 as of April 1; titles 28–41 as of July 1; and titles 42–50 as of October 1. The volumes usually come out two to four months after these cutoff dates. The *CFR* pages shown in Exhibits 7–5 and 7–6 are current as of July 1, 2006, and appear in a volume published in September 2006.

The *CFR* is available in several electronic formats. The official version at GPO Access <www.gpoaccess.gov/cfr/> replicates the paper edition and is updated on the same basis. Sections can be retrieved by citation, and either individual titles or the entire *CFR* can be searched. As with the *Federal Register*, documents can be viewed and printed as PDF files. These PDF images can thus provide the official source required for a citation.

GPO Access also offers a "beta test site" version of a much more current *Electronic Code of Federal Regulations*, or e-CFR <www.gpoaccess.gov/ecfr/>. This edition incorporates new amendments from the *Federal Register* within a day or two. While the site explains that this is a "demonstration project" and not an official legal edition of the *CFR*, it represents a significant improvement in the government's timely delivery of regulatory information.

Regularly updated versions of the *CFR* are also available online from Westlaw and LexisNexis. Like the e-CFR, these files are updated on an ongoing basis to reflect changes published in the *Federal Register*. Both incorporate amendments within a few days of their appearance in the *Register*. Westlaw's *CFR* is even more up to date, because it includes "Regulatory Action" red flags linking affected sections to *Federal Register* documents the same day they are published.

To determine what regulations were in force at a particular time, older editions of the *CFR* are sometimes needed. GPO Access retains older editions as new versions are added, with coverage starting with selected 1996 volumes. Westlaw and LexisNexis provide more extensive historical access, with older editions of the *CFR* back to the early 1980s. HeinOnline fills the rest of the gap, with coverage beginning with the original 1938 edition and extending through 1983. Most large law libraries also have microform collections of older *CFR*s back to 1938.

c. Finding and Updating Regulations

Federal regulations can be found through several methods. The *Federal Register* and the *Code of Federal Regulations* have indexes, and both publications can be searched through GPO Access or other databases including Lexis and Westlaw. Numerous other sources provide references to relevant regulations, including both annotated editions of the United States Code. Agency websites provide links to regulations, either on their own sites or at GPO Access, and references are often found in cases, texts, and articles. One relevant regulation provides easy leads to other versions, through cross-references in *Federal Register* preambles and *CFR* notes.

Most research into the regulations of a federal agency begins with the *Code of Federal Regulations*, rather than the daily *Federal Register*. The *CFR* includes an annually revised *Index and Finding Aids* volume providing access by agency name and subject. This index is far less thorough than most statutory indexes, and it lists parts rather than specific sections. It covers a very broad area in relatively terse fashion, so it can be rather difficult to use. The regulation on prison emergencies shown in Exhibit 7–3 on page 282, for example, is indexed only under "Prisons Bureau–General management and ad-ministration–Scope of rules." Much more detailed subject access is provided in the annual four-volume *West's Code of Federal Regulations General Index*. This index, available on Westlaw as the *RegulationsPlus Index*, has a specific entry to the Exhibit 7–3 regulation under "Correctional institutions–Emergencies."

Online keyword searches are one of the most effective ways to find regulations, through GPO Access or one of the commercial databases. Because the CFR is so volumi-nous and wide-ranging, it is often more effective to search within a particular title or a topical file if you can narrow your search. GPO Access offers options of search-ing the entire CFR or specific titles, while Westlaw and Lexis have files for regulations in topical areas such as banking, environmental law, and securities.

If you have a statute and need to find regulations promulgated under its authority or related to it, the simplest method is to check the *U.S. Code Annotated* (in print or on Westlaw) or *U.S. Code Service* (in print or on Lexis). Cross-references to relevant *CFR* parts or sections follow individual sections in both codes. The online versions of the statutes have hypertext links from the statute to the regulation. The *CFR*'s *Index and Finding Aids* volume also has a "Parallel Table of Authorities and Rules" that lists every statute and presidential document cited by an agency as authority for its rules, taken from the rulemaking authority citation in *CFR*. On GPO Access, the Parallel Table of Authorities and Rules is one of the links at the top of the "Browse and/or search the CFR" screen.

Another option for finding regulations is to check federal agency websites. Many agencies provide the text of the statutes under which they operate as well as their current body of regulations and information on any current proposed rules. Agency sites may be updated less regularly than GPO Access, so some caution is necessary in using this approach.

For some agencies, regulations are reprinted in treatises and looseleaf services covering their topical area. Topical looseleaf services focusing on the work of particular agencies (such as the Internal Revenue Service or the Securities and Exchange Commission) provide currently supplemented and well annotated texts of both substantive and procedural regulations of their subject agencies.

Finding relevant regulations, however, is only the first step of research. The next step is to verify that the regulations are current. For users of the e-CFR, commercial databases, or looseleaf services, this is a relatively simple task because the *CFR* versions available through these sources are regularly updated. For others, it is necessary to update a regulation from the most recent annual *CFR* edition. The key tool for this purpose is a monthly pamphlet accompanying the *CFR* entitled *LSA: List of CFR Sections Affected* (also available through GPO Access <www.gpoaccess.gov/lsa/>).

LSA lists *Federal Register* pages of any new rules affecting *CFR* sections, and indicates the nature of the change with notes such as "amended," "removed," or "revised." *LSA* also includes references to proposed rules, listed separately by part rather than by specific section. Exhibit 7–7 on page 286 shows a page from the May 2005 *LSA*, indicating that several sections of 28 C.F.R. had been revised, removed, or added since the July 1, 2004 revision. This pamphlet includes several references to the final rule shown in Exhibit 7–2 on page 281, providing the specific pages where the revised sections appeared in the *Federal Register*.

Each *LSA* issue cumulates all changes since the latest *CFR* edition, so it is usually not necessary to examine more than the most recent monthly issue. (The exception is if the latest *CFR* volume is more than a year old.) *LSA* brings a search for current regulations up to date within a month or so. The most recent changes not yet covered in *LSA* can then be found by using the cumulative "List of CFR Parts Affected" in the latest *Federal Register* issue, as well as in the last issue of any month not yet covered by *LSA*. This somewhat cumbersome updating process was the standard procedure until quite recently, but now it is much simpler to check a commercial database or the e-CFR to see if it lists any *Federal Register* issues more recent than the latest annual revision among its sources.

Because regulations change so frequently, it is not uncommon to hit a dead end when trying to track down a *CFR* reference from a case or article. The cited regulations may have been repealed or moved to another *CFR* location. In the back of each volume, the *CFR* publishes tables to help trace what has happened to regulations, indicating all sections that have been repealed, transferred, or otherwise changed since 2001. Earlier changes from 1949 to 2000 are listed in a separate series of *List of CFR Sections Affected* volumes for the entire *CFR*, and are included in HeinOnline's *Federal Register* collection.

The official CFR, whether used in print or online (including the e-CFR), contains no annotations of court decisions like those in *United States Code Annotated* or *United States Code Service*. Yet a court may invalidate a regulation or provide an important interpretation of key provisions, and identifying relevant cases is an essential part of regulatory research.

The most convenient way to find court decisions is to use Westlaw's version of the CFR, which includes notes of decisions similar to those in *United States Code Annotated*, as well as references to relevant agency decisions, statutes, and secondary sources. Westlaw in effect gives regulations basically the same treatment that it does statutes, providing a springboard from the text to a wide range of research references. The Westlaw display for 28 C.F.R. § 501.1 is shown in Exhibit 7–8 on page 287. Thomson West provides similar coverage in print of selected *CFR* titles, to date having published titles 8 (immigration), 29 (labor law), and 49 (transportation), as well as chapter IV of title 42 (Medicare/Medicaid).

Lexis provides an unannotated CFR, but a "Shepardize" link at the top of the display allows you to find citing cases and law review articles. Comparable coverage in print is provided by *Shepard's Code of Federal Regulations Citations*. As with its coverage of statutes, Shepard's references are listed under the particular subsection cited. This can make it more difficult to do comprehensive research on an entire section, but is a great time-saver for someone looking for references to a specific provision.

§ 7–4. Guidance Documents

Regulations published in the *Federal Register* and *CFR* are the most authoritative sources of agency law, but in recent years the creation of regulations has become increasingly time-consuming and complicated. As a result of this "ossification" of the rulemaking process, agencies now are just as likely to create new rules through guidance documents, policy statements, or manuals that do not require notice-and-comment procedures and publication in the *Federal Register*. Guidance documents do not have the same binding force as regulations, but they can be important indications of how an agency perceives its mandate and how it will respond in a specific situation.

Most guidance documents do not appear in the *Federal Register*, the *CFR*, or any other widely available published source, but many are available through agency websites. The Electronic Freedom of Information Act Amendments of 1996 (e-FOIA) mandates that agencies make policy statements, manuals, and frequently requested information available to the public electronically.

Website organization and ease of access vary considerably from agency to agency. The Bureau of Prisons has a rather straightforward site, with a Policy/Forms link leading to PDF versions of program statements that provide more detailed procedural information than is available in the Bureau's regulations. Exhibit 7–9 on page 288 shows the BOP page providing links to its various series of program statements. The "Search" link at the bottom of the screen can be used to search the entire website or can be limited to a keyword search of policy documents.

The form and impact of guidance documents can vary widely from agency to agency. A familiarity with the material an agency makes available on its website is necessary, but it is also essential to understand the role of guidance documents and policy statements in its decisionmaking processes.

Even though agency websites have greatly increased access to government information, a vast store of unpublished additional documentation such as internal records, correspondence, and staff studies still exists. The Freedom of Information Act and the Privacy Act have dramatically expanded the public's access to government files by providing that individuals can request copies of most documents (although it may take weeks or months to receive a reply and there are broad exceptions of material that agencies need not disclose). The first place to check for policies and procedures is the specific department or agency's website, which should have a Freedom of Information or FOIA link somewhere on the front page.

Several more general resources are available for assistance in filing FOIA requests. The Reporters Committee for Freedom of the Press <rcfp.org/foia/> includes a useful guide and a fill-in-the-blank FOI Letter Generator. The House Committee on Government Reform publishes a concise handbook with sample request forms, *A Citizen's Guide on Using the Freedom of Information Act and the Privacy Act of 1974 to Request Government Records,* H.R. Rep. 109–226 (2005) (available online from GPO Access and through the Federation of American Scientists <www.fas.org/sgp/foia/citizen.pdf>). Several books provide more extensive treatment of the history and interpretation of FOIA and the Privacy Act, including procedures and sample forms for filing requests and suing to compel disclosure. One of the most current and practical is an American Bar Association publication by Stephen P. Gidiere, *The Federal Information Manual: How the Government Collects, Manages, and Discloses Information Under FOIA and Other Statutes* (2006), which includes a chapter on "The Elements of a Successful FOIA Request."

§ 7–5. Administrative Decisions and Rulings

Besides promulgating regulations and general guidance documents, administrative agencies also have quasi-judicial functions in which they hold hearings and issue decisions involving specific parties. The procedures and precedential value of these decisions vary among agencies, as do means of publication and ease of access.

About fifteen regulatory commissions and other agencies publish their decisions in a form similar to official reports of court decisions. These reports are usually published first in advance sheets or slip decisions and eventually cumulated into bound volumes. The volumes may include indexes, digests and tables, but most of these aids are noncumulative and of limited research value.

Commercial looseleaf services and topical reporters are major sources of administrative decisions in their subject fields. Various Securities and Exchange Commission decisions and releases, for example, are printed in CCH's *Federal Securities Law Reporter*, and National Labor Relations Board decisions appear in BNA's *Labor Relations Reporter*. These services, which will be discussed in Chapter 9, usually appear more promptly and contain better indexing than the official reports, and they combine these administrative decisions with other related sources such as statutes, regulations, and court decisions.

A growing number of administrative decisions are available on the Internet, but there is little consistency in how agencies provide access to these documents. One of the most extensive and current listings of websites with decisions is available from the University of Virginia Library   <www.lib.virginia.edu/govdocs/fed_decisions _agency.html>. Westlaw and LexisNexis include decisions of several dozen agencies in topical databases. Online coverage includes many administrative decisions that are not published in either official reports or looseleaf services, and generally extends much earlier than official websites.

Attorney General opinions deserve special mention. As the federal government's law firm, the Department of Justice provides legal advice to the president and to other departments. Traditionally these opinions were signed by the U.S. Attorney General and published in a series entitled *Opinions of the Attorneys General of the United States*; this function is now delegated to the Office of Legal Counsel (OLC), which has published *Opinions of the Office of Legal Counsel* since 1977. Opinions of both the Attorney General and OLC are also available online through Westlaw and LexisNexis, and OLC opinions are on the Internet <www.usdoj.gov/olc/opinions.htm> from 1992 to date.

A researcher specializing in a particular area must be familiar with decisions of relevant agencies. For nonspecialists, the easiest way to learn of administrative decisions is through the annotations in *United States Code Service. USCS* includes notes of decisions from more than fifty commissions and board. *United States Code Annotated* does not include references to administrative decisions but does cite opinions of the Attorney General and Office of Legal Counsel.

KeyCite and Shepard's both have coverage of selected administrative decisions. They list these decisions among other citing references to court decisions, statutes, and other sources, and they also provide references to later documents that affect or cite administrative decisions. In print, Shepard's coverage is split among *Shepard's United States Administrative Citations*, which lists citations to the decisions and orders of more than a dozen major administrative tribunals, and several of its topical citators such as *Shepard's Federal Energy Law Citations, Federal Tax Citator*, and *Labor Law Citations.*

§ 7–6. Presidential Lawmaking

In addition to supervising the executive departments and agencies, the President of the United States also has several lawmaking roles. The president sends legislative proposals to Congress, approves or vetoes bills which have passed both houses, and issues a range of legally binding documents.

A number of reference sources provide background information on the presidency, addressing political and historical aspects of the institution. The most extensive is Leonard W. Levy & Louis Fisher, eds., *Encyclopedia of the American Presidency* (4 vols., 1994), with more than 1,000 articles, including discussion of presidential powers, relations with Congress, and key legislation. Michael Nelson, ed., *Congressional Quarterly's Guide to the Presidency* (2 vols., 3d. ed. 2002) is another major reference work, arranged topically rather than alphabetically. Part III, "Powers of the Presidency," discusses the president's various roles and actions; and Part VI, "Chief Executive and the Federal Government," analyzes relations with Congress, the Supreme Court, and the federal bureaucracy.

The major legal documents issued by the president are *executive orders* and *proclamations*. While the distinction between the two can be blurred, executive orders usually involve an exercise of presidential authority related to government business while proclamations are announcements of policy or of matters requiring public notice. Proclamations are often ceremonial or commemorative, but some have important legal effects such as implementing trade agreements or declaring treaties to be in force.

Executive orders and proclamations are issued in separate numbered series and published in the *Federal Register*. A variety of other presidential documents are also printed in the *Federal Register* but not included in either of these series. Presidential determinations, issued pursuant to particular statutory mandates, are also issued in a numbered series, and other unnumbered documents include various memoranda and notices. Many, but not all, of these documents deal with foreign affairs. Exhibit 7–10 on page 289 shows an executive order on improving agency disclosure of information, as printed in the *Federal Register*.

Presidential documents in the *Federal Register* are available online from GPO Access <www.gpoaccess.gov/fr> and from the commercial databases. Westlaw has executive orders since 1936 and other presidential documents since 1984, and LexisNexis has all presidential documents since 1981. Older documents can also be found in the *CIS Index to Presidential Executive Orders and Proclamations* (covering 1787–1983, and accompanied by a microfiche set of all documents indexed) and *CIS Federal Register Index* (1984–98).

The Office of the Federal Register website has a disposition table of all executive orders since 1937 <www.archives.gov/federal-register/executive-orders/>, with information on their amendment, revocation, and current status. For executive orders since 1993, the site also includes subject indexes and links to full text at GPO Access.

Executive orders and proclamations are reprinted in a number of locations, including an annual compilation of Title 3 of the *Code of Federal Regulations*. Because each annual edition of Title 3 is a unique set of documents rather than an updated codification, older volumes remain part of the current *CFR* set. Documents from the years 1936 to 1975 have been recompiled into multiyear hardcover editions, and all volumes from 1936 through 2001 are available online as part of HeinOnline's U.S. Presidential Library. The *CFR* is the preferred *Bluebook* and *ALWD Citation Manual* source for presidential documents it contains.

Proclamations, but not executive orders, are printed in the annual *Statutes at Large* volumes. Major orders and proclamations are also reprinted after relevant statutory provisions in the *U.S. Code*, *USCA*, and *USCS*; tables in each version of the code list presidential documents by number and indicate where they can be found. Reorganization plans, an older form of presidential action no longer in use, were published in the *Federal Register*, *CFR*, and *Statutes at Large*, and many are reprinted in all three versions of the code (in appendices to Title 5 in the *U.S. Code* and *USCA*, and following 5 U.S.C.S. § 903).

A variety of other presidential documents are also printed in the *Federal Register* but not included in either of these series. Presidential determinations, issued pursuant to particular statutory mandates, are also issued in a numbered series, and other unnumbered documents include various memoranda and notices. Most of these documents deal with foreign affairs.

Not all presidential directives, of course, are published in the *Federal Register*. Some relate to national security issues and are classified information. The Federal Register Act only requires publication of proclamations and executive orders, so other documents can be used to advance presidential goals without being published.

The president issues several other documents with legal significance that do not appear in the *Federal Register*. Messages to Congress, explaining proposed legislation or vetoes, reporting on the state of the nation, or serving other functions, are published in the *Congressional Record* and as House Documents. Signing statements are often issued when approving legislation, and may provide the president's interpretation of a statute. Although their value as legislative history is disputed, since 1986 these statements have been reprinted with the committee reports in *USCCAN*.

Most of these various presidential documents, including those published in the *Federal Register*, appear in the official *Weekly Compilation of Presidential Documents* along with speeches, transcripts of news conferences, and other material. The *Weekly Compilation of Presidential Documents* is available from GPO Access <www. gpoaccess.gov/wcomp/>, back to 1993, and HeinOnline has comprehensive coverage back to the first volume in 1965.

Public Papers of the Presidents is an official publication cumulating the contents of the *Weekly Compilation of Presidential Documents*. Series of annual volumes have been published for Herbert Hoover and for all presidents after Franklin D. Roosevelt, and cumulated indexes for the papers of each administration are available. Papers of Roosevelt and most earlier presidents are generally available in commercially published editions. GPO Access provides access to *Public Papers* volumes beginning with 1991 <www.gpoaccess.gov/pubpapers/>, and searchable retrospective collections of the entire set and earlier compilations are available from HeinOnline and from the American Presidency Project at the University of California, Santa Barbara <www.presidency.ucsb.edu>.

Coverage of proclamations, executive orders, and reorganization plans is included in KeyCite and Shepard's (in print in *Shepard's Code of Federal Regulations Citations*). Shepard's provides references to citing court decisions and law review articles, while KeyCite's more extensive coverage adds subsequent amendments and citations in administrative materials and court documents. Amendments and revocations are also noted in *LSA: List of CFR Sections Affected*.

§ 7–7. State Administrative Law

Like the federal government, the states have experienced a dramatic increase in the number and activity of their administrative agencies. In most states, however, publication of agency rules and decisions is far less systematic than it is on the federal level.

State websites are often the best starting point to determine the jurisdiction of relevant agencies and their publications. There is unfortunately no standard URL for state homepages, but they can be easily found through searches such as "[state name] government." The form <www.[state].gov> works for most states, and many general legal research sites include links to state homepages. The Library of Congress's "State Government Information" page <www.loc.gov/rr/news/stategov/> can provide a good starting point.

Nearly all states publish official manuals paralleling the *United States Government Manual* and providing quick access to information about government agencies and officials. These directories vary in depth and quality; some describe state agency functions and publications, while others simply serve as government phone directories. They are listed and described in the "General State Government Information" sections of the annual *State Legislative Sourcebook*, along with information about Internet sites, general reference works, statistical abstracts, and other sources. The Bradley University Library has a "State Blue Books" page <wiki.bradley.

edu/library_reference/index.php/State_Blue_Books> that links to online versions of these resources.

In addition, a number of directories provide multistate access to officials' names and numbers. CQ Press's *State Information Directory* (2002) is arranged by state and provides contact information for dozens of agencies in each state, including websites, fax numbers and names and e-mail addresses of directors and commissioners. More extensive listings are provided by *Carroll's State Directory* (three times a year) and Leadership Directories' *State Yellow Book* (quarterly); like the federal directories described on page 252, these are also available as subscription-based Internet services. The Council of State Governments' annual *CSG State Directory III: Administrative Officials* lists officials by function, rather than by state, and may be the most convenient source for someone needing to contact similar officials in several states. CSG's biennial *Book of the States* supplements these directories with more than 170 tables presenting a broad range of information on government operations in each of the fifty states.

a. Regulations

Almost every state issues a subject compilation of its administrative regulations, and most supplement these with weekly, biweekly or monthly registers. While the states generally follow the paradigm established by the *CFR* and *Federal Register*, few state administrative codes and registers are as organized and accessible as their federal counterparts. Some simply compile a variety of material submitted by individual agencies, and some have incomplete coverage. Indexing is often inadequate, sometimes even nonexistent.

The *Bluebook* and *ALWD Citation Manual* identify administrative codes and registers in their lists of basic primary sources for each state. More detailed information is available in William H. Manz, *Guide to State Legislative and Administrative Materials* (2002 ed.), which lists print, online, and CD–ROM sources for each state's administrative code. The annual two-volume *CAL INFO Guide to the Administrative Regulations of the States & Territories* provides the tables of contents for each administrative code, making it easier to identify relevant regulations in order to know which title or code volume is needed.

Although fewer states provide Internet access to regulations than to statutes, more than forty administrative codes and registers are available on state government sites. One of the easiest ways to find available sites is through the National Association of Secretaries of State's list of administrative code and register links <www.nass. org/acr/html/internet.html>. Westlaw and LexisNexis also have administrative codes from most of the states, and Westlaw also has a "50 State Regulatory Surveys" database (REG–SURVEYS) providing citations and links for each state's administrative code provisions on about 150 topics.

Some of the administrative codes and registers include executive orders or similar legal pronouncements from governors. Several governors include the text of executive orders on their websites, which can be accessed through state government homepages or by links from the National Governors Association <www.nga.org>.

b. Decisions and Rulings

Decisions of some state agencies, especially those dealing with banking, insurance, public utilities, taxation, and workers' compensation, may be published in official form in chronological series. A few looseleaf services and topical reporters also include state administrative decisions, and a growing number of state agency decisions are included in the online databases and on agency websites. Manz's *Guide to State Legislative and Administrative Materials* and Cheryl Rae Nyberg, *State Administrative Law Bibliography: Print and Electronic Sources* (2000) both list publications and online sources for agency rulings, decisions, and orders.

The opinions of state attorneys general, issued in response to questions from government officials, can have considerable significance in legal research. Although attorney general opinions are advisory in nature and do not have binding authority, they are given considerable weight by the courts in interpreting statutes and regulations. Most states publish attorney general opinions in slip opinions and bound volumes. Many attorney generals have recent opinions on their websites, which can be found through links at the National Association of Attorneys General website <www.naag.org>. State attorney general opinions are also available online in LexisNexis and Westlaw, with coverage in most states beginning in 1977 or earlier. Some attorney general opinions are included in the annotations in state codes, but coverage varies from state to state. KeyCite (but not Shepard's) includes attorney general opinions as citing sources in its coverage of cases, statutes, and other sources, but does not provide the option to KeyCite these opinions themselves to find later references.

Like the federal government, each state has open records laws under which unpublished information can be obtained upon request. Information on each state's laws and procedures is available from the National Freedom of Information Coalition <www.nfoic.org/resources/states/> and the Reporters Committee for Freedom of the Press's Open Government Guide <rcfp.org/ogg/>.

§ 7–8. Local Law

Cities and counties are administrative units of the states, with lawmaking powers determined by state constitution or by legislative delegation of authority. They create a variety of legal documents which can be important in legal research. *Charters* are the basic laws creating the structure of local government, and *ordinances* are local enactments governing specific issues. In addition many localities have administrative agencies which issue rules or decisions.

Often, local law sources can be quite difficult to locate. Most large cities and counties publish collections of their charters and ordinances, with some attempt at regular supplementation. For many smaller cities and counties, however, there is still no accessible, up-to-date compilation, and individual ordinances must be obtained from the local clerk's office.

A growing number of county and city codes are available on the Internet. State and Local Government on the Net <www.statelocalgov.net> provides convenient links to county and city homepages, which usually provide background and contact information, as well as the text of ordinances and regulations in some instances.

The Seattle Public Library <www.spl.org/default.asp?pageID=collection_municodes> and the Municipal Code Corporation <www.municode.com> have the most extensive sets of links to collections of local ordinances.

Together they cover cities from almost every state; the Seattle site also includes links to several other publishers with online county and city codes.

State and local law often incorporates industry codes on areas such as construction and fire safety. The International Code Council <www.iccsafe.org> publishes a series of fourteen codes on building and related codes, and the construction industry site First Source's Building Code Library <reedfirstsource.com/codes/> provides a database to identify the codes in force in specific states and major cities.

Because much local law information is not available in print or on the Internet, direct contact by telephone or e-mail may be essential. Directories with information on local governments throughout the country include *Carroll's County Directory*, *Carroll's Municipal Directory*, and *Municipal Yellow Book*. These directories are all updated twice a year and are available to subscribers through their publishers' websites (<www.govsearch.com> and <www.leadershipdirectories.com>).

§ 7–9. Conclusion

The extensive literature of regulations and other agency documents play an essential role in legal research, one that until recently was often a cause for frustration and confusion. Before the Internet, access was largely limited to resources such as the *Federal Register*, the *Code of Federal Regulations,* commercial looseleaf services, and major online databases such as Westlaw and LexisNexis. Today, however, the availability of online government information has flourished, and the astute researcher can develop greater insights into agency action than would have been considered possible just a few years ago.

Administrative law cannot be considered an isolated discipline separate from other forms of lawmaking. It is important to remember that administrative agency actions often implement specific statutory provisions, and you often need to consult court decisions to clarify the meaning of regulations or to determine the validity of agency decisions. Administrative law research is rarely completed in a vacuum, and the sources listed in this chapter are best treated as one part of an integrated research plan.

nated by the president. Investigates threats against these protectees; protects the White House, vice president's residence, and foreign missions; and plans and implements security designs for national special security events. Investigates violations of laws relating to counterfeiting of U.S. currency; financial crimes, including access device fraud, financial institution fraud, identity theft, and computer fraud; and computer-based attacks on the financial, banking, and telecommunications infrastructure.

Sentencing and Corrections

Federal Bureau of Prisons *(Justice Dept.)*, 320 1st St. N.W., #654 20534; (202) 307-3250. Fax, (202) 514-6878. Harley G. Lappin, Director. Press, (202) 307-3198. Inmate locator service, (202) 307-3126.
Web, www.bop.gov

Supervises operations of federal correctional institutions, community treatment facilities, and commitment and management of federal inmates; oversees contracts with local institutions for confinement and support of federal prisoners. Regional offices are responsible for administration; central office in Washington coordinates operations and issues standards and policy guidelines. Central office includes Federal Prison Industries, a government corporation providing prison-manufactured goods and services for sale to federal agencies, and the National Institute of Corrections, an information and technical assistance center on state and local corrections programs.

Federal Bureau of Prisons *(Justice Dept.)*, *Health Services*, 320 1st St. N.W., #1054 20534; (202) 307-3055. Fax, (202) 307-0826. Mary Ellen Thoms, Assistant Director; Dr. Newton E. Kendig, Medical Director.
Web, www.bop.gov

Administers health care and treatment programs for prisoners in federal institutions.

Federal Bureau of Prisons *(Justice Dept.)*, *Industries, Education, and Vocational Training—UNICOR*, 400 1st St. N.W. 20534 (mailing address: 320 1st St. N.W., Washington, DC 20534); (202) 305-3500. Fax, (202) 305-7340. Steve Schwalb, Chief Operating Officer. Customer Service, (800) 827-3168.
Web, www.unicor.gov

Administers program whereby inmates in federal prisons produce goods and services that are sold to the federal government.

Federal Bureau of Prisons *(Justice Dept.)*, *National Institute of Corrections*, 320 1st St. N.W., #5007 20534 (mailing address: 500 1st St. N.W., 7th Floor, Washington, DC 20534); (202) 307-3106. Fax, (202) 307-3361. Morris L. Thigpen, Director. Toll-free, (800) 995-6423.
Web, www.nicic.org

Offers technical assistance and training for upgrading state and local corrections systems through staff development, research, and evaluation of correctional operations and programs. Acts as a clearinghouse on correctional information.

Justice Dept. (DOJ), *Pardon Attorney*, 1425 New York Ave. N.W., #1100 20530; (202) 616-6070. Fax, (202) 616-6069. Roger C. Adams, Pardon Attorney.
Web, www.usdoj.gov/pardon

Receives and reviews petitions to the president for all forms of executive clemency, including pardons and sentence reductions; initiates investigations and prepares the deputy attorney general's recommendations to the president on petitions.

Office of Justice Programs (OJP), *(Justice Dept.)*, *Justice Assistance*, 810 7th St. N.W., 4th Floor 20531; (202) 616-6500. Fax, (202) 305-1367. Domingo Herraiz, Director. Information, (202) 514-4887.
General e-mail, askbja@usdoj.gov
Web, www.ojp.usdoj.gov/bja

Provides states and communities with funds and technical assistance for corrections demonstration projects.

Office of Justice Programs (OJP), *(Justice Dept.)*, *National Institute of Justice*, 810 7th St. N.W., 7th Floor 20531; (202) 307-2942. Fax, (202) 307-6394. Glenn Schmitt, Director (Acting).
Web, www.ojp.usdoj.gov/nij

Conducts research on all aspects of criminal justice, including crime prevention, enforcement, adjudication, and corrections. Maintains the National Criminal Justice Reference Service, which provides information on corrections research: (800) 851-3420; in Maryland, (301) 519-5500; Web, www.ncjrs.org.

U.S. Parole Commission *(Justice Dept.)*, 5550 Friendship Blvd., #420, Chevy Chase, MD 20815-7286; (301) 492-5990. Fax, (301) 492-5307. Edward F. Reilly Jr., Chair.
Web, www.usdoj.gov/uspc

Makes release decisions for all federal prisoners serving sentences of more than one year for offenses committed after October 31, 1987, and for D.C. Code offenders serving parolable offenses. Oversees compliance with conditions of release by paroled federal and D.C. Code offenders sentenced to supervised release.

U.S. Sentencing Commission, 1 Columbus Circle N.E., #2-500 South Lobby 20002-8002; (202) 502-4500. Fax, (202) 502-4699. Ricardo H. Hinojosa, Chair.
Web, www.ussc.gov

Establishes sentencing guidelines and policy for all federal courts, including guidelines prescribing the appropriate form and severity of punishment for those convicted of federal crimes. Provides training and research on sentencing-related issues. Serves as an information resource. Library open to the public.

Exhibit 7–1. Washington Information Directory 2006–2007, at 530 (2006).

Fed Agency Info Access

Federal Bureau of Prisons *(continued)*

Internal Affairs Chief **John Dignam** Room 600 . . . . (202) 307-3286

Senior Deputy Assistant Director for Program Review
    Michael W. Garrett Room 254 . . . . (202) 307-1076
                                                    Fax: (202) 616-2100

Ombudsman **Marcus Martin** Room 129 . . . . (202) 307-2266

Assistant Director/General Counsel
    Kathleen M. Kenney Room 958 . . . . (202) 307-3062
    Education: Catholic U 1988 BA;   Fax: (202) 307-2995
    Notre Dame 1992 JD

Deputy General Counsel **James Ropelewski** . . . . (202) 307-3062

Assistant Director for Administrative Division
    Bruce K. Sasser . . . . (202) 307-3123
    500 First Street, NW, 7th Floor,   Fax: (202) 514-9481
    Washington, DC 20530
    Education: William & Mary 1971 BA; Catholic U

Assistant Director for Correctional Programs Division
    John M. Vanyur Room 554 . . . . (202) 307-3226
    Education: Scranton MA; Maryland PhD   Fax: (202) 307-0509

Assistant Director for Health Services Division
    Newton E. Kendig Room 1054 . . . . (202) 307-3055
                                                    Fax: (202) 307-0826

Assistant Director for Human Resource Management
    Division **Whitney I. LeBlanc, Jr.** Room 454 . . . . (202) 307-3082
                                                    Fax: (202) 514-7015

Assistant Director for Industries, Education and
    Vocational Training Division **Steven B. Schwalb** . . . . . . (202) 305-3501
    400 First Street, NW, 8th Floor,   Fax: (202) 305-7340
    Washington, DC 20534
    Education: Washington U (MO) 1972 BA

Assistant Director for Information Policy and Public
    Affairs **Thomas R. Kane** Room 641 . . . . (202) 514-6537
    Education: SUNY (Albany) 1972 BA, 1981 MA,   Fax: (202) 616-2093
    PhD

Affirmative Action Administrator **Sandra Burks Farrior**
    Room 443 . . . . (202) 307-3175

Chief Public Information Officer **Traci Billingsley**
    Room 629 . . . . (202) 514-6551

US Public Health Service Commissioned Officer
    Newton E. Kendig Room 1054 . . . . (202) 307-3055
                                                    Fax: (202) 307-0826

Librarian **Denise W. Lomax** 7th Floor . . . . (202) 307-3029
    · E-mail: dlomax@bop.gov

Exhibit 7–2.   FEDERAL YELLOW BOOK 594 (Winter 2007).

29189

Rules and Regulations

Federal Register

Vol. 70, No. 97

Friday, May 20, 2005

DEPARTMENT OF JUSTICE

Bureau of Prisons

28 CFR Part 501

[BOP Docket No. 1117–F]

RIN 1120–AB17

Bureau of Prisons Emergencies

AGENCY: Bureau of Prisons, Justice.

ACTION: Final rule.

SUMMARY: The Bureau of Prisons (Bureau) makes this final rule to clarify that, when there is an institutional or system-wide Bureau emergency which the Director or designee considers a threat to human life or safety, the Director or designee may suspend the operation of the rules in this chapter as necessary to handle the emergency. This rule clarifies that the Director may suspend Bureau rules as needed in light of any emergency affecting the Bureau, and the Warden may do so to deal with emergencies at the institution level. This rule change clarifying the Director's authority to modify Bureau rules to handle emergencies is especially necessary in light of the recent terrorist attacks, threats to national security, threats of anthrax surrounding mail processing, and other events occurring on and after September 11, 2001.

DATES: This rule is effective June 20, 2005.

ADDRESSES: Rules Unit, Office of General Counsel, Bureau of Prisons, 320 First Street, NW., Washington, DC 20534.

FOR FURTHER INFORMATION CONTACT: Sarah Qureshi, Office of General Counsel, Bureau of Prisons, phone (202) 307–2105.

SUPPLEMENTARY INFORMATION: In this document, the Bureau finalizes an interim final rule we published on this subject on April 16, 2003 (68 FR 18544).

This Final rule clarifies that, when there is an institutional or system-wide Bureau emergency which the Director or designee considers a threat to human life or safety, the Director or designee may suspend the operation of the rules in this chapter as necessary to handle the emergency. This rule change clarifying the Director's authority to modify Bureau rules to handle emergencies is especially necessary in light of the continued threats of terrorist attacks, dangers to national security, and other events occurring on and after September 11, 2001.

Response to Comments

We received a total of four comments which raised similar issues. We will therefore address each of the issues raised instead of addressing each comment separately.

Authority To Suspend Rules

One commenter claimed that "[t]here is no authority to suspend the rules." This rule was promulgated on June 29, 1979 (44 FR 38244) and proposed on May 23, 1977 (42 FR 26334), along with several other core Bureau regulations. There were no amendments made to this rule after 1979, until the interim final rule was published in 2003. When we proposed this rule in 1977, we referred to 18 U.S.C. 4001 and 4042 as the authority for the rule.

18 U.S.C. 4001(b)(1) states that the Attorney General "shall promulgate rules for the government" of Federal penal and correctional institutions. Subsection (b)(2) also gives the Attorney General the authority to "provide for [inmates'] proper government, discipline, treatment, care, rehabilitation, and reformation." The Attorney General delegates these statutory rulemaking and custodial authorities to the Director of the Federal Bureau of Prisons in 28 CFR 0.96(o). 18 U.S.C. 4042(a) gives the Director of the Bureau of Prisons the authority to manage and regulate all Federal penal and correctional institutions and provide for the "safekeeping, care and subsistence" of inmates.

The Bureau's authority to promulgate rules, together with its authority to provide for the care and safekeeping of inmates, gives the Bureau implicit authority to create a rule that allows for the suspension of other rules as necessary in the limited situation of an emergency that threatens human life or safety.

Notice to Inmates

A commenter suggested that when rules are suspended, inmates should receive notice of the suspension immediately, including a description of the rules being suspended, a clear reason for the suspension and authority for suspension.

Because the reason for suspending the rules will necessarily involve an emergency, it will not always be practical or possible to provide notice to inmates of the specific circumstances surrounding suspension. However, the Bureau intends that inmates will be notified as soon as practicable of the suspension.

Administrative Remedies

Two commenters incorrectly assume that there is no way for an inmate to grieve a suspension of the rules. One commenter asked, "If the rules are suspended, does BOP waive any claim to administrative remedies regarding any incident occurring during the suspension period?" The Bureau will not waive claim to administrative remedies because inmates are permitted to follow the Administrative Remedy rules as set forth in 28 CFR part 542 to register complaints regarding incidents occurring during the suspension period.

Freedom of Information Act

A commenter asked whether the notice of suspension of rules, provided by the Warden to the Director, would be subject to release under the Freedom of Information Act (FOIA). The Warden's notice to the Director regarding suspension of the rules will be treated as any other Bureau document for the purposes of FOIA. Certain FOIA exemptions may apply, depending on the content of the notice.

Suspension of Rules Relating to Inmate Rights

Three commenters claimed that rule suspension would mean denial of Constitutional rights, such as attorney visits or other due process. Commenters asserted that there should never be a suspension of rules relating to other inmate programs or privileges, such as the Inmate Financial Responsibility Program, religious programs,

Exhibit 7–3.   Bureau of Prison Emergencies, 70 Fed. Reg. 29,189 (2005) (to be codified at 28 C.F.R. pt. 501).

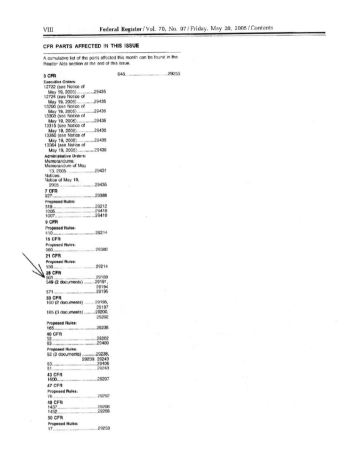

Exhibit 7–4. CFR Parts Affected in This Issue, FEDERAL REGISTER, May 20, 2005, at viii.

SUBCHAPTER A—GENERAL MANAGEMENT AND ADMINISTRATION

PART 500—GENERAL DEFINITIONS

AUTHORITY: 5 U.S.C. 301; 18 U.S.C. 3621, 3622, 3624, 4001, 4042, 4081, 4082 (Repealed in part as to offenses committed on or after November 1, 1987), 5006-5024 (Repealed October 12, 1984 as to offenses committed after that date), 5039; 28 U.S.C. 509, 510; 28 CFR 0.95-0.99.

§ 500.1 Definitions.

As used in this chapter,

(a) The *Warden* means the chief executive officer of a U.S. Penitentiary, Federal Correctional Institution, Medical Center for Federal Prisoners, Federal Prison Camp, Federal Detention Center, Metropolitan Correctional Center, or any federal penal or correctional institution or facility. *Warden* also includes any staff member with authority explicitly delegated by any chief executive officer.

(b) *Staff* means any employee of the Bureau of Prisons or Federal Prison Industries, Inc.

(c) *Inmate* means all persons in the custody of the Federal Bureau of Prisons or Bureau contract facilities, including persons charged with or convicted of offenses against the United States; D.C. Code felony offenders; and persons held as witnesses, detainees, or otherwise.

(d) *Institution* means a U.S. Penitentiary, a Federal Correctional Institution, a Federal Prison Camp, a Federal Detention Center, a Metropolitan Correctional Center, a Metropolitan Detention Center, a U.S. Medical Center for Federal Prisoners, a Federal Medical Center, or a Federal Transportation Center.

(e) *Shall* means an obligation is imposed.

(f) *May* means a discretionary right, privilege, or power is conferred.

(g) *May not* means a prohibition is imposed.

(h) *Contraband* is material prohibited by law, or by regulation, or material which can reasonably be expected to cause physical injury or adversely affect the security, safety, or good order of the institution.

(i) *Qualified health personnel* includes physicians, dentists, and other professional and technical workers who engage in activities within their respective levels of health care training or experience which support, complement, or supplement the administration of health care.

[44 FR 38244, June 29, 1979, as amended at 48 FR 48969, Oct. 21, 1983; 56 FR 31530, July 10, 1991; 63 FR 55775, Oct. 16, 1998; 66 FR 55065, Oct. 31, 2001]

PART 501—SCOPE OF RULES

Sec.
501.1 Bureau of Prisons emergencies.
501.2 National security cases.
501.3 Prevention of acts of violence and terrorism.

AUTHORITY: 5 U.S.C. 301; 18 U.S.C. 3621, 3622, 3624, 4001, 4042, 4081, 4082 (Repealed in part as to offenses committed on or after November 1, 1987), 4161-4166 (Repealed as to offenses committed on or after November 1, 1987), 5006-5024 (Repealed October 12, 1984 as to offenses committed after that date), 5039; 28 U.S.C. 509, 510.

§ 501.1 Bureau of Prisons emergencies.

(a) *Suspension of rules during an emergency.* The Director of the Bureau of Prisons (Bureau) may suspend operation of the rules in this chapter as necessary to handle an institutional emergency or an emergency affecting the Bureau. When there is an institutional emergency which the Director or Warden considers a threat to human life or safety, the Director or Warden may suspend the operation of the rules in this chapter as necessary to handle the emergency.

(b) *Responsibilities of the Warden*—(1) *Notifying the Director.* If the Warden suspends operation of the rules, the Warden must, within 24 hours of the suspension or as soon as practicable, notify the Director by providing written documentation which;

(i) Describes the institutional emergency that threatens human life or safety;

525

Exhibit 7–5. 28 C.F.R. §§ 500.1–501.1 (2006).

§ 501.2

(ii) Sets forth reasons why suspension of the rules is necessary to handle the institutional emergency;

(iii) Estimates how long suspension of the rules will last; and

(iv) Describes criteria which would allow normal rules application to resume.

(2) *Submitting certification to Director of continuing emergency.* 30 days after the Warden suspends operation of the rules, and every 30 days thereafter, the Warden must submit to the Director written certification that an institutional emergency threatening human life or safety and warranting suspension of the rules continues to exist. If the Warden does not submit this certification to the Director, or if the Director so orders at any time, the suspension of the rules will cease.

[70 FR 29191, May 20, 2005]

§ 501.2 National security cases.

(a) Upon direction of the Attorney General, the Director, Bureau of Prisons, may authorize the Warden to implement special administrative measures that are reasonably necessary to prevent disclosure of classified information upon written certification to the Attorney General by the head of a member agency of the United States intelligence community that the unauthorized disclosure of such information would pose a threat to the national security and that there is a danger that the inmate will disclose such information. These special administrative measures ordinarily may include housing the inmate in administrative detention and/or limiting certain privileges, including, but not limited to, correspondence, visiting, interviews with representatives of the news media, and use of the telephone, as is reasonably necessary to prevent the disclosure of classified information. The authority of the Director under this paragraph may not be delegated below the level of Acting Director.

(b) Designated staff shall provide to the affected inmate, as soon as practicable, written notification of the restrictions imposed and the basis for these restrictions. The notice's statement as to the basis may be limited in the interest of prison security or safety or national security. The inmate shall

sign for and receive a copy of the notification.

(c) Initial placement of an inmate in administrative detention and/or any limitation of the inmate's privileges in accordance with paragraph (a) of this section may be imposed for a period of time as determined by the Director, Bureau of Prisons, up to one year. Special restrictions imposed in accordance with paragraph (a) of this section may be extended thereafter by the Director, Bureau of Prisons, in increments not to exceed one year, but only if the Attorney General receives from the head of a member agency of the United States intelligence community an additional written certification that, based on the information available to the agency, there is a danger that the inmate will disclose classified information and that the unauthorized disclosure of such information would pose a threat to the national security. The authority of the Director under this paragraph may not be delegated below the level of Acting Director.

(d) The affected inmate may seek review of any special restrictions imposed in accordance with paragraph (a) of this section through the Administrative Remedy Program, 28 CFR part 542.

(e) Other appropriate officials of the Department of Justice having custody of persons for whom special administrative measures are required may exercise the same authorities under this section as the Director of the Bureau of Prisons and the Warden.

[62 FR 33732, June 20, 1997, as amended at 66 FR 55065, Oct. 31, 2001]

§ 501.3 Prevention of acts of violence and terrorism.

(a) Upon direction of the Attorney General, the Director, Bureau of Prisons, may authorize the Warden to implement special administrative measures that are reasonably necessary to protect persons against the risk of death or serious bodily injury. These procedures may be implemented upon written notification to the Director, Bureau of Prisons, by the Attorney General or, at the Attorney General's direction, by the head of a federal law enforcement agency, or the head of a member agency of the United States intelligence community, that there is a

Exhibit 7–6.   28 C.F.R. §§ 501.1–501.3 (2006).

MAY 2005

CHANGES JULY 1, 2004 THROUGH MAY 31, 2005

NOTE: **Boldface page numbers indicate 2004 changes.**

Exhibit 7–7. LSA: List of CFR Sections Affected, May 2005, at 35.

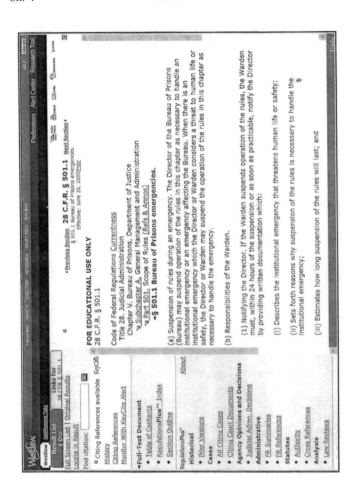

Exhibit 7–8.   28 C.F.R. § 501.1 (2006), WL 28 CFR § 501.1.

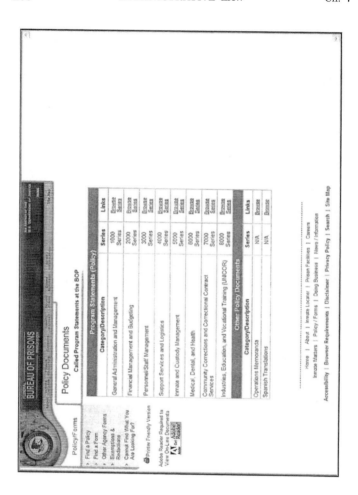

Exhibit 7–9. Policy Documents, Federal Bureau of Prisons <www.bop.gov>.

75373

Federal Register

Vol. 70, No. 242

Monday, December 19, 2005

Presidential Documents

Title 3—

The President

Executive Order 13392 of December 14, 2005

Improving Agency Disclosure of Information

By the authority vested in me as President by the Constitution and the laws of the United States of America, and to ensure appropriate agency disclosure of information, and consistent with the goals of section 552 of title 5, United States Code, it is hereby ordered as follows:

Section 1. *Policy.*

(a) The effective functioning of our constitutional democracy depends upon the participation in public life of a citizenry that is well informed. For nearly four decades, the Freedom of Information Act (FOIA) has provided an important means through which the public can obtain information regarding the activities of Federal agencies. Under the FOIA, the public can obtain records from any Federal agency, subject to the exemptions enacted by the Congress to protect information that must be held in confidence for the Government to function effectively or for other purposes.

(b) FOIA requesters are seeking a service from the Federal Government and should be treated as such. Accordingly, in responding to a FOIA request, agencies shall respond courteously and appropriately. Moreover, agencies shall provide FOIA requesters, and the public in general, with citizen-centered ways to learn about the FOIA process, about agency records that are publicly available (e.g., on the agency's website), and about the status of a person's FOIA request and appropriate information about the agency's response.

(c) Agency FOIA operations shall be both results-oriented and produce results. Accordingly, agencies shall process requests under the FOIA in an efficient and appropriate manner and achieve tangible, measurable improvements in FOIA processing. When an agency's FOIA program does not produce such results, it should be reformed, consistent with available resources appropriated by the Congress and applicable law, to increase efficiency and better reflect the policy goals and objectives of this order.

(d) A citizen-centered and results-oriented approach will improve service and performance, thereby strengthening compliance with the FOIA, and will help avoid disputes and related litigation.

Sec. 2. *Agency Chief FOIA Officers.*

(a) *Designation.* The head of each agency shall designate within 30 days of the date of this order a senior official of such agency (at the Assistant Secretary or equivalent level), to serve as the Chief FOIA Officer of that agency. The head of the agency shall promptly notify the Director of the Office of Management and Budget (OMB Director) and the Attorney General of such designation and of any changes thereafter in such designation.

(b) *General Duties.* The Chief FOIA Officer of each agency shall, subject to the authority of the head of the agency:

(i) have agency-wide responsibility for efficient and appropriate compliance with the FOIA;

(ii) monitor FOIA implementation throughout the agency, including through the use of meetings with the public to the extent deemed appropriate by the agency's Chief FOIA Officer, and keep the head of the agency, the chief legal officer of the agency, and the Attorney General appropriately informed of the agency's performance in implementing the FOIA, including the extent to which the agency meets the milestones

Exhibit 7–10. Exec. Order No. 13,392, 70 Fed. Reg. 75,373 (2005).

CHAPTER 8

COURT RULES AND PRACTICE

§ 8–1.   Introduction

This chapter covers a number of resources dealing with court proceedings and legal practice. Some, such as the rules governing trial procedures and lawyer conduct, have the force of law. Others, such as briefs and docket sheets, contain background information on decided cases or pending lawsuits. A third group, the directories and formbooks, provide practical assistance for lawyers or anyone else who needs to contact courts, draft documents, or transact other legal business.

Any litigator should be familiar with these materials, but their value extends to other legal research situations as well. All lawyers, of course, must follow rules of professional conduct, and sources such as briefs and model jury instructions can provide important information about substantive legal issues.

§ 8–2. Court Rules

Rules regulating court proceedings have the force of law, but they generally cannot supersede or conflict with statutes. Most jurisdictions have sets of rules governing trial and appellate procedure, as well as rules for specialized tribunals or for particular actions such as admiralty or habeas corpus. These rules are created in a variety of ways. Some are enacted by statute, but most are promulgated by the courts themselves or by conferences of judges.

a. Federal Rules

Under the Rules Enabling Act, 28 U.S.C. § 2072, federal courts have the power to adopt rules governing their procedures as long as they do not "abridge, enlarge, or modify any substantive right." Individual federal courts have had rules since the beginning of the judicial system, but the modern era of rules of national scope began with the adoption of the Federal Rules of Civil Procedure in 1938. These rules were prepared by a judicial advisory committee and approved by the Supreme Court, as were subsequent sets of rules governing criminal procedure (1946) and appellate procedure (1968). The Federal Rules of Evidence were originally drafted by judges, but they were enacted by Congress in 1975 due to their potential impact on substantive rights.

Most court rules are available at free Internet sites, but usually without the helpful commentary and annotations found in the treatises or annotated codes. The House Committee on the Judiciary provides PDF copies of the Federal Rules of Appellate Procedure, Civil Procedure, Criminal Procedure, and Evidence <judiciary. house.gov/Printshop.aspx?Section=1>. The Administrative Office of the U.S. Courts website has a section on rules <www.uscourts.gov.rules/>, which includes links to these sources as well as information on proposed amendments and numerous other documents.

Federal court rules are also available in a variety of pamphlets and reference publications. All of the major sets of rules are printed in the *U.S. Code*, accompanied by the advisory committee's explanatory comments after each section. *USCA* (in print and on Westlaw) and *USCS* (in print and on LexisNexis) also include annotations of cases in which the rules have been applied or construed, as well as other research aids such as references to treatises, law review articles, and legal encyclopedias. These annotations can be quite extensive; the Federal Rules of Civil Procedure, for example, occupy ten volumes in *USCA*.

A somewhat less overwhelming source of annotated federal rules is the *United States Supreme Court Digest, Lawyers' Edition*. Volumes 17 to 22 of this set include the text of the major rules series, as well as rules for specialized federal courts, accompanied by advisory committee comments, scholarly commentaries by National Institute for Trial Advocacy professors, and annotations of Supreme Court cases. While this is a less comprehensive source, it may be a useful starting point for someone seeking significant judicial interpretations of the rules.

The most extensive scholarly sources for analysis of the federal rules are the treatises on federal procedure,

Wright & Miller's *Federal Practice and Procedure* (1969–date) and *Moore's Federal Practice* (3d ed. 1997–date). These works are organized rule-by-rule, providing the texts and official comments accompanied by historical background and extensive discussion of cases. Both analyze the civil, criminal, and appellate rules; *Federal Practice and Procedure* also covers the Federal Rules of Evidence. These treatises are among the secondary sources most often cited by the federal courts. *Federal Practice and Procedure* is available on Westlaw, and *Moore's Federal Practice* is on LexisNexis. *Weinstein's Federal Evidence* (2d ed. 1997–date), also on LexisNexis, provides similar rule-by-rule treatment of the Federal Rules of Evidence.

Individual courts also have local rules to supplement the national sets of rules. Local court rules often detail procedural matters such as the time allowed to file papers, the format of documents, and the fees for filing various documents. The Supreme Court's rules are available online <www.supremecourtus.gov/ctrules/ctrules. html> and are also included in the *U.S. Code*, *USCA*, and *USCS*. The rules for each of the Courts of Appeals are also published in *USCA*, *USCS*, and several other sources including *Federal Procedure Rules Service* (which publishes a separate volume for each circuit).

Local rules from the entire country are published in a seven-volume looseleaf set, *Federal Local Court Rules* (3d ed. 2001–date). Local U.S. District Court rules are usually available in court rules pamphlets published for individual states. Exhibit 8–1 on page 311 shows Local Rule 83.5 of the United States District Court for the Northern District of Georgia, on the prohibition of weapons in the courthouse. This is from an annual publication called

Georgia Rules of Court Annotated, containing both state and federal rules. Note the case note and research references at the top of the page; some, but not all, state pamphlets include such annotations. Local court rules are also available on Westlaw and LexisNexis, although they may be found in databases with state court rules rather than with other federal materials.

Local rules are available on most individual courts' websites, and some sites also include answers to frequently asked questions about filing requirements and trial procedures. Links to local pages are also available through the U.S. Courts website <www.uscourts. gov/courtlinks.html>, and Law Library Resource Xchange provides a "Court Rules, Forms and Dockets" page <www.llrx.com/courtrules> listing more than 1,400 federal and state sources for these materials.

KeyCite and Shepard's coverage of federal court rules is similar to that for statutes. KeyCite begins with the annotations from *USCA*, but expands this to include additional cases and secondary sources. Shepard's treatment can be accessed online or in *Shepard's Federal Statute Citations*, and covers local rules as well as the major national sets.

The Federal Sentencing Guidelines are not court rules, but they occupy a similar position in the hierarchy of legal authorities. They were originally promulgated in 1987 by the U.S. Sentencing Commission, which was created by Congress as an independent agency within the judicial branch. The sentencing guidelines are not published with the official *U.S. Code*, but the commission publishes an annual *Guidelines Manual* in print and on the Internet <www.ussc.gov/guidelin.htm>.

Both *USCA* and *USCS* include annotated versions of the sentencing guidelines, accompanied by notes of court decisions and other references. Westlaw has the guidelines as part of the USCA database, annotated and covered by KeyCite, and in a separate Federal Criminal Justice—Federal Sentencing Guidelines (FCJ–FSG) database without notes or KeyCite references. The LexisNexis version, in the USCS file or in a folder of "Federal Sentencing, RICO & Class Action Materials," includes annotations and Shepard's links. In print, the guidelines are covered in *Shepard's Federal Statute Citations*.

Federal Practice and Procedure and *Moore's Federal Practice* do not cover sentencing guidelines, but shorter works such as Roger W. Haines, Jr., et al., *Federal Sentencing Guidelines Handbook: Text and Analysis*, and Thomas W. Hutchison et al., *Federal Sentencing Law and Practice*, provide similar treatment, combining the text of the guidelines with commentary and analysis of cases. Both of these are published in annual paperback editions, and the latter volume is available as the FSLP database on Westlaw.

b. State Rules

There are significant differences in rules and procedures from state to state, although these distinctions have decreased with the adoption by many states of provisions modeled on the federal rules. A few states have court procedures governed by statutory codes rather than rules.

The rules governing proceedings in state courts are usually included in the annotated state codes, accompanied by notes of relevant cases, as well as on Westlaw and LexisNexis. Coverage of state court rules in KeyCite and Shepard's is similar to that for statutes, with references to citations in federal and state court decisions, law reviews, and other sources.

Most states also have annual paperback volumes providing convenient access to rules and procedural statutes. Many of these publications are unannotated, but some contain useful case notes and comments by scholars or drafting committees. More elaborate practice sets in many jurisdictions include all of these features, often accompanied by procedural forms. Like *Federal Practice and Procedure* or *Moore's Federal Practice*, the best of these provide a scholarly commentary on the rules and extensive analysis of relevant case law.

Most state court websites provide convenient access to rules and other procedural information. The National Center for State Courts' "Court Web Sites" <www.ncsconline.org/D_KIS/info_court_web_sites.html> provides access to these sites.

§ 8–3. Legal Ethics

In most jurisdictions, courts are responsible for governing the professional activities of lawyers, although in some states that power is delegated to bar associations or oversight boards. The materials in this area are found in a distinct body of literature consisting of codified rules of conduct, ethics opinions, and disciplinary decisions. An ethics opinion is an advisory document, usually issued by a bar association, analyzing how lawyers or judges should handle a particular or hypothetical problem, while disciplinary decisions punish specific acts of misconduct.

While rules vary from state to state, most jurisdictions have adopted some form of the Model Rules of Professional Conduct, promulgated by the American Bar Association in 1983. A few states still have rules based on the ABA's older Model Code of Professional Responsibility (1969). The rules in force are usually included in the volumes containing a state's court rules, although in some states they are incorporated into longer sets of rules and can be a bit difficult to find. Only a few of these sources are annotated with notes of decisions under the rules. The *National Reporter on Legal Ethics and Professional Responsibility* (1982–date), a looseleaf service, reprints the unannotated rules for every state as well as the District of Columbia and Puerto Rico. The American Legal Ethics Library at Cornell's Legal Information Institute <www.law.cornell.edu/ethics/> provides links to websites providing the rules in force in each state.

Annotated Model Rules of Professional Conduct (5th ed. 2003) provides the text of the ABA rules with comments, legal background, and notes of decisions from various jurisdictions. Although it contains the ABA's rules rather than those adopted in any specific state, this is a useful source for comparative analysis and commentary. The annotated rules are available online from Westlaw; LexisNexis has the Model Rules with official comments but no background notes and annotations. The ABA Center for Professional Responsibility <www.abanet.org/cpr/> has the text of both Code and Rules, as well as a directory of lawyer disciplinary agencies and a wide range of other information and documents on legal ethics.

The American Law Institute has also formulated basic rules of legal ethics in its *Restatement of the Law: The Law Governing Lawyers* (2000), and the two approaches have been compared in an ABA publication by Thomas D. Morgan, *Lawyer Law: Comparing the ABA Model Rules of Professional Conduct with the ALI Restatement (Third) of the Law Governing Lawyers* (2005). For a more general discussion, the leading modern treatise on legal ethics is Geoffrey C. Hazard, Jr. & W. William Hodes, *The Law of Lawyering* (3d ed. 2000–date).

Ethics opinions, generally prepared in response to inquiries from attorneys, are issued by the American Bar Association and by state and local bar associations. ABA opinions are available on Westlaw and LexisNexis, as are opinions from selected state and local bars. Ethics opinions can also be found in the *National Reporter on Legal Ethics and Professional Responsibility*, and most state bars have some sort of publication either summarizing their opinions or reprinting them in full text.

State bars and disciplinary agencies generally have websites providing information about procedures for filing complaints and resolving problems with lawyers, and some of these include the text of rules and ethics opinions. The ABA and Cornell sites mentioned above both include links to these sites.

The *ABA/BNA Lawyers' Manual on Professional Conduct* (1984–date) is often a good place to begin research. This looseleaf service includes an extensive commentary with background and practical tips, as well as news of developments and abstracts of new decisions.

Judges are governed by a separate set of rules, in almost every jurisdiction based either on the ABA's 1990 Model Code of Judicial Conduct or its 1972 predecessor. These rules are generally published in state court rules pamphlets with the rules of professional conduct. The Model Code is available on the ABA Center for Professional Responsibility's website <www.abanet.org/cpr/>, and Cornell's American Legal Ethics Library provides links to state versions. The ABA has published an *Annotated Model Code of Judicial Conduct* (2004), and Jeffrey M. Shaman et al., *Judicial Conduct and Ethics* (3d ed. 2000), provides extensive analysis of issues in this area.

§ 8–4.   Records and Briefs

The materials submitted by the parties in appellate court cases are often available for research use. Briefs are the written arguments and authorities cited by the attorneys for the parties on appeal. Records are documents from the lower court proceeding, including pleadings, motions, trial transcripts, and judgments, usually reprinted as an appendix to the briefs. Records and briefs are usually filed by the docket number of the case in which they were submitted. These documents enable researchers to study in detail the arguments and facts of significant decisions.

Print United States Supreme Court records and briefs go to several libraries around the country, while many more libraries subscribe to microform editions. Free online sources include FindLaw <supreme.lp.findlaw.com/supreme_court/briefs/>, which has current and recent briefs back to 1999, and the Curiae Project <curiae.law.yale.edu>, which provides access to documents filed in major historical cases. Filings since 1979 are available online through LexisNexis, and Westlaw coverage begins in 1990. Retrospective electronic coverage is offered by Thomson Gale's *The Making of Modern Law: U.S. Supreme Court Records and Briefs, 1832–1978* <www.gale.com/SupremeCourt/>. Many cases have a substantial number of briefs, often with filings by *amici curiae* ("friends of the court") supporting one side or the other.

Transcripts of Supreme Court oral arguments are also available in various formats. Microform collections begin with the 1953 term, and online coverage starts in 1979 (LexisNexis) or 1990 (Westlaw). The Supreme Court website <www.supremecourtus.gov> provides PDF transcripts of arguments available later the same day, with older arguments beginning with the 2000 term. Oyez: U.S. Supreme Court Media <www.oyez.com> has more than 3000 hours of recorded arguments dating back to 1955.

Briefs and argument transcripts for hundreds of major cases, dating back to the 19th century, are reprinted in *Landmark Briefs and Arguments of the Supreme Court of the United States: Constitutional Law* (1975–date). Cases through the 1973 term are covered in the first eighty volumes of this set, and about a dozen new cases are added each year.

One way to determine the status of a Supreme Court case or to identify documents is through the Court's website <www.supremecourtus.gov>, which provides information on cases pending on the docket, schedules of upcoming oral arguments, and other information. The docket, which provides for each case a chronological listing of documents filed and actions taken, has current coverage and historical information back to 2001.

Another source for information on the Supreme Court's docket is *The United States Law Week*, which publishes a record of the Court's proceedings and reports on arguments and other developments. *Law Week* includes a "Topical Index and Table of Cases," which provides references to cases on the Court's docket. These entries can be confusing at first, because page references are provided only if an opinion has been issued. Other entries (for cases pending on the docket or those in which review has been denied) simply provide a docket number; to find more information it is necessary to turn to a "Case Status Report" table for page references. These index features are indicated in Exhibit 8–2 on page 312, showing entries referring to *Muscarello v. United States*, the case shown in Chapter 3. *U.S. Law Week* is also available online as a subscription-based Internet service <www.bna.com/products/lit/uslw.htm>. The *Supreme Court Today* section of the site provides several ways to track Supreme Court cases and is continuously updated with new decisions, filings, and other developments.

Records and briefs of the U.S. Courts of Appeals and state appellate courts are not as widely available as those from the U.S. Supreme Court, but briefs in many recent cases are now available on Westlaw. Coverage for some courts extends back into the 1970s, while for others it does not start until 2004. Some court websites also provide access to recent briefs. For federal courts, the fee-based information system PACER (Public Access to Court Electronic Records) provides docket information and some briefs and other documents. Each court has its own PACER site, but the system has a central registration process <pacer.psc.uscourts.gov> and a national index of cases by party name. The main PACER site has links to the individual courts' sites.

In most instances, appellate court records and briefs can also be found in local law libraries within the circuit or state. For some cases, however, it may be necessary to contact the court or a judicial records center to obtain copies. Michael Whiteman & Peter Scott Campbell, *A Union List of Appellate Court Records and Briefs: Federal and State* (1999) provides contact information for court clerks and libraries, with notes indicating the scope and format of each library's holdings and its lending policy.

Some briefs are available on the Internet even if not on court websites. Parties or *amici curiae* may post their briefs in major cases, and high profile documents are often available from sites such as FindLaw <news.findlaw.com> or CNN <www.cnn.com>. The "Resources–Legal Cases and Documents" link on the U.S. Department of Justice homepage <www.usdoj.gov> provides access to briefs and other materials prepared by the department's divisions and offices, including Solicitor General briefs in the Supreme Court since 1997. "A Brief Summary: Finding Briefs on the Web" <www.legaline.com/freebriefslinks.html> provides links to several dozen sites where briefs may be available.

§ 8–5. Other Case Information

Appellate cases generally follow a standard path and produce documentation consisting of the parties' briefs, the lower court record, and the court's opinion. Material from trial court litigation, on the other hand, may be harder to identify and find. Some cases result in judges' opinions, such as a decision granting a motion for summary judgment, but many matters are decided without a written opinion. Cases may be decided by jury verdict, summary disposition, or settlement agreement. Some cases produce dozens of memoranda or briefs submitted to support or oppose motions before, during and after trial, while others go to trial without any written submissions on points of law. It may be possible to examine a trial transcript; this can be an essential but voluminous source of information. News reports may provide some discussion of trial court proceedings, but to obtain a transcript or other documents it is usually necessary to contact the court directly. For cases since 2000, Westlaw has a growing collection of pleadings, memoranda, and trial motions from both federal and state courts.

Documents submitted in a case are kept on file at the courthouse or a records center. Many courts are developing electronic systems in which pleadings and other documents are submitted and retained online, but paper filings remain common. Determining the case number or docket number is usually the first step in obtaining documents. This number may be mentioned in a published decision or secondary source, but it might be necessary to ask the court clerk to consult an index by party name. Each case has a docket sheet listing the proceedings and documents filed, providing the information needed to obtain documents. Some courts accept requests electronically or by telephone, while for others it is necessary to apply by mail or in person.

In many instances, access to docket sheet information for pending cases is available electronically. The federal courts' PACER system <pacer.psc.uscourts.gov> covers each of the U.S. District Courts and Bankruptcy Courts, in addition to the Courts of Appeals. As electronic filing becomes the norm, more and more pleadings, motions, and other documents are available through PACER along with docket information.

While docket information for some state courts is available online, for others it may be more difficult to obtain.

Most states have electronic docket systems, but means of access vary. In 2002 the Center for Democracy & Technology prepared an extensive state-by-state guide <www. cdt.org/publications/020821courtrecords.shtml> indicating the information available and providing links to court sites in each jurisdiction.

Westlaw can be used to monitor docket information in the federal courts and in some state courts. Its dockets databases, including DOCK–ALL combining federal and state dockets, provide a broader range of search options than official sites, and individual dockets can be tracked for e-mailed updates of new developments. Other commercial subscription services, such as Legal Dockets Online <www.legaldockets.com> and LexisNexis CourtLink <courtlink.lexisnexis.com>, may also provide more convenient and current access to docket information.

Access methods for both federal and state courts are explained in *The Sourcebook to Public Record Information: The Comprehensive Guide to County, State, & Federal Public Records Sources* (annual). This book also explains how to obtain access to other public records, such as property and licensing information, much of which is now available through state and local government websites. Links to free public record sites are available from Pretrieve <www.pretrieve.com> and BRB Publications <www.brbpub.com/pubrecsites.asp>. Extensive public record databases are also available through subscription-based commercial services, including Westlaw and LexisNexis, although access through academic subscriptions may be limited.

§ 8–6. Directories of Courts and Judges

Court directories serve a number of purposes. They provide contact information for clerks' offices, and some include judges' biographical data. This can be useful information for litigants appearing before a particular judge or panel; in law schools, the heaviest use of court directories is by students applying for clerkships after graduation. Most court websites also provide names and contact information, and sometimes biographies; these are accessible through portals such as the "Court Links" section of the federal judiciary homepage <www.uscourts.gov/courtlinks/>.

A number of directories provide information about federal courts and judges. *Judicial Staff Directory* and *Judicial Yellow Book* (both semiannual) include basic biographical information for judges, as well as extensive listings of court personnel such as clerks and staff attorneys. Like other volumes in the Staff Directories and Yellow Books series, these are available electronically as well as in print. A two-volume looseleaf publication, *Almanac of the Federal Judiciary*, is the most thorough source for biographical information, including noteworthy rulings, media coverage, and lawyers' evaluations of the judge's ability and temperament. CQ Press's *Federal-State Court Directory* (annual) provides a concise listing of contact information for federal judges, clerks, and other court personnel.

Several directories cover both federal and state courts. *BNA's Directory of State and Federal Courts, Judges, and Clerks* (annual) provides addresses and telephone numbers, and includes a list of Internet sites and a personal name index. *The American Bench* (annual) is the most comprehensive biographical source, covering almost every judge in the United States. It includes an Alphabetical Name Index indicating the jurisdictions for all judges listed. *Judicial Yellow Book* includes state appellate courts but not trial courts, and *Federal-State Court Directory* has just one page per state listing a few key officials. CQ Press provides more thorough coverage in its *Directory of State Court Clerks & County Courthouses* (annual). As noted in Chapter 3 on page 87, *BNA's Directory* and CQ Press's *Federal-State Court Directory* both include charts explaining the structure of each court's judicial system.

Sometimes information is needed about a judge involved in an older case or sitting on a particular court. If only the last name at the head of an opinion is known, the first step may be to determine a judge's full name. This can be found in tables in the front of most reporter volumes. For example, since 1882 the *Federal Reporter* has listed the sitting federal judges, with footnotes indicating any changes since the previous volume. Similar listings appear in each of West's regional reporters and in most official state reports. Biographical information on most appellate judges can be found in standard sources such as *American National Biography* (1999) or *Who Was Who in America* (1943–date). The Federal Judicial Center website <www.fjc.gov> has a database providing biographical information about all life-tenured federal judges since 1789. Entries include links to information about manuscript sources and lists of more extensive biographical sources, where available.

§ 8–7. Formbooks and Jury Instructions

In the course of legal practice, many basic transactions and court filings occur with regularity. Rather than redraft these documents each time, attorneys frequently work from sample versions of standard legal documents and instruments. Model forms are available from a variety of sources, in both printed collections and electronic products. Some sets of forms are annotated with discussion of the underlying laws, checklists of steps in completing the forms, and citations to cases in which the forms were in issue.

Several multivolume compilations of forms, with extensive indexing, notes and cross-references, are published. Some of these are comprehensive national works containing both procedural forms, such as complaints and motions, and transactional forms, such as contracts and wills. Most, however, are limited to particular jurisdictions or particular types of forms.

Two of the major national form sets are published as adjuncts to *American Jurisprudence 2d* and are linked to that encyclopedia by frequent cross-references. *American Jurisprudence Legal Forms 2d* (1971–date) provides forms of instruments such as contracts, leases, and wills, and *American Jurisprudence Pleading and Practice Forms* (rev ed., 1966–date) focuses on litigation and other practice before courts and administrative agencies. Both sets are divided into several hundred topical chapters mirroring the organization of *Am. Jur. 2d*. Exhibit 8–3 on page 312 shows a page from *Am. Jur. Pleading and Practice Forms*, containing the beginning of a model complaint by a city or county against handgun manufacturers and distributors.

Other comprehensive sets include Jacob Rabkin & Mark H. Johnson, *Current Legal Forms, with Tax Analysis* (1948–date), and *West's Legal Forms* (2d ed. 1981–date). Unlike the *Am. Jur.* sets, these are arranged by broad practice area such as estate planning or real estate. They may be better for understanding a wider range of related issues than for finding forms on very fact-specific topics.

Three major sets devoted to forms used in federal practice are *Bender's Federal Practice Forms* (1951– date), *Federal Procedural Forms, Lawyers' Edition* (1975–date) and *West's Federal Forms* (1952–date). Each of these has a different structure. *Bender's Federal Practice Forms* is arranged by court rule. *Federal Procedural Forms, Lawyers' Edition* is a companion to Thomson West's encyclopedic *Federal Procedure, Lawyers' Edition*, and is organized similarly, with several dozen subject chapters. *West's Federal Forms* is arranged instead by court, with separate volumes covering forms needed in the Supreme Court, Courts of Appeals, District Courts, Bankruptcy Courts, and specialized national courts such as the Court of Federal Claims.

Sets of forms, varying in complexity and size, are also published for most states and for particular subject areas. Some sets, such as *Bender's Forms of Discovery* (1963–date), are geared toward specific stages of litigation. Practice-oriented treatises and manuals frequently include appendices of sample forms, and in some states compilations of official forms are issued in conjunction with statutory codes.

Several sets of forms are available online and on CD– ROM, streamlining the drafting process by eliminating the need to retype. LexisNexis provides access to *Bender's Federal Practice Forms* and *Bender's Forms of Discovery*, while Westlaw has both *Am. Jur.* form sets, *Federal Procedural Forms*, and numerous state-specific collections. Westlaw has two broad multi-jurisdictional databases, FORMS–ALL combining the various publish-ed sets and ALLFRMS with more than 45,000 official forms from federal and state courts and agencies.

A more limited range of forms is available from free Internet sites, but these may be satisfactory for simple transactions or court filings. LexisONE <www.lexisone. com> provides free access to more than 6,000 forms, listed topically and by jurisdiction. FindLaw <forms.lp.findlaw.com> has links to official sites for federal circuits and states, as well as an extensive list of sites providing free and fee-based legal forms. Before using any form, particularly one found at a free website, it is necessary to make sure that it conforms with the law of the jurisdiction.

Most jurisdictions have published sets of *model* or *pattern jury instructions*, used by judges to explain the applicable law to jurors before they weigh the evidence and reach their decisions. Model jury instructions can be useful as forms, and they also provide a concise summary of a jurisdiction's ruling law on the issues covered. Some of these sets of instructions are published by state court systems, and others by bar associations. Still others are unofficial but highly respected, such as Kevin F. O'Mal-ley et al., *Federal Jury Practice and Instructions* (5th & 6th eds. 2000–date). The subject heading used by the Library of Congress and in most online catalogs for these sets is "Instructions to juries–[Jurisdiction]." Exhibit 8–4 on page 314 shows a page from *Federal Jury Practice and Instructions* with a sample instruction for the defini-tion of "uses or carries a firearm."

Some court websites provide model jury instructions, and both Westlaw and LexisNexis include instructions for federal courts and for several states. Westlaw has

Federal Jury Practice and Instructions and publications for about twenty-eight states, while LexisNexis provides the competing *Modern Federal Jury Instructions* and instructions for about seventeen states. Westlaw also has a growing collection of actual jury instruction filings used in recent cases.

§ 8–8. Conclusion

Court rules have taken a back seat in earlier chapters to more substantive sources such as judicial decisions and statutes, but they have the force of law and can be vital in determining procedural rights. Some rules, such as those establishing the principles of legal ethics, must be known and followed by every practicing attorney.

Many of the other materials discussed in this chapter are primarily of use in litigation, but a working knowledge is essential in dealing with many other aspects of the legal system as well. Court documents and docket information can be useful for evaluating potential clients or commercial partners, and forms for contracts, deeds and other instruments can be just as valuable and time-saving as litigation forms.

LR 83.4. RESTRICTIONS ON MEDIA AND RELEASE OF INFORMATION.

A. *Television and Radio Broadcasting, Tape Recording, or Photographing Judicial Proceedings.* — The taking of photographs and operation of tape recorders in the courthouse and radio or television broadcasting from the courthouse during the progress of or in connection with judicial proceedings, including proceedings before a United States Magistrate Judge, whether or not court is actually in session, is prohibited. A judicial officer may, however, permit (1) the use of electronic or photographic means for the presentation of evidence or the perpetuation of a record, and (2) the broadcasting, televising, recording, or photographing of investiture, ceremonial, or naturalization proceedings.

Cameras and/or any electronic devices equipped with cameras, including cellular telephones, personal digital assistants and laptop computers, will not be allowed into the courthouses of this district except by court order or by direct escort and supervision of an employee of a federal agency whose offices are located therein.

To facilitate the enforcement of this rule, no photographic, broadcasting, sound or recording equipment other than the recording equipment of the United States magistrate judges and the official court reporters, will be permitted to be operated on the floors of the courthouse occupied by the court, except as otherwise permitted by order of the judicial officer before whom the particular case or proceeding is pending.

Portable computers, cellular telephones, pagers and personal communication devices without cameras may be transported onto floors occupied by the court; however, these devices shall not be operated in any courtroom or hearing room nor shall they be operated in any public area where their operation is disruptive of any court proceeding unless otherwise permitted by order of the court.

All electronic photographic, broadcasting, sound or recording equipment brought into the courthouses shall be subject to inspection by the United States Marshals' Service.

B. *Provisions for Special Orders in Widely Publicized or Sensational Civil Cases.* — In a widely publicized or sensational civil case, the court, on motion of either party or on its own motion, may issue a special order governing such matters as extra-judicial statements by parties and witnesses likely to interfere with the rights of the parties or the rights of the accused to a fair trial by an impartial jury; the seating and conduct in the courtroom of spectators and news media representatives; the management and sequestration of jurors and witnesses; and any other matters which the court may deem appropriate for inclusion in such an order.

Editor's notes. — This rule was amended effective March 1, 2006.

JUDICIAL DECISIONS

es, 659 F.2d

1078 (5th Cir. 1981).

RESEARCH REFERENCES

Am. Jur. 2d. — 7 Am. Jur. 2d, Attorneys at Law, §§ 41, 119. 75 Am. Jur. 2d, Trial, §§ 196-204. **C.J.S.** — 7 C.J.S., Attorneys at Law, § 52. 16

C.J.S., Constitutional Law, § 213. 23 C.J.S., Criminal Law, § 1134-1141.

LR 83.5. WEAPONS NOT ALLOWED IN COURTHOUSE.

A. *Weapons Not Allowed.* — Firearms or other weapons shall not be worn or brought into the courtrooms of this court or into the buildings in which they are located, except with the specific authorization of the court. The court has excused, to the extent hereinafter stated, the following persons or groups from this rule:

(1) The United States Marshal and his duly assigned deputy marshals, court security officers and other security personnel engaged by the U.S. Marshal.

(2) Federal Protective Service officers on assignment or upon call.

(3) Any federal law enforcement officer presenting a prisoner before a magistrate judge for initial appearance.

Exhibit 8–1. N.D. Ga. R. 83.4–83.5, *reprinted in* GEORGIA RULES OF COURT ANNOTATED 1181 (LexisNexis 2007).

Firearms and other weapons

Drug offenses, gun use in relation to

—Guilty pleas, subsequent ruling decriminalizing facts upon which plea based, defendant may collaterally attack conviction if able to overcome procedural default by showing actual innocence, 96-8516; ▶ 4346; no ruling in companion cases, 96-1440; 97-1721

--Locked glove compartment or trunk is "carrying," 96-1654; 96-8837; ▶ 4459

—Pickup bed, truck driven by trafficker, "carrying." 97-1623

Murphy v. Sofamor Danek Group Inc., 97-1265
Murphy v. United Parcel Service Inc., 97-1992
Murphy Bros. Inc. v. Michetti Pipe Stringing Inc., 97-1909
Murr v. U.S., 97-11
Murray; Lawson v., 97-1790
Murray v. Trans Union Corp., 97-51
Muscarello v. U.S., 96-1654; ▶ 66:4459
Musco Corp. v. Qualite Inc., 96-1889
Muskogee, Okla. v. Allen, 97-978

96-1653	filed (4/17/97) 66:3026, sum 66:3054, rev den (10/06/97) 66:3254
96-1654	filed (4/18/97) 66:3026, sum 66:3045, rev grant (12/12/97) 66:3416, interim order (03/09/98) 66:3590, oral arg (03/23/98) 66:3673, dec (06/08/98) ▶ 66:4459
96-1661	filed (4/15/97) 66:3026, sum 66:3064, rev den (10/06/97) 66:3254
96-1680	filed (4/21/97) 66:3026, sum 66:3047, judg aff (10/06/97) 66:3253

Exhibit 8–2. Excerpts from THE UNITED STATES LAW WEEK Supreme Court Index, Table of Cases, and Case Status Report (1997–98).

§ 9 Complaint, petition, or declaration—By political subdivision—Against manufacturers and distributors of handguns, and their trade associations— Dangerous instrumentalities; handguns—Products liability; unreasonably dangerous and negligent design; inadequate warning; unjust enrichment; nuisance abatement; negligence

[Title of Court]

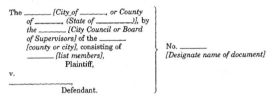

The _____ *[City of _____, or County of _____, (State of _____)], by the _____ [City Council or Board of Supervisors]* of the _____ *[county or city],* consisting of _____ *[list members],*
          Plaintiff,

v.

_____,
          Defendant.

No. _____
[Designate name of document]

COMPLAINT

I. NATURE OF THE CASE

1. _____ *[Name of mayor],* the duly elected and present Mayor of the City of _____, brings this action on behalf of _____ *[himself or herself]* and the City of _____ (sometimes here referred to as "the City"), and respectfully represents that under the Charter of the City of _____, the Mayor is charged with the duty to "define, prohibit, abate, suppress, and prevent all things detrimental to the health, morals, conduct, safety, convenience and welfare of the inhabitants of the City, and all nuisances and causes thereof."

2. Pursuant to the Charter of the City of _____ and under the Constitution of the State of _____, the Mayor and the City of _____ are responsible for the general health, safety, and welfare of its citizens. The Mayor has a duty to protect the interests of the general public.

3. As a result of the manufacturing, marketing, promotion, and sale of firearms which, under _____ *[state]* law, are defective in design and fail to incorporate firearm safety features designed to prevent harm caused by foreseeable human error making the firearms unreasonably dangerous, the City and its citizens have suffered harm and have incurred substantial expenses. In addition to the defective designs and failure to incorporate feasible safety features, defendants' guns are unreasonably dangerous as they can be and are fired by unauthorized users, including, but not limited to children, criminals, mentally unstable persons, and others who put themselves and/or others at risk when they possess a firearm.

4. This action is brought to recover damages and other equitable relief as may be obtained, for the harm unjustly, intentionally and wrongfully done and that continues to be done to the City and its citizens by defendants, who have been and continue to be unjustly enriched by such harm at the expense of the City and its residents.

115

Exhibit 8–3. 25 AM. JUR. PLEADING & PRACTICE FORMS *Weapons and Firearms* § 9 (2001).

purposes and a determination of the elements of that offense. Taylor, 495 U.S. at 602, 110 S.Ct. at 2160.

The Eighth Circuit held in United States v. Matra, 841 F.2d 837, 843 (8th Cir.1988), that possession of cocaine with intent to distribute is a "drug trafficking crime" within the meaning of Section 924(c). Affirming the defendant's conviction, the Eighth Circuit wrote,

> Section 924(c)(2) defines a "drug trafficking crime" as "any felony violation of Federal law involving the distribution, manufacture, or importation of any controlled substance." 18 U.S.C.A. § 924(c)(2) (Supp.1987). "When we find the terms of a statute unambiguous, judicial inquiry is complete.... " Rubin v. United States, 449 U.S. 424, 430, 101 S.Ct. 698, 701, 66 L.Ed.2d 633 (1981). (footnote omitted) Giving effect to the plain language of this statute, we conclude that violations "involving" the distribution, manufacture, or importation of controlled substances must be read as including more than the crimes of distribution, manufacture, or importation. The crime of possession of cocaine with intent to distribute, of which Matra stands convicted, requires proof of the defendant's specific intent to distribute. It is clearly a crime "involving" the distribution of cocaine.

§ 39.20 "Uses or Carries a Firearm"—Defined

The phrase "uses or carries a firearm" means having a firearm, or firearms, available to assist or aid in the commission of the crime alleged in Count ___ of the indictment.

In determining whether Defendant _____ used or carried a firearm, you may consider all of the factors received in evidence in the case including the nature of the underlying crime of violence or drug trafficking alleged, the proximity of the defendant to the firearm in question, the usefulness of the firearm to the crime alleged, and the circumstances surrounding the presence of the firearm.

The government is not required to show that Defendant _____ actually displayed or fired the weapon. The government is required, however, to prove beyond a reasonable doubt that the firearm was in the defendant's possession or under the defendant's control at the time that a crime of violence or drug trafficking crime was committed.

95

Exhibit 8–4. 2A FEDERAL JURY PRACTICE AND INSTRUCTIONS § 39.20 (Kevin F. O'Malley et al. eds., 5th ed. 2000).

CHAPTER 9

TOPICAL RESEARCH SOURCES

―――――――――

―――――――――

§ 9–1. Introduction

The resources many lawyers turn to most often are tools narrowly designed for use in specialized areas of law, rather than the general codes, digests, and databases discussed thus far. Topical looseleaf and electronic services make lawyers' work easier by compiling related statutes, cases, and regulations in one location, along with explanations, forms, and other research aids. These services also provide the current awareness lawyers need to respond to and anticipate new legal developments, such as recently decided cases or proposed regulations. These are essential tools for specialists, and other researchers can make profitable use of them as well.

Specialized insights beyond those available from a general research guide such as this *Nutshell* may be available in works focusing on specific topics. Many guides (sometimes called "pathfinders") have been published in legal bibliography journals such as *Law Library Journal*, *Legal Reference Services Quarterly*, and LLRX.com <www.llrx.com>; and law library websites often provide guidance on legal research issues in their home jurisdictions. Penny A. Hazelton, ed., *Specialized Legal Research* (1987–date), covers more than a dozen topics, with chapters on admiralty, banking law, copyright, customs, environmental law, government contracts, immigration, income tax, labor and employment law, military and veterans law, patents and trademarks, securities regulation, and the Uniform Commercial Code. The volume also includes a bibliography of other specialized legal research sources. Tax research is the focus of several published works, including Robert L. Gardner et al., *Tax Research Techniques* (7th ed. 2005), and Barbara H. Karlin, *Tax Research* (3d ed. 2006).

§ 9–2. Looseleaf Services

A looseleaf service is a resource published in a binder and frequently supplemented, focusing on a specific subject area and containing primary legal sources, finding aids, and secondary material. The best looseleaf services provide coordinated access to a diverse collection of documents as well as prompt notice of developments in the courts, legislatures, and agencies. Even though more research is now done online than with print resources, many lawyers keep looseleaf services near their desks because they provide such convenient and comprehensive coverage of a specialized area.

The first looseleaf services were issued just before World War I to facilitate research in the new federal income tax law. By the 1930s other services had developed in heavily regulated areas such as labor law, antitrust, and securities. Services are now also published in such varied areas as criminal law, environmental protection, health care, and products liability.

There are several ways to determine whether a service is published in a particular area of interest. References to looseleaf services may appear in law review articles and cases, and lawyers or professors specializing in a field can provide helpful advice. The annual directory *Legal Looseleafs in Print* includes regularly supplemented services, although it also lists numerous publications that are not updated very frequently. At the end of this volume, Appendix C provides a selected list of looseleaf and electronic services in fields of major interest.

There are two basic types of looseleaf services, *newsletter* and *interfiled*. In a newsletter service, new issues simply supplement the existing compilation and do not replace pages already filed. Newsletter services are useful in areas where it is necessary to monitor new developments from a variety of sources. *The United States Law Week*, published by the Bureau of National Affairs (BNA), is representative of the genre. Other BNA services, such as *Antitrust & Trade Regulation Report*, *Criminal Law Reporter*, *Family Law Reporter*, and *Securities Regulation & Law Report,* serve as major current awareness tools in their fields.

Interfiled services, on the other hand, are updated by replacing superseded material with revised pages. New pages are inserted where appropriate, rather than simply added at the end. Page numbering is designed to facilitate filing of new material and can be rather convoluted; pages 603–1 to 603–24 may be inserted, for example, between pages 603 and 604. To help researchers find specific references, many interfiled services assign *paragraph numbers* to each section of material. A "paragraph" in this sense can vary in length from a few sentences to several pages. Each code section, for example, may be assigned one paragraph number, regardless of its length. It retains this number no matter how many new pages are added to the service. Paragraph numbers, not page numbers, are generally used in indexes and cross-references.

Interfiled services are well suited to areas in which it is essential to integrate recent legal developments with a large body of primary sources such as statutes or regulations. CCH (formerly Commerce Clearing House) publishes a wide variety of interfiled services, such as *Federal Securities Law Reports*, *Standard Federal Tax Reports*, and *Trade Regulation Reports*.

Some services have the attributes of both newsletter and interfiled services, with current awareness pamphlets and regularly updated compilations of primary sources. Whatever form it takes, a looseleaf service must be frequently supplemented if it is to be a trustworthy resource. Most of the major services are updated weekly or biweekly. Many treatises are also published in looseleaf binders, but they are not looseleaf *services* if they are only updated once or twice a year.

Looseleaf services cover a wide range of subjects, and no two services are exactly alike. The access methods and organization vary according to the nature of the primary sources, the characteristics of the legal field, and the editorial approach. In areas where one major statute dominates the legal order, the service may be arranged by statutory sections or divisions. Most federal tax services, for example, are structured according to the sections of the Internal Revenue Code. If several statutes are significant, the service can be divided into areas by the relevant statutes. Labor law services, for example, offer separate treatment of the Labor Management Relations Act, Title VII of the Civil Rights Act of 1964, and the Fair Labor Standards Act. In other fields where common law or judicial rules predominate, or where there is a mixture of case and statutory law (such as family law, trusts and estates, or corporations), the service may be arranged by subject.

Despite differences in organization, looseleaf services share several common features. They present all relevant primary authority in one place, regardless of its original source and form of publication. This may include decisions of federal and state courts; statutes, both federal and state; and regulations, decisions, and other documents from administrative agencies in the field. It could be quite time-consuming, even online, to check all of these various sources when beginning each research project.

Looseleaf services also summarize and analyze primary sources. Some contain detailed analytical notes by topic, which function like case digests in explaining and providing access to the primary sources. Exhibits 9–1 to 9–3 on pages 334–336 show sample pages from CCH's *Standard Federal Tax Reporter*, a typical interfiled service. Exhibit 9–1 provides part of 26 U.S.C. § 692, the statute governing the abatement of income taxes of members of the armed forces, astronauts, and terrorist victims on death, followed by excerpts from legislative history materials.

Exhibit 9–2 on page 335 contains part of the regulation implementing this code section and the beginning of the publisher's explanation of these provisions, and Exhibit 9–3 on page 336 shows the end of the explanation and annotations of court decisions. Much of this material is available elsewhere in law libraries, but the looseleaf service brings it together along with an explanatory overview and news of new developments.

Looseleaf and topical reporters often contain cases that are not published in Thomson West's National Reporter System, such as trial court decisions and rulings of state and federal administrative agencies. These decisions and rulings are generally published first in weekly looseleaf inserts. Some services then publish permanent bound volumes of decisions, while others issue transfer binders for storage of older material.

In addition to publishing court and administrative decisions, looseleaf services also provide systems for digesting and indexing them. This coverage is similar to West's key-number digest system, but a specialized system can respond more quickly to developments in a particular area and may offer a more sophisticated analysis of topics within its expertise. The West system had just one key number for child labor, for example, but BNA's *Labor Relations Reporter* digests have more than ten distinct subdivisions, including classifications for specific exemptions such as newspaper delivery, agricultural labor, and acting and performing.

The cases in most topical reporters can be updated online through KeyCite or Shepard's Citations, as well as in several specialized Shepard's print citators. Citing references to decisions in BNA's *Environment Reporter Cases* and the Environmental Law Institute's *Environ-*

mental Law Reporter, for example, can be found online and in *Shepard's Environmental Law Citations*.

One of the most valuable features of looseleaf services is their coverage of proposed legislation, pending litigation, and other legal developments. Approaches vary from service to service. Many services include weekly or biweekly newsletters. *Standard Federal Tax Reporter* has several current awareness approaches, including weekly "CCH Comments" articles, a *Taxes on Parade* newsletter, and extra issues providing the text of important new documents such as tax reform bills and congressional committee reports.

Detailed, regularly updated indexes provide fast and convenient access to looseleaf services. A typical service includes several types of indexes. The general or *topical index* provides detailed subject access. In many services, an additional index known as a "Current Topical Index" or "Latest Additions to Topical Index" covers new material between the periodic recompilations of the main index. Newsletter services such as BNA's *Antitrust & Trade Regulation Report* or *Family Law Reporter* generally have just one index, which is updated every two or three months. Exhibit 9–4 on page 337 shows a page from the topical index for the *Standard Federal Tax Reporter*, with a reference under "Armed Forces of the U.S." to the material shown in Exhibits 9–1 to 9–3 on pages 334–336. Note that the index includes very detailed references to annotations of court decisions and administrative rulings.

Finding lists provide direct references to particular statutes, regulations, or cases by their citations. These can be particularly useful in searching for numerically designated agency materials, such as IRS rulings or SEC releases. Some of these lists also serve as citator services, providing information on the current validity of materials listed.

Note that Exhibits 9–1 to 9–3 have both page numbers at the top (46,287 to 46,298) and paragraph numbers at the bottom (¶ 24,920 to ¶ 24,922.10). It is easy to be misled by the page numbers, but remember that they are used only for filing purposes and that the paragraph numbers are the points of reference used in indexes and finding lists.

Another device used in some services is the *cumulative index*. This is not a subject index but a tool providing cross-references from the main body of the service to current material. Under paragraph number listings, cumulative indexes update each topic with leads to new materials which have not yet been incorporated into the main discussion.

Detailed instructions, often entitled "How to Use This Reporter" or "About This Publication," are frequently provided at the beginning of the first volume of a looseleaf service. A particular service may include features that appear confusing at first but are very useful to the experienced researcher. New users often neglect these instructions, but a few moments of orientation can save considerable time and frustration.

§ 9–3. Topical Electronic Resources

Looseleaf services remain the preferred research tools of many specialists, and they are the topical resources most likely to be available to public law library patrons. An increasing number of lawyers and other researchers, however, rely on electronic services to perform similar functions. Several of the major looseleaf publishers have online systems providing comprehensive access to the material available in the print products.

Like looseleaf services, topical Internet or CD resources provide both the texts of primary sources and explanatory or analytical material. Keyword searching provides more flexibility than looseleaf indexes, and hypertext links allow for moving conveniently back and forth between various documents. Some of the information available through these services is only issued electronically, but many online services have counterparts in print. The *Standard Federal Tax Reporter* discussed in the preceding section, for example, is part of CCH's Tax Research Network <cchgroup.com/network>, and the competing *United States Tax Reporter* is available through RIA Checkpoint <checkpoint.riag.com>. BNA provides subscriber access to almost all of its services through its website <www.bna.com>.

Most of these topical resources provide access to primary material, commentary, and regular notification of new developments. Some of them also include major secondary sources such as securities or tax treatises. RIA Checkpoint has not only the *United States Tax Reporter* but other major looseleaf services such as *Federal Tax Coordinator,* several tax journals, and editorial analysis of major tax legislation. Exhibit 9–5 on page 338 shows an introductory screen of Checkpoint, indicating the broad array of resources available, and Exhibit 9–6 on page 339 shows the display of a section of a *Tax Planning and Practice Guide* analysis of the Military Family Tax Relief Act of 2003.

Many electronic services are also available on CD. These eliminate the need for laborious filing of replace-

ment pages, but new discs are generally issued less
frequently than looseleaf supplements. CD users must
usually finish updating their research through an online
system or by other means. Internet-based services, on
the other hand, can be constantly updated without the
need for new discs or other supplementation.

The annual *Directory of Law–Related CD–ROMs* provides an extensive listing of more than 1,600 electronic
services, and indicates which services are available on the
Internet. Appendix C in this volume, listing major services, includes coverage of both Internet and CD services.

LexisNexis and Westlaw have numerous topical electronic libraries with cases, statutes, regulations, and
other sources in specialized areas. Both systems, for
example, have files combining federal tax cases, legislation, regulations, and administrative rulings. Their tax
libraries also provide access to treatises, newsletters, and
other secondary sources. These libraries do not, however,
integrate the primary sources and commentary in the
same way that the major looseleaf or electronic services
do.

§ 9–4.   Current Awareness Sources

It is essential that lawyers be aware of activity in their
areas of expertise, not just new court decisions but also
legislative and regulatory changes. Several approaches
are available to keep on top of current activities, recent
scholarly literature, and new developments in the law.

Much current awareness information is generated by
searches set up to run automatically and provide notice
of new results, like WestClip and LexisNexis Alerts.
Some arrive by e-mail. Many people subscribe to RSS

("really simple syndication") feeds and use feed reader or aggregator programs such as Bloglines <www.bloglines. com> or NewsGator <www.newsgator.com> to monitor developments from numerous sites.

a.　Legal Newsletters and Newspapers

Looseleaf services are often excellent sources of current information in particular fields. Many include newsletters summarizing developments; the *Fair Employment Practices* and *Standard Federal Tax Reporter* newsletters noted in § 9–2 are just two examples.

A large number of separate current awareness newsletters are also published for this express purpose, in some instances delivered by fax or e-mail instead of in print. Some are freely available, but many are quite expensive. Weekly newsletters may cost $1000 or more per year. Specialized newsletters often have a limited circulation and can be hard to find in academic or public law libraries. Nevertheless, they may be the best available sources for learning about newly developing areas of law. Newsletters are often the forum through which practitioners in a very specialized area share information and documents. A newsletter may, for example, include photocopies of pleadings or of trial court decisions that will never be published in the regular court reports.

Among the leading newsletter publishers are several companies that make their products available through Westlaw and LexisNexis. Westlaw has more than fifty Andrews Publications reporters, including court documents as well as news, on specific areas of litigation such as corporate corruption, nursing homes, and tire defects. LexisNexis has several dozen similar newsletters from

Mealey Publications, on issues ranging from antidepressant drugs to welding rods.

In addition to its looseleaf services, BNA publishes about two dozen daily newsletters in areas such as environmental law, labor law, and taxation. Some of these are available in both print and electronic versions, but others are electronic-only publications.

Numerous law firms produce newsletters for their clients and other readers. These may serve primarily as marketing tools for their firms, but many also provide useful information about developing areas of law. They are generally available through law firm websites, and may be identified through topical browsing or keyword searches in resources such as Mondaq <www.mondaq.com>.

A leading source for identifying available newsletters is the annual *Legal Newsletters in Print*. This directory describes more than 2,200 newsletters, with information about subscription prices and Internet access. A subject index provides topical access to its listings. This publication is available to online subscribers, along with *Legal Looseleafs in Print* and *Directory of Law–Related CD–ROMs*, as part of the LawTRIO database <www.infosourcespub.com>.

News on developments in the law is also available from a number of daily and weekly legal newspapers. These vary considerably in coverage. Some serve primarily as vehicles for local court calendars and legal announcements, but others include new court decisions and articles on developing legal topics. Westlaw and LexisNexis provide access to several major newspapers. Westlaw coverage includes two national weekly newspapers, the *National Law Journal* and *Legal Times*, as well as several dailies including the *New York Law Journal*. Lexis-Nexis has the *Chicago Daily Law Bulletin* and several *Lawyers Weekly* publications for various states.

One of the leading Internet sources for legal news is law.com <www.law.com>, with stories from *American Lawyer*, *National Law Journal*, and regional newspapers. Many legal newspapers, including the *National Law Journal* <www.nlj.com>, have their own websites, and FindLaw Legal News <news.findlaw.com> provides law-related stories from the AP and Reuters wire services.

b. Current Scholarship

Specialists need to know about scholarly as well as legal developments. A new article directly on a topic of concern may appear in any of the hundreds of law reviews and other legal journals published in this country. Some lawyers scan new issues of journals in their area of expertise, but more systematic ways of surveying the vast majority of journal literature are also available.

One of the principal resources for information about new journal issues is *Current Index to Legal Periodicals* <lib.law.washington.edu/cilp/cilp.html>, published weekly by the University of Washington's Marian Gould Gallagher Law Library. This index covers more than 600 law reviews, indexing articles under about a hundred subject headings and listing each issue's table of contents. Subscribers can receive customized weekly e-mail updates limited to particular subjects and journal titles. Online access is also available through Westlaw's CILP database.

Other resources also provide free notice of new contents, without subject indexing but searchable for particular authors' names or title keywords. Current Law

Journal Content <lawlib.wlu.edu/CLJC/> has tables of contents to nearly 1300 law journals, and provides weekly alerts of new articles. The Tarlton Law Library at the University of Texas also provides table of contents access to more than 750 law-related journals, updated daily <tarlton.law.utexas.edu/tallons/content_search.html>.

Many specialists rely on services such as the Social Science Research Network (SSRN) <www.ssrn.com> and the Berkeley Electronic Press <www.bepress.com> to learn of new scholarly work in their area. These networks serve as forums for scholars in various disciplines, including law, to share recent articles and working papers. New abstracts are delivered to subscribers by e-mail, and searchable Internet archives include free access to several thousand downloadable full-text documents.

c. Blogs and Listservs

In recent years, blogs have increasingly become a major vehicle for timely dissemination of information and opinion. Law blogs (sometimes called "blawgs") are written on a variety of topics, some by individuals and some with several contributors at particular institutions. Some blogs have become leading sources of current information. SCOTUSblog <www.scotusblog.com>, for example, often is the first available source with breaking news about the Supreme Court.

To find blogs on particular topics, you can use directories at sites such as BlawgSearch <blawgsearch. justia.com> (focusing on law) or Technorati <www. technorati.com> (tracking millions of blogs on all subjects). These sites can also be used to search blog postings for specific topics, as can Google Blog Search <blog search.google.com>. Blawg Republic <www. blawgrepublic.com> provides a regularly updated digest of new items from the legal blogging community.

The University of Akron Law Library's law weblogs pathfinder <www.uakron.edu/law/library/blawg.php> provides a good introductory overview of blogs, an annotated listing of several dozen major blogs, and information on aggregators, blog search engines, and directories.

E-mail listservs provide another effective way to keep on top of developments in a particular area, and can also be used to seek assistance with difficult research issues. Some listservs disseminate information by organizations or government agencies, while others are designed for specialists, professors, and others interested in an area to share news and ideas. Posing questions to a list often yields results that would otherwise elude most researchers. Chances are that some list subscriber may be able to help with a thorny legal issue or can identify a source for an obscure document. Older messages to a list, if available in a searchable Internet archive, may form a valuable repository of information in the area.

Hundreds of listservs on legal topics are maintained. Resources such as CataList <www.lsoft.com/lists/ listref.html> and Topica <lists.topica.com> can be used to find lists on legal and nonlegal topics of interest.

A number of courts and state legislatures now provide automatic e-mail notification when a particular case or bill is acted upon, and several government agencies have mailing lists summarizing new developments. These include several dozen EPA lists <https://lists.epa.gov/ read/>, the FCC Daily Digest <www.fcc. gov/updates.html>, and more than twenty FDA mailing

lists <www.fda.gov/emaillist.html>. Other agency websites may provide information about similar listservs in
their fields.

§ 9–5. Legal History Resources

Most legal research involves determining the law now
in effect, but many researchers need information on legal
developments occurring decades or centuries ago. These
materials are of interest to historians and other scholars,
but the background of a court decision, statute, or constitutional provision can also affect its current interpretation and is thus of more than historical interest.

Many of the resources discussed in earlier chapters are
invaluable in legal history research. Westlaw and Lexis-
Nexis have judicial opinions back to the 18th century,
and access to older law review literature is available
through the comprehensive backfiles of HeinOnline (going back as far as 1788) and Index to Legal Periodicals
Retrospective, covering 1918–81. Historical material from
Congress is available in sources such as the digitized
Serial Set publications from LexisNexis and Readex, and
in the Library of Congress's "A Century of Lawmaking
for a New Nation: U.S. Congressional Documents and
Debates" <memory.loc.gov/ammem/amlaw>.

Other resources are specifically designed for historical
inquiry. The Making of Modern Law: Legal Treatises,
1800–1926 <www.gale.com/ModernLaw/> provides full
text access to more than 20,000 English and American
works from the nineteenth and early twentieth centuries.
HeinOnline <www.heinonline.org> has a more selective
collection of about a thousand titles in its "Legal Clas-
sics" library. Even earlier books can be found through
Eighteenth Century Collections Online (ECCO) <www.

gale.com/EighteenthCentury/> and Early English Books Online (EEBO) <eebo.chadwyck.com>, and items published in the American colonies and the early republic are in Early American Imprints (Series I: Evans, 1639–1800 and Series II: Shaw–Shoemaker, 1801–1819) <www.readex.com>. Together these resources provide access to works ranging from Sir Thomas Littleton's *Tenures* (c. 1481) to Sir William Blackstone's *Commentaries on the Laws of England* (4 vols., 1765–69) down to Oliver Wendell Holmes's *The Common Law* (1881). Major works such as these are also available in modern facsimile editions, and some fortunate researchers may be able to use the original editions in rare book collections.

Other historical resources have been digitized in recent years, vastly increasing access to contemporary accounts of major legal developments. Accounts of the drafting and ratification of the U.S. Constitution, for example, can be found in America's Historical Newspapers, 1690–1922 <www.readex.com>, while the course of more modern developments such as the New Deal and civil rights litigation can be followed in ProQuest Historical Newspapers <www.proquest.com>, covering several major national newspapers including the *New York Times* and *Washington Post*. Another subscription site, Newspaper-ARCHIVE.com <newspaperarchive.com>, covers hundreds of papers from around the country from as early as 1759.

Printed collections of historical legal documents are available on a variety of topics, and include such works as Helen Tunnicliff Catterall, ed., *Judicial Cases Concerning American Slavery and the Negro* (5 vols., 1926–37), and Maeva Marcus, ed., *The Documentary History of the Supreme Court of the United States, 1789–1800* (8 vols., 1985–2007). Library online catalogs and footnote references can lead to many others.

Legal history researchers have a broad array of scholarly monographs from which to choose, from wide-ranging sources such as Lawrence M. Friedman, *A History of American Law* (3d ed. 2005) to much more specific studies. One of the most extensive and valuable works in American legal history is the multivolume Oliver Wendell Holmes Devise *History of the Supreme Court of the United States* (1971–date). The Holmes Devise is perhaps the closest American counterpart to W. S. Holdsworth's monumental *A History of English Law* (17 vols., 1903–72).

Guides and bibliographies can be invaluable resources in discovering historical materials. Works such as Michael G. Chiorazzi, ed., *Prestatehood Legal Materials: A Fifty–State Research Guide, Including New York City and the District of Columbia* (2 vols., 2005), can provide information on available resources for specific jurisdictions. The predecessor to the *Index to Legal Periodicals*, entitled *Index to Legal Periodical Literature* (6 vols., 1888–1939), sometimes called the Jones–Chipman index after the names of its editors, covers articles as far back as 1770. Morris L. Cohen, *Bibliography of Early American Law* (7 vols. 1998–2003) provides a comprehensive record of American legal publications up to 1860.

§ 9–6. Conclusion

Looseleaf and electronic services, current awareness tools, and other specialized materials are some of the most important resources for practicing lawyers. Unlike more general sources such as court reports and codes, these materials are not published in one standardized format. Learning what resources are available in a particular area may require preliminary research into indexes and directories. Although it may take some time to use these specialized resources effectively, they can lead directly to more productive research and to a better understanding and anticipation of legal developments.

Information about specialized legal topics may be more important for practicing attorneys on a day-to-day basis than scholarly research and historical information, but these resources provide a context and background for today's legal topics. Scholarly and historic information also help to make the law more than simply a trade but rather a discipline with rich and continuing traditions.

INCOME TAXES—ARMED FORCES—§ 692 [¶ 24,920]   **46,287**

be computed by only taking into account the items of income, gain, or other amounts attributable to—

(A) deferred compensation which would have been payable after death if the individual had died other than as a specified terrorist victim, or

(B) amounts payable in the taxable year which would not have been payable in such taxable year but for an action taken after September 11, 2001.

(4) SPECIFIED TERRORIST VICTIM.—For purposes of this subsection, the term 'specified terrorist victim' means any decedent—

(A) who dies as a result of wounds or injury incurred as a result of the terrorist attacks against the United States on April 19, 1995, or September 11, 2001, or

(B) who dies as a result of illness incurred as a result of an attack involving anthrax occurring on or after September 11, 2001, and before January 1, 2002.

Such term shall not include any individual identified by the Attorney General to have been a participant or conspirator in any such attack or a representative of such an individual.

(5) RELIEF WITH RESPECT TO ASTRONAUTS.—The provisions of this subsection shall apply to any astronaut whose death occurs in the line of duty, except that paragraph (3)(B) shall be applied by using the date of the death of the astronaut rather than September 11, 2001.

.01 Amended by P.L. 108-121, P.L. 107-134, P.L. 99-514, P.L. 98-369, P.L. 98-259, P.L. 97-448, P.L. 94-569, P.L. 94-455 (Deadwood Act), and P.L. 93-597. For details, see the Code Volumes.

Joint Committee Summary of P.L. 108-121 (Military Family Tax Relief Act of 2003)

.019 Extension of certain tax relief provisions to astronauts.—The bill extends the exclusion from income tax, the exclusion for death benefits, and the estate tax relief available under the Victims of Terrorism Tax Relief Act of 2001 to astronauts who lose their lives on a space mission (including the individuals who lost their lives in the space shuttle Columbia disaster).

Effective Date—The provision is generally effective for qualified individuals whose lives are lost in the line of duty after December 31, 2002.—Technical Explanation of the "Military Family Tax Relief Act of 2003," November 7, 2003 (JCX-99-03).

Joint Committee Summary of P.L. 107-134 (Victims of Terrorism Tax Relief Act of 2001)

.02 Income taxes of victims of terrorist attacks.—The bill extends relief similar to the present-law treatment of military or civilian employees of the United States who die as a result of terrorist or military activity outside the United States to individuals who die as a result of wounds or injury which were incurred as a result of the terrorist attacks that occurred on September 11, 2001, or April 19, 1995, and individuals who die as a result of illness incurred due to an attack involving anthrax that occurs on or after September 11, 2001, and before January 1, 2002. Under the bill, such individuals generally are exempt from income tax for the year of death and for prior taxable years beginning with the taxable year prior to the taxable year in which the wounds or injury occurred.[10] The exemption applies to these individuals whether killed in an attack (e.g., in the case of the September 11, 2001,

attack in one of the four airplanes or on the ground) or in rescue or recovery operations.

The provision provides a minimum tax relief benefit of $10,000 to each eligible individual regardless of the income tax liability of the individual for the eligible tax years. If an eligible individual's income tax for years eligible for the exclusion under the provision is less than $10,000, the individual is treated as having made a tax payment for such individual's last taxable year in an amount equal to the excess of $10,000 over the amount of tax not imposed under the provision.

Subject to rules prescribed by the Secretary, the exemption from tax does not apply to the tax attributable to (1) deferred compensation which would have been payable after death if the individual had died other than as a specified terrorist victim, or (2) amounts payable in the taxable year which would not have been payable in such taxable year but for an action taken after September 11, 2001. Thus, for example, the exemption does not apply to amounts payable from a qualified plan or individual retirement arrangement to the beneficiary or estate of the individual. Similarly, amounts payable only as death or survivor's benefits pursuant to deferred compensation preexisting arrangements that would have been paid if the death had occurred for another reason are not covered by the exemption. In addition, if the individual's employer makes adjustments to a plan or arrangement to accelerate the vesting of restricted property or the payment of nonqualified deferred compensation after the date of the particular attack, the exemption does not apply to income received as a result of that action.[11] Also, if the individual's beneficiary cashed in savings bonds of the decedent, the exemption does not apply. On the other hand, the exemption does apply, for example, to a final paycheck of the individual or dividends on stock held by the individual

---

[10] The bill does not provide relief from self-employment tax liability.

[11] Such amounts may, however, be excludable from gross income under the death benefit exclusion provided in section 102 of the bill.

2007(10) CCH—Standard Federal Tax Reports   Reg. § 692(d)(5) ¶ 24,920

Exhibit 9–1. I.R.C. § 692, [2007] 10 Stand. Fed. Tax Rep. (CCH) ¶ 24,920.

INCOME TAXES—ARMED FORCES—§ 692 [¶ 24,920]   **46,291**

⇛→ *Caution: Reg. § 1.692-1 does not reflect recent law changes. For details, see ¶ 24,921.01.*

such spouse may agree. Should they agree to treat such estimated tax, or any portion thereof, as the estimated tax of such individual, the estimated tax so paid shall be credited or refunded as an overpayment for the taxable year ending with the date of his death.

(d) For the purpose of determining the tax which is unpaid at the date of death, amounts deducted and withheld under chapter 24, subtitle C of the Internal Revenue Code of 1954, or under subchapter D, chapter 9 of the Internal Revenue Code of 1939 (relating to income tax withheld at source on wages), constitute payment of tax imposed under subtitle A of the Internal Revenue Code of 1954 or under chapter 1 of the Internal Revenue Code of 1939, as the case may be.

(e) This section shall have no application whatsoever with respect to the liability of an individual as a transferee of property of a taxpayer where such liability relates to the tax imposed upon the taxpayer by subtitle A of the Internal Revenue Code of 1954 or by chapter 1 of the Internal Revenue Code of 1939. [Reg. § 1.692-1.]

.01 Historical Comment: Proposed 6/27/56. Adopted 10/7/57 by T.D. 6257. Amended 5/4/78 by T.D. 7543. [Reg. § 1.692-1 does not reflect P.L. 98-259 (1984), P.L. 98-369 (1984), P.L. 99-514 (1986) or P.L. 107-134 (2002). See ¶ 24,920.021 et seq. and ¶ 24,922 et seq.]

[¶ 24,922]   Income Taxes of Members of Armed Forces, Astronauts and Terrorist Victims On Death

• • *CCH Explanation*

Table of Contents

.01 Synopsis - combat zone tax forgiveness.—The United States has long had a policy of forgiving federal income tax liability for U.S. military personnel who die while serving in a combat zone or as a result of wounds, disease, or injury incurred while so serving. An area must be designated as a combat zone in an executive order signed by the President of the United States (Code Sec. 112). See ¶ 7082.03. The forgiveness of tax applies to the year of death and to any prior year ending on or after the first day that the individual served in a combat zone (Code Sec. 692(a)). For example, if a taxpayer died in 2005, but was in the combat zone from 2003, no tax liability would be owed for tax years 2003, 2004 and 2005.

In the case of joint return, only the decedent's portion of the income tax liability is forgiven. Reg. § 1.692-1(b) sets forth a method for allocating the joint income tax liability between spouses. Under this method, the portion of the decedent's joint income tax liability that can be forgiven is the joint tax liability

Exhibit 9–2. Income Taxes of Members of Armed Forces, Astronauts and Terrorist Victims on Death: CCH Explanation, [2007] 10 Stand. Fed. Tax Rep. (CCH) ¶ 24,922.

46,298   INCOME TAXES—ARMED FORCES—§692 [¶ 24,920]

Income Taxes of Members of Armed Forces, Astronauts and Terrorist Victims On Death

• • CCH Explanation

MA 01888. For those using a private delivery service, the returns should be sent to: IRS, 310 Lowell St., Stop 661, Andover, Mass. 01810.

The IRS will provide a free copy of prior year tax returns to survivors or executors of disaster victims estates. The free copy can be obtained by filling out Form 4506, "Request for Copy or Transcript of Tax Form," writing "DISASTER" in the top margin, attaching Testamentary Letters or other evidence of authorization to act for the estate and mailing it as instructed in the form instructions.— CCH.

• • • *Annotations by Topic*

.10 Community income.—The surviving spouse of a serviceman who died while serving in a combat zone is entitled to a refund of income taxes paid that are attributable to her community share of her husband's military compensation.

Rev. Rul. 68-393, 1968-2 CB 292.

.11 Estate of serviceman.—Under former Code Sec. 421, the income taxes of the estate of a deceased serviceman were abated on the serviceman's share of partnership income that was paid to the estate for the period from the date of his death to the end of the partnership's fiscal year that ended in the calendar year of death. This section was construed as forgiving the income taxes of deceased for the full tax year in which death occurred and was applicable to the estate, even though both the combat zone and the estate were separate taxable entities.

R. Lupia Est., CA-2, 54-2 USTC ¶49,049, 214 F2d 942. Aff'd, *per curiam,* SCt, 55-1 USTC ¶49,097, 348 US 956.

The above decision was under former Code Sec. 421, which was applicable during World War II. However, the decision is also applicable under Code Sec. 692 because the language contained in these laws is substantially the same.— CCH.

.12 Income taxes defined.—Amounts withheld for income taxes in 1970 for a member of the Armed Services who first entered a combat zone in 1971, was reported missing in 1971, and presumed dead in 1974 are not subject to the provisions of section 692(a)(1) of the Code and thus the amounts withheld are refundable only

to the extent of any overpayment. The amount of any tax liability in excess of the amount withheld will not be assessed under section 692(a)(2). FICA taxes deducted for years 1972 through 1974 will be refunded.

Rev. Rul. 76-355, 1976-2 CB 201.

Administrative tax relief has been provided to military and support personnel involved in Operation Iraqi Freedom. Guidelines, in a question-and-answer format, address the tax relief that is being extended to those serving in the combat zone, which encompasses the "Arabian Peninsula Areas." In addition to clarifying the scope of the exclusion from income for military pay and the extension of deadlines for performing certain tax-related acts; the guidelines state that deadline extensions generally apply to both those serving in the combat zone and their spouses who are in the United States. The extensions also apply to support personnel, such as merchant marines on vessels under the control of the Defense Department, Red Cross personnel, accredited correspondents, and civilian personnel acting under the direction of the Armed Forces.

Notice 2003-21, 2003-1 CB 818.

The IRS has released guidance for representatives of federal employees who die from injuries sustained in a terrorist or military action. It discusses the requirements for securing income tax forgiveness for the deceased taxpayer under Code Sec. 692(c)(1) and for claiming related refunds. It also sets down procedures for determining whether a terrorist or military action, as defined by Code Sec. 692(c)(2), has occurred.

Rev. Proc. 2004-26, 2004-1 CB 890.

¶24,922.10 Reg. §1.692-1(e)

Exhibit 9–3. Income Taxes of Members of Armed Forces, Astronauts and Terrorist Victims on Death: Annotations by Topic, [2007] 10 Stand. Fed. Tax Rep. (CCH) ¶¶ 24,922.10–24,922.12.

10,246

ARC

Exhibit 9–4. Topical Index, [2007 Index] Stand. Fed. Tax Rep. (CCH) 10,246.

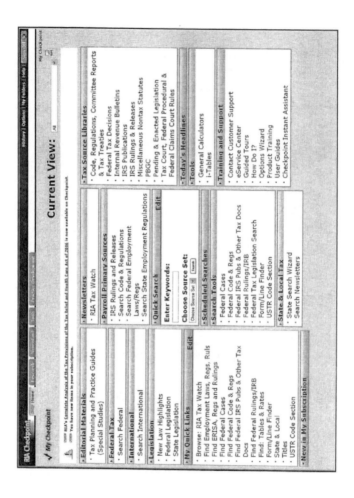

Exhibit 9–5. Introductory screen, RIA Checkpoint <checkpoint.riag.com>.

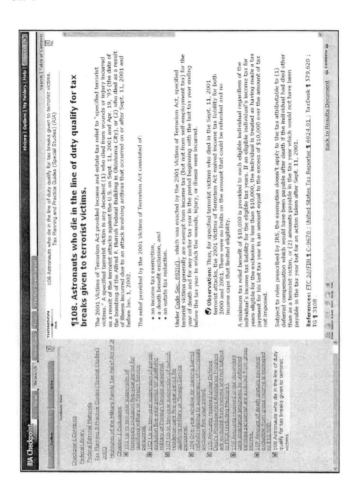

Exhibit 9–6. Highlights of the Military Family Relief Act of 2003, ¶ 108, RIA Checkpoint <checkpoint.riag.com>.

CHAPTER 10

REFERENCE RESOURCES

---

§ 10–1. Introduction

This brief chapter serves two purposes. First, it looks at legal resources designed to provide answers to relatively simple questions. Some reference sources, such as dictionaries and multistate surveys, have been discussed in prior chapters, but there are additional reference materials with which lawyers should be familiar. These are not sources for lengthy legal analysis but for telephone numbers, addresses, facts, and statistics. Knowing how to find this information quickly can save valuable time.

The chapter also introduces more general reference sources for interdisciplinary research. Many law students focus so intently on legal literature that they neglect information from other disciplines. General sources, however, can provide essential background information, and scholarship in the sciences and social sciences may add valuable perspectives and insights in analyzing legal issues.

§ 10–2. Legal Directories

Chapters 6 through 8 discussed directories covering federal and state governments, including legislatures, administrative agencies, and courts. The law does not live by government alone, however, and directories of lawyers and legal organizations can also be valuable sources of information. Legal directories provide background information about other lawyers and can help in establishing contacts within the profession. Organizations interested in particular issues may provide networking opportunities or insights unavailable in any printed or electronic sources.

Numerous directories provide contact and biographical information for lawyers. Most focus on individual states or particular specialties, but two comprehensive directories of the legal profession exist. These are published by divisions of the parent companies of LexisNexis and Westlaw, and each covers close to a million lawyers. Neither, however, includes every single lawyer in the country.

The more established source, and the only one available in print format, is the *Martindale-Hubbell Law Directory*. This annual publication contains twelve large volumes listing lawyers and law firms, arranged by state and city. At the beginning of each volume are blue pages containing "Practice Profiles," with a one-line entry for each lawyer indicating date of birth, date of admission to practice, college, law school, and address or affiliation. "Professional Biographies" provide fuller descriptions of those lawyers and firms who purchase space beyond the simple alphabetical listings. Lawyers in corporate law departments are listed geographically and have fuller listings in a "Corporate Law Departments" section; selected lawyers in other countries are covered by *Martindale-Hubbell International Law Directory*.

One useful feature of *Martindale-Hubbell* is its rating system, which evaluates U.S. lawyers based on interviews with their peers. Legal ability ratings range from A (Very High to Preeminent) to C (Good to High), and these are published only if accompanied by an ethical standards rating of V (Very High). Ratings are not provided for all lawyers listed in the directory.

The *Martindale-Hubbell Law Directory* is available on CD, online through LexisNexis, and on the Internet as the Martindale–Hubbell Lawyer Locator <www.martindale.com>. A related site designed for clients and the public, lawyers.com <www.lawyers.com>, is limited to lawyers and firms with paid listings. Its modified version of the *Martindale-Hubbell* ratings indicates only whether a lawyer is "Peer Review Rated" without being more specific.

The other comprehensive directory of attorneys, West Legal Directory (WLD), is published only electronically on CD, through Westlaw, and on the Internet as the FindLaw Lawyer Directory <lawyers.findlaw.com>. Like *Martindale-Hubbell*, WLD has both simple free listings and more extensive paid entries. Coverage in the two sources is comparable, although only WLD includes telephone numbers in its basic listings. Westlaw's PROFILER–WLD database links directory information to relevant cases, briefs, pleadings, and other documents, as well as summaries of litigation history.

Several other national directories of lawyers and law firms are available, although none is as comprehensive as *Martindale-Hubbell* or WLD. *Who's Who in American Law* (biennial) is a useful source of biographical information on prominent attorneys and legal scholars, and the *Law Firms Yellow Book* (semiannual) provides information on the management and recruiting personnel of major law firms. The National Association for Law Placement's annual *Directory of Legal Employers* <www.nalpdirectory.com> is designed primarily for job-seeking law students and has basic data on firms and their attorneys. Law firm websites, of course, usually include information about the firm's attorneys and their practices.

Other directories focus on attorneys working outside of law firms. *Directory of Corporate Counsel* (2 vols., annual) has biographical information on lawyers working for corporations and nonprofit organizations. Directories of public interest and government law offices include *Directory of Legal Aid and Defender Offices in the United States* and *National Directory of Prosecuting Attorneys* (both updated irregularly).

Interest groups, professional organizations, and trade associations can be invaluable sources of information in their areas of concern. Links to legal organization websites, including state bar associations, are available from several websites including FindLaw <www.findlaw.com /06associations/> and WashLaw Web <www.washlaw. edu/bar/>. Broader coverage of legal and nonlegal organizations is provided by the *Encyclopedia of Associations* (4 vols., annual), with contact information for nearly 24,000 national organizations. The *Encyclopedia of Associations* is also available through Westlaw and LexisNexis, and as part of the Thomson Gale *Associations Unlimited* online database <www.galenet.com/servlet/AU>. Exhibit 10–1 on page 354 shows the *Associations Unlimited* entry for the International Handgun Metallic Silhouette Association (IHMSA). Note that entries include website addresses, if available, and information on organizations' publications and meetings. Another directory, *National Trade and Professional Associations of the United States* (annual, online by subscription <www.associationexecs.com>), is less extensive than the *Encyclopedia of Associations* but just as useful for finding addresses and telephone numbers of business-related organizations.

While most directories are somewhat specialized, a few try to provide answers to a wider range of inquiries. *Law and Legal Information Directory* (annual) is a large volume covering legal organizations and bar associations as well as other resources such as law libraries, lawyer referral services, and a variety of federal and state government agencies. A handier desktop work by Arlene L. Eis, *The Legal Researcher's Desk Reference* (biennial), has an impressive array of directory information including government offices, courts, and bar associations, and also includes other resources such as state court organization charts and lists of Internet sites.

§ 10–3. Statistics

Lawyers need demographic and statistical information for many purposes, from preparing for cross-examination of an expert witness to supporting a discrimination claim. Statistics are published in a variety of sources, some focused on legal matters and some more general.

Statistics relating to law include data on courts, lawyers, and the criminal justice system. Information about court caseloads can be found in the Administrative Office of the U.S. Courts' annual *Judicial Business of the United States Courts* (also available online <www.uscourts.gov/judbususc/judbus.html>), and the National Center for State Courts' annual *State Court Caseload Statistics* <www.ncsconline.org/D_Research/csp/CSP_Main_Page.html>. The composition of the U.S. legal profession is analyzed in *The Lawyer Statistical Report*, published periodically by the American Bar Foundation; the most recent report, published in 2004, provides data as of 2000. The American Bar Association's Market Research Department provides links to various websites with statistics on lawyers and the legal profession <www.abanet.org/marketresearch/resource.html>.

Criminal statistics are widely available from both federal and state governments. Each year the U.S. Department of Justice publishes two major sources in print and on the Internet. The Federal Bureau of Investigation issues *Uniform Crime Reports* (also known as *Crime in the United States*) <www.fbi.gov/ucr/ucr.htm>, focusing on criminal activities, and the Bureau of Justice Statistics issues *Sourcebook of Criminal Justice Statistics* <www.albany.edu/sourcebook/>, providing a broader survey of the social and economic impacts of crime.

Most people are familiar with the U.S. Census Bureau <www.census.gov> from its decennial census of population, but it also conducts an extensive economic census every five years and provides a vast range of statistical information on business and industry. The key to finding relevant economic information from the Census Bureau and other sources is determining the appropriate North American Industry Classification System (NAICS) code for an industry <www.census.gov/epcd/www/naics. html>.

The *Statistical Abstract of the United States*, published annually by the Census Bureau in print, on CD, and on the Internet <www.census.gov/compendia/statab/>, is a general reference source with which any legal researcher should be familiar. It covers a wide range of economic and demographic statistics, and is particularly useful because it gives source information for each table. It thus serves as a convenient lead to agencies and publications with more extensive coverage of specific areas. Exhibit 10–2 on page 355 shows a table from the *Statistical Abstract*, providing information about the number of law degrees conferred per year, from 1970 to 2004. Note that the table includes a source reference to the annual publication *Digest of Education Statistics*, where more detailed information may be available.

The *Statistical Abstract* website provides previous editions of the publication, all the way back to 1878. A less exhaustive, but more convenient, source for older statistics is Susan B. Carter et al., eds., *Historical Statistics of the United States: Earliest Times to the Present* (5 vols., 2006). Another source for statistics from government agencies is the FedStats website <www.fedstats.gov>, with links to numerous federal statistical sources by topic and by agency.

Annual reports and other publications of trade associations, labor unions, financial institutions, public interest groups, and government agencies generally contain statistical data relating to their work and interests. Much of this material is now available on organizations' websites, but a subject index can provide helpful guidance on where to look. *American Statistics Index* (1973–date, covering U.S. government sources) and *Statistical Reference Index* (1980–date, covering state government and private sources) are available in print and as part of LexisNexis Statistical <web.lexis-nexis.com/statuniv/>.

Information about public opinion and polls is available through a number of print and electronic sources. Leading free sources include the Gallup Organization <www.galluppoll.com> and the Harris Poll Library <www.harrisinteractive.com/harris_poll/>. Both sites allow keyword searching of questionnaires and poll analyses, and provide access to some in-depth poll results on topics such as the Supreme Court and election results. The subscription sources Polling the Nations <www.orspub.com> and the Roper Center for Public Opinion Research <www.ropercenter.uconn.edu> provide more extensive compilations of polls and survey data.

§ 10–4. News and Business Information

Every practicing lawyer must keep abreast of developments in business, politics, and society. Legal newspapers, discussed in Chapter 9, focus on law-related activity, but for a broader picture it is necessary to monitor more general sources such as major newspapers or news websites. In addition to providing current awareness, news stories can also be rich sources for factual research or background information.

Two of the most convenient news sources for law students are Westlaw and LexisNexis. Westlaw provides access to hundreds of newspapers, as well as wire services and business publications; and LexisNexis's news library has the text of newspapers, magazines, trade journals, newsletters, and wire services. The two systems have considerable overlap in coverage; both, for example, have the *New York Times* and the *Washington Post*, while only LexisNexis has the full text of the *Wall Street Journal*. Back issues of these and other newspapers are usually available in large libraries on microfilm, and ProQuest Historical Newspapers <www.proquest.com> provides subscription-based web access to PDF images of several major newspapers as far back as 1849.

Other electronic sources of news abound, including websites for newspapers (such as <www.wsj.com> and <www.nyt.com>) and multisource subscription databases such as Factiva <www.factiva.com>. Google News <news.google.com> provides free and very current coverage of a wide range of newspapers, magazines, and wire services. Websites for newspapers and other news sources can be found through sites such as NewsLink <newslink.org> or NewsVoyager <www.newsvoyager. com>.

Business developments are a major focus of research in news sources. Company information is also available through a number of other print and electronic directories and databases. The leading provider of data on both public and private businesses is Dun & Bradstreet, which publishes several directories as well as in-depth profiles of individual companies. D & B material is available through Westlaw and LexisNexis (but not on most law school accounts), and as a subscription website <www. dnb.com>. LexisNexis and Westlaw provide law schools access to numerous other directories. Both have *Standard & Poor's Register of Corporations, Directors & Executives*, which provides basic data and biographical information, and S & P's more extensive *Corporate De-*

scriptions Plus News database with more extensive background and financial information. Parent and subsidiary companies can be identified in the *Directory of Corporate Affiliations*, available on LexisNexis. Other Internet sources for basic information include Hoover's <www. hoovers.com>, ThomasNet <www.thomasnet.com>, and Yahoo Finance <finance.yahoo.com>. Harvard Business School's Baker Library produces an extensive collection of research guides <www.library.hbs.edu/guides/> for assistance in doing more extensive business research.

Publicly traded companies must submit a wide range of financial information to the Securities and Exchange Commission, much of which is available through the SEC's EDGAR (Electronic Data Gathering Analysis and Retrieval) system. EDGAR resources are available directly from the SEC <www.sec.gov/edgar.shtml> and through several commercial services including Westlaw and LexisNexis.

§ 10–5. Interdisciplinary Research

Legal research is rarely confined to the insular world of cases, statutes, and law review articles. It is important for researchers to be able to find information in a wide variety of disciplines.

Periodical indexes. Several indexes to nonlegal periodical literature can provide valuable leads. Some of these are specialized indexes in particular disciplines, while others provide comprehensive coverage of a wide range of sources (including legal journals). The online versions of many indexes link directly to full-text PDF versions of the articles listed.

Indexes from other disciplines such as *ABI/INFORM* (business and economics), *PAIS International* (public policy), or *PsycINFO* (psychology and related disciplines) may provide background information or interdisciplinary perspectives. A few indexes are available free on the Internet, such as the National Library of Medicine's *PubMed* version of *MEDLINE*, the comprehensive index of biomedical journals <www.pubmed.gov>. Most, however, are accessible by subscription only. A number of indexes are available through Westlaw, and researchers in university libraries usually have access to many more through subscription websites.

Thomson Scientific (formerly the Institute for Scientific Information) publishes several citation indexes which function like Shepard's in other academic disciplines and can be used to find articles citing a particular author or source. These very broad indexes cover thousands of journals and can also search for articles by author or keyword. They are available on CD and online as ISI Web of Knowledge <www.isiwebofknowledge.com>. The most useful in legal research is *Social Sciences Citation Index* (covering 1966–date), which includes extensive coverage of law journals. The others are *Science Citation Index* (1955–date) and *Arts & Humanities Citation Index* (1976–date). These databases are also available through other systems, including Westlaw, where they are known as *Social Scisearch (SOCSCISRCH)*, *Scisearch*, and *Arts & Humanities Search (ART–HUM)*. ISI also publishes several subject-based editions of *Current Contents*, weekly print or electronic services providing the tables of contents of new scholarly journal issues; the *Social & Behavioral Sciences* edition includes numerous law-related titles.

Web of Knowledge is just one of several major multi-disciplinary indexes available by subscription at most large academic libraries; others include Thomson Gale's Academic OneFile and InfoTrac OneFile <www.gale.com>. IngentaConnect <www.ingentaconnect.com> also provides comprehensive coverage of current journal literature, with tables of contents information from more than 30,000 publications. Searching is free, and articles are available for electronic or fax delivery for a fee. JSTOR <www.jstor.org> was mentioned in Chapter 2 as a source for retrospective coverage of several dozen legal journals; it also provides full-text comprehensive coverage of several hundred other non-law scholarly journals. Two other subscription web services providing access to older journal articles back as far as 1770 are *Periodicals Archive Online* (full text of some 400 journals, <pao.chadwyck.com>) and *Periodicals Index Online* (indexing of more than 4000 other journals, <pio.chadwyck.com>).

Dissertations. One of the most extensive bodies of scholarly research can be found in doctoral dissertations, which are usually the product of several years of work and often provide extensive references to published and manuscript sources. Until recently, reading a dissertation required searching a *Dissertations Abstracts* database or publication and then obtaining a copy through purchase or interlibrary loan. Now, however, ProQuest Dissertations & Theses Database <www.proquest.com> makes available the full PDF text of most dissertations since 1997. (It also includes abstracts to older dissertations since 1980, and subject, title and author information for works going back to 1861.) Digital access has transformed dissertations from esoteric and hard-to-find items to readily available research tools.

Online catalogs. No law library has every possible text, so research limited to one library's holdings may miss important works. WorldCat provides access to records for more than a billion items, in more than 10,000 libraries worldwide. This database is available in two forms. One <www.worldcat.org> is free to the public and identifies holding libraries, but it has only simple search options and basic information. The other <www. oclc.org/firstsearch/> is available through subscribing libraries and provides more sophisticated search capabilities as well as more extensive bibliographic information about items found.

Specific library catalogs can also be searched. One of the most extensive individual library catalogs is that of the Library of Congress <catalog.loc.gov>, and Find-Law's list of law schools by state <stu.findlaw.com/ schools/usaschools/> includes direct links to library websites and online catalogs. Even more catalogs are accessible through resources such as lib-web-cats <www. librarytechnology.org/libwebcats/>, which lists links to libraries worldwide, geographically or by type of library (including law and other specialties).

Other reference sources. Most disciplines have an extensive literature of encyclopedias, dictionaries, bibliographies, research guides, directories, indexes, and other sources that can be valuable in a research project. The standard, comprehensive source for identifying available reference materials is the American Library Association's *Guide to Reference Books* (11th ed. 1996). The *Guide* describes basic resources in hundreds of disciplines, providing just enough background to help the legal researcher know where to look. A new online edition, *Guide to Reference Sources*, is scheduled for publication in 2007.

§ 10–6. Conclusion

This chapter's introductory survey has presented just a small sampling of the many resources available for answering factual questions and for expanding research into other disciplines. Indexes and bibliographies can provide further leads, and reference librarians can suggest other sources and research approaches.

The legal system impacts and is impacted by other aspects of society. Legal arguments may be swayed by sociological or psychological research, for example, and many aspects of economic and social life are subject to legal control. Researchers who do not limit their scope to legal materials will find that the resources of other disciplines can make for more a complete and accurate answer to many legal problems.

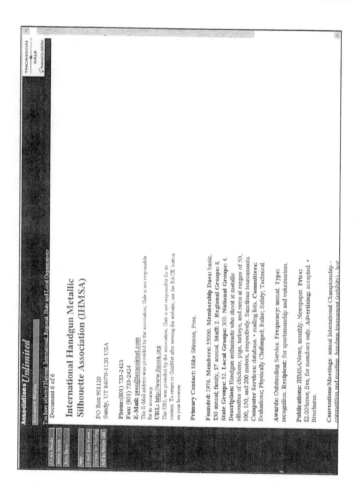

Exhibit 10–1. International Handgun Metallic Silhouette Association (IHMSA), Associations Unlimited <www.galenet.com/servlet/AU>.

Table 293. **First Professional Degrees Earned in Selected Professions: 1970 to 2004**

[First professional degrees include degrees which require at least 6 years of college work for completion (including at least 2 years of preprofessional training). Based on survey; see Appendix III]

Type of degree and sex of recipient	1970	1975	1980	1985	1990	1995	2000	2002	2003	2004
Medicine (M.D.):										
Institutions conferring degrees.....	86	104	112	120	124	119	118	118	118	118
Degrees conferred, total.........	8,314	12,447	14,902	16,041	15,075	15,537	15,286	15,237	15,034	15,442
Percent to women...........	8.4	13.1	23.4	30.4	34.2	38.8	42.7	44.4	45.3	46.4
Dentistry (D.D.S. or D.M.D.):										
Institutions conferring degrees.....	48	52	58	59	57	53	54	53	53	53
Degrees conferred, total.........	3,718	4,773	5,258	5,339	4,100	3,897	4,250	4,239	4,344	4,335
Percent to women...........	0.9	3.1	13.3	20.7	30.9	36.4	40.1	38.5	38.9	41.6
Law (LL.B. or J.D.):										
Institutions conferring degrees.....	145	154	179	181	182	183	190	192	194	195
Degrees conferred, total.........	14,916	29,296	35,647	37,491	36,485	39,349	38,152	38,981	39,067	40,209
Percent to women...........	5.4	15.1	30.2	38.5	42.2	42.6	45.9	48.0	49.0	49.4
Theological (B.D., M.Div., M.H.L.):										
Institutions conferring degrees.....	(NA)	(NA)	(NA)	(NA)	(NA)	192	198	191	196	200
Degrees conferred, total.........	5,298	5,095	7,115	7,221	5,851	5,978	6,129	5,195	5,351	5,332
Percent to women...........	2.3	6.8	13.8	18.5	24.8	25.7	29.2	32.9	34.6	34.2

NA Not available.

Source: U.S. National Center for Education Statistics, *Digest of Education Statistics*, annual.

Exhibit 10–2. U.S. CENSUS BUREAU, STATISTICAL ABSTRACT OF THE UNITED STATES 186 tbl. 293 (126th ed. 2007).

CHAPTER 11

INTERNATIONAL LAW

---

§ 11–1. Introduction

Public international law is the body of law which governs relations among nations. Although its primary historical functions have been the preservation of peace and regulation of war, international law now governs an ever broader range of transnational activities. It regulates matters from copyright protection to the rights of refugees, and agreements such as the Convention on

Contracts for the International Sale of Goods (CISG) have made international law an inherent aspect of commercial activity. *Public international law* is distinguished from *private international law* (or conflict of laws), which determines where, and by whose law, controversies involving more than one jurisdiction are resolved, as well as how foreign judgments are enforced.

A modern legal practice often requires knowledge of international law. Lawyers representing an American firm investing in another country, for example, must be aware of treaties between the two nations as well as the investment and trade laws of both the United States and the other country. They may also need to examine jurisdictional issues in resolving disputes or in determining the application of one country's rules in the other's courts. This chapter focuses on international law, while research in the law of foreign countries is the subject of Chapter 12.

The classic statement of the sources of international law doctrine is found in Article 38 of the Statute of the International Court of Justice. *Treaties* and *international custom* are generally considered the two most important sources. If a treaty is relevant to a problem involving its signatories, it is the primary legal authority. International custom consists of the actual conduct of nations, when that conduct is consistent with the rule of law. Custom is not found in a clearly defined collection of sources, but is established instead by evidence of state practices. Other sources include *judicial decisions* and *scholarly writings*, although these are subsidiary to treaties and international custom. Judicial decisions are not considered binding precedents in subsequent disputes, but they are evidence of international practice and can aid in treaty interpretation and in the definition of customary law.

The Internet has had a dramatic impact on international legal research. International law sources have traditionally been difficult to identify and locate, but many are now widely available through the websites of the United Nations and other international organizations. This chapter discusses some specific resources available electronically and also provides general Internet sites that can serve as useful starting points for further research.

International law has its own terminology, and a dictionary may be an essential research tool. Two leading works are John P. Grant & J. Craig Barker, eds., *Parry and Grant Encyclopaedic Dictionary of International Law* (2d ed. 2004), and James R. Fox, *Dictionary of International and Comparative Law* (3d ed. 2003). More specialized works, such as H. Victor Condé, *A Handbook of International Human Rights Terminology* (2d ed. 2004), are also available.

§ 11–2. International Organizations

While national governments are the major parties in international law, the field cannot be studied without understanding the vital role of intergovernmental organizations. Worldwide and regional organizations establish norms, promote multilateral conventions, and provide mechanisms for the peaceful resolution of conflicts. Several have established adjudicatory bodies by whose decisions nations agree to be bound. Even when not acting as lawmaking bodies, international organizations compile and publish many of the most important research sources in international law.

a. United Nations

The United Nations, founded in 1945 as a successor to the League of Nations, has greatly influenced the development of international law by providing an organizational forum and a center for the preparation and promotion of legislation and conventions. Its six principal organs are the General Assembly, Security Council, Economic and Social Council, Trusteeship Council, Secretariat, and International Court of Justice (ICJ). This section provides a general introduction to the UN; its treaty work and the ICJ will be discussed in greater detail in §§ 11–3 and 11–4.

The United Nations website <www.un.org> provides a wealth of information about the organization, including news, descriptive overviews of its activities, and access to numerous documents. The best printed source for basic information on the UN's structure and membership is *United Nations Handbook*, published annually by the New Zealand Ministry of External Relations and Trade. More in-depth treatments include Edmund Jan Osmańczyk, *Encyclopedia of the United Nations and International Agreements* (4 vols., 3d ed. 2003), a substantial reference work with the texts of major documents and research references for most entries.

The *Yearbook of the United Nations* is one of the best starting points for historical research on UN activities. Although coverage is delayed two or three years, this publication summarizes major developments, reprints major documents, and provides references to other sources for the year covered. Each volume includes a thorough index.

Among the most important documents for UN research are the *General Assembly Official Records* (GAOR). The records of the meetings of the assembly and its committees are accompanied by *Annexes* containing the more important documents produced during the session, and by *Supplements* containing annual reports submitted by the Secretary–General, the Security Council, the International Court of Justice, and various committees. The final supplement each year compiles all the resolutions passed by the General Assembly during the session.

Resolutions are also reprinted in the *Yearbook of the United Nations* and are available on the Internet. The Official Document System of the United Nations <documents.un.org> is a searchable database with the full text of resolutions from the General Assembly, Security Council, and Economic and Social Council since 1946, as well as other documents beginning in 1993. The UN Documentation Centre <www.un.org/documents/> provides access to major documents, including all General Assembly and Security Council resolutions since 1946, and may be easier to use because it can be browsed by year and document number.

The UN produces a broad range of other publications, including specialized yearbooks, statistical compilations, and conference proceedings. Documents since 1979 are indexed in UNBISNET (the United Nations Bibliographic Information System) <unbisnet.un.org>, with earlier material covered by the printed *UNDEX* (1974–78) and *United Nations Documents Index* (1950–73). The commercial database *Access UN: Index to United Nations Documents and Publications* <infoweb.newsbank.com>

has comprehensive retrospective coverage back to 1946, and includes the full text of several thousand documents.

Much of the work of the United Nations in particular subject fields is conducted by related international organizations, such as the Food and Agriculture Organization, the World Health Organization, and UNESCO. These organizations are referred to by the UN Charter as "specialized agencies" and submit their reports to the Economic and Social Council, which forwards them to the General Assembly. Several of these agencies have extensive law-related activities which produce documentation useful to the legal researcher. The United Nations System website locator <www.unsystem.org> provides access to sites for more than a hundred specialized organizations.

United Nations Documentation: Research Guide <www.un.org/Depts/dhl/resguide/> provides a concise introduction to UN resources, including an explanation of its document symbols, discussion of the major organizational units, and more in-depth coverage of some topics such as human rights and international law. Several more extensive guides are published, including Peter I. Hajnal, ed., *International Information: Documents, Publications, and Electronic Information of International Governmental Organizations* (2 vols., 2d ed. 1997–2001).

b. World Trade Organization

The World Trade Organization <www.wto.org>, the successor to the General Agreement on Tariffs and Trade (GATT), was established in 1995 as the principal international body for administering trade agreements among member states. The WTO acts as a forum for negotiations, seeks to resolve disputes, and oversees national trade policies. It is governed by a Ministerial Conference, which meets every two years, while most operations are handled by its General Council.

The basic documents governing WTO operations are reprinted in *The Results of the Uruguay Round of Multilateral Trade Negotiations: The Legal Texts* (1994) and are available on the organization's website. The WTO's *Annual Report* (1996–date, <www.wto.org/english/res_e/ reser_e/annual_report_e.htm>) provides trade statistics and a commentary on the organization's work every year. The WTO Secretariat has published *Guide to the Uruguay Round Agreements* (1999), a fairly concise work that is the only official explanation of the treaties. Mitsuo Matsushita et al., *The World Trade Organization: Law, Practice, and Policy* (2d ed. 2006) provides an extensive commentary on the WTO, and Joseph F. Dennin, ed., *Law and Practice of the World Trade Organization* (5 vols., 1995–date) is an extensive collection of treaties, dispute resolution decisions, and commentary.

The "Dispute Settlement" section of the WTO website includes panel decisions and appellate body reports, as well as information about rules and procedures. These decisions are also available in several commercial sources, including *International Trade Law Reports* (1996–date), *World Trade Organization Dispute Settlement Decisions: Bernan's Annotated Reporter* (1998–date), and Westlaw and LexisNexis. The subscription website WorldTradeLaw.net <www.worldtradelaw.net> provides summaries and text of decisions as well as various other WTO documents. Subject access is provided by *WTO Appellate Body Repertory of Reports and Awards, 1995–2005* (2006).

c. European Union and Other Regional Organizations

For American lawyers, the European Union (EU) <europa.eu> is probably the most frequently encountered of the world's many regional organizations. The EU was established in 1993 by the Maastricht Treaty, as the more ambitious successor to the European Communities (European Atomic Energy Community, European Coal and Steel Community, and European Economic Community). With the enlargement of the EU by the addition of ten new member states in 2004 and the ongoing consideration of a Constitution for Europe, the EU can be seen more as a supranational government than as a regional organization.

The major institutions of the EU are the European Parliament, a large elected body exercising mostly advisory powers; the Council, the major decision-making body consisting of one minister from each member country; the Commission, a permanent executive body responsible for implementing the organizing treaties and managing the Union; and the European Court of Justice (which will be discussed in § 11–3 with other regional courts). The monthly *Bulletin of the European Union* <europa.eu/bulletin/en/welcome.htm> reviews activities and reprints selected documents, and the annual *General Report on the Activities of the European Union* <europa.eu/generalreport/en/welcome.htm> provides an overview of developments.

The *Official Journal of the European Union* consists of two series, *Legislation* (L) and *Information and Notices* (C), and the semiannual *Directory of Community Legislation in Force* provides subject access to treaties, regulations, directives and other legislative actions. These and other major texts are available online through EUR–Lex, the EU's law portal <eur-lex.europa.eu>. Commercial databases such as Westlaw and LexisNexis also provide extensive access to the EU's treaties, legislation, and case law.

Several introductory reference works are available. Desmond Dinan, ed., *Encyclopedia of the European Union* (updated ed. 2000) is an alphabetically arranged overview of major topics and institutions, with bibliographies after most articles providing further leads. Other useful one-volume works include K.P.E. Lasok & Dominik Lasok, *Law and Institutions of the European Union* (7th ed. 2001), and P.S.R.F. Mathijsen, *A Guide to European Union Law* (8th ed. 2004). The annual *European Union Encyclopedia and Directory* provides explanations of EU terminology and activities, as well as contact information for EU institutions and officials.

CCH's *European Union Law Reporter* is one of the most useful starting points for American lawyers, because of its familiar looseleaf format, broad scope, and frequent supplementation. In addition to its primary emphasis on the European Union, it also provides limited coverage of other regional organizations and summarizes the domestic legislation of European countries on a variety of subjects.

Two works providing detailed analysis of the treaties creating the European Union are *Smit & Herzog on the Law of the European Union* (4 vols., 2005–date), and Neville March Hunnings, ed., *Encyclopedia of European Union Law: Constitutional Texts* (7 vols., 1996–date). *European Current Law: Monthly Digest* (1992–date) provides information on legal developments in the EU and throughout Europe, and is cumulated as the *European Current Law Year Book*.

Several guides to EU research are available, including the University of California Library's extensive collection

of links to EU Internet resources <www.lib.berkeley.edu/
doemoff/govinfo/intl/gov_eu.html>   and   Marylin   J.
Raisch's "European Union Law: An Integrated Guide to
Electronic and Print Research" <www.llrx.com/features/
eulaw2.htm>.

Other important regional organizations include the
Organization of American States (OAS) <www.oas.org>,
often considered the oldest regional organization; and the
Council of Europe <www.coe.int>, the major advocate of
democracy and the rule of law in Europe. Both of these
organizations draft and promote multilateral treaties
among their member states, and work to protect human
rights in their regions. Their activities in these areas will
be discussed in the following sections. G. Pope Atkins,
Encyclopedia of the Inter–American System (1997) provides a one-volume overview of the OAS and other Western Hemisphere organizations.

Information on major intergovernmental organizations
is included as Part One of the *Europa World Year Book*
(2 vols., annual; available online as Europa World Plus
<www.europaworld.com>), which also provides exten-
sive background information and statistics on the nations of the world. The *Yearbook of International Organizations* (6 vols., annual; also available on CD and online
<www.uia.org/organizations/>)   contains   descriptions
and directory information for thousands of international
groups and associations, with indexes by name, country
and subject; and U.S.-based organizations interested in
international issues are listed by subject in Congressional
Quarterly's *International Information Directory* (1999).

§ 11–3. Treaties

Treaties are formal agreements between countries. *Bilateral* treaties are those between two governments, and *multilateral* treaties (or *conventions*) are those entered into by more than two governments. The initial signatures to a treaty establish the parties' agreement that its text is authentic and definitive, but nations are not bound until they approve the treaty through ratification (such as approval by the United States Senate), accession (joining a treaty already negotiated by other states), or some other procedure. Parties may add reservations excluding certain provisions, or declarations providing their own interpretations of treaty terms. The texts of treaties usually identify the point at which they enter into force, often (in the case of multilateral conventions) when a specified number of nations have indicated their ratification or accession.

Treaties have legal significance for both international and domestic purposes. Article VI of the U.S. Constitution provides that treaties are part of the supreme law of the land, giving them the same legal effect and status as federal statutes. Treaties and statutes can supersede each other as the controlling law within the United States, but a treaty no longer valid as the law of the land may still be binding between the U.S. and another country. Treaties of the United States are negotiated and drafted by the executive branch but require approval by two-thirds of the Senate. Most treaty sources also cover executive agreements, which are made with other countries by the President without Senate consent.

Treaty research generally involves several aspects: (1) finding its text in an authoritative source; (2) determining whether it is in force and with what parties and reservations; and (3) interpreting its provisions, with the aid of commentaries, judicial decisions, and legislative history. What resources to use may depend in large part on whether the United States is a party to a treaty or convention, so answering that question is an important first step.

a. Sources

Treaties are published in a variety of forms–official and unofficial, national and international, current and retrospective. The *Bluebook* generally specifies citation of bilateral treaties to an official U.S. source (usually *United States Treaties and Other International Agreements*, or *UST*), and of multilateral treaties to an official international source as well (usually the *United Nations Treaty Series*, or *UNTS*). Not all treaties, however, appear in these standard sources, and it may be necessary to check journals, commercially published compilations, and electronic sources for the texts of agreements.

Sometimes the hardest step in researching a treaty is identifying its *UST* and *UNTS* citations. For this purpose, the law review databases of Westlaw and LexisNexis are great time-savers. Searching the law reviews for the title or subject of a treaty will usually lead to numerous footnotes providing the necessary references. Lists of major treaties, such as the University of Minnesota Law School's "Frequently–Cited Treaties and Other International Instruments" <www.law.umn.edu/library/tools/pathfinders/most-cited.html>, can also be invaluable.

U.S. sources. Until 1949, treaties were published in the *Statutes at Large* for each session of Congress. These have been reprinted in a definitive, official compilation,

Bevans' Treaties and Other International Agreements of the United States of America 1776–1949 (13 vols., 1968–75). This set contains four volumes of multilateral treaties (arranged chronologically), eight volumes of bilateral treaties (arranged alphabetically by country), and indexes by country and subject.

Beginning in 1950, *UST* has been the official, permanent form of publication for all treaties and executive agreements to which the United States is a party. *UST* volumes are published after a long delay of more than twenty years. Exhibit 11–1 on page 389 shows the first page of a treaty between the United States and Iraq, as published in *UST*.

Treaties and agreements are issued first in a slip format in the preliminary series, *Treaties and Other International Acts Series (TIAS)*. Slip treaties are consecutively numbered and issued in separately paginated pamphlets, containing the treaty text in English and in the languages of the other parties. *TIAS* publication is more current than *UST*, but still involves a time lag of more than ten years.

HeinOnline's Treaties and Agreements Library <www.heinonline.org> provides comprehensive online access to all of these sources (*Statutes at Large, Bevans, UST, TIAS*) as well as more recent treaties and a variety of guides, indexes, and other materials. Its search screen, shown in Exhibit 11–2 on page 390, provides a template for retrieving treaties by number, country, title, or date, as well as by full-text words or phrases.

Because of the long delays in the publication of *TIAS* and *UST*, commercial services are important sources for current access to treaties. Westlaw and LexisNexis are among the most comprehensive and up-to-date collections; Westlaw's USTREATIES database and the "U.S. Treaties on LEXIS" file both have documents dating back to 1778 and are regularly updated. Another extensive online source, *Treaties and International Agreements Online*, is available as a subscription website from Oceana Publications <www.oceanalaw.com>.

Hein's United States Treaties and Other International Agreements Current Service (1990–date), on microfiche, and *Consolidated Treaties & International Agreements: United States* (1990–date), in print, both provide copies of new treaties and agreements, with indexing by country and subject. The American Society of International Law's bimonthly *International Legal Materials* (1962–date) contains the texts of treaties of major significance and sometimes provides drafts before final agreement; its contents are available through Westlaw, LexisNexis, and HeinOnline.

General sources. The most comprehensive source for modern treaties is the *United Nations Treaty Series* (*UNTS*), containing more than 2,000 volumes. Since 1946 this series has published all treaties registered with the United Nations by member nations (including the U.S.) in their original languages, as well as in English and French translations. Exhibit 11–3 on page 391 shows the first page of the 1980 Convention on Prohibitions or Restrictions on the Use of Certain Conventional Weapons Which May be Deemed to be Excessively Injurious or to Have Indiscriminate Effects, as published in *UNTS*. Note that footnote 1 identifies the twenty ratifications that caused the convention to enter into force in 1983.

On the Internet, the United Nations Treaty Collection <untreaty.un.org> has the text of more than 30,000 treaties, searchable by name, subject, date, or parties, available on a subscription basis. Free sources for the texts of major multilateral treaties and conventions include the Multilaterals Project at the Fletcher School, Tufts University <fletcher.tufts.edu/multilaterals.html> and the University of Minnesota Human Rights Library <www1.umn.edu/humanrts/>.

Treaties predating the creation of the United Nations can be found in two older series. The *League of Nations Treaty Series (LNTS)* (1920–46) is similar in scope to the *UNTS*, and is included in the online United Nations Treaty Collection. A retrospective compilation, *Consolidated Treaty Series (CTS)* (1969–86) contains all treaties between nation states from 1648 to 1918. *CTS* prints treaties in the language of one of the signatories, usually accompanied by an English or French translation. Although there is no subject index, the set includes a chronological list and an index to parties.

Regional organizations also publish compilations of treaties among their members. Both the OAS <www.oas.org/DIL/> and the Council of Europe <conventions.coe.int> provide Internet access to major treaties. The Hague Conference on Private International Law <www.hcch.net> has the text of several dozen conventions it has drafted on issues such as international civil procedure and recognition of judgments. Treaties among European states are published in *European Conventions and Agreements* (1971–date); new agreements often appear in the annual *European Yearbook*, which also reports on the activities of more than a dozen regional organizations. Many countries publish current treaties in their official gazettes and on government websites, and new treaties are often printed in international law yearbooks and journals.

b. Indexes and Guides

Treaties are generally published chronologically rather than by subject, so finding tools or indexes are needed to identify agreements on a particular topic. Many of these same resources also provide information on treaty status.

Treaties in Force <www.state.gov/s/l/treaty/treaties>, an annual publication of the Department of State, is the official index to current United States treaties and agreements. It provides citations to all of the major treaty publications, including *Bevans*, *UST*, and the *LNTS* and *UNTS*. The first section of *Treaties in Force* lists bilateral treaties by country and, under each country, by subject; and the second section lists multilateral treaties by subject. Exhibits 11–4 and 11–5 on pages 392–393 show portions of each section, covering the bilateral and multilateral agreements in Exhibits 11–1 and 11–3 on pages 389 and 391.

A commercially published *Guide to the United States Treaties in Force* is also issued annually and provides several additional means of access to current treaties, including subject and country indexes to both bilateral and multilateral treaties. This can be a valuable resource, particularly because the official *Treaties in Force* has no subject index to bilateral treaties.

In addition to *Treaties in Force*, the State Department's Treaty Affairs website <www.state.gov /s/l/treaty/> also includes "Treaty Actions," a monthly compilation of new developments. This information was previously found in the publications *US Department of State Dispatch* (1990–99) and *Department of State Bulletin* (1939–89), both available through Hein-Online.

The major collections and series of U.S. treaties and international agreements are indexed in Igor I. Kavass, ed., *United States Treaty Index: 1776–2000 Consolidation* (13 vols., 1991–2002). This work includes a numerical guide to treaties and agreements, and indexes by subject, date, and country. The consolidated index is updated semiannually by the *Current Treaty Index*, and cumulative electronic access to both publications is available through *Hein's United States Treaty Index on CD–ROM*.

The *United Nations Treaty Series*, the major international source for treaties, has no cumulative official index. Initially, indexes were published for every one hundred volumes of *UNTS*; more recent indexes cover fifty volumes apiece and are published after a time lag of several years. Retrospective coverage back to 1946 is provided by a commercial publication, *United Nations Cumulative Treaty Index* (15 vols., 1999), and an electronic *United Nations Master Treaty Index on CD–ROM*.

The leading index for finding multilateral conventions is Christian L. Wiktor, *Multilateral Treaty Calendar, 1648–1995* (1998). This lists more than 6,000 agreements chronologically, identifies sources in more than a hundred publications, and provides information on treaty status. The *Multilateral Treaty Calendar* entry for the Conventional Weapons Convention in Exhibit 11–3 on page 391 is shown in Exhibit 11–6 on page 394. Note that it lists more than a dozen sources for the text of the treaty, including the *UNTS* and several national treaty series and journals, but that it does not list the nations that are parties to the agreement.

The source for determining the status of, and identifying the parties to, major conventions is the annual *Multilateral Treaties Deposited with the Secretary–General,* published by the United Nations. This listing of nearly 500 treaties is arranged by subject, and provides citations, information on status, a list of parties with dates of signature and ratification, and the text of any reservations imposed by individual parties. Coverage is limited to treaties concluded under UN auspices or for which the Secretary–General acts as depository, so it excludes such major agreements as the Geneva Conventions of 1949 or the Convention on International Trade in Endangered Species (CITES). Exhibit 11–7 on page 395 shows the first page of the entry for the Conventional Weapons Convention as of December 31, 2005, with nearly ninety countries now parties to the convention. Individual countries' declarations, reservations, and objections are noted on following pages after the list of parties. Subscribers to the United Nations Treaty Collection <untreaty.un.org> have access to an online version that is updated daily.

Two other sources are useful for identifying older treaties, but neither has been updated in several years. M.J. Bowman & D.J. Harris, *Multilateral Treaties: Index and Current Status* (1984, with 11th cum. supp. 1995), provides information on sources and lists parties. It covers more than 1,000 agreements, including some predating or not deposited with the UN. The *World Treaty Index*, compiled by Peter H. Rohn (5 vols., 2d ed. 1983–84) provides comprehensive coverage of some 44,000 bilateral and multilateral treaties from 1900 to 1980, indexing *UNTS*, *LNTS*, and numerous other sources by country, subject, date, and international organization. An online version of *World Treaty Index* has been updated to 1999 with 25,000 additional treaty citations <depts. washington.edu/hrights/Treaty/trindex.html>.

c. Interpretation

Treaties often contain ambiguities which can lead to controversies in interpretation and application. Several resources provide assistance in understanding the terms of a treaty. Among the most important are court decisions interpreting a treaty and documents produced during its drafting and consideration.

The easiest way to find court decisions on a treaty's meaning or effect is a Westlaw or LexisNexis case database full-text search for the treaty name, because neither KeyCite nor Shepard's covers citations to treaties. (*Shepard's Federal Statute Citations* includes coverage of treaties in its 1996 volumes, but not in more recent supplements.) The *United States Code Service* includes two useful volumes: *International Agreements*, containing the texts of about two dozen major conventions and treaties, accompanied by research references and case annotations; and *Annotations to Uncodified Laws and Treaties*, which has no treaty texts but provides broader coverage of decisions interpreting U.S. treaties, including sections for treaties with Native American nations, multilateral treaties (listed by date), and bilateral treaties (listed by country).

For United States treaties, Senate deliberation provides another valuable source of documentation on an agreement's terms and meaning. *Treaty Documents* (until 1980, called *Senate Executive Documents*) contain the text of treaties as they are transmitted to the Senate for its consideration. These documents usually contain messages from the President and the Secretary of State. The Senate Foreign Relations Committee analyzes treaties, may hold hearings, and issues *Senate Executive Reports* containing its recommendations. Both Treaty Documents and Senate Executive Reports are issued in numbered series which identify the Congress and sequence in which they were issued. Note in Exhibit 11–6 on page 394 that two of the sources the *Multilateral Treaty Calendar* lists for the text of the Conventional Weapons Convention are Treaty Docs. No. 103–25 and 105–1.

THOMAS <thomas.loc.gov> provides legislative history summaries of congressional treaty action since the 90th Congress (1967–68). The best list of currently pending treaties, with actions taken, is available from the Senate Foreign Relations Committee website <foreign. senate.gov/treaties.pdf>. The looseleaf *Congressional Index* also includes a table of treaties pending before the Senate, with references to Treaty Documents, Executive Reports, hearings, and ratifications.

Another source available for the interpretation of some multilateral conventions is the *travaux preparatoires* (documents created during the drafting process such as reports and debates). These are recognized under the 1969 Vienna Convention on Treaties as a source for clarifying ambiguous treaty terms, and U.S. courts frequently rely on such sources. *Travaux* for some conventions have been published, e.g. Marc J. Bossuyt, *Guide to the "Travaux Preparatoires" of the International Covenant on Civil and Political Rights* (1987), or Paul Weis, *The Refugee Convention, 1951: The Travaux Preparatoires Analysed with a Commentary* (1995).

§ 11–4. Dispute Resolution

Although most disputes between nations are resolved by direct negotiation between the parties, some are submitted to international tribunals, arbitral bodies, or temporary commissions convened for particular disputes. Adjudications by international courts are generally recognized as authoritative, even if they lack effective enforcement procedures.

Nations are not the only parties to significant international law cases. Courts established by regional organizations resolve disputes between nations and their citizens, and have developed a growing body of international human rights law. Decisions of domestic courts on matters of international law can also be important evidence of international legal custom, and commercial arbitration is increasingly prevalent in international business.

a. International Courts

The preeminent international tribunal is the International Court of Justice (also known as the World Court), which succeeded the Permanent Court of International Justice of the League of Nations. The ICJ settles legal controversies between countries and resolves a limited number of other cases involving major questions of international law.

ICJ decisions are published initially in individual slip opinions and later in the bound volumes of *Reports of Judgments, Advisory Opinions and Orders*. The ICJ website <www.icj-cij.org> has all of the Court's decisions, basic documents, and information on its current docket. The best printed source for recent decisions is the American Society of International Law's bimonthly *International Legal Materials*. Exhibit 11–8 on page 396 shows the first page of a recent order in a case involving the United States, as published officially by the Court.

The leading commentaries on the ICJ are Shabtai Rosenne, *The Law and Practice of the International*

Court, 1920–1996 (4 vols., 3d ed. 1997), and Andreas Zimmermann et al., eds., *The Statute of the International Court of Justice: A Commentary* (2006). Rosenne was also the original author of a shorter volume, Terry D. Gill et al., *Rosenne's The World Court: What It Is and How It Works* (6th ed. 2003), and editor of a compilation of source material, *Documents on the International Court of Justice* (3d ed. 1991). Arthur Eyffinger, *The International Court of Justice 1946–1996* (1996) is an extensively illustrated overview of the ICJ's procedures and history, with biographies of every judge during its first fifty years.

The annual *Yearbook of the International Court of Justice* contains a summary of the Court's work since 1946, basic information about the Court, and summaries of judgments and opinions issued during the year. Other Court publications include *Summaries of Judgments, Advisory Opinions and Orders of the International Court of Justice: 1948–1991* (1992, with supplements covering 1992–96 and 1997–2002); and *Pleadings, Oral Arguments and Documents*, containing the briefs and documents submitted by the parties.

The ICJ website includes decisions of the Permanent Court of International Justice (PCIJ), its predecessor as World Court. An unofficial compilation of PCIJ decisions was published as *World Court Reports*, edited by Manley O. Hudson (4 vols., 1934–43), and PCIJ decisions are available on HeinOnline. *International Law Reports* (1956–date), succeeding *Annual Digest and Reports of Public International Law Cases* (1932–55), is a widely used reporter of international decisions, including all PCIJ and ICJ decisions. It also prints selected decisions of regional and national courts on international law issues.

The ICJ is not the only court of global scope. The United Nations Convention on the Law of the Sea established an International Tribunal for the Law of the Sea (ITLOS), which issued its first judgment in 1999. Information on ITLOS procedures and cases are available on its website <www.itlos.org>, and publications include an annual *Reports of Judgments, Advisory Opinions, and Orders* and *Yearbook*, as well as *Basic Texts 2005* printing the rules and other documents.

An International Criminal Court <www.icc-cpi.int> with jurisdiction over war crimes, genocide, and crimes against humanity had its first session in 2003, without United States participation. Background information and documents are available on the Court's website and in works such as Antonio Cassese et al., eds., *The Rome Statute of the International Criminal Court: A Commentary* (3 vols., 2002), and M. Cherif Bassiouni, ed., *The Legislative History of the International Criminal Court* (3 vols., 2005). Bassiouni is also the editor of *International Criminal Law* (3 vols., 2d ed. 1999), the leading treatise in this area.

In addition to the International Criminal Court, more focused courts address violations of international humanitarian law in specific countries. These include the International Criminal Tribunal for the former Yugoslavia (ICTY) <www.un.org/icty/>, the International Criminal Tribunal for Rwanda (ICTR) <www.ictr.org>, and the Special Court for Sierra Leone <www.sc-sl.org>. Documents and judgments are available on the court websites, and their work is discussed in sources such as John R.W.D. Jones & Steven Powles, *International Criminal Practice* (2003) and William Schabas, *UN International*

Criminal Tribunals: The Former Yugoslavia, Rwanda, and Sierra Leone (2006).

Cases of the criminal tribunals can be found in *Annotated Leading Cases of International Criminal Tribunals* (1999–date), and the case law is summarized in collections such as *Genocide, War Crimes and Crimes Against Humanity: A Topical Digest of the Case Law of the International Criminal Tribunal for the Former Yugoslavia* (2006) (also available online <hrw.org/reports/2006/icty0706/>).

b. Regional and National Courts

The decisions of the courts of regional organizations have assumed growing importance in international law, as the range of disputes over which they exercise jurisdiction grows. Among the most important of these regional courts are the European Court of Justice, the European Court of Human Rights, and the Inter–American Court of Human Rights.

The European Court of Justice <curia.europa.eu>, an organ of the European Union, resolves disputes between EU institutions and member states over the interpretation and application of EU treaties and legislation. A subordinate Court of First Instance was established in 1988 to handle certain classes of cases and reduce the Court of Justice's workload. The official *Reports of Cases Before the Court of Justice and the Court of First Instance* includes decisions from both courts. Commercial publications of these decisions include the CCH *European Union Law Reporter* and *Common Market Law Reports* (1962–date). All decisions since 1954 are also available online from the ECJ website, as well as from Westlaw and LexisNexis.

The European Court of Human Rights <www.echr.coe.int> was created under the European Convention of Human Rights of 1950, which established a system for the international protection of the rights of individuals. The Court's decisions are available on its website, and are published officially in *Reports of Judgments and Decisions* and commercially in *European Human Rights Reports* (1979–date, available online from Westlaw). Cases are summarized in *Human Rights Case Digest* (1990–date, bimonthly), published by the British Institute of Human Rights, and a variety of documents and decisions appear in the annual *Yearbook of the European Convention on Human Rights* (1958–date).

The Inter–American Commission on Human Rights <www.cidh.oas.org> was created in 1959 and hears complaints of individuals and institutions alleging violations of human rights in the American countries. The Commission, or a member state, can refer matters to the Inter–American Court of Human Rights <www.corteidh.or.cr>, created in 1978. Twenty-one countries (not including the United States) have accepted its jurisdiction. The Court's decisions are reported on its website, in two series of judgments (advisory opinions in Series A, *Judgments and Opinions*, and contentious cases in Series C, *Decisions and Judgments*). The *Inter-American Yearbook on Human Rights* (1985–date) covers the work of both the Commission and the Court and includes selected decisions and other documents.

Judicial decisions of national courts on matters of international law are also valuable sources of information. While any U.S. court may be faced with international legal issues, one with a particular expertise is the U.S. Court of International Trade (CIT). Its decisions are reported officially in the *U.S. Court of International Trade Reports*, as well as in the *Federal Supplement* and in BNA's *International Trade Reporter* (1980–date), which also includes cases from other courts (including the Court of Appeals for the Federal Circuit reviewing CIT decisions), administrative agencies, and binational panels under the North American Free Trade Agreement. CIT decisions are also available from LexisNexis and Westlaw, and the court's website <www.cit.uscourts.gov> provides copies of slip opinions since 1999.

Cases from the U.S. and other countries under the Convention on Contracts for the International Sale of Goods (CISG) are available online and in print from UNILEX <www.unilex.info>, which also provides a bibliography of books and articles on CISG and the UNIDROIT Principles of International Commercial Contracts. International law cases from some countries are published or summarized in national yearbooks, periodicals, and digests of international law, as well as a few specialized case reporters (such as *British International Law Cases* and *Commonwealth International Law Cases*). As noted earlier, *International Law Reports* includes selected decisions of domestic courts as well as those of international tribunals.

c. Arbitrations

An increasing number of disputes, between nations and between commercial partners, are settled by arbitration. The Hague Peace Conferences of 1899 and 1907 created standards for international arbitration and established the Permanent Court of Arbitration. Its early decisions were published in the *Hague Court Reports*, edited by James B. Scott (2 vols., 1916–32). This set has been continued by the United Nations series, *Reports of*

International Arbitral Awards (1948–date), with retrospective coverage back to the end of Scott's reports (available on HeinOnline). The awards are printed in either English or French, with bilingual headnotes. The UN series includes agreements reached by mediation or conciliation, as well as awards resulting from contested arbitrations, but it is limited to disputes in which states are the parties.

Reference works include *Repertory of International Arbitral Jurisprudence* (3 vols., 1989–91), arranging arbitral decisions from 1794 to 1987 by subject; A.M. Stuyt, ed., *Survey of International Arbitrations, 1794–1989* (3d ed. 1990); providing an extensive digest of decisions; and P. Hamilton et al., eds., *The Permanent Court of Arbitration: International Arbitration and Dispute Resolution* (1999), summarizing the work of twentieth-century arbitral tribunals and commissions.

Several sources cover international arbitrations between private parties, including *Yearbook: Commercial Arbitration* (1975–date) and Hans Smit & Vratislav Pechota, eds., *World Arbitration Reporter* (1986–date). Some coverage is provided in *International Legal Materials*, and selected decisions appear in the *American Review of International Arbitration* (1990–date). Two major current awareness services in this area are BNA's *World Arbitration & Mediation Report* (1990–date, monthly) and *Mealey's International Arbitration Report* (1986–date, monthly, available through LexisNexis). The leading one-volume treatise in the area is Alan Redfern & Martin Hunter, *Law and Practice of International Commercial Arbitration* (4th ed. 2004). A variety of major sources are available online from the subscription site Kluwer Arbitration <www.kluwerarbitration.com>.

§ 11–5. Secondary Sources and Document Collections

As in other areas of law, it is often best to begin international law research with a reference work or law review article for background information and for help in analyzing the issues involved. A general treatise, such as Peter Malanczuk, *Akehurst's Modern Introduction to International Law* (8th ed. 2002) or Ian Brownlie, *Principles of Public International Law* (6th ed. 2003), can provide an overview of international law doctrine.

The *Encyclopedia of Public International Law*, edited by Rudolf Bernhardt and published under the auspices of the Max Planck Institute for Comparative Public Law and International Law, provides a comprehensive view of international law issues. Its articles, by leading scholars in the field, include brief bibliographies for further research. The set was originally published in 12 volumes (1981–90), with each volume devoted to one or more specific subjects, and was then reissued in one alphabetical sequence (5 vols., 1992–2003), with some additional articles and addenda.

Shorter reference works and texts include Anthony Aust, *Handbook of International Law* (2005); Ian Brownlie, *Principles of Public International Law* (6th ed. 2003); and Malcolm N. Shaw, *International Law* (5th ed. 2003). The American Bar Association publishes Lucinda A. Low et al., eds., *International Lawyer's Deskbook* (2d ed. 2002), designed as an introductory starting point for lawyers facing international law issues.

To study state practice in international law, it is best to turn to sources summarizing or explaining how a particular nation has acted in the past. Reference works such as Bruce W. Jentleson & Thomas G. Paterson, eds.,

Encyclopedia of U.S. Foreign Relations (4 vols., 1997), can provide a background understanding. More detailed discussion of United States practice can be found in a series of encyclopedic digests of international law published by the Department of State and available on HeinOnline. These digests are based on treaties, decisions, statutes and other documents reflecting the U.S. position on major issues of international law, and are essentially official restatements of American international law.

The most current U.S. digest (although long outdated) is Marjorie M. Whiteman's *Digest of International Law* (15 vols., 1963–73), focusing largely on the period from the 1940s to the 1960s. The Whiteman *Digest* is supplemented by a Department of State series called *Digest of United States Practice in International Law*. Current developments are summarized in "Contemporary Practice of the United States Relating to International Law," a feature in each quarterly issue of the *American Journal of International Law*.

The earlier digests of international law published by the Department of State, with slight variations in title, were by the following compilers: Francis Wharton (3 vols., 1886; 2d ed. 1887); John Bassett Moore (8 vols., 1906), covering the period 1776 to 1906 and effectively superseding Wharton; and G.H. Hackworth (8 vols., 1940–44), covering the period 1906 to 1939. Since material in Moore and Hackworth is not reprinted in later digests, they retain their research value for the period covered.

More extensive documentation of U.S. practice can be found in *Foreign Relations of the United States* (1861–date), a series prepared by the Historical Office of the

Department of State to provide a comprehensive record of material relating to such issues as treaty negotiation and international conflicts. Unfortunately, there is a time lag of more than thirty years between the original (often confidential) issuance of these documents and their publication in this series. Some volumes, from the Kennedy through Nixon administrations, are available online <www.state.gov/r/pa/ho/frus/>.

The American Law Institute's *Restatement (Third) of the Foreign Relations Law of the United States* (2 vols., 1987) is an unofficial but respected summary of American law and practice in international law and foreign relations. The *Restatement (Second) of Conflict of Laws* (4 vols., 1971–80) covers private international law from an American perspective. Appendices to both Restatements include abstracts of citing court decisions.

Researchers can find information about the practices of other nations in annual publications such as the *British Yearbook of International Law* or the *Annuaire Français de Droit International*. Most of these yearbooks also include scholarly articles on international law and reprint selected major documents. Several countries also publish documentary compilations similar to the U.S. foreign relations collections, some as large retrospective collections primarily useful for historical research and others providing continuing series of contemporary materials.

Several collections reprint a variety of important international law documents, including Ian Brownlie, ed., *Basic Documents in International Law* (5th ed. 2002); Ian Brownlie & Guy S. Goodwin–Gill, eds., *Basic Documents on Human Rights* (5th ed. 2006); John P. Grant & J. Craig Barker, eds., *International Criminal Law Desk-*

book (2006); and Philippe Sands & Paolo Galizzi, eds., *Documents in International Environmental Law* (2d ed. 2004). The most extensive of these collections is Burns H. Weston & Jonathan C. Carlson, eds., *International Law and World Order: Basic Documents* (9 vols., 1994–date).

§ 11–6. Sources for Further Information

Materials involved in international law issues are often published in diverse, elusive sources, and specialized bibliographies and research guides can be valuable finding aids. One of the most useful of these, and most frequently updated, is the American Society of International Law's *ASIL Guide to Electronic Resources for International Law*, available in print and online <www. asil.org/resource/home.htm>, with sections on the United Nations, treaties, and several topical areas. In total it provides annotated links to thousands of Internet resources in international law.

The American Society of International Law also produces "The Electronic Information System for International Law" (EISIL) <www.eisil.org>, which contains links to primary documents and major web sites in thirteen major subject areas. A "More Information" link under each reference includes some background information and legal citations.

Another major Internet source for international law information is Law Library Resource Xchange, or LLRX, which publishes heavily linked research guides on specific topics. Its International Law Guides page <www.llrx. com/international_law.html> lists several dozen guides in the area. GlobaLex, based at the New York University

School of Law <www.nyulawglobal.org/globalex/>, provides a similar range of research guides on international, comparative, and foreign law.

Several international law research guides are available. The most current and regularly updated is *Guide to International Legal Research*, a substantial volume published annually by the George Washington University Journal of International Law and Economics.

The *Index to Foreign Legal Periodicals* (1960–date, quarterly, available through Westlaw and other database systems) is principally an index of journals published in countries outside the common law system, but it also indexes articles on international law in selected American law reviews. *Public International Law: A Current Bibliography of Books and Articles* (1975–date, semiannual) is a comprehensive index of the literature in the field. Each issue of the *American Journal of International Law* contains an extensive section reviewing or noting new works in the field, and the *International Journal of Legal Information* regularly publishes bibliographies devoted to specific areas of foreign and international law.

§ 11–7. Conclusion

This brief survey of international law highlights the extent and variety of available sources. With the increasingly global nature of business and legal relationships, and the frequent treatment of transnational legal issues by American courts, international law research is no longer an exotic specialty known only to a few practitioners.

In researching international law in this increasingly global age, it is important for American lawyers *not* to limit their inquiry to U.S. sources. Materials from international organizations and other countries can provide new perspectives and present solutions that may not be readily apparent from within the U.S. legal tradition. A facility with other languages assists greatly in broadening the scope of research, but as this chapter has shown there are a large number of English-language resources available for substantial international law study.

IRAQ

Cultural Relations

Agreement signed at Baghdad January 23, 1961;
Entered into force August 13, 1963.

CULTURAL AGREEMENT BETWEEN THE UNITED STATES OF AMERICA AND THE REPUBLIC OF IRAQ

The Government of the United States of America and the Government of the Republic of Iraq:

In consideration of the bonds of friendship and understanding existing between the peoples of the United States of America and of the Republic of Iraq;

In view of the expressed desire of both Governments for an agreement which would encourage and further stimulate the present cultural exchange between the two countries;

Inspired by the determination to increase mutual understanding between the peoples of the United States of America and the Republic of Iraq;

Agree as follows:

Article I

Each Government shall encourage the extension within its own territory of a better knowledge of the history, civilization, institutions, literature and other cultural accomplishments of the people of the other country by such means as promoting and facilitating the exchange of books, periodicals and other publications; the exchange of musical, dramatic, dance and athletic groups and performers; the exchange of fine art and other exhibitions; the exchange of radio and television programs, films, phonograph records and tapes; and by the establishment of university courses and chairs and language instruction.

Article II

The two Governments shall promote and facilitate the interchange between the United States of America and the Republic of Iraq of prominent citizens, professors, teachers, technicians, students and other qualified individuals from all walks of life.

Exhibit 11–1. Cultural Agreement between the United States of America and the Republic of Iraq, Jan. 23, 1961, 14 U.S.T. 1168.

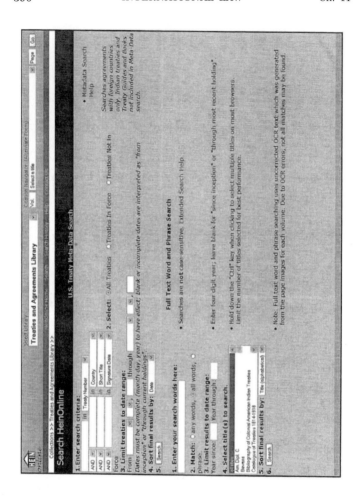

Exhibit 11–2. HeinOnline Treaties and Agreements Library search screen.

CONVENTION[1] ON PROHIBITIONS OR RESTRICTIONS ON THE USE OF CERTAIN CONVENTIONAL WEAPONS WHICH MAY BE DEEMED TO BE EXCESSIVELY INJURIOUS OR TO HAVE INDISCRIMINATE EFFECTS

The High Contracting Parties,

Recalling that every State has the duty, in conformity with the Charter of the United Nations, to refrain in its international relations from the threat or use of force against the sovereignty, territorial integrity or political independence of any State, or in any other manner inconsistent with the purposes of the United Nations,

Further recalling the general principle of the protection of the civilian population against the effects of hostilities,

Basing themselves on the principle of international law that the right of the parties to an armed conflict to choose methods or means of warfare is not unlimited, and on the principle that prohibits the employment in armed conflicts of weapons, projectiles and material and methods of warfare of a nature to cause superfluous injury or unnecessary suffering,

Also recalling that it is prohibited to employ methods or means of warfare which are intended, or may be expected, to cause widespread, long-term and severe damage to the natural environment,

---

[1] The Convention, including the three Protocols, came into force on 2 December 1983 in respect of the following States, i.e., six months after the date of deposit of the twentieth instrument of ratification, acceptance, approval or accession with the Secretary-General of the United Nations, in accordance with article 5 (1) and (3):

State	Date of deposit of the instrument of ratification, acceptance (A) or accession (a) and of acceptance of Protocols I, II and III	State	Date of deposit of the instrument of ratification, acceptance (A) or accession (a) and of acceptance of Protocols I, II and III
Austria	14 March 1983	Japan	9 June 1982 A
Bulgaria	15 October 1982	Lao People's Democratic Republic	3 January 1983 a
Byelorussian Soviet Socialist Republic	23 June 1982	Mexico	11 February 1982
China	7 April 1982	Mongolia	8 June 1982
Czechoslovakia	31 August 1982	Poland	2 June 1983
Denmark	7 July 1982	Sweden	7 July 1982
Ecuador	4 May 1982	Switzerland	20 August 1982
Finland	8 April 1982	Ukrainian Soviet Socialist Republic	23 June 1982
German Democratic Republic	20 July 1982	Union of Soviet Socialist Republics	10 June 1982
Hungary	14 June 1982	Yugoslavia	24 May 1983

Subsequently, the Convention came into force for the following State six months after the date on which it deposited its instrument of ratification, acceptance, approval or accession with the Secretary-General of the United Nations, in accordance with article 5 (2):

State	Date of deposit of the instrument of ratification and of acceptance of Protocols I, II and III
Norway (With effect from 7 December 1983.)	7 June 1983

Exhibit 11–3.   Convention on Prohibitions or Restrictions on the Use of Certain Conventional Weapons Which May be Deemed to be Excessively Injurious or to Have Indiscriminate Effects, Oct. 10, 1980, 1342 U.N.T.S. 163.

IRAQ

CLAIMS

Agreement concerning claims resulting from attack on the U.S.S. *Stark*. Exchange of notes at Baghdad March 27 and 28, 1989; entered into force March 28, 1989.
TIAS 12030.

COMMERCE (See also ECONOMIC AND TECHNICAL COOPERATION)

Treaty of commerce and navigation. Signed at Baghdad December 3, 1938; entered into force June 19, 1940.
54 Stat. 1790; TS 960; 9 Bevans 7; 203 LNTS 107.

CULTURAL RELATIONS

Cultural agreement. Signed at Baghdad January 23, 1961; entered into force August 13, 1963.
14 UST 1168; TIAS 5411; 488 UNTS 163.

CUSTOMS

Agreement relating to the privilege, on a reciprocal basis, of free entry to all articles imported for the personal use of consular officers. Exchange of notes at Washington March 14, May 15, June 19, and August 8, 1951; entered into force August 8, 1951.
5 UST 657; TIAS 2956; 229 UNTS 185.

DEFENSE

Agreement confirming understanding of Iraq that paragraphs 1 and 4 of the military assistance agreement of April 21, 1954 apply to equipment or materials transferred by the United States to Iraq on a reimbursable basis.

Exhibit 11–4. U.S. DEP'T STATE, TREATIES IN FORCE: A LIST OF TREATIES AND OTHER INTERNATIONAL AGREEMENTS OF THE UNITED STATES IN FORCE ON JANUARY 1, 2006, at 154 (2006).

WEAPONS

Convention on prohibitions or restrictions on the use of certain conventional weapons which may be deemed to be excessively injurious or to have indiscriminate effects. Adopted at Geneva October 10, 1980; entered into force December 2, 1983; for the United States September 24, 1995.
TIAS

Protocol on non-detectable fragments (Protocol I). Adopted at Geneva October 10, 1980; entered into force December 2, 1983; for the United States September 24, 1995.
TIAS

Protocol on prohibitions or restrictions on the use of mines, booby-traps and other devices (Protocol II). Adopted at Geneva October 10, 1980; entered into force December 2, 1983; for the United States September 24, 1995.[1]
TIAS
Parties:
Albania
Argentina
Australia
Austria
Bangladesh
Belarus
Belgium
Benin [2]
Bolivia
Bosnia-Herzegovina
Brazil
Bulgaria
Burkina Faso
Cambodia
Canada [3]
Cape Verde
Chile
China [4]
Colombia
Costa Rica
Croatia
Cuba
Cyprus
Czech Republic
Denmark
Djibouti
Ecuador
El Salvador
Estonia [2]
Finland
France

Exhibit 11–5. TREATIES IN FORCE 2006, at 536.

October 10, 1980   **Rules of Warfare**
Convention on prohibitions or restrictions on the use of certain conventional weapons which may be deemed to be excessively injurious or to have indiscriminate effects, with protocols (I to IV). *Convention sur l'interdiction ou la limitation de l'emploi de certaines armes classiques qui peuvent être considérées comme produisant des effets traumatiques excessifs ou comme frappant sans discrimination, avec protocoles (I à IV).*

    Concluded at Geneva (U.N.) October 10, 1980

    Printed text: 1342 UNTS 137, 163 (E), 173 (F); US Treaty Doc. 103-25, p. 6; US Treaty Doc. 105-1, pp. 37, and subs. (protocols II to IV); BTS 105(1996), Cm. 3497; CTS 1994/19; ATS 1984/6; SDIA 28:124 (1980); JORF 1988:13843; RTAF 1988/62; 73 VBD A904; UNJY 1980:113; 19 ILM 1523, 1524 (text)

    Depository: United Nations

    Entered into force: December 2, 1983

    Status: 57 parties (UN Status, Dec. 1995, p. 865; 19 UNDY 286)

    Note: Adopted by the United Nations Conference on Prohibitions or Restrictions of Use of Certain Conventional Weapons Which May be Deemed to be Excessively Injurious or to Have Indiscriminate Effects on October 10, 1980, and annexed to the final act as annexes A to D; opened for signature at New York (U.N.) April 10, 1981; refers to U.N. Charter of JUNE 26, 1945, and Geneva conventions of AUGUST 12, 1949; protocol I concerns nondetectable fragments, protocol II the prohibitions or restrictions on the use of mines, boobytraps and other devices, and protocol III the prohibitions or restrictions on the use of incendiary weapons; protocol II was amended on MAY 3, 1996 (see text in US Treaty Doc. 105-1, p. 37; BPP Misc. 2(1997), Cm. 3507; 35 ILM 1206, 1209; 100 RGDIP 1138); see also protocol IV on blinding laser weapons of OCTOBER 13, 1995.

Exhibit 11–6. CHRISTIAN L. WIKTOR, MULTILATERAL TREATY CALENDAR 1648–1995, at 1192 (1998).

2. CONVENTION ON PROHIBITIONS OR RESTRICTIONS ON THE USE OF CERTAIN CONVENTIONAL WEAPONS WHICH MAY BE DEEMED TO BE EXCESSIVELY INJURIOUS OR TO HAVE INDISCRIMINATE EFFECTS (WITH PROTOCOLS I, II AND III)

Geneva, 10 October 1980

ENTRY INTO FORCE:	2 December 1983 in accordance with article 5 (1) and (3).
REGISTRATION:	2 December 1983, No. 22495
STATUS:	Signatories: 50. Parties: 100.
TEXT:	United Nations, Treaty Series, vol. 1342, p. 137; depositary notifications C.N.356.1981. TREATIES-7 of 14 January 1982 (procès-verbal of rectification of the Chinese authentic text) and C.N.320.1982. TREATIES-11 of 21 January 1983 (procès-verbal of rectification of the Final Act).

Note: The Convention and its annexed Protocols were adopted by the United Nations Conference on Prohibitions or Restrictions of the Use of Certain Conventional Weapons Which May Be Deemed Excessively Injurious or to Have Indiscriminate Effects, held in Geneva from 10 to 28 September 1979 and from 15 September to 10 October 1980. The Conference was convened pursuant to General Assembly resolutions 32/152 of 19 December 1977 and 33/70 of 14 December 1978. The original of the Convention with the annexed Protocols, of which the Arabic, Chinese, English, French, Russian and Spanish texts are equally authentic, is deposited with the Secretary-General of the United Nations. The Convention was open for signature by all States at United Nations Headquarters in New York for a period of twelve months from 10 April 1981.

Participant	Signature	Ratification, Acceptance (A), Approval (AA), Accession (a), Succession (d)	Participant	Signature	Ratification, Acceptance (A), Approval (AA), Accession (a), Succession (d)
Afghanistan	10 Apr 1981		Guatemala		
Albania		28 Aug 2002 a	Holy See		
Argentina	2 Dec 1981	2 Oct 1995	Honduras		30 Oct 2003 a
Australia	8 Apr 1982	29 Sep 1983	Hungary	10 Apr 1981	14 Jun 1982
Austria	10 Apr 1981	14 Mar 1983	Iceland	10 Apr 1981	
Bangladesh		6 Sep 2000 a	India	15 May 1981	1 Mar 1984
Belarus	10 Apr 1981	23 Jun 1982	Ireland	10 Apr 1981	13 Mar 1995
Belgium	10 Apr 1981	7 Feb 1995	Israel		22 Mar 1995 a
Benin		27 Mar 1989 a	Italy	10 Apr 1981	20 Jan 1995
Bolivia		21 Sep 2001 a	Japan	22 Sep 1981	9 Jun 1982 A
Bosnia and Herzegovina[1]		1 Sep 1993 d	Jordan		19 Oct 1995 a
Brazil		3 Oct 1995 a	Lao People's Democratic Republic[5]		3 Jan 1983 a
Bulgaria	10 Apr 1981	15 Oct 1982	Latvia		4 Jan 1993 a
Burkina Faso		26 Nov 2003 a	Lesotho		6 Sep 2000 a
Cambodia		25 Mar 1997 a	Liberia		16 Sep 2005 a
Canada	10 Apr 1981	24 Jun 1994	Liechtenstein	11 Feb 1982	16 Aug 1989
Cape Verde		16 Sep 1997 a	Lithuania		3 Jun 1998 a
Chile		15 Oct 2003 A	Luxembourg	10 Apr 1981	21 May 1996
China[2]	14 Sep 1981	7 Apr 1982	Maldives		7 Sep 2000 a
Colombia		6 Mar 2000 a	Mali		24 Oct 2001 a
Costa Rica		17 Dec 1998 a	Malta		26 Jun 1995 a
Croatia[1]		2 Dec 1993 d	Mauritius		6 May 1996 a
Cuba	10 Apr 1981	2 Mar 1987	Mexico	10 Apr 1981	11 Feb 1982
Cyprus		12 Dec 1988 a	Monaco		12 Aug 1997 a
Czech Republic[3]		22 Feb 1993 d	Mongolia	10 Apr 1981	8 Jun 1982
Denmark	10 Apr 1981	7 Jul 1982	Morocco	10 Apr 1981	19 Mar 2002
Djibouti		29 Jul 1996 a	Nauru		12 Nov 2001 a
Ecuador	9 Sep 1981	4 May 1982	Netherlands[6]	10 Apr 1981	18 Jun 1987 A
Egypt	10 Apr 1981		New Zealand	10 Apr 1981	18 Oct 1993
El Salvador		26 Jan 2000 a	Nicaragua	20 May 1981	5 Dec 2000
Estonia		20 Apr 2000 a	Niger		10 Nov 1992 a
Finland	10 Apr 1981	8 Apr 1982	Nigeria	26 Jan 1982	
France	10 Apr 1981	4 Mar 1988	Norway	10 Apr 1981	7 Jun 1983
Georgia		29 Apr 1996 a	Pakistan	26 Jan 1982	1 Apr 1985
Germany[4]	10 Apr 1981	25 Nov 1992	Panama		26 Mar 1997 a
Greece	10 Apr 1981	28 Jan 1992	Paraguay		22 Sep 2004 a
			Peru		3 Jul 1997 a

Exhibit 11–7. 2 UNITED NATIONS, MULTILATERAL TREATIES DEPOSITED WITH THE SECRETARY-GENERAL: STATUS AS AT 31 DECEMBER 2005, at 414 (2006).

152

INTERNATIONAL COURT OF JUSTICE

2003
10 September
General List
No. 89

10 September 2003

CASE CONCERNING QUESTIONS OF INTERPRETATION AND APPLICATION OF THE 1971 MONTREAL CONVENTION ARISING FROM THE AERIAL INCIDENT AT LOCKERBIE

(LIBYAN ARAB JAMAHIRIYA *v.* UNITED STATES OF AMERICA)

ORDER

The President of the International Court of Justice,

Having regard to Article 48 of the Statute of the Court and to Article 88 of the Rules of Court,

Having regard to the Application filed in the Registry of the Court on 3 March 1992, by which the Great Socialist People's Libyan Arab Jamahiriya instituted proceedings against the United States of America in respect of a "dispute between Libya and the United States concerning the interpretation or application of the Montreal Convention" of 23 September 1971 for the Suppression of Unlawful Acts against the Safety of Civil Aviation,

Having regard to the Order of 19 June 1992, by which the Court fixed 20 December 1993 and 20 June 1995 as the time-limits for the filing, respectively, of the Memorial of Libya and the Counter-Memorial of the United States,

Having regard to the Memorial filed by Libya and the preliminary objections submitted by the United States, within the time-limits thus fixed,

Having regard to the Judgment of 27 February 1998, by which the Court gave its decision on the preliminary objections,

4

Exhibit 11–8. Case Concerning Questions of Interpretations and Application of the 1971 Montreal Convention Arising from the Aerial Incident at Lockerbie (Libya v. U.S.), 2003 I.C.J. 152 (Sept. 10).

CHAPTER 12

THE LAW OF OTHER COUNTRIES

---

§ 12–1. Introduction

Expanded foreign communication, travel, and trade have made the law of other countries increasingly significant to American social and economic life. The law of a foreign country may be relevant in American court proceedings involving international transactions, and scholars and lawmakers can study other legal systems to better understand and improve our own. The extent to which American courts should cite precedent from other countries is the subject of a vigorous debate. Foreign law sources are also essential to the study of comparative law, in which differences among national legal systems are analyzed.

The legal systems of most foreign countries can be described as either *common law* or *civil law*. Each system has its own history, its own fundamental principles and procedures, and its own forms of publication for legal sources. Under the common law, as explained in Chapter 1, legal doctrine is derived from specific cases decided by judges rather than from broad, abstractly articulated codifications. Judicial decisions are traditionally the most important and vital source of new legal rules in a common law system.

The civil law system refers to the legal tradition, arising out of Roman law and the European codes, which characterizes the countries of continental Europe, Latin America, and parts of Africa and Asia. There are several distinctive characteristics of the civil law system: the predominance of comprehensive and systematic codes governing large fields of law (civil, criminal, commercial, civil procedure, and criminal procedure); the strong influence of concepts, terms and principles from Roman law; little weight for judicial decisions as legal authority; and great influence of legal scholars who interpret, criticize and develop the law in their writings, particularly through commentaries on the codes.

Some countries do not fit clearly into either the civil law or common law systems, but are strongly influenced by customary law or traditional religious systems, particularly Hindu or Islamic law. The law of these countries (e.g. India, Israel, Pakistan and Saudi Arabia) may be a mixture of civil *or* common law and the religious legal system.

The differences between the common law and civil law systems have become less marked in recent years, as each system adopts features of the other. Codes have been enacted in some American jurisdictions, for example, while judicial decisions are being given greater weight in some civil law countries. Nonetheless, basic differences remain in how legal issues are perceived and research is conducted.

This chapter begins by surveying resources useful in learning about foreign legal systems generally, whether common law or civil law. It then focuses more specifically on English, Canadian, and Australian materials, before finishing with a brief overview of research in civil law jurisdictions.

§ 12–2.   Reference Sources in Foreign and Comparative Law

While thorough research on a foreign law issue can only be undertaken in original sources, print and online reference resources can provide a working knowledge of the major legal issues. It is usually best to begin with an encyclopedia or treatise for a general introduction to a national legal system, or, if possible, to the specific legal subject. A research guide for the jurisdiction or subject, describing available primary and secondary sources, can help clarify the range of research options.

Encyclopedias and Legal Guides. Several encyclopedic works provide coverage of legal topics in various nations. The most comprehensive work in English, the *International Encyclopedia of Comparative Law* (1971– date), is still incomplete after more than thirty years. Most of the encyclopedia covers specific legal topics such as contracts or civil procedure, but volume 1 contains a series of "National Reports" on individual countries, with references to the main sources of law and topical bibliographies for each country. Most of these reports, however, were published in pamphlets in the 1970s and have never been updated. Depending on the jurisdiction, much of their information may be of historical value only.

Two recent one-volume reference works provide broad and more current coverage of comparative law issues. Both Jan M. Smits, ed., *Elgar Encyclopedia of Comparative Law* (2006) and Reinhard Zimmermann & Mathias Reimann, eds., *The Oxford Companion to Comparative Law* (2006) contain chapters by leading scholars analyzing the legal systems of specific countries or regions as well as studies of particular topics and subject areas.

Another series of comparative law works, *International Encyclopaedia of Laws*, consists of several sets focusing on specific subjects with separate monographic pamphlets for individual countries. The oldest and most extensive of these works, *International Encyclopaedia for Labour Law and Industrial Relations* (1977–date), covers more than sixty countries. Newer sets covering fewer countries are available in almost two dozen other areas. These sets currently consist of one to ten volumes each, but they are growing steadily. Their areas of focus, and the year each began publication, are: civil procedure (1994), commercial and economic law (1993), constitutional law (1992), contracts (1993), corporations and partnerships (1991), criminal law (1993), cyber law (2004), energy law (2001), environmental law (1991), family and succession law (1997), insurance law (1992), intellectual property (1997), intergovernmental organizations (1996), medical law (1993), private international law (2000), property and trust law (2000), social security law (1994), sports law (2004), sub-national constitutional law (1999), tort law (2002), and transport law (1994). These can be excellent scholarly resources, although the chances of finding a specific country covered in a specific subject area are not always promising. Information on which countries are covered in each set is available online <www.cer-leuven.be/cerleuven/iel/published. htm>.

Surveys of the legal systems of more than 170 jurisdictions are included in Kenneth R. Redden & Linda L. Schlueter, eds., *Modern Legal Systems Cyclopedia* (1984–date). These vary considerably in length, from three to more than a hundred pages, and in quality. The dates of chapters are not indicated, but some are now clearly obsolete. This set includes a few chapters on legal research methods as well.

A much more current but less extensive publication, Herbert M. Kritzer, ed., *Legal Systems of the World: A Political, Social, and Cultural Encyclopedia* (4 vols. 2002), provides an introductory overview by subject and jurisdiction. Articles on countries discuss history, major legal concepts, and the current structure of the legal system. Most also include charts showing the structure of court systems, and each article provides references for further reading.

The United States government publishes several useful guides to the legal and business environments in foreign countries. The Central Intelligence Agency's *World Factbook* <https://www.cia.gov/cia/publications/factbook/> has basic demographic and economic information about the countries of the world. More extensive legal and commercial guides for specific countries and industries are available from the International Trade Administration's Export Portal <www.export.gov/mrktresearch/> and the USDA Foreign Agricultural Service's

Global Agriculture Information Network (GAIN) <www.
fas.usda.gov/agx/market_research/market_research_
resources.asp>.

Bibliographies and Research Guides. When starting research in the law of another country, it is essential
to have some sense of what publications are available
and in what sources research is best conducted. A wide
variety of guides to foreign law research are published.
Some cover several subjects and many jurisdictions,
while others are specialized bibliographic surveys of particular countries, regions, or subjects.

One of the best starting points is Thomas H. Reynolds
& Arturo A. Flores, *Foreign Law: Current Sources of
Codes and Basic Legislation in Jurisdictions of the World*
(8 vols., 1989–date), covering almost every country in the
world. A separate section for each country contains a
description of its legal system, notes on the major codifications, gazettes, and sources for legislation and court
decisions (including those available in English or on the
Internet), and a detailed listing of codes and laws covering specific subject areas. Exhibit 12–1 on page 423
shows a page from the Paraguay section of *Foreign Law*,
with information about basic primary sources. Note that
the entries include references to English summaries and
online sources. *Foreign Law* is also available online by
subscription <www.foreignlawguide.com>.

GlobaLex <www.nyulawglobal.org/globalex/> and Law
Library Resource Xchange (LLRX) <www.llrx.
com/comparative_and_foreign_law.html> have each published guides to researching the legal systems of more
than fifty countries. These guides generally summarize
the legal system, describe available documentation, and
provide extensive links to electronic resources.

Germain's Transnational Law Research: A Guide for Attorneys (1991–date) describes sources in international and foreign law, including translations, digests, and current awareness materials. Chapters introducing major procedural and substantive issues are followed by more detailed treatment of sources in more than three dozen subject areas and in seventeen European countries. Most chapters include helpful "where to start" sections listing key resources.

Summaries and Translations of Foreign Law. The growing literature on foreign law includes many multinational summaries and digests of laws on specific subjects, as well as translations of actual laws. While summaries and translations cannot substitute for the original sources, they can provide some familiarity with the basic concepts and issues of a foreign law problem.

The simplest and most convenient starting point may be the annual *Martindale-Hubbell International Law Digest*, which has summaries of basic laws and procedures for more than seventy countries. Topics covered include business regulation, foreign trade, family law, property, and taxation. Most national digests are prepared by lawyers in that nation, and include references to codes, laws, and other sources. The *International Law Digest* is available online through LexisNexis.

The basic laws of government structure and individual liberties are found in national constitutions. The most comprehensive printed collection of current constitutions in English translation is the looseleaf set, *Constitutions of the Countries of the World* (1971–date). For some foreign-language countries, the original text of the constitution is included as well. Robert L. Maddex, *Constitutions of the World* (2d ed. 2001) provides summaries of constitutions and brief constitutional histories for one hundred countries.

International Constitutional Law at the University of Bern <www.oefre.unibe.ch/law/icl/> has more than eighty constitutions in English, with introductory pages providing constitutional background and history. The Constitution Finder at the University of Richmond <confinder.richmond.edu> links to constitutions from more than 200 nations and territories, some in more than one language. The most extensive collections of constitutions are those assembled by Professor Horst Dippel of the University of Kassel: *Constitutions of the World, 1850 to the Present* (2002–date) is a set of modern constitutions on microfiche, and *Constitutions of the World from the Late 18th Century to the Middle of the 19th Century* (2005–date) is a print compilation with a companion website, *The Rise of Modern Constitutionalism, 1776–1849* <www.uni-kassel.de/∽dippel/projekt/>.

Laws affecting international business are the most likely sources to be available in English. Several collections covering specific topics are published, including *Digest of Commercial Laws of the World* (rev. ed. 1998–date), *Investment Laws of the World* (1973–date), and *International Securities Regulation* (1986–date).

Most larger countries have both free and subscription-based legal databases similar to those available in the United States. The World Legal Information Institute (WorldLII) <www.worldlii.org> provides links to resources at member LII sites and a much larger catalog of links to materials by country and subject. Other websites with links to legal resources by country include Hieros Gamos <www.hg.org>, the Law Library of Congress's "Nations of the World" <www.loc.gov/law/guide/

nations.html> and Cornell Law School's "Law by Source: Global" <www.law.cornell.edu/world/>. Each of these provides access to constitutions, government websites, and other resources.

Citation forms for foreign legal materials can be very confusing for American lawyers. The *Bluebook* includes citation information for more than thirty countries, covering of statutory, judicial, and other frequently cited sources. More extensive coverage is provided by *Guide to Foreign and International Legal Citations* (2006) (available free online <www.law.nyu.edu/journals/jilp/gfilc.html>), which has profiles and citation guides for forty-five countries as well as for international organizations, international and regional tribunals, and treaties.

§ 12–3. English and Commonwealth Law

The common law system originated in England and spread to its colonies around the world. Most of these nations, now known as the Commonwealth, still have legal systems modeled on the English common law. This chapter looks at three major common law jurisdictions: England (which is part of the United Kingdom but has a separate body of law from Northern Ireland and Scotland), Canada, and Australia.

While related, the legal systems of these countries are quite distinct. The United Kingdom has an "unwritten constitution," meaning that its basic constitutional principles are not found in one specific document. The UK has been part of the European Union (formerly the European Communities) since 1973 and is increasingly governed by EU treaties and legislation. The Canadian and Australian systems have federal governments and written constitutions. Canada's Constitution, dating back to 1867, was dramatically changed when the Constitution Act 1982 added an extensive new Charter of Rights and Freedoms. The Australian Constitution has been in effect, with relatively few amendments, since 1901. Further information is available in overviews such as Stephen Bailey et al., *Smith, Bailey and Gunn on the Modern English Legal System* (4th ed. 2002); Richard Ward & Amanda Wragg, *Walker & Walker's English Legal System* (9th ed. 2005); Gerald L. Gall et al., *The Canadian Legal System* (5th ed. 2004); or John Carvan, *Understanding the Australian Legal System* (5th ed. 2005).

Although the laws of England and its former colonies have developed separately, common law countries share a heritage which gives their decisions more persuasive value in each other's courts than that generally afforded to the law of other countries. English cases have continued to influence American law on issues such as tort causation and contract formation. Similarities in language, publication, and research procedures make information about English legal doctrine easily accessible to researchers in the United States and other common law countries.

a.   Case Law

Court reports are central to legal research in England and other common law countries, and research is simplified by the relatively small number of published decisions compared to the fifty state jurisdictions and federal system in the United States. England has one straightforward structure of trial and appellate courts, with the House of Lords as the court of last resort. The Canadian and Australian federal court systems are more like that of the United States, although fundamental differences exist. U.S. state supreme courts, for example, are the final arbiters on issues of state law, while any decision from a Canadian provincial court or an Australian state court is generally subject to review by the highest federal court in its country.

Publication of Cases. As in the United States, new decisions in most other common law countries are published first in weekly or monthly advance sheets and later in permanent bound volumes. Official or authorized series of reports are published, but unofficial commercial reporters and online services often provide quicker access to new cases. Westlaw and LexisNexis have extensive coverage of judicial decisions from the United Kingdom, Canada, and Australia, as do other commercial systems based in those countries. Free Internet access to decisions is provided by the British and Irish Legal Information Institute (BAILII) <www.bailii.org>, the Canadian Legal Information Institute (CanLII) <www.canlii.org>, and the Australasian Legal Information Institute (AustLII) <www.austlii.edu.au>.

English law reporting has had a long and varied history. The recording of cases began with fragmentary reports in the *Plea Rolls*, dating from the reign of Richard I in 1189. The *Year Books*, covering the long period from 1285 to 1537, include both reports of proceedings and brief summaries of decisions. Following the *Year Books* came the *nominate* or *nominative* reports, that is, court reports named for the person who recorded or edited them. The earliest known reporter was probably James Dyer, whose reports were published around 1550. *Plowden's Reports*, first published in 1571, are considered among the finest and most accurate, while the reports of

Sir Edward Coke were probably the most influential of the period.

Most nominative reports were cumulated into *The English Reports*, covering cases from 1220 to 1865 in 176 volumes. This invaluable set contains about 100,000 decisions originally published in some 275 series of nominative reporters. The volumes are arranged by court, star-paged to the original reporter, and accessible by a two-volume alphabetical table of cases. There is no subject index, but the subscription sites HeinOnline <www.heinonline.org> and Justis <www.justis.com> provide keyword access to the entire set and PDFs of cases. Another compilation of older cases, the *Revised Reports*, covers 1785 to 1866 in 149 volumes and includes some decisions not found in *The English Reports*.

Exhibit 12–2 on page 424 shows a decision of the Court of Exchequer (which was abolished in 1875) in *Fletcher v. Rylands*, as published in *The English Reports*. Note the bracketed star paging reference to page 774 of the original nominative reporter, Hurlstone & Coltman's *Exchequer Reports* (cited as H. & C.).

For decisions since 1865, the standard source is the semi-official *Law Reports*, which now consists of four series: *Appeal Cases* (House of Lords and the Judicial Committee of the Privy Council); *Queen's Bench Division*; *Chancery Division*; and *Family Division*. Before appearing in these four separate series, new cases are published in *Weekly Law Reports*, which also includes some decisions unreported in the four *Law Reports* series.

All England Law Reports (1936–date) is a commercially published reporter which often issues new cases sooner than the *Weekly Law Reports* and contains some decisions which are not published elsewhere. As in the United States, numerous specialized subject reporters are also available.

Canada and Australia both have authorized reports for their national courts of last resort (*Canada Supreme Court Reports*, and *Commonwealth Law Reports* for the High Court of Australia). Both nations also have lower federal courts with trial and appellate jurisdiction, and courts in each province or state. In Canada, the commercially published *National Reporter* contains decisions of the Supreme Court and the Federal Court of Appeal, and *Dominion Law Reports* contains decisions from both federal and provincial courts. The High Court of Australia's decisions are also published in the *Australian Law Reports*, along with lower federal court cases and state court cases on federal issues; *Federal Law Reports* duplicates some of this coverage of lower court decisions. In addition, each country has reporters for the supreme courts of its provinces or states, as well as topical reporters in specialized subject areas.

Case Research Tools. Much case research in other common law countries is done by keyword through free and commercial database systems, including versions of Westlaw and LexisNexis. Online research is supplemented by many of the same types of digesting and updating tools that are found in the United States.

Each country has a major national digest, somewhat similar to the West digest system: *The Digest: Annotated British, Commonwealth and European Cases* (3d ed. 1971–date); the *Canadian Abridgment* (3d ed. 2003–date, available on Westlaw); and the *Australian Digest* (3d ed. 1988–date). All three sets include consolidated indexes and tables of cases, and each is updated regularly by bound or looseleaf supplements. The Canadian and Australian digests are further updated in the monthly issues of *Canadian Current Law Case Law Digests* and the *Australian Legal Monthly Digest*.

KeyCite and *Shepard's Citations* do not have direct counterparts in other countries, but there are tools for finding later cases that have considered an earlier decision. *Current Law* is an English service useful for both finding and updating cases. Its *Monthly Digest* contains summaries of new court decisions arranged by subject and a table of cases which have been judicially considered. The case summaries cumulate at the end of the year into the *Current Law Year Book*, and the case tables into the *Current Law Case Citator*. The *Case Citator*, which consists of four volumes and an annual paperback supplement, lists, by name, cases decided or cited since 1947. For those cases which have been judicially considered, the effect of each later case is indicated with notes such as "Overruled," "Applied," or "Considered."

Updating Canadian and Australian cases is possible through *Canadian Case Citations* and the *Australian Case Citator* (as well as through online citators). Like their English counterpart, tables in these works are arranged alphabetically by case name and are useful for finding citations as well as for determining later treatment of cited decisions.

b. Statutes and Regulations

Statutes in other common law jurisdictions are published both in session laws and in compilations of statutes in force. The compilations, however, generally reprint acts alphabetically by name or chronologically, rather than by subject. There is no official counterpart to the *United States Code*, in which each part of an act is systematically assigned a title and section number as part of a general subject compilation of statutes. Instead, acts are usually identified by their original name and date of enactment.

The current national session law publications are *Public General Acts* (for Britain), *Statutes of Canada*, and *Acts of the Parliament of the Commonwealth of Australia*; each is published in annual volumes with subject indexes or tables of acts for each year. Statutes of the individual Canadian provinces and Australian states are published in similar annual volumes.

The standard historical collection of English statutes is the *Statutes of the Realm* (11 vols., 1810–22), covering 1235 to 1713. Several other chronological collections were published during the 19th century under the title *Statutes at Large*, extending coverage to the beginning of the modern *Public General Acts* in 1866. Justis <www.justis.com> provides subscription online coverage to these early statutes, with retrospective coverage back to 1235.

The first step in identifying and finding an older English statute is deciphering its citation. Acts before 1963 are generally cited not by calendar year but by regnal year (the year of a monarch's rule). Tables to convert regnal years to calendar years are printed in reference works such as *Black's Law Dictionary*, and a Regnal Year Calculator is available online <www.albion.edu/english/calendar/regnal.htm>. (Even more confusing to many American researchers is the division of the English legal year into four terms: Michaelmas, Hilary, Easter, and Trinity. This calendar dates back to the

1200s and is still used today <www.judiciary.
gov.uk/keyfacts/legal_year/term_dates.htm>).

The source most frequently used for English statutory
research is *Halsbury's Statutes of England and Wales*
(4th ed. 1985–date), an unofficial compilation similar to
U.S. annotated codes, with footnote annotations to judicial decisions. *Halsbury's* is a well-indexed encyclopedic
arrangement of acts in force, updated with annual bound
supplements and looseleaf volumes (*Current Statutes Service*, containing annotated versions of new statutes, and
Noter-Up Service, providing references to developments
since the latest annual supplement). A *Consolidated Index* and several pamphlets of tables are published annually. Exhibit 12–3 on page 425 shows a page from *Halsbury's Statutes* containing the beginning of an 1883 act
still in force as amended. Notes provide explanations and
cross-references to related acts, and a parenthetical reference at the top provides the regnal year citation. "46 &
47 Vict c 3" means that this was the third chapter of the
Public General Acts for the parliamentary session spanning the forty-sixth and forty-seventh years of Queen
Victoria's reign.

Current English statutes are also available on Westlaw
and LexisNexis, as well as free from the UK Statute Law
Database <www.statutelaw.gov.uk>. The government
also provides online access to all Public Acts beginning in
1988 <www.opsi.gov.uk/acts.htm>. The Parliament website <www.parliament.uk> provides information about
procedures, debates, and pending legislation.

Current Law Statute Citator, part of the *Current Law*
service, contains a chronological list of British statutes,
with each followed by references to later statutes and
cases which affect it. Coverage includes any statutes

amended, repealed, or considered in judicial decisions since 1947. This set is updated annually, with more current coverage in *Current Law Monthly Digest*.

Canadian and Australian statutes are available online, but neither country has an annotated, regularly updated publication similar to *Halsbury's Statutes*. The Consolidated Statutes of Canada are available from the Department of Justice Canada <laws.justice.gc.ca>, and CanLII <www.canlii.org> provides links to provincial sources. AustLII <www.austlii.edu.au> has a wealth of legislative information, including Commonwealth Consolidated Acts and state statutes. Coverage of much of this material is also available from LexisNexis, Westlaw, and other commercial databases.

Recent legislative activity by Canadian federal and provincial governments is noted in *Canadian Current Law Legislation*, and references to citing cases can be found by using *Canadian Statute Citations*. In Australia, *Commonwealth Statutes Annotations* and *Federal Statutes Annotations* both provide references to amendments and to cases citing federal statutes. Similar works are available for some Australian states, and information on federal and state legislative developments is available in such publications as the *Australian Legal Monthly Digest* and *Australian Current Law Legislation*.

While parliamentary debates and other legislative documents are also published in each of these countries, legislative history materials are generally considered less persuasive than in the United States for purposes of statutory interpretation. Some use of parliamentary materials, however, has now been accepted by courts in most countries. Parliamentary websites (<www.

parliament.uk>,   <www.parl.gc.ca>,   <www.aph.gov.
au>) provide information on available sources.

As in the United States, delegated legislation such as
administrative or local law plays a vital role in the legal
system of Commonwealth nations. Regulations, the most
common form of delegated legislation, are known in
Britain as *statutory instruments* and in Australia as *statutory rules*. The most useful printed source for research
in English statutory instruments is the unofficial *Halsbury's Statutory Instruments* (4th ed. 1978–date). Westlaw and LexisNexis have all statutory instruments of
general effect currently in force, including many not
printed in *Halsbury's*, and instruments since 1987 are
available online for free <www.opsi.gov.uk/stat.htm>.
Current Law lists new instruments and includes them in
its subject digests, and the *Current Law Legislation
Citators* covers statutory instruments, noting amendments or revocations as well as other references. Access
to Canadian regulations and Australian statutory rules is
similar to that for statutes, with links to current resources available at CanLII <www.canlii.org> and Aust-
LII <www.austlii.edu.au>.

c.   Secondary Sources

The secondary literature of other common law countries parallels that of the United States, with a variety of
treatises, practitioners' handbooks, looseleaf services,
and other materials. This section examines only a few
basic resources.

Encyclopedias. Like *Am. Jur. 2d* and *C.J.S.*, legal
encyclopedias in other nations contain concise statements of ruling law and extensive footnote references to
primary sources. Foreign legal encyclopedias are often

more useful than those from one's own country, since they summarize unfamiliar legal doctrines and provide convenient references to materials that might otherwise be difficult to find.

Halsbury's Laws of England (4th ed. 1973–date) is more definitive than the American legal encyclopedias, in part because it covers just one jurisdiction and can encompass statutes and administrative sources as well as case law. Access to the set is provided by a subject index and by tables of cases and statutes cited. The encyclopedia is updated by annual cumulative supplements and *Current Service* looseleaf volumes, which include a "Monthly Review" summarizing new developments. *Halsbury's Laws* is available online in Britain, but most U.S. LexisNexis subscriptions include only the "Monthly Review." Exhibit 12–4 on page 426 shows a page from *Halsbury's Laws*, summarizing statutory provisions and providing references to several cases.

While there is no general legal encyclopedia for all of Canada, two regional encyclopedias include coverage of Canadian federal law: *Canadian Encyclopedic Digest (Ontario)* (3d ed. 1973–date), and *Canadian Encyclopedic Digest (Western)* (3d ed. 1979–date). The CED database on Westlaw provides access to both Canadian encyclopedias. There are two competing comprehensive Australian legal encyclopedias, *Halsbury's Laws of Australia* (1991–date) and *The Laws of Australia* (1993–date).

Martindale-Hubbell International Law Digest is hardly a substitute for an encyclopedic treatment and original sources, but it provides convenient summaries of major legal principles and references to primary sources for England, Canada, and Australia, as well as each Canadian province, Northern Ireland, Scotland, and several other common law countries.

Periodicals and Treatises. No other country has a profusion of legal periodicals to match that in the United States, but the forms of publication are similar. Each nation has a variety of academic law reviews and professional journals. Many are available through either Westlaw or LexisNexis. The major American indexes (*Index to Legal Periodicals and Books* and *Current Law Index/Legal Resource Index*) include coverage of most of the world's major English-language journals, but indexes published in other countries may provide more precise coverage of domestic legal issues. *Legal Journals Index*, covering more than 400 British publications, is available through Westlaw, and references to recent English books and articles appear in *Current Law*. The most comprehensive Canadian index is *Canadian Legal Literature* (1981–date), and recent Australian material is listed in *Australian Legal Monthly Digest* and *Australian Current Law Reporter*.

Dictionaries and research guides. Reference works can help considerably in researching another country's laws. Legal dictionaries ensure that words are understood in their proper context, and foreign research guides contain more detailed and precise discussion than is possible in an American treatment.

The major British legal dictionary is *Jowitt's Dictionary of English Law* (2 vols., 2d ed. 1977, with 1985 supp.); two shorter, more current works are E.A. Martin & Jonathan Law, *A Dictionary of Law* (6th ed. 2006), and *Osborn's Concise Law Dictionary* (10th ed. 2005). Daphne A. Dukelow, *The Dictionary of Canadian Law* (3d ed. 2004) is the most substantial treatment of Canadian legal definitions, and Australian legal terms are defined in *Butterworths Australian Legal Dictionary* (1997). David M. Walker's *Oxford Companion to Law* (1980) is a cross between a dictionary and an encyclopedia, providing concise explanations of basic common and civil law concepts, documents, events, and institutions.

English legal research materials are discussed in Guy Holborn, *Butterworths Legal Research Guide* (2d ed. 2001), and John Knowles & Philip A. Thomas, *Effective Legal Research* (2006). Similar treatment for Canada and Australia is offered by works such as Douglass T. MacEllven, *Legal Research Handbook* (5th ed. 2003) and Robert Watt, *Concise Legal Research* (5th ed. 2004). Guides to citation format in other common-law include *OSCOLA: The Oxford Standard for Citation Of Legal Authorities* (2006) <denning.law.ox.ac.uk/published/oscola.shtml> and the McGill Law Journal's *Canadian Guide to Uniform Legal Citation* (6th ed. 2006). Raistrick's *Index to Legal Citations and Abbreviations* (2d ed. 1993) and Cardiff Index to Legal Abbreviations <www.legalabbrevs. cardiff.ac.uk> are particularly useful for deciphering citations to English sources.

§ 12–4. Civil Law

An American lawyer or law student researching the law of a civil law country must be cognizant of the major differences between the civil and common law systems, and the effect of these differences on how legal problems are evaluated and researched. Instead of searching for precedents in factually similar judicial decisions, a civil lawyer looks first to the abstract provisions of the code for a logical and appropriate legal principle. Among the most important sources are extensive article-by-article commentaries on the major codes; the most scholarly and reputable of these commentaries are themselves sources of the law. Other laws, such as legislation, regulations, and decrees, are most often found in official gazettes, which are comparable to but usually broader in scope than the *Federal Register*. Court decisions are published, but they are generally of secondary importance.

Research approaches in civil law vary by country and by topic. Translations and summaries of foreign law in English, such as those discussed in § 12–2, may be quite helpful, but translated texts of legal materials are no substitute for the original documents. The most effective research in any legal system is conducted in the language of its sources.

Introductory study in an encyclopedia, treatise, or journal article may provide leads to original sources. The next step is to consult the relevant code (preferably in an edition accompanied by extensive commentary) or other statutes applicable to the problem. You should then find administrative orders and judicial decisions implementing or interpreting the legislative norms. Remember that research usually begins with the code itself, and almost never, as in the United States, with a review of judicial decisions.

Basic Legal Sources. Most countries in the civil law system have several separately published codes. These include the basic general codes (civil, criminal, commercial, civil procedure and criminal procedure), and minor codes which are often simply statutory compilations on specific subjects (such as taxation, labor law, and family law). The codes are usually published in frequent unannotated editions, and also in larger editions with scholarly commentary and annotations.

In many countries, daily or weekly official gazettes contain the texts of new laws, decrees and administrative orders. The University of Michigan's "Government Gazettes Online" site <www.lib.umich.edu/govdocs/gazettes/> provides links to gazettes from sixty countries, with summary information about their contents and searchability. The American Library Association's *Guide to Official Publications of Foreign Countries* (2d ed. 1997) provides an annotated listing of gazettes, statistical yearbooks, court reports, and other publications for more than 170 countries; commercially published guides, bibliographies, and directories are included as well as official sources.

Because judicial decisions carry less weight in civil law countries, most jurisdictions have fewer court reports and less developed means for finding cases by subject. In many countries, legal periodicals publish court decisions in addition to articles and other legal news. In France, for example, the leading legal periodicals, *Recueil Dalloz* (1808–date) and *La Semaine Juridique* (1927–date), provide both legislative texts and judicial decisions, as well as scholarly articles.

Online access to civil law sources in English is not very extensive, although commercial laws of some countries are available through LexisNexis, Westlaw, and other databases. The official French site Legifrance <www.legifrance.gouv.fr> has searchable English translations of major French codes, updated each year. The Institute of Global Law at the University of London provides English translations of French and German statutes and court decisions <www.ucl.ac.uk/laws/global_law/>, and the German Law Archive <www.iuscomp.org/gla/> has numerous sources in English including statutes, court decisions, and secondary sources. The Institute for Transnational Law at the University of Texas <www. utexas.edu/law/academics/centers/transnational/work/> has English translations of Austrian, French, German, and Israeli legal materials.

Secondary Materials. Under the civil law system, scholarly commentaries and treatises by recognized experts have considerable weight as persuasive authority. They are discussed as "secondary materials" here in keeping with our own notion of authority, but in many instances they have greater weight than judicial decisions. The range of available texts, as in common law countries, is quite broad in both subject and quality. There are comprehensive scholarly treatises, highly specialized monographs on narrow topics, pragmatic manuals and guides for practitioners, and simplified texts for students and popular use.

Foreign legal encyclopedias, particularly the French *répertoires* published by Dalloz, are often of higher quality and reputation than those in this country. Their articles are frequently written by leading legal scholars. Civil law countries also have a multitude of legal periodicals covering legal developments and often printing primary sources. The *Index to Foreign Legal Periodicals* (1960–date, quarterly; available through various database systems including Westlaw commercial subscriptions) covers more than 500 journals from seventy-five countries, as well as *festschriften* and other collections of essays.

Reference Aids. Part of the difficulty of doing legal research in the civil law system stems from differences in language. Legal dictionaries can help somewhat, although a dictionary alone can provide only a superficial sense of the differences in meaning and usage.

Numerous bilingual dictionaries are available for assistance in translating foreign terms into English. *Dahl's Law Dictionary: Spanish to English/English to Spanish* (4th ed. 2005) and *Dahl's Law Dictionary: French to English/English to French* (2d ed. 2001) are also represented (in older editions) in LexisNexis. Several multilingual law dictionaries are also published. The standard work in English, French, and German is Robert Herbst & Alan G. Readett, *Dictionary of Commercial, Financial and Legal Terms* (3 vols., 3d–6th eds. 1998–2003). *West's Law and Commercial Dictionary in Five Languages* (2 vols., 1985) adds Italian and Spanish as well. *World Dictionary of Legal Abbreviations* (4 vols., 1991–date), has extensive lists of foreign abbreviations, with separate sections for Bulgarian, Chinese, French, German, Hebrew, Italian, Japanese, Korean, Portuguese, and Spanish.

A number of guides to the legal systems of specific civil law countries or regions are published in English. These generally explain legal institutions and summarize major doctrines. A sample of recently published titles includes Ilias Bantekas, *Law and Legal System of Uzbekistan* (2005); William Burnham et al., *Law and Legal System of the Russian Federation* (3d ed. 2004); Daniel C. K. Chow, *The Legal System of the People's Republic of China in a Nutshell* (2003); Catherine Elliott et al., *French Legal System* (2d ed. 2006); and Elena Merino–Blanco, *Spanish Law and Legal System* (2d ed. 2006).

§ 12–5. Conclusion

Any serious legal problem involving another jurisdiction will require consultation with a lawyer trained and licensed in that jurisdiction. The resources discussed in this chapter, however, can provide a solid starting point for the American researcher.

Other than availability of materials, there is little hindrance to research in English, Canadian, or Australian law. These countries have legal research resources that are quite similar to our own and are easily accessible to American legal researchers, either for comparative study or for analysis of legal problems arising in those nations.

In researching the law of civil law countries, lawyers limited to English-language materials will be seriously handicapped. However, the increasing availability of secondary sources in English and translations now allows preliminary study of most foreign legal problems. Such study may help the American lawyer to determine the general nature of a problem, and can facilitate communication with the foreign law specialist who may be called in to assist.

4. Criminal Code

Código penal. Ley 1,160 of 16 Oct 1997 in *Registro oficial* 26 Nov 1997. Official text available at <http://www.itacom.com.py/ministerio_publico/codigo_penal>. In force 26 Nov 1998. Replacing the 1914 codification.

5. Code of Criminal Procedure

Código de procedimientos penales. Ley 1,286 of 8 Jul 1998 in *Registro oficial* 14 Jul 1998. Full text available in Spanish, with English summary, at <http://www.glin.gov/>.‡ Replacing 1980 code over a transitional period that concluded 28 Feb 2003. Compare with Ley 1,444 of 25 Jun 1999. Full text available in Spanish, with English summary, at <http://www.glin.gov/>.‡

OFFICIAL GAZETTE

Registro oficial de la República del Paraguay. [Vol. 1]– , 1869/70– . Asunción, 1887– (cited herein as *Registro oficial).* This is actually a separate section of the *Gaceta oficial* containing laws, decrees, resolutions and regulatory legislation. The other section is titled "Avisos y anuncios" and is of little legal interest. One can approach the *Gaceta oficial* online at <http://www2.paraguaygobierno.gov.py/gacetaoficial>.

COMPILATIONS OR OFFICIAL CODIFICATIONS

Legislación paraguaya: recopilación de leyes, decrtetos-leyes, y decretos vigentes.... [2a.ed.] Asunción Universidad Catolica, 1981– (no more published).

Coleción legislación paraguaya. Asunción, Intercontinental Editora, 1989– (this is the publisher's series of currently issued and irregularly revised subject compilations, e.g., *Legislación mercantil, Legislación bancaria, Código civil,* etc.).

SESSION LAWS

Session laws appear in regular numbers of the *Registro oficial.*

Exhibit 12–1. Thomas H. Reynolds & Arturo A. Flores, 1–A Foreign Law: Current Sources of Codes and Legislation in Jurisdictions of the World *Paraguay* 9 (2005).

any part of the journey. That principle was recognized and adopted in *Scothorn v. The South Staffordshire Railway Company* (8 Exch. 341). [Martin, B. The decision of the House of Lords in *The Bristol and Exeter Railway Company v. Collins* (7 H. L. Cas. 194) is conclusive of this case.]

Grove (Horatio Lloyd with him), in support of the rule. Pickford & Co. were the agents not of the defendants, but of the London and North Western Railway Company, and had a direct interest in sending goods by that Company. The contract of the defendants was to carry the clock to Stafford and there deliver it to the London and North Western Railway Company. [Bramwell, B. Suppose a parcel was delivered to the South Western Railway at Reading addressed to a person at Dover, "per London, Chatham and Dover Railway," which Company would have been liable if it was lost?] The South Western Railway Company would have performed their contract when they delivered the goods to the London, Chatham and Dover Railway. There was no proof of a contract by the plaintiff with the defendants. The plaintiff's contract **[774]** was with Pickford & Co., who contracted with the defendants. *Muschamp v. The Lancaster, &c., Railway Company* (8 M. & W. 421) only decided that where nothing is said about the route, there is primâ facie one contract to carry the whole distance.

Cur. adv. vult.

POLLOCK, C. B., now said,—The question in this case was, whether the Great Western Railway Company were liable to the plaintiff for damage done to his clock during the transit from Worcester to Chester. I am of opinion with the rest of the Court that there was evidence for the jury of one contract only and not two contracts. The jury have so found, and we think there was evidence to warrant their finding. The rule must therefore be discharged.

Rule discharged.

FLETCHER *v.* RYLANDS AND HORROCKS. May 3, 4, 5, 1865.—The defendant made a reservoir for water on his land, and in the selection of the site and the planning and construction of the reservoir employed a competent engineer and competent contractors. In excavating the bed of the reservoir five old shafts were met with, running vertically downwards to old coal workings under the site of the reservoir, and communicating with the plaintiff's colliery by means of other old coal workings under intervening lands. These shafts were filled with soil of the same kind as that which immediately surrounded them, and it was not known to or suspected by the defendant, or the persons employed by him in planning or constructing the reservoir, that they were shafts which had been made for the purpose of getting coal under the land beneath the reservoir, or that they led down to coal workings under its site. When the reservoir was completed, and partially filled with water, one of these shafts burst downwards, in consequence of which the water flowed into the old workings underneath the reservoir, and by means of the underground communications, into the plaintiff's colliery, and flooded it. There was no personal negligence or default on the part of the defendant, but reasonable and proper care and skill were not exercised by the persons employed, with reference to the shafts, to provide for the sufficiency of the reservoir to bear the pressure of water which, when filled, it would have to bear.—Held, that under these circumstances, the defendant was not responsible for the damage done to the plaintiff by the water from the reservoir flooding his colliery : per Pollock, C. B., and Martin, B. Dissentiente Bramwell, B.—Per Bramwell, B. That the defendant was responsible, on the ground that he had caused water to flow into the plaintiff's colliery which but for the defendants' act would not have gone there.

[S. C. 34 L. J. Ex. 177; 11 Jur. (N. S.) 714; 13 W. R. 992: reversed 1866, 4 H. & C. 263; L. R. 1 Ex. 265; 35 L. J. Ex. 154; 12 Jur. (N. S.) 603; 14 W. R. 799: the latter decision affirmed 1868, L. R. 3 H. L. 330; 37 L. J. Ex. 161; 19 L. T. 220: referred to in numerous cases. Applied, *Jones* v. *Festiniog Railway*, 1868, L. R. 3 Q. B. 736. Not applied, *The Thetis*, 1869, L. R. 2 Adm. & Ec. 369. Distinguished, *Carstairs v. Taylor*, 1871, L. R. 6 Ex. 221; *Wilson v. Newberry*, 1871, L. R. 7 Q. B. 33; *Boughton v. Midland Great Western*

Ex. Div. xv.—24

Exhibit 12–2. Fletcher v. Rylands, 159 Eng. Rep. 737 (Ex. 1865).

EXPLOSIVE SUBSTANCES ACT 1883

(46 & 47 Vict c 3)

An Act to amend the Law relating to Explosive Substances   [10 April 1883]

Extent   See s 9 post.

General information   For an overview of the legislation relating to the title Criminal Law, see the Preliminary Note ante.

1   Short title   [182]

This Act may be cited as the Explosive Substances Act 1883.

NOTES

Additional information   See the Introductory Note(s) to this Act.

[2   Causing explosion likely to endanger life or property   [183]

A person who in the United Kingdom or (being a citizen of the United Kingdom and Colonies) in the Republic of Ireland unlawfully and maliciously causes by any explosive substance an explosion of a nature likely to endanger life or to cause serious injury to property shall, whether any injury to person or property has been actually caused or not, be guilty of an offence and on conviction on indictment shall be liable to imprisonment for life.]

NOTES

Amendments

Substituted by the Criminal Jurisdiction Act 1975, s 7(1), (3).

United Kingdom   Ie Great Britain and Northern Ireland; see the Interpretation Act 1978, s 5, Sch 1, Vol 41, title Statutes. "Great Britain" means England, Scotland and Wales by virtue of the Union with Scotland Act 1706, preamble, Art I, Vol 10, title Constitutional Law (Pt 1), as read with s 22(1) of, and Sch 2, para 5(a) to, the 1978 Act. Neither the Channel Islands nor the Isle of Man is within the United Kingdom.

Citizen of the United Kingdom and Colonies   This expression is defined, for the purposes of enactments passed before 1983, by the British Nationality Act 1981, s 51(3)(a), Vol 31, title Nationality and Immigration. As to references to ceasing to be such a citizen, see s 51(3)(b) of that Act.

Republic of Ireland   Ie that part of Ireland previously known as Eire and originally called the Irish Free State; see the Ireland Act 1949, s 1(1), (3), Vol 7, title Commonwealth and Other Territories, in conjunction with the Eire (Confirmation of Agreements) Act 1938, s 1 (repealed).

Conviction on indictment   All proceedings on indictment are to be brought before the Crown Court; see the Supreme Court Act 1981, s 46(1), Vol 11, title Courts and Legal Services.

Offences under this section   Offences under this section are extra-territorial offences for the purposes of the Criminal Jurisdiction Act 1975; see s 1 of, and Sch 1, paras 8, 12(1), (3) to, that Act, Vol 31; title Northern Ireland (Pt 2).

An offence under this section is always a serious arrestable offence for the purposes of the Police and Criminal Evidence Act 1984, see s 116(2)(b) of, Sch 5, Pt II, para 1 to, that Act post.

An offence under this section is a "qualifying offence" for the purposes of the Criminal Justice Act 2003, s 62 (right of appeal in respect of evidentiary rulings) post; see s 62(9) of, Sch 4, Pt 1, para 26 to, that Act post (and see also Sch 4, Pt 2 thereto post).

An offence under this section is a "qualifying offence" for the purposes of the Criminal Justice Act 2003, Pt 10 (retrial for serious offences) post; see s 75(8) of, Sch 5, Pt 1, para 23 to, that Act post (and see also Sch 5, Pt 3 thereto post).

By the Criminal Justice Act 2003, s 224 post, an offence is a "specified offence" for the purposes of Chapter 5 (dangerous offenders) of Pt 12 of that Act if it is a specified violent offence or a specified sexual offence. Further, an offence is a "serious offence" for the purposes of that Chapter if and only if it is a specified offence, and it is, apart from s 225, punishable in the case of a person aged 18

Exhibit 12–3. Explosive Substances Act 1883, 46 & 47 Vict., ch. 70 (Eng.), *reprinted in* 12(1) HALSBURY'S STATUTES OF ENGLAND AND WALES 185 (4th ed. 2005 reissue).

10 *R v Cramp* (1880) 5 QBD 307, CCR. See also *R v Hennah* (1877) 13 Cox CC 547; *R v Cato* [1976] 1 All ER 260, 62 Cr App Rep 41, CA (heroin held to be a noxious thing because it is liable to cause injury in common use); *R v Marcus* [1981] 2 All ER 833, 73 Cr App Rep 49, CA (sedatives added to bottle of milk; whether noxious a question of fact and degree). Cf *R v Weatherall* [1968] Crim LR 115 (small quantity of sedative not noxious).

11 *R v Harley* (1830) 4 C & P 369.

12 *R v Michael* (1840) 9 C & P 356, CCR; *R v Lewis* (1833) 6 C & P 161.

13 *R v Wilkins* (1861) Le & Ca 89, CCR. As to the administration of stupefying drugs see paras 122 ante, 230 post.

(v) Injury by Explosion, Corrosives, Mantraps etc

125.   Causing bodily injury by explosion. Any person who unlawfully and maliciously[1] by the explosion of gunpowder or other explosive substance[2] burns, maims, disfigures, disables or does any grievous bodily harm[3] to any person is guilty of an offence and liable on conviction on indictment to imprisonment for life or for any shorter term[4].

1 For the meaning of 'maliciously' see para 119 text to notes 12–15 ante.

2 As to the meaning of 'explosive substance' in a related offence under the Offences against the Person Act 1861 see para 126 post.

3 For the meaning of 'grievous bodily harm' see para 119 ante.

4 Offences against the Person Act 1861 s 28; Criminal Justice Act 1948 s 1(1); Criminal Law Act 1967 s 12(5)(a). This offence is one of those specified in the Terrorism Act 2000 s 63B (as added) for the purposes of the extra-territorial jurisdiction provisions (terrorist acts abroad by United Kingdom nationals or residents): see s 63B(1), (2)(b) (as added); and para 474 post. As to procedural provisions applying where an offence involving bodily injury to a child or young person is charged see para 1164 post.

   This offence may be constituted by an act done in connection with the offence of hijacking committed or attempted on board an aircraft: see AVIATION vol 2(3) (Reissue) para 1088. The offence may also constitute an 'act of violence' for the purposes of the Aviation Security Act 1982 s 2: see AVIATION vol 2(3) (Reissue) para 1091.

126.   Causing explosion. Any person who unlawfully and maliciously[1]:

(1) causes any gunpowder or other explosive substance[2] to explode[3];

(2) sends or delivers to, or causes to be taken or received by, any person any explosive substance or any other dangerous or noxious thing[4]; or

(3) puts or lays at any place, or casts or throws at or upon or otherwise applies to any person, any corrosive fluid, or any destructive or explosive substance[5],

with intent, in any such case, to burn, maim, disfigure, or disable[6] any person, or to do some grievous bodily harm[7] to any person, whether any bodily injury is effected or not, is guilty of an offence and liable on conviction on indictment to imprisonment for life or for any shorter term[8].

1 For the meaning of 'maliciously' see para 119 text to notes 12–15 ante.

2 A petrol bomb is an 'explosive substance' within the meaning of the Offences against the Person Act 1861 s 29: *R v Howard* [1993] Crim LR 213, CA (following *R v Bouch* [1983] QB 246, 76 Cr App Rep 11, CA (see para 127 note 7 post)).

3 Offences against the Person Act 1861 s 29; Criminal Law Act 1967 s 12(5)(a).

4 Offences against the Person Act 1861 s 29; Criminal Law Act 1967 s 12(5)(a).

5 Offences against the Person Act 1861 s 29; Criminal Law Act 1967 s 12(5)(a). Boiling water was held be 'a destructive matter' for the purposes of the Offences Against the Person Act 1837 s 5 (*R v Crawford* (1845) 2 Car & Kir 129, CCR) but subsequently it was held that it was not a 'destructive substance' for the purposes of the Offences against the Person Act 1861 (*R v Crawford* (1877) 62 LT Jo 372 per Huddleston B).

6 Where an intent to disable is alleged, the prosecution need not prove that the defendant intended to disable permanently: *R v James* (1979) 70 Cr App Rep 215, CA.

7 For the meaning of 'grievous bodily harm' see para 119 ante.

Exhibit 12–4. 11(1) HALSBURY'S LAWS OF ENGLAND *Criminal Law, Evidence and Procedure* ¶¶ 125–126 (4th ed. 2006 reissue).

APPENDIX A

SOURCES FOR STATE APPELLATE COURT CASES

Most state appellate court cases are published in both official reports and the National Reporter System, but there are significant exceptions. Regional reporters did not begin publication until 1879 or later, and several states have discontinued official reports in recent decades and now rely on regional reporter coverage of their courts. The inclusion of volume numbers in this table indicates a reporter series that is no longer published.

This table shows major published and electronic sources for the decisions of state courts of last resort and intermediate appellate courts. Internet sites are listed if they have current coverage, provide free access to cases, and maintain archives for more than just a few weeks or months. Most of the sites listed are official state sites, but commercial sites are included if they provide coverage or features unavailable from the official site. Those free sites that permit keyword searching (beyond a general website search engine) are indicated.

Another source for recent decisions, not listed here, is lexisONE <www.lexisone.com>, which provides free access to the most recent five years of cases from all state appellate courts. These can be retrieved using LexisNexis search techniques.

In some instances, entries include earlier courts with similar functions to the current courts listed. Some court systems have changed dramatically under new state constitutions, e.g., New York in 1846 and South Carolina in 1868, but the earlier courts are not listed separately. For more precise information it may be necessary to turn to a state legal research guide (see Appendix B).

The Bluebook: A Uniform System of Citation (18th ed. 2005, pp. 198–239) has listings of state nominative reports (with abbreviations); and Cohen, Berring & Olson, *How to Find the Law* (9th ed. 1989, pages 614–662) includes more extensive coverage of nominative reports, miscellaneous reports, and sources for state trial court cases.

ALABAMA

Supreme Court

Nominative reports, 1820–39

1–295 *Alabama Reports*, 1840–1976

Southern Reporter, 1887 [80 Ala.]–date

LexisNexis and Westlaw, 1820–date

Loislaw, 1916–date

Court of Civil Appeals

1–57 *Alabama Appellate Court Reports*, 1911–76

Southern Reporter, 1911 [1 Ala. App.]–date

LexisNexis and Westlaw, 1916–date

Loislaw, 1916–date

Court of Criminal Appeals

1–57 *Alabama Appellate Court Reports*, 1911–76

Southern Reporter, 1911 [1 Ala. App.]–date

LexisNexis and Westlaw, 1911–date

Loislaw, 1916–date

ALASKA

Supreme Court

Pacific Reporter, 1959–date

LexisNexis, Loislaw, and Westlaw, 1959–date

Court of Appeals

Pacific Reporter, 1980–date

LexisNexis, Loislaw, and Westlaw, 1980–date

ARIZONA

Supreme Court

Arizona Reports, 1866–date

Pacific Reporter, 1866 [1 Ariz.]–date

LexisNexis and Westlaw, 1866–date

Loislaw, 1925–date

<www.supreme.state.az.us/opin/>, 1998–date

Court of Appeals

1–27 *Arizona Appeals Reports*, 1965–76

Arizona Reports, 1976–date

Pacific Reporter, 1965 [1 Ariz. App.]–date

LexisNexis, Loislaw, and Westlaw, 1965–date

Division One <www.cofad1.state.az.us>, 2000–date

Division Two <www.apltwo.ct.state.az.us>, 2002–date

ARKANSAS

Supreme Court

Arkansas Reports, 1837–date

South Western Reporter, 1887 [47 Ark.]–date

LexisNexis and Westlaw, 1837–date

Loislaw, 1924–date

<courts.state.ar.us/opinions/opinions.html>,   1994–date [searchable]

Court of Appeals

Arkansas Appellate Reports, 1979–date (bound with *Arkansas Reports*)

South Western Reporter, 1979 [1 Ark. App.]–date

LexisNexis, Loislaw, and Westlaw, 1979–date

<courts.state.ar.us/opinions/opinions.html>,   1994–date [searchable]

CALIFORNIA

Supreme Court

California Reports, 1850–date

Pacific Reporter, 1883 [64 Cal.]–date)

California Reporter, 1960 [53 Cal. 2d]–date)

LexisNexis and Westlaw, 1850–date

Loislaw, 1899–date

<www.lexisnexis.com/clients/CACourts/>,   1850–date [searchable]

Courts of Appeal

California Appellate Reports, 1905–date

Pacific Reporter, 1905 [1 Cal. App.]–1959 [175 Cal. App. 2d]

California Reporter, 1960 [176 Cal. App. 2d]–date

LexisNexis, Loislaw, and Westlaw, 1905–date

<www.lexisnexis.com/clients/CACourts/>,   1850–date [searchable]

COLORADO

Supreme Court

1–200 *Colorado Reports*, 1864–1980

Pacific Reporter, 1884 [7 Colo.]–date

LexisNexis and Westlaw, 1864–date

Loislaw, 1924–date

<www.findlaw.com/11stategov/co/coca.html>,   1998–
date

Court of Appeals

1–44 *Colorado Court of Appeals Reports*, 1891–1915,
1970–80

Pacific Reporter, 1891 [1 Colo. App.]–1915, 1970–date

LexisNexis and Westlaw, 1891–1915, 1970–date

Loislaw, 1970–date

<www.findlaw.com/11stategov/co/coca.html>,   1998–
date

CONNECTICUT

Supreme Court

Nominative reports, 1786–1813

Connecticut Reports, 1814–date

Atlantic Reporter, 1886 [53 Conn.]–date

LexisNexis and Westlaw, 1786–date

Loislaw, 1899–date

<www.jud.state.ct.us/opinions.htm>,   2000–date
[searchable]

Appellate Court

Connecticut Appellate Reports, 1983–date

Atlantic Reporter, 1983 [1 Conn. App.]–date

LexisNexis, Loislaw, and Westlaw, 1983–date

<www.jud.state.ct.us/opinions.htm>,   2000–date
[searchable]

DELAWARE

Supreme Court

1–3 *Delaware Cases*, 1795–1830

1–59 *Delaware Reports*, 1832–1966

Atlantic Reporter, 1886 [12 Del.]–date

LexisNexis and Westlaw, 1795–date

Loislaw, 1948–date

<courts.state.de.us/opinions>, 2000–date [searchable]

DISTRICT OF COLUMBIA

Court of Appeals

Atlantic Reporter, 1942–date

LexisNexis, Loislaw, and Westlaw, 1942–date

<www.dcappeals.gov/dccourts/appeals/opinions_mojs.jsp>. 1998–date [searchable]

FLORIDA

Supreme Court

1–160 *Florida Reports*, 1846–1948

Southern Reporter, 1887 [22 Fla.]–date

LexisNexis and Westlaw, 1846–date

Loislaw, 1925–date

<www.floridasupremecourt.org/decisions/index.shtml>, 1999–date

<www.findlaw.com/11stategov/fl/flca.html>, 1995–date

District Courts of Appeal

Southern Reporter, 1957–date

LexisNexis, Loislaw, and Westlaw, 1957–date

First District <opinions.1dca.org>, 2004–date

Second District <www.2dca.org/opinions.htm>, 2001–date

Third District <www.3dca.flcourts.org>, 2001–date

Fourth District <www.4dca.org/recentopfrm.html>, 2005–date

Fifth District <www.5dca.org/opinions.shtml>, 2001–date

GEORGIA

Supreme Court

Georgia Reports, 1846–date

South Eastern Reporter, 1887 [77 Ga.]–date

LexisNexis and Westlaw, 1846–date

Loislaw, 1939–date

Court of Appeals

Georgia Appeals Reports, 1907–date

South Eastern Reporter, 1907 [1 Ga. App.]–date

LexisNexis and Westlaw, 1907–date

Loislaw, 1939–date

HAWAI'I

Supreme Court

Hawai'i Reports, 1847–date

Pacific Reporter, 1884 [43 Haw.]–date

LexisNexis and Westlaw, 1847–date

Loislaw, 1924–date

<www.hawaii.gov/jud/ctops.htm>, 1998–date

Intermediate Court of Appeals

1–10 *Hawai'i Appellate Reports*, 1980–94

Hawai'i Reports, 1994–date

Pacific Reporter, 1980 [1 Haw. App.]–date

LexisNexis, Loislaw, and Westlaw, 1980–date

<www.hawaii.gov/jud/ctops.htm>, 1998–date

IDAHO

Supreme Court

Idaho Reports, 1866–date

Pacific Reporter, 1881 [2 Idaho]–date

LexisNexis and Westlaw, 1866–date

Loislaw, 1924–date

<www.findlaw.com/11stategov/id/idca.html>,   1998–date

Court of Appeals

Idaho Reports, 1982–date

Pacific Reporter, 1982 [102 Idaho]–date

LexisNexis, Loislaw, and Westlaw, 1982–date

<www.findlaw.com/11stategov/id/idca.html>,   1998–date

ILLINOIS

Supreme Court

Illinois Reports, 1819–date

North Eastern Reporter, 1884 [112 Ill.]–date

LexisNexis and Westlaw, 1819–date

Loislaw, 1925–date

<www.state.il.us/court/Opinions/>, 1996–date [searchable]

Appellate Court

Illinois Appellate Reports, 1877–date

North Eastern Reporter, 1936 [284 Ill. App.]–date

LexisNexis and Westlaw, 1877–date

Loislaw, 1924–date

<www.state.il.us/court/Opinions/>, 1996–date [searchable]

INDIANA

Supreme Court

Nominative reports, 1817–47

1–275 *Indiana Reports*, 1848–1981

North Eastern Reporter, 1885 [102 Ind.]–date

LexisNexis and Westlaw, 1817–date

Loislaw, 1923–date

<www.findlaw.com/11stategov/in/inca.html>,   1998–date

<www.ai.org/judiciary/opinions/>, 1999–date

Court of Appeals

1–182 *Indiana Court of Appeals Reports*, 1891–1979

North Eastern Reporter, 1891 [1 Ind. App.]–date

LexisNexis and Westlaw, 1891–date

Loislaw, 1921–date

<www.findlaw.com/11stategov/in/inca.html>,   1998–date

<www.ai.org/judiciary/opinions/>, 1999–date

IOWA

Supreme Court

Nominative reports, 1839–54

1–261 *Iowa Reports*, 1855–1968

North Western Reporter, 1879 [51 Iowa]–date

LexisNexis and Westlaw, 1839–date

Loislaw, 1924–date

<www.judicial.state.ia.us>, 1998–date

Court of Appeals

North Western Reporter, 1977–date

LexisNexis, Loislaw, and Westlaw, 1977–date

<www.judicial.state.ia.us>, 1998–date

KANSAS

Supreme Court

Nominative reports, 1858–61

Kansas Reports, 1862–date

Pacific Reporter, 1883 [30 Kan.]–date

LexisNexis and Westlaw, 1858–date

Loislaw, 1949–date

<www.kscourts.org/kscases/>, 1996–date [searchable]

Court of Appeals

Kansas Court of Appeals Reports, 1895–1901, 1977–date

Pacific Reporter, 1895 [1 Kan. App.]–1901, 1977–date

LexisNexis and Westlaw, 1895–1901, 1977–date

Loislaw, 1977–date

<www.kscourts.org/kscases/>, 1996–date [searchable]

KENTUCKY

Supreme Court

1–314 *Kentucky Reports*, 1785–1951

South Western Reporter, 1886 [84 Ky.]–date

LexisNexis and Westlaw, 1785–date

Loislaw, 1925–date

<www.kycourts.net/Supreme/SC_Opinions.shtm>, 1999–date [searchable]

Court of Appeals

South Western Reporter, 1976–date

LexisNexis, Loislaw, and Westlaw, 1976–date

<www.kycourts.net/Supreme/SC_Opinions.shtm>, 1996–date [searchable]

LOUISIANA

Supreme Court

Nominative reports, 1813–30, 1841–46

1–19 *Louisiana Reports*, 1830–41

1–52 *Louisiana Annual Reports*, 1846–1900

104–263 *Louisiana Reports*, 1900–72

Southern Reporter, 1887 [39 La. Ann.]–date

LexisNexis and Westlaw, 1813–date

Loislaw, 1924–date

Courts of Appeal

Nominative reports, 1881–85, 1903–23

1–19 *Louisiana Courts of Appeals Reports*, 1924–32

Southern Reporter, 1928 [9 La. App.]–date

LexisNexis and Westlaw, 1881–date

Loislaw, 1941–date

First Circuit <www.la-fcca.org/published_opinions.htm>, 2000–date

Second Circuit <www.lacoa2.org/opinions.htm>, 2001–date [searchable]

Third Circuit <www.la3circuit.org/opinions.htm>, 2003–date

Fourth Circuit <4thcir-app.state.la.us/opinions2.aspx>, 2001–date

Fifth Circuit <www.fifthcircuit.org/published_opinions.html>, 2002–date

MAINE

Supreme Judicial Court

1–161 *Maine Reports*, 1820–1965

Atlantic Reporter, 1886 [77 Me.]–date

LexisNexis and Westlaw, 1820–date

Loislaw, 1923–date

<www.courts.state.me.us/opinions/supreme/>,   1997–date [searchable]

MARYLAND

Court of Appeals

Nominative reports, 1787–1851

Maryland Reports, 1851–date

Atlantic Reporter, 1886 [63 Md.]–date

LexisNexis and Westlaw, 1787–date

Loislaw, 1899–date

<www.courts.state.md.us/opinions.html>,   1995–date [searchable]

Court of Special Appeals

Maryland Appellate Reports, 1967–date

Atlantic Reporter, 1967 [1 Md. App.]–date

LexisNexis, Loislaw, and Westlaw, 1967–date

<www.courts.state.md.us/opinions.html>,   1995–date [searchable]

MASSACHUSETTS

Supreme Judicial Court

Massachusetts Reports, 1804–date

North Eastern Reporter, 1885 [139 Mass.]–date

LexisNexis and Westlaw, 1804–date

Loislaw, 1899–date

<www.malawyersweekly.com/masjc.cfm>,   1997–date [searchable]

Appeals Court

Massachusetts Appeals Court Reports, 1972–date

North Eastern Reporter, 1972 [1 Mass. App.]–date

LexisNexis, Loislaw, and Westlaw, 1972–date

<www.malawyersweekly.com/macoa.cfm>,   1997–date [searchable]

MICHIGAN

Supreme Court

Nominative reports, 1838–47

Michigan Reports, 1847–date

North Western Reporter, 1879 [41 Mich.]–date

Westlaw, 1838–date

LexisNexis, 1843–date

Loislaw, 1924–date

<courtofappeals.mijud.net/resources/opinions.htm>, 2001–date [searchable]

<government.westlaw.com/miofficial/historical/>, 1942–2000 [searchable]

Court of Appeals

Michigan Appeals Reports, 1965–date

North Western Reporter, 1965 [1 Mich. App.]–date

LexisNexis, Loislaw, and Westlaw, 1965–date

<courtofappeals.mijud.net/resources/opinions.htm>, 2001–date [searchable]

<government.westlaw.com/miofficial/historical/>, 1977–2000 [searchable]

MINNESOTA

Supreme Court

1–312 *Minnesota Reports*, 1851–1977

North Western Reporter, 1879 [26 Minn.]–date

LexisNexis and Westlaw, 1851–date

Loislaw, 1924–date

<www.lawlibrary.state.mn.us/archive/>,   1996–date
[searchable]

Court of Appeals

North Western Reporter, 1983–date

LexisNexis, Loislaw, and Westlaw, 1983–date

<www.lawlibrary.state.mn.us/archive/>,   1996–date
[searchable]

MISSISSIPPI

Supreme Court

1–254 *Mississippi Reports*, 1818–1966

Southern Reporter, 1887 [64 Miss.]–date

LexisNexis and Westlaw, 1818–date

Loislaw, 1924–date

<www.mssc.state.ms.us/decisions/search/default.asp>,
1996–date [searchable]

Court of Appeals

Southern Reporter, 1995–date

LexisNexis, Loislaw, and Westlaw, 1995–date

<www.mssc.state.ms.us/decisions/search/default.asp>,
1996–date [searchable]

MISSOURI

Supreme Court

1–365 *Missouri Reports*, 1821–1956

South Western Reporter, 1886 [89 Mo.]–date

LexisNexis and Westlaw, 1821–date

Loislaw, 1919–date

<www.courts.mo.gov/courts/pubopinions.nsf>,   1997–date [searchable]

Courts of Appeals

1–241 *Missouri Appeal Reports*, 1876–1952

South Western Reporter, 1902 [93 Mo. App.]–date

LexisNexis and Westlaw, 1876–date

Loislaw, 1919–date

<www.courts.mo.gov/courts/pubopinions.nsf>,   1997–date [searchable]

MONTANA

Supreme Court

Montana Reports, 1868–date

Pacific Reporter, 1884 [4 Mont.]–date

LexisNexis and Westlaw, 1868–date

Loislaw, 1924–date

<searchcourts.mt.gov>, 1981–date [searchable]

NEBRASKA

Supreme Court

Nebraska Reports, 1860s–date

North Western Reporter, 1879 [8 Neb.]–date

LexisNexis and Westlaw, 1860s–date

Loislaw, 1949–date

Court of Appeals

Nebraska Appellate Reports, 1992–date

North Western Reporter, 1992 [1 Neb. App.]–date

LexisNexis, Loislaw, and Westlaw, 1992–date

NEVADA

Supreme Court

Nevada Reports, 1865–date

Pacific Reporter, 1884 [17 Nev.]–date

LexisNexis and Westlaw, 1865–date

Loislaw, 1924–date

<www.findlaw.com/11stategov/nv/nvca.html>, 1998–2003, 2005–date

NEW HAMPSHIRE

Supreme Court

Nominative reports, 1803–16

New Hampshire Reports, 1816–date

Atlantic Reporter, 1886 [63 N.H.]–date

LexisNexis and Westlaw, 1816–date

Loislaw, 1874–date

<www.courts.state.nh.us/supreme/opinions/>, 1995–date

NEW JERSEY

Supreme Court

1–137 *New Jersey Law Reports*, 1789–1948

1–142 *New Jersey Equity Reports*, 1830–1948

New Jersey Reports, 1948–date

Atlantic Reporter, 1885 [47 N.J. Law, 40 N.J. Eq.]–date

LexisNexis and Westlaw, 1789–date

Loislaw, 1924–date

<lawlibrary.rutgers.edu/search.shtml>, 1994–date [searchable]

Superior Court, Appellate Division

New Jersey Superior Court Reports, 1948–date

Atlantic Reporter, 1948 [1 N.J. Super.]–date

LexisNexis, Loislaw, and Westlaw, 1948–date

<lawlibrary.rutgers.edu/search.shtml>, 1995–date [searchable]

NEW MEXICO

Supreme Court

New Mexico Reports, 1852–date

Pacific Reporter, 1883 [3 N.M.]–date

LexisNexis and Westlaw, 1852–date

Loislaw, 1924–date

<www.supremecourt.nm.org>, 1998–date

Court of Appeals

New Mexico Reports, 1966–date

Pacific Reporter, 1966 [78 N.M.]–date

LexisNexis, Loislaw, and Westlaw, 1966–date

<www.supremecourt.nm.org>, 1998–date

NEW YORK

Court of Appeals

Nominative reports, 1791–1847

New York Reports, 1847–date

North Eastern Reporter, 1885 [99 N.Y.]–date

New York Supplement, 1956 [1 N.Y.2d]–date

LexisNexis and Westlaw, 1791–date

Loislaw, 1847–date

<www.law.cornell.edu/ny/ctap/>, 1992–date [searchable]

<government.westlaw.com/nyofficial/>, 1997–date [searchable]

Supreme Court, Appellate Division

Appellate Division Reports, 1896–date

New York Supplement, 1896 [1 App. Div.]–date

LexisNexis, Loislaw, and Westlaw, 1896–date

<government.westlaw.com/nyofficial/>, 1997–date [searchable]

NORTH CAROLINA

Supreme Court

North Carolina Reports, 1778–date

South Eastern Reporter, 1884 [96 N.C.]–date

LexisNexis, Loislaw, and Westlaw, 1778–date

<www.aoc.state.nc.us/www/public/html/opinions. htm>, 1997–date [searchable]

Court of Appeals

North Carolina Court of Appeals Reports, 1968–date

South Eastern Reporter, 1968 [1 N.C. App.]–date

LexisNexis, Loislaw, and Westlaw, 1968–date

<www.aoc.state.nc.us/www/public/html/opinions. htm>, 1996–date [searchable]

NORTH DAKOTA

Supreme Court

1–6 *Dakota Reports*, 1867–89

1–79 *North Dakota Reports*, 1890–1953

North Western Reporter, 1867 [1 Dak.]–date

LexisNexis and Westlaw, 1867–date

Loislaw, 1924–date

<www.court.state.nd.us/court/opinions.htm>, 1967–date [searchable]

OHIO

Supreme Court

1–20 *Ohio Reports*, 1821–52

Ohio State Reports, 1852–date

North Eastern Reporter, 1885 [43 Ohio St.]–date

LexisNexis and Westlaw, 1821–date

Loislaw, 1923–date

<www.sconet.state.oh.us/rod/>, 1992–date [searchable]

Courts of Appeals

Ohio Appellate Reports, 1913–date

North Eastern Reporter, 1923 [20 Ohio App.]–date

LexisNexis and Westlaw, 1913–date

Loislaw, 1926–date

<www.sconet.state.oh.us/rod/>, 2001–date [searchable]

OKLAHOMA

Supreme Court

1–208 *Oklahoma Reports*, 1890–1953

Pacific Reporter, 1890 [1 Okla.]–date

LexisNexis, Loislaw, and Westlaw, 1890–date

<www.oscn.net>, 1890–date [searchable]

Court of Criminal Appeals

1–97 *Oklahoma Criminal Reports*, 1908–53

Pacific Reporter, 1980 [1 Okla. Crim.]–date

LexisNexis, Loislaw, and Westlaw, 1908–date

<www.oscn.net>, 1908–date [searchable]

Court of Civil Appeals

Pacific Reporter, 1968–date

LexisNexis, Loislaw, and Westlaw, 1968–date

<www.oscn.net>, 1968–date [searchable]

OREGON

Supreme Court

Oregon Reports, 1853–date

Pacific Reporter, 1884 [11 Or.]–date

LexisNexis and Westlaw, 1853–date

Loislaw, 1924–date

<www.publications.ojd.state.or.us/supreme.htm>, 1998–date

Court of Appeals

Oregon Reports, Court of Appeal, 1969–date

Pacific Reporter, 1969 [1 Or. App.]–date

LexisNexis, Loislaw, and Westlaw, 1969–date

<www.publications.ojd.state.or.us/appeals.htm>, 1998–date

PENNSYLVANIA

Supreme Court

Nominative reports, 1754–1845

Pennsylvania State Reports, 1845–date

Atlantic Reporter, 1886 [108 Pa. St.]–date

LexisNexis and Westlaw, 1754–date

Loislaw, 1924–date

<www.courts.state.pa.us/Index/Opinions/Index Opinions.asp>, 1996–date [searchable]

Superior Court

Pennsylvania Superior Court Reports, 1895–date

Atlantic Reporter, 1930 [102 Pa. Super.]–date

LexisNexis and Westlaw, 1895–date

Loislaw, 1923–date

<www.courts.state.pa.us/Index/Opinions/Index Opinions.asp>, 1997–date [searchable]

Commonwealth Court

1–168 *Pennsylvania Commonwealth Court Reports*, 1970–94

Atlantic Reporter, 1970 [1 Pa. Commw.]–date

LexisNexis, Loislaw, and Westlaw, 1970–date

<www.courts.state.pa.us/Index/Opinions/Index Opinions.asp>, 1997–date [searchable]

PUERTO RICO

Tribunal Supremo

1–100 *Puerto Rico Reports*, 1899–1972

Decisiones de Puerto Rico, 1899–date

LexisNexis and Westlaw, 1899–date

<www.tribunalpr.org/opiniones/index–2.html>, 1998–date

Tribunal de Apelaciones

LexisNexis, 1995–date

Westlaw, 2001–date

RHODE ISLAND

Supreme Court

1–122 *Rhode Island Reports*, 1828–1980

Atlantic Reporter, 1886 [15 R.I.]–date

LexisNexis, Loislaw, and Westlaw, 1828–date

<www.courts.state.ri.us/supreme/publishedopinions. htm>, 1999–date

SOUTH CAROLINA

Supreme Court

Nominative reports, 1783–1868

South Carolina Reports, 1868–date

South Eastern Reporter, 1886 [25 S.C.]–date

Westlaw, 1783–date

LexisNexis, 1868–date

Loislaw, 1900–date

<www.judicial.state.sc.us/opinions/>, 1997–date

Court of Appeals

South Carolina Reports, 1983–date

South Eastern Reporter, 1983–date

LexisNexis, Loislaw, and Westlaw, 1983–date

<www.judicial.state.sc.us/opinions/>, 1999–date

SOUTH DAKOTA

Supreme Court

1–6 *Dakota Reports*, 1867–89

1–90 *South Dakota Reports*, 1890–1976

North Western Reporter, 1867 [1 Dak.]–date

LexisNexis and Westlaw, 1867–date

Loislaw, 1931–date

<www.sdjudicial.com>, 1996–date [searchable]

TENNESSEE

Supreme Court

1–225 *Tennessee Reports*, 1791–1971

South Western Reporter, 1886 [85 Tenn.]–date

LexisNexis and Westlaw, 1791–date

Loislaw, 1925–date

<www.tsc.state.tn.us/opinions/tsc/oplsttsc.htm>,
1995–date

Court of Appeals

1–63 *Tennessee Appeals Reports*, 1925–71

South Western Reporter, 1932 [16 Tenn. App.]–date

LexisNexis, Loislaw, and Westlaw, 1925–date

<www.tsc.state.tn.us/opinions/tca/oplsttca.htm>,
1995–date

Court of Criminal Appeals

1–4 *Tennessee Criminal Appeals Reports*, 1967–71

South Western Reporter, 1967 [1 Tenn. Crim. App.]–
date

LexisNexis and Westlaw, 1967–date

Loislaw, 1971–date

<www.tsc.state.tn.us/opinions/tcca/oplstcca.htm>,
1995–date

TEXAS

Supreme Court

Nominative reports, 1840–45

1–163 *Texas Reports*, 1846–1963

South Western Reporter, 1886 [66 Tex.]–date

LexisNexis and Westlaw, 1840–date

Loislaw, 1890–date

<www.supreme.courts.state.tx.us>,   1997–date
[searchable]

Court of Criminal Appeals

1–30 *Texas Court of Appeals Cases*, 1876–92

31–172 *Texas Criminal Reports*, 1892–1963

South Western Reporter, 1886 [21 Tex. App.]–date

LexisNexis and Westlaw, 1876–date

Loislaw, 1892–date

<www.cca.courts.state.tx.us>, 1998–date [searchable]

Courts of Appeals

1–63 *Texas Civil Appeals Reports*, 1892–1911

South Western Reporter, 1892 [1 Tex. Civ. App.]–date

LexisNexis and Westlaw, 1892–date

Loislaw, 1892–date

<www.courts.state.tx.us/courts/coa.asp>,   2001–date [searchable]

UTAH

Supreme Court

1–123, 1–30 2d *Utah Reports*, 1861–1974

Pacific Reporter, 1884 [3 Utah]–date

LexisNexis and Westlaw, 1861–date

Loislaw, 1923–date

<www.utcourts.gov/opinions/>, 1996–date [searchable]

Court of Appeals

Pacific Reporter, 1987–date

LexisNexis, Loislaw, and Westlaw, 1987–date

<www.utcourts.gov/opinions/>, 1997–date [searchable]

VERMONT

Supreme Court

Nominative reports, 1789–1826

Vermont Reports, 1826–date

Atlantic Reporter, 1885 [58 Vt.]–date

Westlaw, 1789–date

LexisNexis, 1826–date

Loislaw, 1923–date

<dol.state.vt.us/www_root/000000/html/supct.html>,
1993–date

VIRGINIA

Supreme Court

Virginia Reports, 1790–date

South Eastern Reporter, 1887 [82 Va.]–date

LexisNexis and Westlaw, 1790–date

Loislaw, 1931–date

<www.courts.state.va.us/opin.htm>, 1995–date

<www.valawyersweekly.com/vasup.cfm>,   1998–date
[searchable]

Court of Appeals

Virginia Court of Appeals Reports, 1985–date

South Eastern Reporter, 1985 [1 Va. App.]–date

LexisNexis, Loislaw, and Westlaw, 1985–date

<www.courts.state.va.us/opin.htm>, 1995–date

<www.valawyersweekly.com/vacoa.cfm>,   1997–date
[searchable]

WASHINGTON

Supreme Court

1–3 *Washington Territory Reports*, 1854–89

Washington Reports, 1889–date

Pacific Reports, 1884 [2 Wash. Terr.]–date

LexisNexis and Westlaw, 1854–date

Loislaw, 1925–date

<www.legalwa.org>, 1854–date [searchable]

Court of Appeals

Washington Appellate Reports, 1969–date

Pacific Reporter, 1969 [1 Wash. App.]–date

LexisNexis, Loislaw, and Westlaw, 1969–date

<www.legalwa.org>, 1969–date [searchable]

WEST VIRGINIA

Supreme Court of Appeals

West Virginia Reports, 1864–date

South Eastern Reporter, 1884 [29 W. Va.]–date

LexisNexis and Westlaw, 1864–date

Loislaw, 1923–date

<www.state.wv.us/wvsca/opinions.htm>, 1991–date [searchable]

WISCONSIN

Supreme Court

Nominative reports, 1839–53

Wisconsin Reports, 1853–date

North Western Reporter, 1879 [46 Wis.]–date

LexisNexis and Westlaw, 1839–date

Loislaw, 1939–date

<www.wicourts.gov/opinions/>, 1995–date [searchable]

<www.wisbar.org/Wis/>, 1995–date [searchable]

Court of Appeals

Wisconsin Reports, 1978–date

North Western Reporter, 1978 [85 Wis. 2d]–date

LexisNexis, Loislaw, and Westlaw, 1978–date

<www.wicourts.gov/opinions/>, 1995–date [searchable]

<www.wisbar.org/WisCtApp/>, 1995–date [searchable]

WYOMING

Supreme Court

1–80 *Wyoming Reports*, 1870–1959

Pacific Reporter, 1884 [3 Wyo.]–date

LexisNexis and Westlaw, 1870–date

Loislaw, 1932–date

<wyomcases.courts.state.wy.us>, 1993–date [searchable]

APPENDIX B

STATE RESEARCH GUIDES

Because of variations in legal materials from state to state, a general research guide like this *Nutshell* cannot provide the necessary detail for specific state sources. These guides are therefore suggested for further information on the materials of individual states. The list includes several journal articles discussing state practice materials and research methods, as well as chapters in a looseleaf volume edited by Frank G. Houdek, *State Practice Materials: Annotated Bibliographies* (2002–date). So far this collection has chapters for eighteen states and the District of Columbia, and its value is increasing with its coverage. The American Association of Law Libraries has issued a series of short but useful guides to state materials or government documents, but these titles are generally listed here only if no other recent guide is available for that state.

Other works listing research guides and other basic resources for each state include William H. Manz, *Guide to State Legislative and Administrative Materials* (2002), and "State Legal Publications and Information Sources," in Kendall F. Svengalis, *Legal Information Buyer's Guide & Reference Manual* (annual).

Alabama   Gary Orlando Lewis, *Legal Research in Alabama: How to Find and Understand the Law in Alabama* (2001).

Scott DeLeve, "Alabama Practice Materials: A Selective Annotated Bibliography" (2005), in *State Practice Materials: Annotated Bibliographies.*

Alaska

Aimee Ruzicka, *Alaska Legal and Law–Related Publications: A Guide for Law Librarians* (1984).

Arizona

A Survey of Arizona State Legal and Law–Related Documents (2006).

Kathy Shimpock–Vieweg & Marianne Sidorski Alcorn, *Arizona Legal Research Guide* (1992).

Arkansas

Kathryn C. Fitzhugh, "Arkansas Practice Materials II: A Selective Annotated Bibliography," 21 U. Ark. Little Rock L.J. 363 (1999).

California

John K. Hanft, *Legal Research in California* (5th ed. 2004).

Judy C. Janes, "California Practice Materials: A Selective Annotated Bibliography" (2006), in *State Practice Materials: Annotated Bibliographies.*

Daniel W. Martin, ed., *Henke's California Law Guide* (8th ed. 2006).

Colorado

Mitch Fontenot, "Colorado Practice Materials: A Selective Annotated Bibliography" (2003), in *State Practice Materials: Annotated Bibliographies.*

Connecticut

Shirley Bysiewicz, *Sources of Connecticut Law* (1987).

Lawrence G. Cheeseman & Arlene C. Bielefeld, *The Connecticut Legal Research Handbook* (1992).

Jonathan Saxon, "Connecticut Practice Materials: A Selective Annotated Bibliography," 91 Law Libr. J. 139 (1999).

Delaware

Patrick J. Charles & David K. King, "Delaware Practice Materials: A Selective Annotated Bibliography," 89 Law Libr. J. 349 (1997).

District of Columbia

Leah F. Chanin, "Legal Research in the District of Columbia," in *Legal Research in the District of Columbia, Maryland and Virginia* (2d ed. 2000).

Michelle Wu, "District of Columbia Practice Materials: A Selective Annotated Bibliography" (2001), in *State Practice Materials: Annotated Bibliographies.*

Florida

Barbara J. Busharis & Suzanne E. Rowe, *Florida Legal Research: Sources, Process, and Analysis* (2d ed. 2002).

Betsy L. Stupski, *Guide to Florida Legal Research* (6th ed. 2001).

Georgia

Leah F. Chanin & Suzanne L. Cassidy, *Guide to Georgia Legal Research and Legal History* (1990).

Nancy P. Johnson & Nancy Adams Deel, "Researching Georgia Law (1998 Edition)," 14 Ga. St. U. L. Rev. 545 (1998).

Hawai'i

Leina'ala R. Seeger, "Hawaii Practice Materials: A Selective Annotated Bibliography" (2003), in *State Practice Materials: Annotated Bibliographies.*

Idaho

Michael J. Greenlee, *Idaho State Documents: A Bibliography of Legal Publications and Related Materials* (2003).

Leina'ala R. Seeger, "Idaho Practice Materials: A Selective Annotated Bibliography," 87 Law Libr. J. 534 (1995).

Illinois

Phill Johnson, "Illinois Practice Materials: A Selective Annotated Bibliography" (2006), in *State Practice Materials: Annotated Bibliographies.*

Laurel Wendt, *Illinois Legal Research Guide* (2d ed. 2006).

Mark E. Wojcik, *Illinois Legal Research* (2003).

Indiana

Richard E. Humphrey, "Indiana Practice Materials: A Selective Annotated Bibliography" (2004), in *State Practice Materials: Annotated Bibliographies.*

Iowa

John D. Edwards, *Iowa Legal Research Guide* (2003).

Kansas

Joseph A. Custer et al., *Kansas Legal Research and Reference Guide* (3d ed. 2003).

Joseph A. Custer, "Kansas Practice Materials: A Selective Annotated Bibliography" (2002), in *State Practice Materials: Annotated Bibliographies.*

Kentucky

Kurt X. Metzmeier et al., *Kentucky Legal Research Manual* (3d ed. 2005).

Louisiana

Win–Shin S. Chiang, *Louisiana Legal Research* (2d ed. 1990).

Catherine Lemann, "Louisiana Practice Materials: A Selective Annotated Bibliography" (2006), in *State Practice Materials: Annotated Bibliographies.*

Maine   Christine I. Hepler & Maureen P. Quinlan, *Maine State Documents: A Bibliography of Legal Publications and Law–Related Materials* (2003).

William W. Wells, *Maine Legal Research Guide* (1989).

Maryland   Pamela J. Gregory, "Legal Research in Maryland," in *Legal Research in the District of Columbia, Maryland and Virginia* (2d ed. 2000).

Massachusetts   Mary Ann Neary, ed., *Handbook of Legal Research in Massachusetts* (rev. ed. 2002).

Michigan   Richard L. Beer & Judith J. Field, *Michigan Legal Literature: An Annotated Guide* (2d ed. 1991).

Pamela Lysaght, *Michigan Legal Research* (2006).

Minnesota   Vicente E. Garces, "Minnesota Practice Materials: A Selective Annotated Bibliography" (2001), in *State Practice Materials: Annotated Bibliographies.*

John Tessner et al., *Minnesota Legal Research Guide* (2d ed. 2002).

Mississippi   Scott D. DeLeve & Anne M. Klingen, "Mississippi Practice Materials: A Selective Annotated Bibliography" (2001), in *State Practice Materials: Annotated Bibliographies.*

Missouri   Mary Ann Nelson, *Guide to Missouri State Documents and Selected Law–Related Materials* (1991).

Montana	Robert K. Whelan et al., *A Guide to Montana Legal Research* (8th ed. 2003) <www.montanacourts.org/library/guides/guide.pdf>.
Nebraska	Kay L. Andrus, *Research Guide to Nebraska Law* (2006 ed.).
	Beth Smith, "Nebraska Practice Materials: A Selective Annotated Bibliography" (2003), in *State Practice Materials: Annotated Bibliographies.*
Nevada	G. LeGrande Fletcher, "Nevada Practice Materials: A Selective Annotated Bibliography," 91 Law Libr. J. 313 (1999).
	Jennifer Larraguibel Gross et al., *Nevada Legal Research Guide* (2005).
New Jersey	Cameron Allen, *A Guide to New Jersey Legal Bibliography and Legal History* (1984).
	Paul Axel–Lute, *New Jersey Legal Research Handbook* (4th ed. 1998), with Web supplement <www.rci.rutgers.edu/?axellute/njlrsupp.html>.
New Mexico	Mary A. Woodward, "New Mexico Practice Materials: A Selective Annotated Bibliography," 84 Law Libr. J. 93 (1992).
New York	William H. Manz, *Gibson's New York Legal Research Guide* (3d ed. 2004).
North Carolina	Mirian J. Baer & James C. Ray, *Legal Research in North Carolina* (2006).
	Jean Sinclair McKnight, *North Carolina Legal Research Guide* (1994).

Ohio	Kenneth S. Kozlowski & Susan N. Elliott, "Ohio Practice Materials: A Selective Annotated Bibliography" (2005), in *State Practice Materials: Annotated Bibliographies.*
	Melanie K. Putnam & Susan Schaefgen, *Ohio Legal Research Guide* (1997).
Oklahoma	Marilyn K. Nicely, *Oklahoma Legal and Law–Related Documents and Publications: A Selected Bibliography* (2d ed. 1997).
Oregon	Mary Clayton & Stephanie Midkiff, "Oregon Practice Materials: A Selective Annotated Bibliography" (2005), in *State Practice Materials: Annotated Bibliographies.*
	Suzanne E. Rowe, *Oregon Legal Research* (2003).
Pennsylvania	Joel Fishman & Marc Silverman, "Pennsylvania Practice Materials: A Selective Annotated Bibliography" (2003), in *State Practice Materials: Annotated Bibliographies.*
	Frank Y. Liu et al., *Pennsylvania Legal Research Handbook* (2001).
Puerto Rico	Luis Muñiz Argüelles & Migdalia Fraticelli Torres, *La Investigación Jurídica en el Derecho Puertorriqueño: Fuentes Puertorriqueñas, Norteamericanas y Españolas* (4th ed. 2006).
Rhode Island	Daniel J. Donovan, *Legal Research in Rhode Island (including Federal and State Research Materials)* (4th ed. 2004).

Gail I. Winson, *State of Rhode Island and Providence Plantations: Survey of State Documents and Law–Related Materials* (2004).

South Carolina

Paula Gail Benson & Deborah Ann Davis, *A Guide to South Carolina Legal Research and Citation* (1991).

Duncan E. Alford, "South Carolina Practice Materials: A Selective, Annotated Bibliography," Legal Reference Services Q., Winter 1999, at 23.

South Dakota

Delores A. Jorgensen, *South Dakota Legal Research Guide* (2d ed. 1999).

Tennessee

Toof Brown, III, "Tennessee Practice Materials: A Selective Annotated Bibliography" (2004), in *State Practice Materials: Annotated Bibliographies.*

Texas

Matthew C. Cordon & Brandon D. Quarles, *Specialized Topics in Texas Legal Research* (2005).

Brandon D. Quarles & Matthew C. Cordon, *Legal Research for the Texas Practitioner* (2003).

Brandon D. Quarles & Matthew C. Cordon, "Texas Practice Materials: A Selective Annotated Bibliography" (2006), in *State Practice Materials: Annotated Bibliographies.*

Utah

Kory D. Staheli, "Utah Practice Materials: A Selective Annotated Bibliography," 87 Law Libr. J. 28 (1995).

Vermont

Virginia Wise, *A Bibliographical Guide to the Vermont Legal System* (2d ed. 1991).

Virginia	John D. Eure & Gail F. Zwirner, eds., *A Guide to Legal Research in Virginia* (5th ed. 2005).
	Leslie A. Lee, "Virginia Practice Materials: A Selective Annotated Bibliography" (2001), in *State Practice Materials: Annotated Bibliographies.*
	Sarah K. Wiant, "Legal Research in Virginia," in *Legal Research in the District of Columbia, Maryland and Virginia* (2d ed. 2000).
Washington	Penny A. Hazelton et al., *Washington Legal Researcher's Deskbook 3d* (2002).
	Julie A. Heintz, *Washington Legal Research* (2005).
West Virginia	Ann Walsh Long, "Washington Practice Materials: A Selective Annotated Bibliography" (2003), in *State Practice Materials: Annotated Bibliographies.*
Wisconsin	Law Librarians Association of Wisconsin, *Introduction to Legal Materials: A Manual for Non–Law Librarians in Wisconsin* (2003) <www.aallnet.org/chapter/llaw/paliguide/index.htm>.
	Ellen J. Platt & Mary J. Koshollek, "Wisconsin Practice Materials: A Selective, Annotated Bibliography," 90 Law Libr. J. 219 (1998).
	Ellen J. Platt & Mary J. Koshollek, *Wisconsin Practice Materials: A Selective, Annotated Bibliography* (1999).
Wyoming	Debora A. Person, *Wyoming State Documents: A Bibliography of State Publications and Related Materials* (2006).

APPENDIX C

TOPICAL LOOSELEAF AND ELECTRONIC SERVICES

This is a selective list of topical services useful in legal research. Most services are available in numerous formats, including print, CD–ROM, and online versions, sometimes with slight variations in name. Electronic options are indicated in brackets, and italic type indicates services available only electronically. Basic criteria for inclusion are frequent supplementation (at least bimonthly) and publication of primary documents (either abstracts or full texts). For regularly updated and more comprehensive listings, see publisher websites or the annual *Legal Looseleafs in Print*.

Abbreviation	Publisher
BNA	Bureau of National Affairs <www.bna.com>
CCH	CCH Inc. <www.cch.com>
LRP	LRP Publications <www.lrp.com>
P&F	Pike & Fischer <www.pf.com>
RIA	Thomson RIA <ria.thomson.com>
West	Thomson West <west.thomson.com>

Accounting

Accounting Policy & Practice Report (BNA), biweekly *[Internet]*

Tax Management Portfolios–Accounting Policy & Practice Series (BNA), *[Internet]*

463

Advertising

Advertising Law Guide (CCH), monthly *[CD, Internet]*

Alcoholic Beverages

Liquor Control Law Reports (CCH), biweekly

Banking

Bank Compliance Guide (CCH), monthly *[CD, Internet]*

Banking Report (BNA), weekly *[Internet]*

Federal Banking Law Reports (CCH), weekly *[CD, Internet]*

Financial Privacy Law Guide (CCH), monthly *[Internet]*

State Banking Law Reports (CCH), monthly *[CD, Internet]*

Bankruptcy

Bankruptcy Law Reporter (BNA), weekly *[Internet]*

Bankruptcy Law Reports (CCH), biweekly

Commercial Law

Consumer Credit Guide (CCH), biweekly *[CD, Internet]*

Mortgage Compliance Guide (CCH), monthly [CD, Internet]

RICO Business Disputes Guide (CCH), monthly *[CD, Internet]*

Secured Transactions Guide (CCH), biweekly *[CD, Internet]*

Communications

Communications Regulation (P & F), weekly *[CD, Internet]*

Media Law Reporter (BNA), weekly

Computers and Internet

Electronic Commerce & Law Report (BNA), weekly *[Internet]*

Guide to Computer Law (CCH), monthly *[CD, Internet]*

Internet Law & Regulation (P & F), monthly *[Internet]*

Corporations

Business Strategies (CCH), monthly

Corporate Practice Series (BNA), weekly *[Internet]*

Corporate Secretary's Guide (CCH), monthly *[Internet]*

Corporation (Aspen Publishers), biweekly *[CD, Internet]*

Mergers & Acquisitions Law Report (BNA), weekly *[Internet]*

Criminal Law

Criminal Law Reporter (BNA), weekly *[Internet]*

Money Laundering, Terrorism and Financial Institutions (Civic Research Institute <www.civic research institute.com>), monthly *[Internet]*

Disabilities

Accommodating Disabilities: Business Management Guide (CCH), monthly *[CD, Internet]*

National Disability Law Reporter (LRP), biweekly

Education Law

Early Childhood Law and Policy Reporter (LRP), monthly

Individuals with Disabilities Education Law Reporter (LRP), biweekly *[CD]*

Election Law

Federal Election Campaign Financing Guide (CCH), monthly

Employee Compensation and Pensions

Benefits Coordinator (RIA), weekly *[Internet]*

COBRA Guide (CCH), monthly *[CD, Internet]*

Compliance Guide for Plan Administrators (CCH), monthly *[CD, Internet]*

Employee Benefits Management (CCH), biweekly *[CD, Internet]*

Executive Compensation and Taxation Coordinator (RIA), monthly *[Internet]*

Fringe Benefits Tax Guide (CCH), monthly *[CD, Internet]*

Individual Retirement Plans Guide (CCH), monthly *[CD, Internet]*

Payroll Administration Guide (BNA), biweekly *[Internet]*

Payroll Guide (RIA), biweekly *[Internet]*

Payroll Management Guide (CCH), weekly *[CD, Internet]*

Pension & Benefits Reporter (BNA), weekly *[Internet]*

Pension Coordinator (RIA), weekly *[Internet]*

Pension Plan Guide (CCH), weekly *[CD, Internet]*

Spencer's Research Reports on Employee Benefits (CCH), weekly *[Internet]*

Employment and Labor Law

Collective Bargaining Negotiations and Contracts (BNA), biweekly

Employment Coordinator (West), monthly *[CD]*

Employment Guide (BNA), biweekly *[CD, Internet]*

Federal Labor Relations Reporter (LRP), biweekly

Government Employee Relations Report (BNA), weekly *[Internet]*

Labor Arbitration Information System (LRP), monthly *[CD]*

Labor Relations (CCH), monthly [CD, Internet]

Labor Relations Reporter (BNA), weekly *[CD, Internet]*

Termination of Employment (West), bimonthly

Wages / Hours Reports (CCH), biweekly *[CD, Internet]*

Employment Discrimination

Employment Discrimination Coordinator (West), biweekly

Employment Practices Guide (CCH), biweekly *[CD, Internet]*

Federal Equal Opportunity Reporter (LRP), biweekly

Energy Law

Energy Management and Federal Energy Guidelines (CCH), monthly

Nuclear Regulation Reports (CCH), biweekly

Utilities Law Reports (CCH), biweekly

Environmental Law

Chemical Regulation Reporter (BNA), weekly *[Internet]*

Environment Reporter (BNA), weekly *[CD, Internet]*

Environmental Due Diligence Guide (BNA), monthly *[Internet]*

Environmental Law Reporter (Environmental Law Institute <www.eli.org>), monthly *[Internet]*

International Environment Reporter (BNA), biweekly *[Internet]*

Toxics Law Reporter (BNA), weekly *[Internet]*

Estate Planning and Taxation

Estate and Personal Financial Planning (West), monthly

Estate Planning and Taxation Coordinator (RIA), biweekly *[CD, Internet]*

Federal Estate and Gift Tax Reports (CCH), weekly *[CD, Internet]*

Financial and Estate Planning (CCH), monthly *[Internet]*

Inheritance, Estate and Gift Tax Reports (CCH), monthly

Tax Management Portfolios–Estates, Gifts & Trusts Library (BNA), monthly *[Internet]*

United States Tax Reporter: Estate and Gift Taxes (RIA), biweekly *[CD, Internet]*

Excise Taxation

Federal Excise Tax Reports (CCH), monthly *[CD, Internet]*

United States Tax Reporter: Excise Taxes (RIA), monthly *[CD, Internet]*

Family Law

Family Law Reporter (BNA), weekly *[Internet]*

Family Law Tax Guide (CCH), monthly

Federal Taxation (General and Income)

CCH Tax Research Network [Internet]

Federal Tax Coordinator 2d (RIA), weekly *[CD, Internet]*

Federal Tax Guide (CCH), monthly *[Internet]*

Federal Tax Research Library / OneDisc (Tax Analysts <www.taxanalysts.com>) *[CD, Internet]*

Standard Federal Tax Reports (CCH), weekly *[CD, Internet]*

Tax Management Portfolios–U.S. Income Library (BNA), biweekly *[CD, Internet]*

United States Tax Reporter (RIA), weekly *[CD, Internet]*

Food and Drug

Food, Drug and Cosmetic Law Reports (CCH), weekly *[Internet]*

Medical Devices Reports (CCH), monthly *[Internet]*

Foundations and Charities

Charitable Giving and Solicitation (RIA), monthly

Exempt Organizations Reports (CCH), monthly *[CD, Internet]*

Franchises

Business Franchise Guide (CCH), monthly *[CD, Internet]*

Government Contracts

Cost Accounting Standards Guide (CCH), monthly *[CD, Internet]*

Federal Contracts Report (BNA), weekly *[Internet]*

Government Contracts Reporter (CCH), monthly [CD, Internet]

Health Care

Health Care Policy Report (BNA), weekly *[Internet]*

Health Law Reporter (BNA), weekly *[Internet]*

Health Care Compliance Reporter (CCH) [Internet]

Medicare–Medicaid Guide (CCH), weekly *[CD, Internet]*

Medicare Report (BNA), weekly *[CD, Internet]*

Housing and Real Estate

Housing and Development Reporter (West), bimonthly *[CD]*

Intellectual Property

Copyright Law Reports (CCH), monthly *[Internet]*

Patent, Trademark & Copyright Journal (BNA), weekly *[Internet]*

International Business and Taxation

International Trade Reporter (BNA), weekly *[Internet]*

Tax Management Portfolios–Foreign Income Library (BNA), bimonthly *[Internet]*

U.S. Taxation of International Operations (RIA), biweekly

Lawyers and Legal Ethics

ABA/BNA Lawyer's Manual on Professional Conduct, biweekly *[Internet]*

Ethics in Government Reporter (CCH), monthly

National Reporter on Legal Ethics and Professional Responsibility (LexisNexis), monthly

Legislation

Congressional Index (CCH), weekly

Native Americans

Indian Law Reporter (American Indian Lawyer Training Program), monthly

Occupational Safety and Health

Employment Safety and Health Guide (CCH), monthly *[CD, Internet]*

Occupational Safety & Health Reporter (BNA), weekly *[CD, Internet]*

Partnerships and S Corporations

Partnership Tax Planning and Practice (CCH), monthly

S Corporations Guide (CCH), monthly

Products Liability and Consumer Safety

Consumer Product Safety Guide (CCH), biweekly *[CD, Internet]*

Product Safety & Liability Reporter (BNA), weekly *[Internet]*

Products Liability Reports (CCH), biweekly *[CD, Internet]*

Securities and Commodities

Blue Sky Law Reports (CCH), bimonthly *[CD, Internet]*

Commodity Futures Law Reports (CCH), biweekly *[Internet]*

Derivatives Regulation Law Reports (CCH), bimonthly

Federal Securities Law Reports (CCH), weekly *[CD, Internet]*

Global Capital Markets Internet Library (CCH) [Internet]

Mutual Funds Guide (CCH), monthly

SEC Compliance: Financial Reporting and Forms (RIA), monthly *[Internet]*

Securities Regulation & Law Report (BNA), weekly *[Internet]*

Securities Transfer Guide (CCH), monthly *[Internet]*

State and Local Taxation

All States Tax Guide (RIA), biweekly *[Internet]*

State Tax Guide (CCH), biweekly *[CD, Internet]*

State Tax Reports (CCH) (for each state) [Internet]

Tax Management Portfolios–State Tax Library (BNA), monthly *[Internet]*

Supreme Court

United States Law Week (BNA), weekly *[Internet]*

Taxation

See Estate Planning and Taxation; Excise Taxation; Federal Taxation (General and Income); State and Local Taxation; and specific subjects

Trade Regulation

Antitrust & Trade Regulation Report (BNA), weekly *[Internet]*

State Unfair Trade Practices Law (CCH), monthly

Trade Regulation Reports (CCH), weekly *[CD, Internet]*

Transportation

Aviation Law Reports (CCH), biweekly *[CD, Internet]*

Federal Carriers Reports (CCH), biweekly

Shipping Regulation (P & F), biweekly

Unemployment Insurance / Social Security

Social Security Reporter (CCH), monthly [CD, Internet]

Unemployment Insurance Reporter (CCH), monthly [CD, Internet]

*

SUBJECT INDEX

References are to Pages

Boldface references are to exhibits

See also title and website indexes

*

TITLE INDEX

References are to Pages

Boldface reference are to exhibits

See also subject and website indexes

487

WEBSITE INDEX

References are to Pages

Boldface references are to exhibits

See also subject and title indexes

Note: This index does not include websites cited in the appendices. A regularly updated set of links to all websites mentioned in the book, listed by page and including the appendices, is available online <www.law.virginia.edu/nutshell>.

†